DYNAMITE ENTERTAINMENT PRESENT

SHERLOCK HOLMES

YEAR ONE

DYNAMITE
ENTERTAINMENT

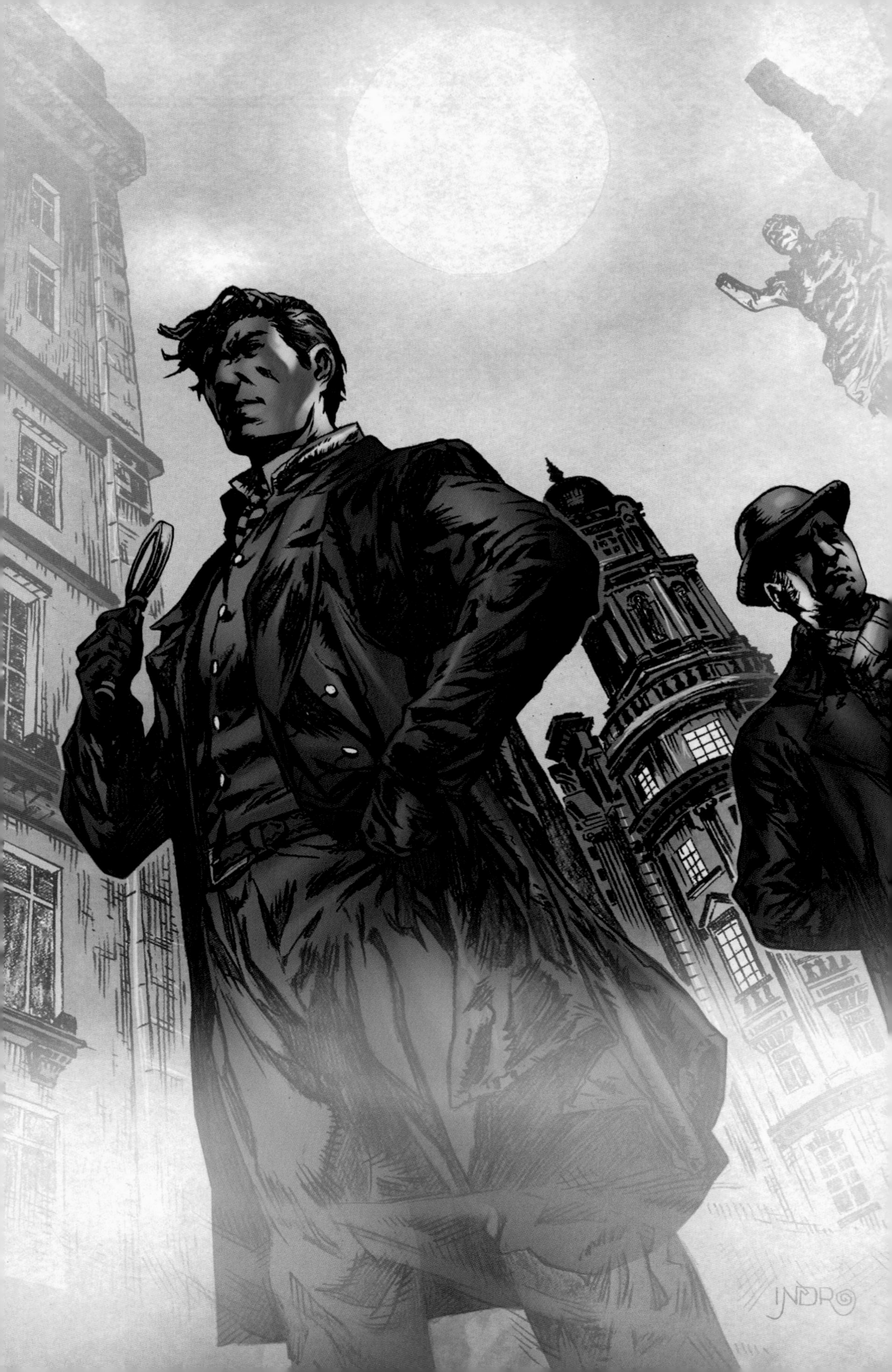
INDRO

DYNAMITE ENTERTAINMENT PRESENTS

SHERLOCK HOLMES YEAR ONE

Written by:
SCOTT BEATTY

Illustrated by:
DANIEL INDRO

Colored by:
TONY AVIÑA

Lettered by:
SIMON BOWLAND

Collection Cover by:
FRANCESCO FRANCAVILLA

Collection Design by:
BILL TORTOLINI

Dedicated to:
SIR ARTHUR CONAN DOYLE

Special thanks to:
LESLIE KLINGER
Editor of The Sherlock Holmes Reference Library

ISBN 10: 1-60690-217-2   ISB13: 978-1-60690-217-2

FIRST PRINTING   10 9 8 7 6 5 4 3 2 1

SHERLOCK HOLMES: YEAR ONE, VOLUME 1. Contains materials originally published in Sherlock Holmes: Year One #1-6. Published by Dynamite Entertainment. 155 Ninth Ave. Suite B, Runnemede, NJ 08078. Sherlock Holmes TM & © 2011 Savage Tales Entertainment, llc. Dynamite, Dynamite Entertainment and the Dynamite Entertainment colophon are ® and © 2011 DFI. All rights reserved. All names, characters, events, and locales in this publication are entirely fictional. Any resemblance to actual persons (living or dead), events or places, without satiric intent, is coincidental. No portion of this book may be reproduced by any means (digital or print) without the written permission of Dynamite Entertainment except for review purposes. The scanning, uploading and distribution of this book via the Internet or via any other means without the permission of the publisher is illegal and punishable by law. Please purchase only authorized electronic editions, and do not participate in or encourage electronic piracy of copyrighted materials. Printed in Canada

Cover by:
FRANCESCO FRANCAVILLA

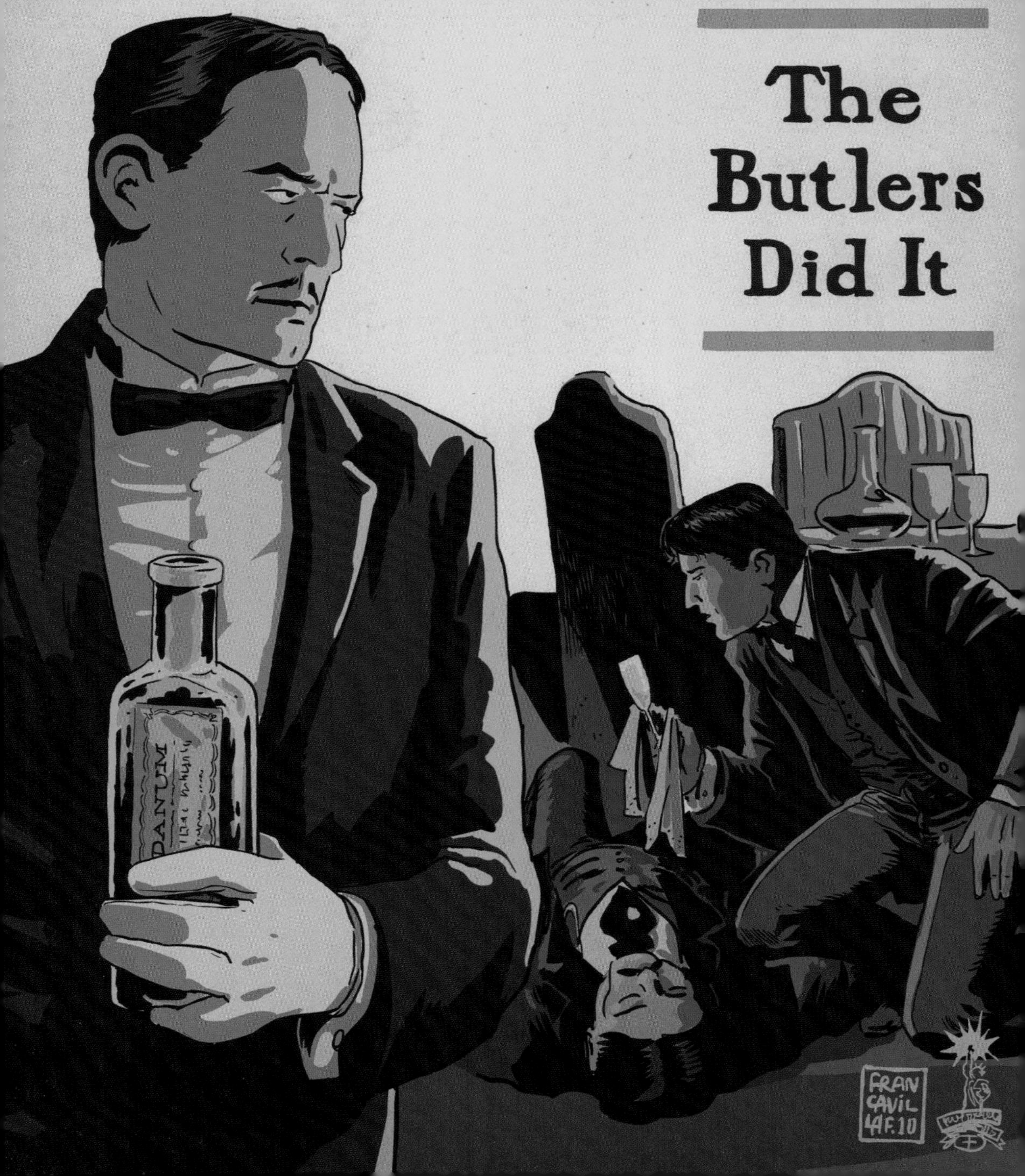
The Butlers Did It
DANUM
FRAN CAVIL LA F.10

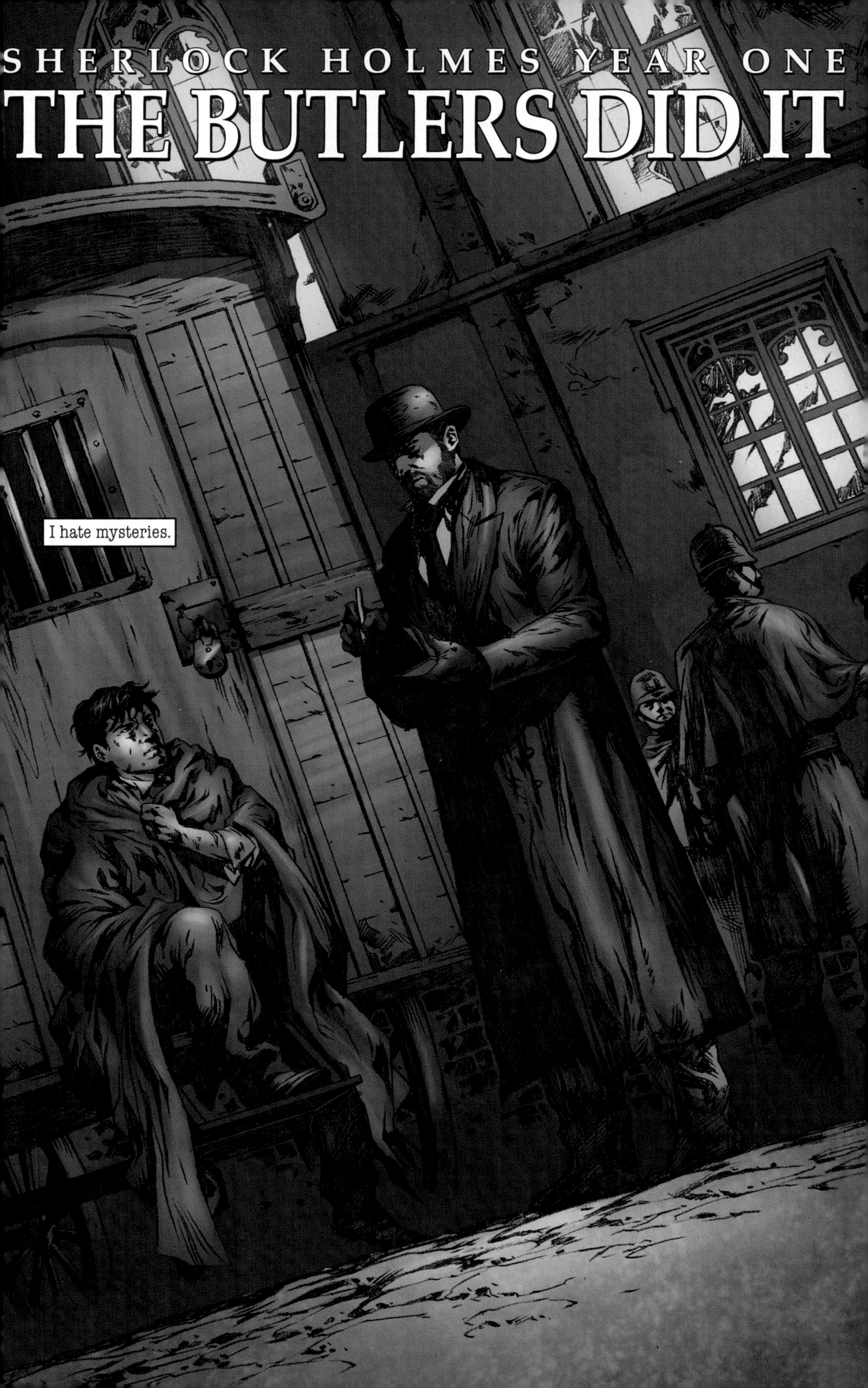
SHERLOCK HOLMES YEAR ONE
THE BUTLERS DID IT
I hate mysteries.

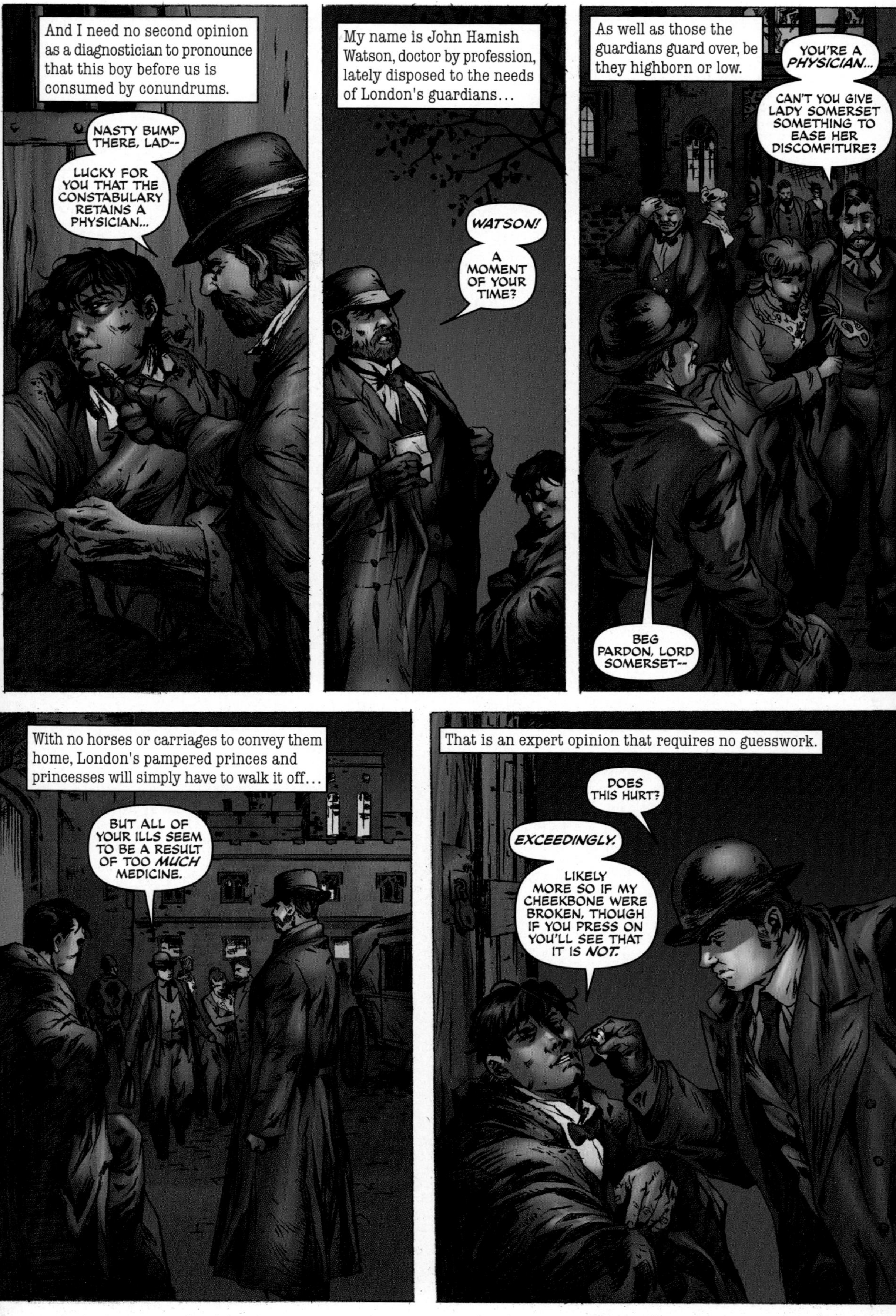
And I need no second opinion as a diagnostician to pronounce that this boy before us is consumed by conundrums.
NASTY BUMP THERE, LAD--
LUCKY FOR YOU THAT THE CONSTABULARY RETAINS A PHYSICIAN...
My name is John Hamish Watson, doctor by profession, lately disposed to the needs of London's guardians...
WATSON!
A MOMENT OF YOUR TIME?
As well as those the guardians guard over, be they highborn or low.
YOU'RE A PHYSICIAN...
CAN'T YOU GIVE LADY SOMERSET SOMETHING TO EASE HER DISCOMFITURE?
BEG PARDON, LORD SOMERSET--
With no horses or carriages to convey them home, London's pampered princes and princesses will simply have to walk it off...
BUT ALL OF YOUR ILLS SEEM TO BE A RESULT OF TOO MUCH MEDICINE.
That is an expert opinion that requires no guesswork.
DOES THIS HURT?
EXCEEDINGLY.
LIKELY MORE SO IF MY CHEEKBONE WERE BROKEN, THOUGH IF YOU PRESS ON YOU'LL SEE THAT IT IS NOT.

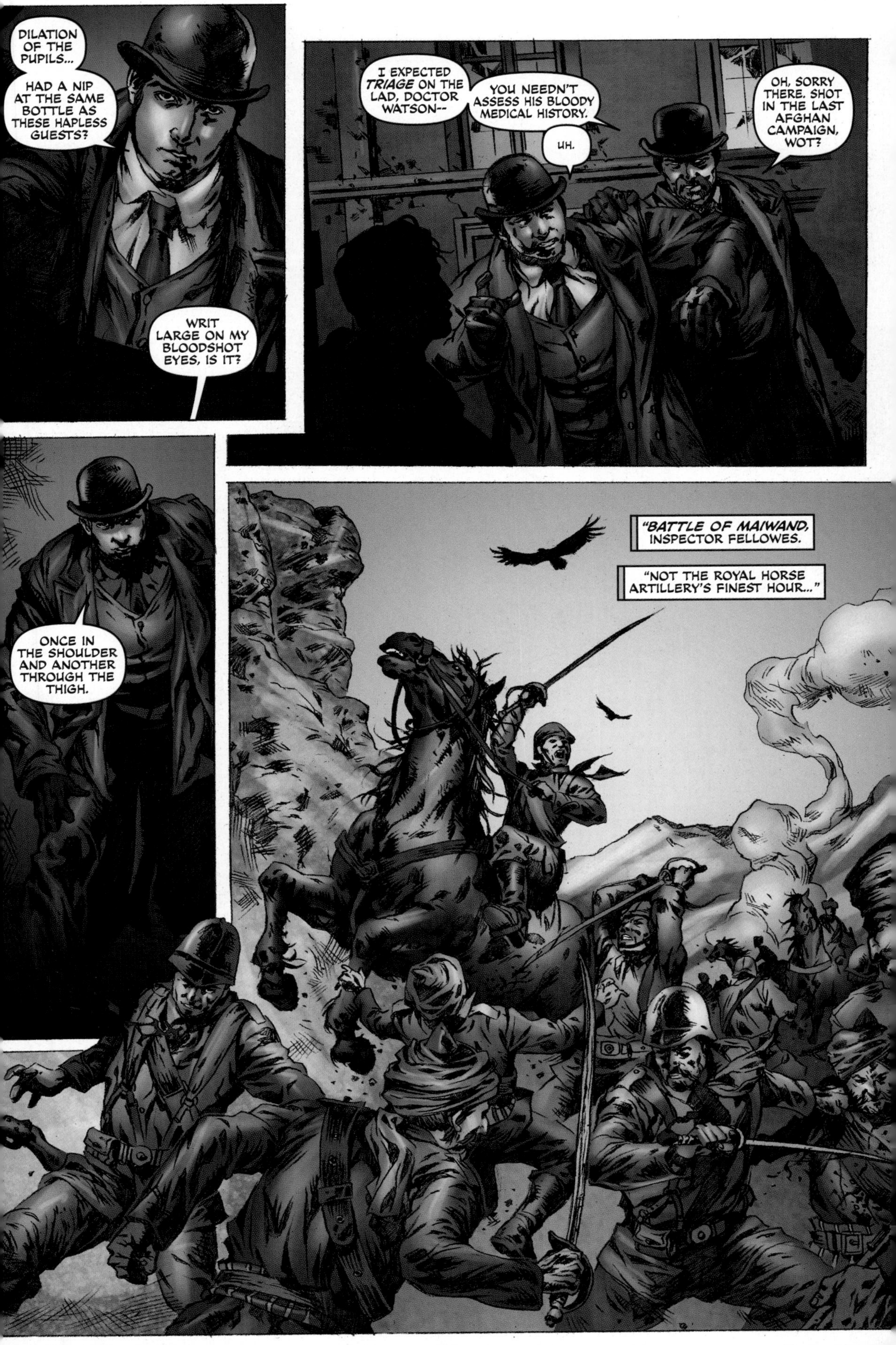
DILATION OF THE PUPILS...
HAD A NIP AT THE SAME BOTTLE AS THESE HAPLESS GUESTS?
WRIT LARGE ON MY BLOODSHOT EYES, IS IT?
I EXPECTED TRIAGE ON THE LAD, DOCTOR WATSON--
YOU NEEDN'T ASSESS HIS BLOODY MEDICAL HISTORY.
UH.
OH, SORRY THERE. SHOT IN THE LAST AFGHAN CAMPAIGN, WOT?
ONCE IN THE SHOULDER AND ANOTHER THROUGH THE THIGH.
"BATTLE OF MAIWAND, INSPECTOR FELLOWES.
"NOT THE ROYAL HORSE ARTILLERY'S FINEST HOUR..."

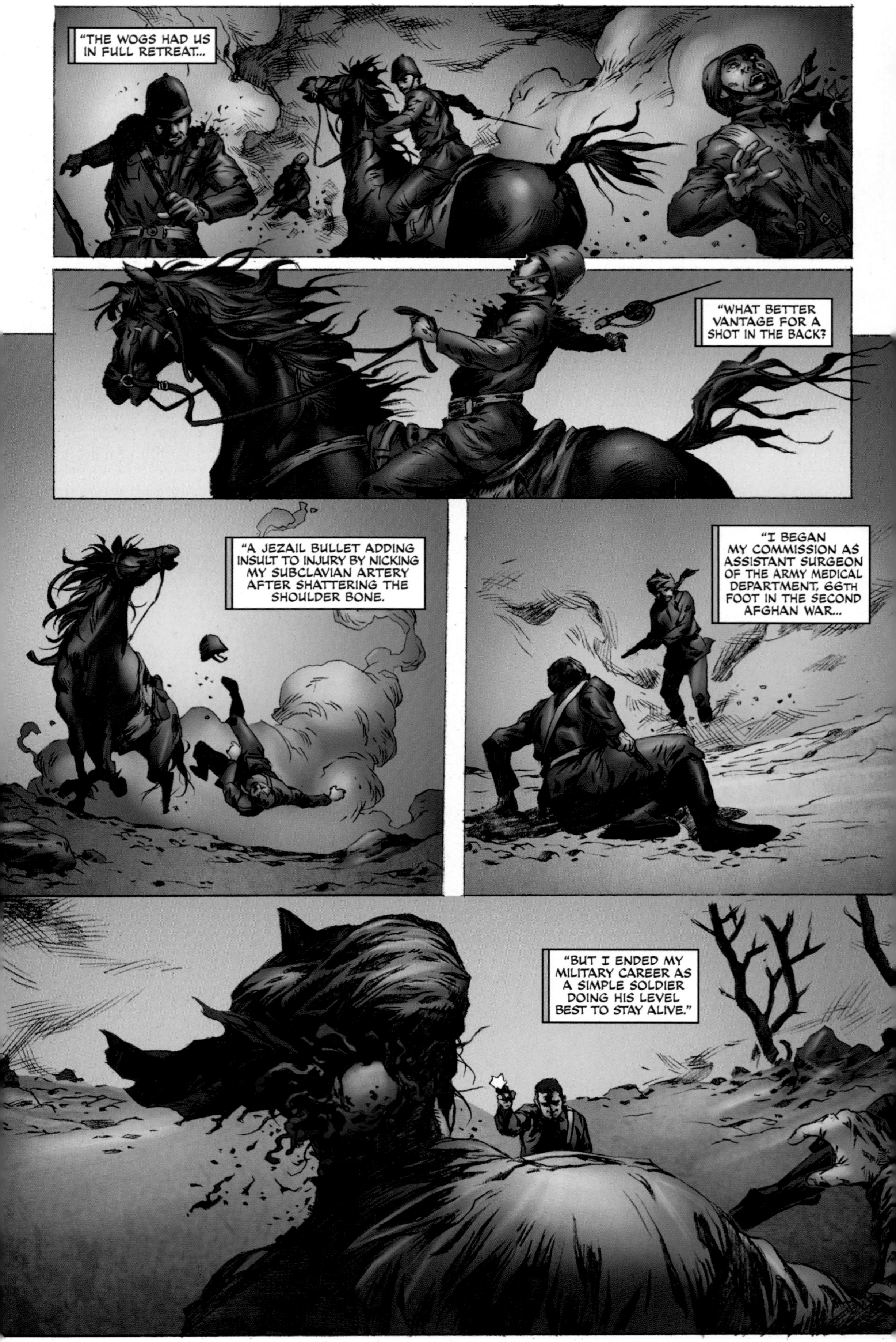
"THE WOGS HAD US IN FULL RETREAT...
"WHAT BETTER VANTAGE FOR A SHOT IN THE BACK?
"A JEZAIL BULLET ADDING INSULT TO INJURY BY NICKING MY SUBCLAVIAN ARTERY AFTER SHATTERING THE SHOULDER BONE.
"I BEGAN MY COMMISSION AS ASSISTANT SURGEON OF THE ARMY MEDICAL DEPARTMENT, 66TH FOOT IN THE SECOND AFGHAN WAR...
"BUT I ENDED MY MILITARY CAREER AS A SIMPLE SOLDIER DOING HIS LEVEL BEST TO STAY ALIVE."

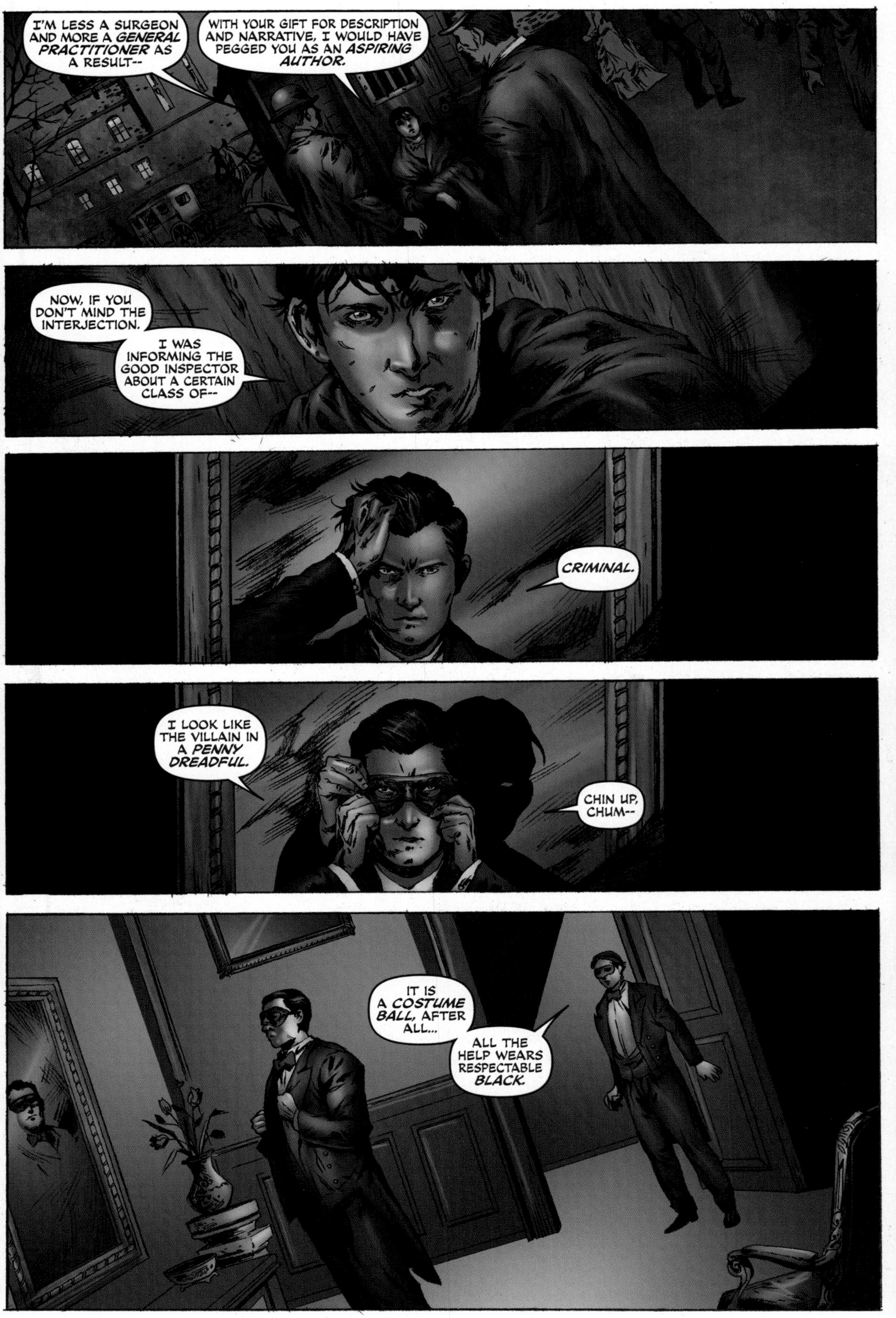
I'M LESS A SURGEON AND MORE A *GENERAL PRACTITIONER* AS A RESULT--
WITH YOUR GIFT FOR DESCRIPTION AND NARRATIVE, I WOULD HAVE PEGGED YOU AS AN *ASPIRING AUTHOR.*
NOW, IF YOU DON'T MIND THE INTERJECTION.
I WAS INFORMING THE GOOD INSPECTOR ABOUT A CERTAIN CLASS OF--
CRIMINAL.
I LOOK LIKE THE VILLAIN IN A *PENNY DREADFUL.*
CHIN UP, CHUM--
IT IS A *COSTUME BALL,* AFTER ALL...
ALL THE HELP WEARS RESPECTABLE *BLACK.*

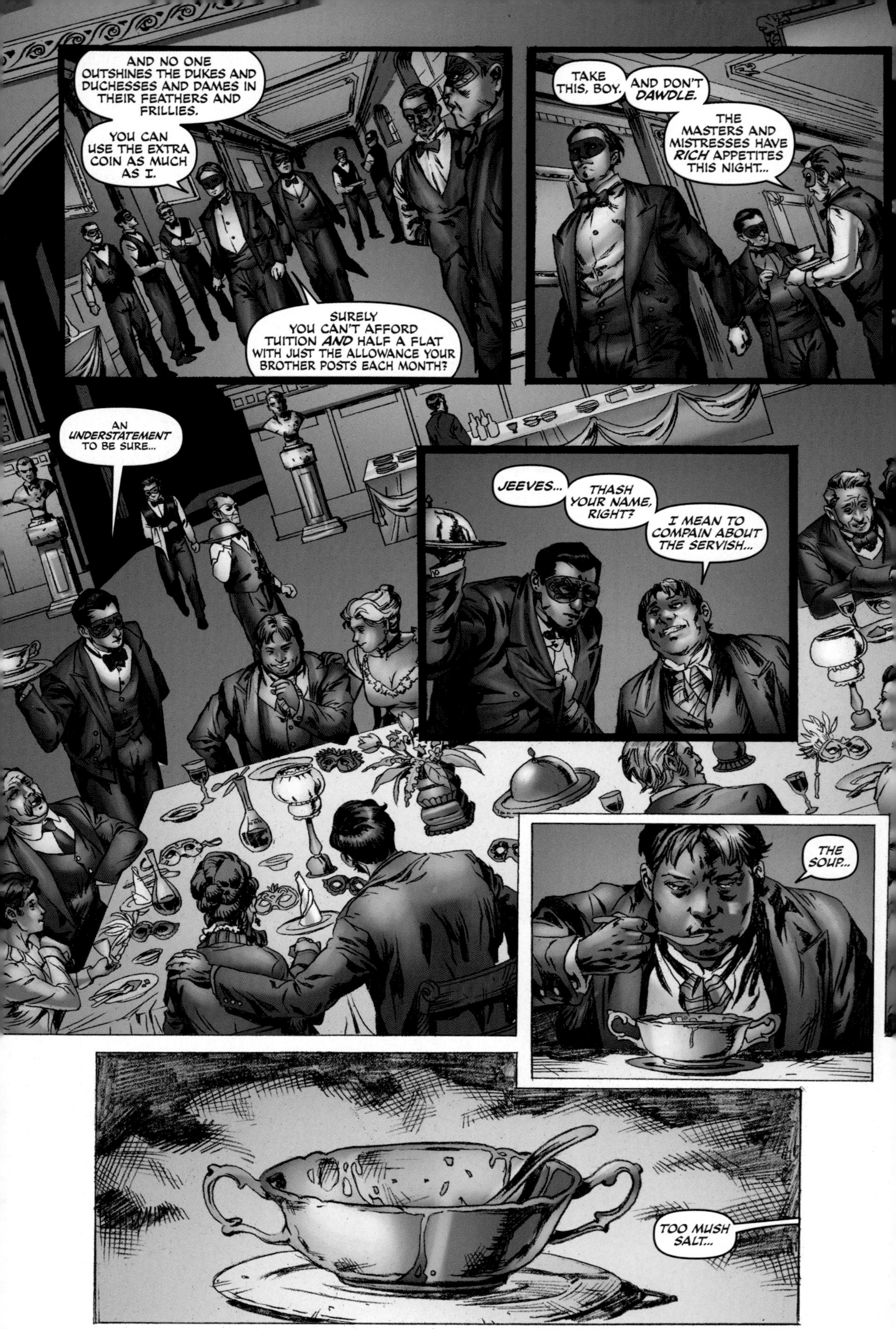

AND NO ONE OUTSHINES THE DUKES AND DUCHESSES AND DAMES IN THEIR FEATHERS AND FRILLIES.
YOU CAN USE THE EXTRA COIN AS MUCH AS I.
SURELY YOU CAN'T AFFORD TUITION AND HALF A FLAT WITH JUST THE ALLOWANCE YOUR BROTHER POSTS EACH MONTH?
TAKE THIS, BOY.
AND DON'T DAWDLE.
THE MASTERS AND MISTRESSES HAVE RICH APPETITES THIS NIGHT...
AN UNDERSTATEMENT TO BE SURE...
JEEVES...
THASH YOUR NAME, RIGHT?
I MEAN TO COMPAIN ABOUT THE SERVISH...
THE SOUP...
TOO MUSH SALT...

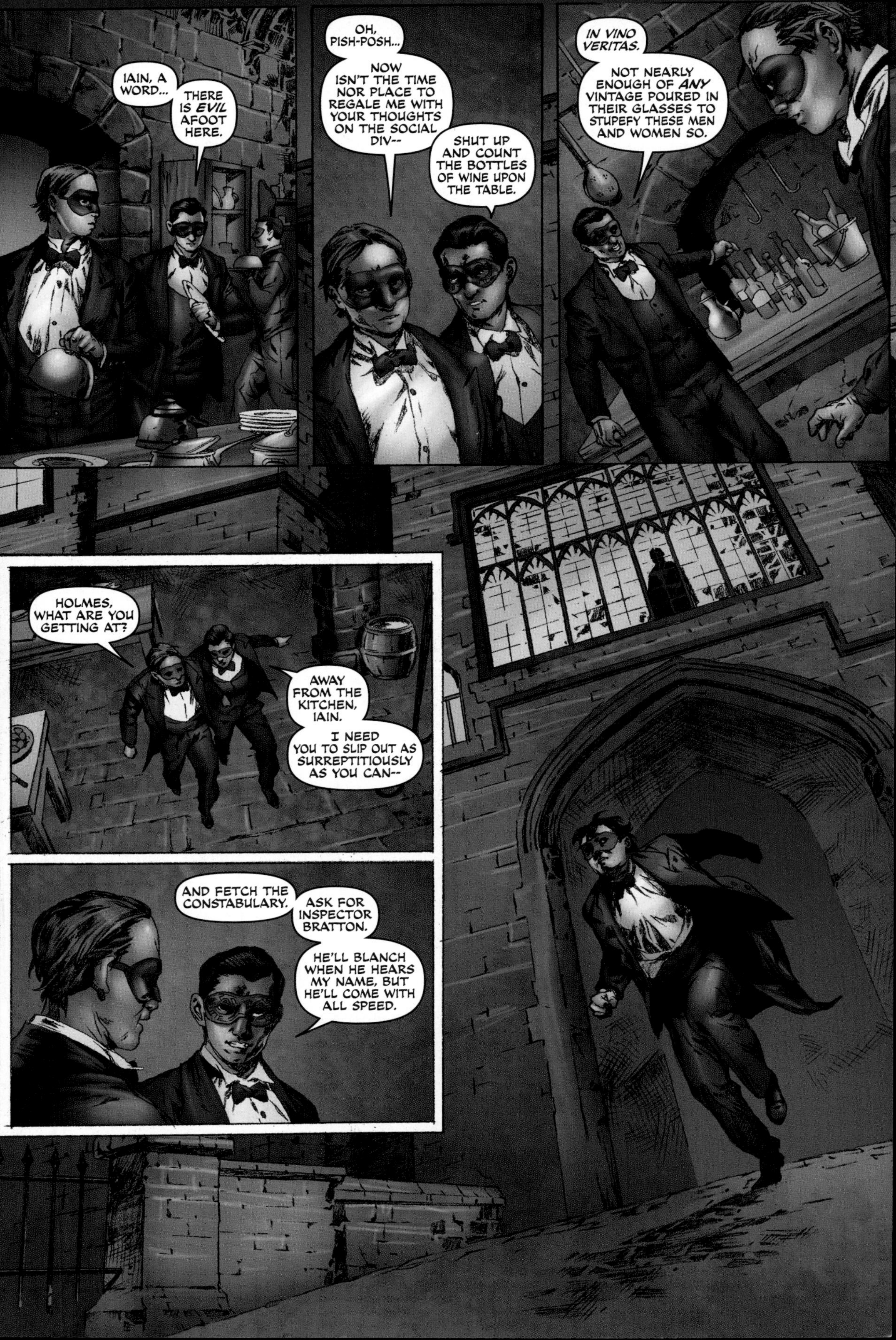
IAIN, A WORD...
THERE IS EVIL AFOOT HERE.
OH, PISH-POSH...
NOW ISN'T THE TIME NOR PLACE TO REGALE ME WITH YOUR THOUGHTS ON THE SOCIAL DIV--
SHUT UP AND COUNT THE BOTTLES OF WINE UPON THE TABLE.
IN VINO VERITAS.
NOT NEARLY ENOUGH OF ANY VINTAGE POURED IN THEIR GLASSES TO STUPEFY THESE MEN AND WOMEN SO.
HOLMES, WHAT ARE YOU GETTING AT?
AWAY FROM THE KITCHEN, IAIN.
I NEED YOU TO SLIP OUT AS SURREPTITIOUSLY AS YOU CAN--
AND FETCH THE CONSTABULARY.
ASK FOR INSPECTOR BRATTON.
HE'LL BLANCH WHEN HE HEARS MY NAME, BUT HE'LL COME WITH ALL SPEED.

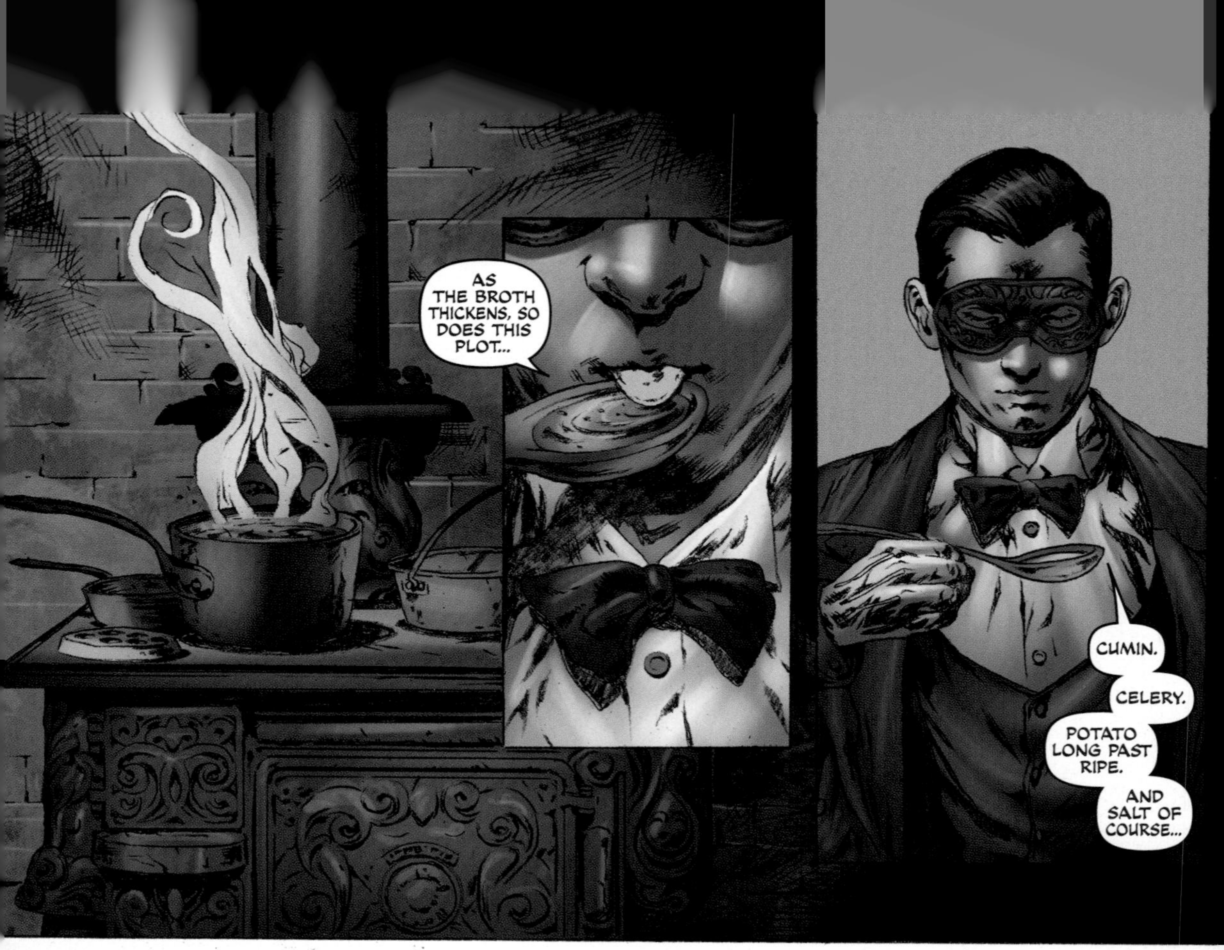
AS THE BROTH THICKENS, SO DOES THIS PLOT...
CUMIN.
CELERY.
POTATO LONG PAST RIPE.
AND SALT OF COURSE...

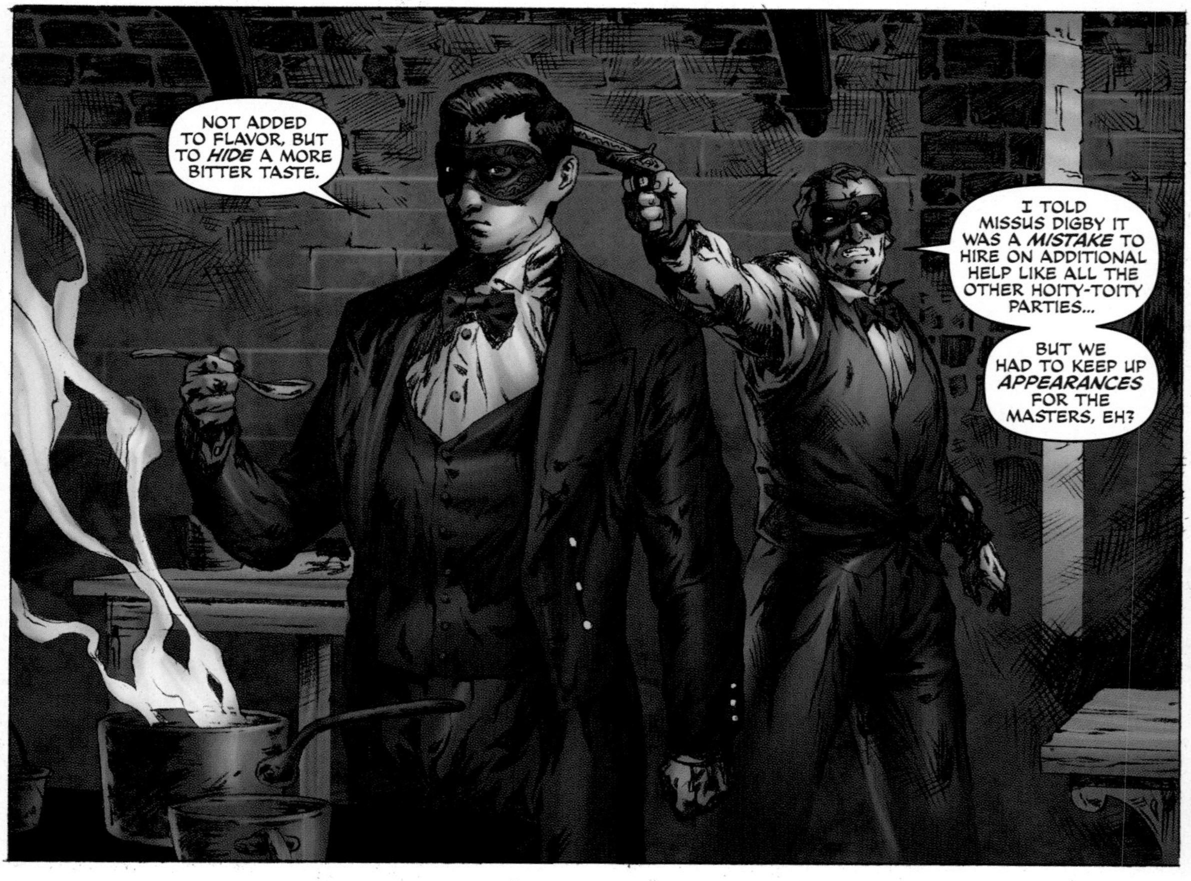
NOT ADDED TO FLAVOR, BUT TO *HIDE* A MORE BITTER TASTE.
I TOLD MISSUS DIGBY IT WAS A *MISTAKE* TO HIRE ON ADDITIONAL HELP LIKE ALL THE OTHER HOITY-TOITY PARTIES...
BUT WE HAD TO KEEP UP *APPEARANCES* FOR THE MASTERS, EH?

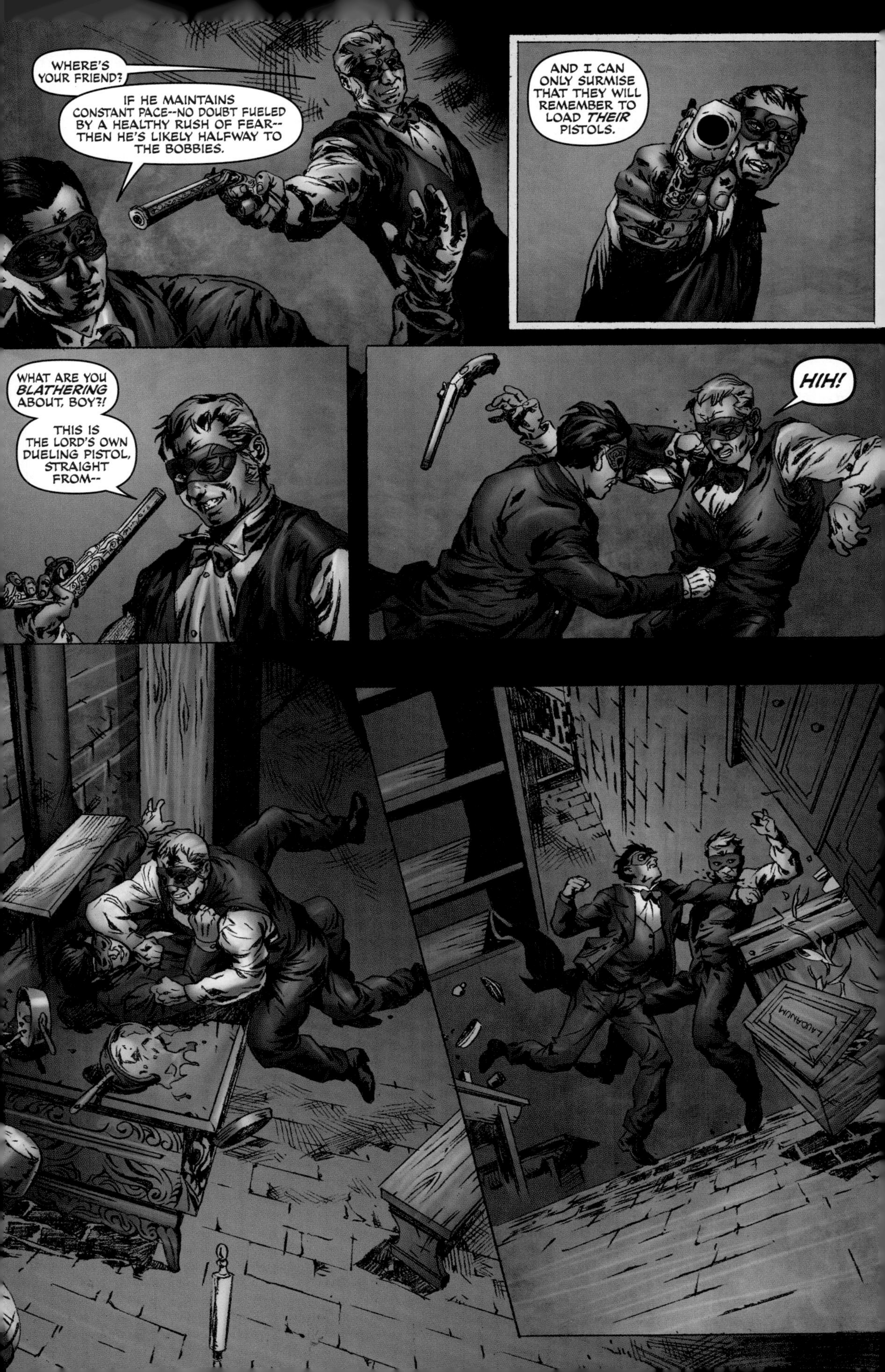
WHERE'S YOUR FRIEND?
IF HE MAINTAINS CONSTANT PACE--NO DOUBT FUELED BY A HEALTHY RUSH OF FEAR--THEN HE'S LIKELY HALFWAY TO THE BOBBIES.
AND I CAN ONLY SURMISE THAT THEY WILL REMEMBER TO LOAD *THEIR* PISTOLS.
WHAT ARE YOU *BLATHERING* ABOUT, BOY?!
THIS IS THE LORD'S OWN DUELING PISTOL, STRAIGHT FROM--
HIH!
LAUDANUM

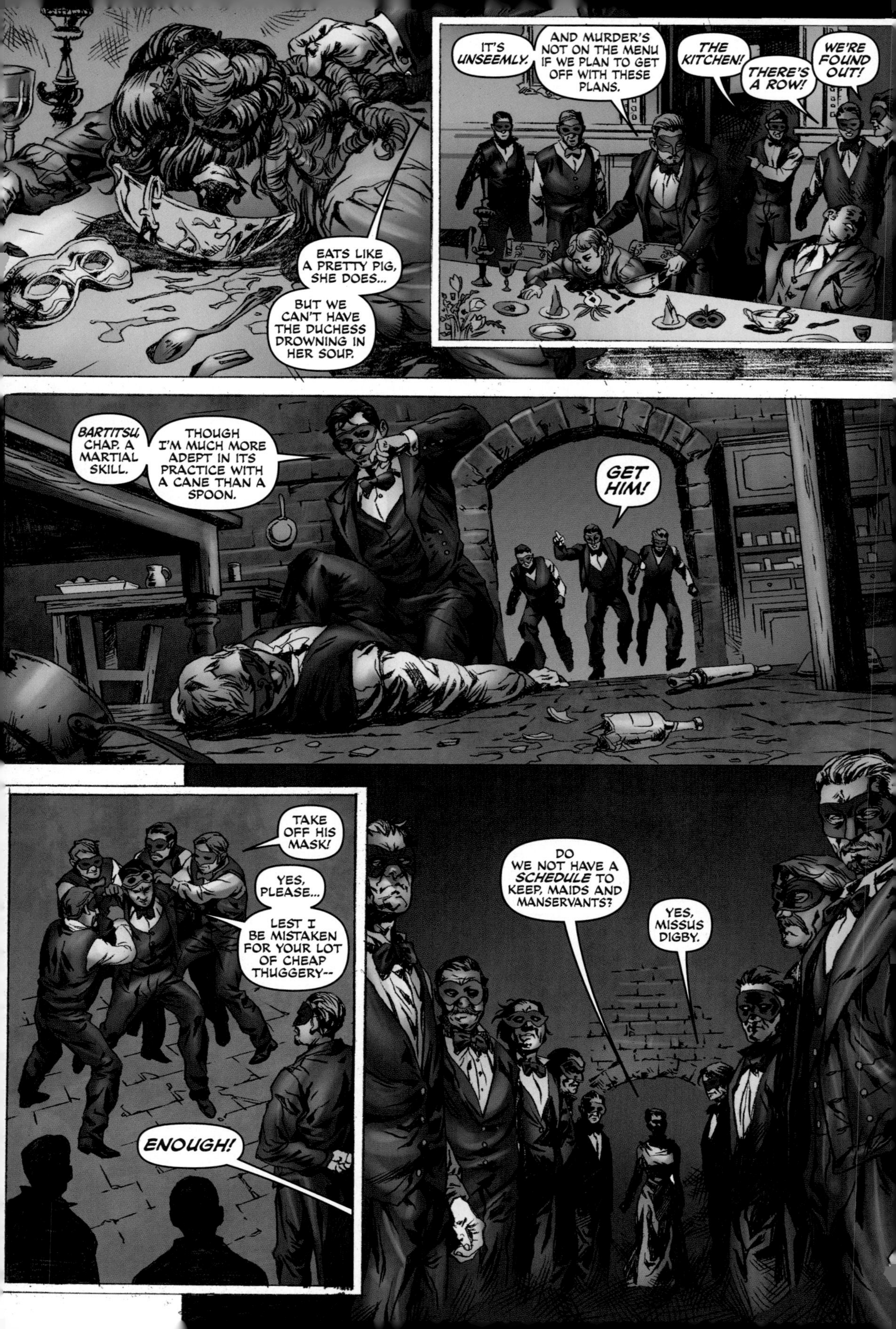
EATS LIKE A PRETTY PIG, SHE DOES...
BUT WE CAN'T HAVE THE DUCHESS DROWNING IN HER SOUP.
IT'S UNSEEMLY.
AND MURDER'S NOT ON THE MENU IF WE PLAN TO GET OFF WITH THESE PLANS.
THE KITCHEN!
THERE'S A ROW!
WE'RE FOUND OUT!
BARTITSU, CHAP. A MARTIAL SKILL.
THOUGH I'M MUCH MORE ADEPT IN ITS PRACTICE WITH A CANE THAN A SPOON.
GET HIM!
TAKE OFF HIS MASK!
YES, PLEASE...
LEST I BE MISTAKEN FOR YOUR LOT OF CHEAP THUGGERY--
ENOUGH!
DO WE NOT HAVE A SCHEDULE TO KEEP, MAIDS AND MANSERVANTS?
YES, MISSUS DIGBY.

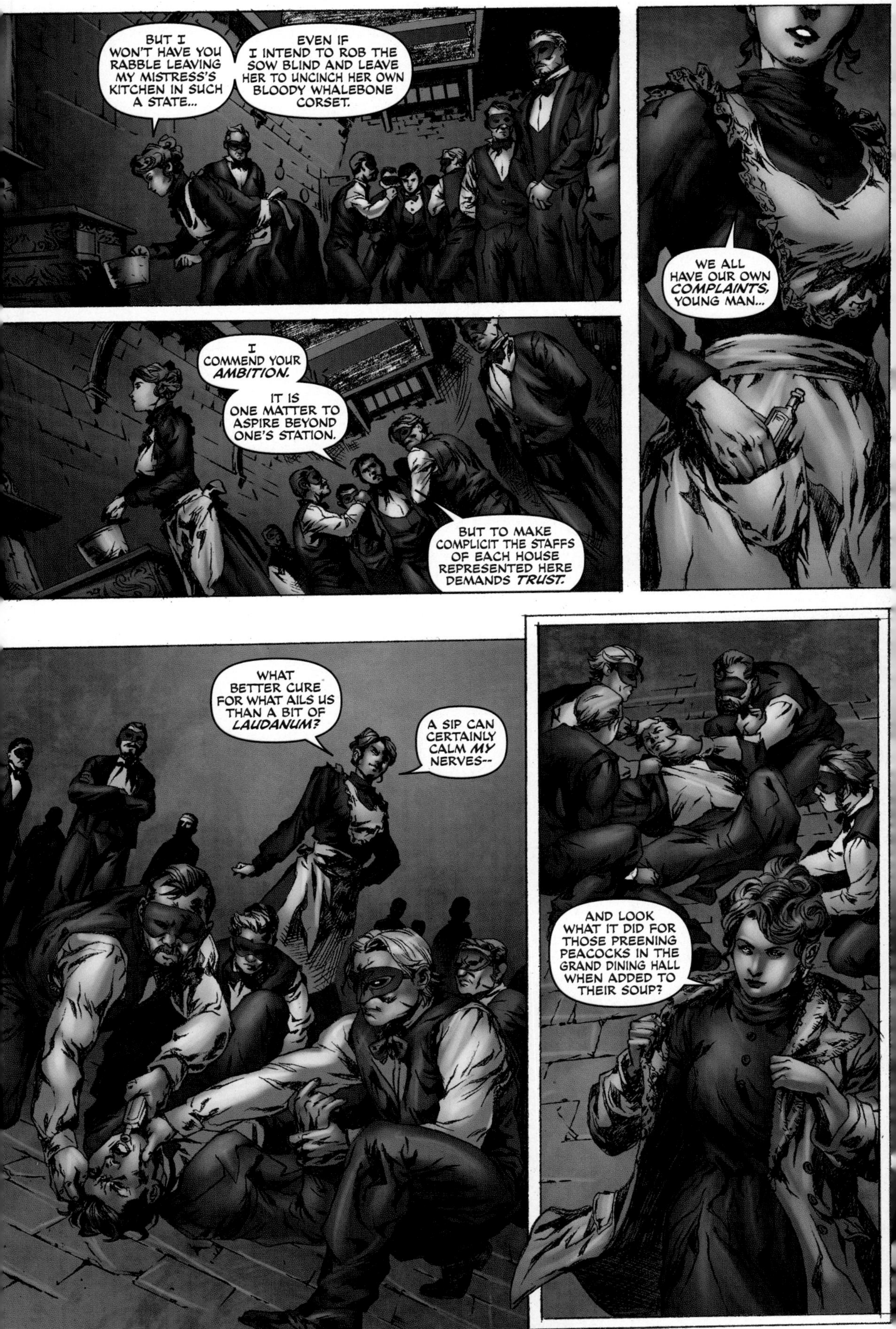
BUT I WON'T HAVE YOU RABBLE LEAVING MY MISTRESS'S KITCHEN IN SUCH A STATE...
EVEN IF I INTEND TO ROB THE SOW BLIND AND LEAVE HER TO UNCINCH HER OWN BLOODY WHALEBONE CORSET.
I COMMEND YOUR AMBITION.
IT IS ONE MATTER TO ASPIRE BEYOND ONE'S STATION.
BUT TO MAKE COMPLICIT THE STAFFS OF EACH HOUSE REPRESENTED HERE DEMANDS TRUST.
WE ALL HAVE OUR OWN COMPLAINTS, YOUNG MAN...
WHAT BETTER CURE FOR WHAT AILS US THAN A BIT OF LAUDANUM?
A SIP CAN CERTAINLY CALM MY NERVES--
AND LOOK WHAT IT DID FOR THOSE PREENING PEACOCKS IN THE GRAND DINING HALL WHEN ADDED TO THEIR SOUP?

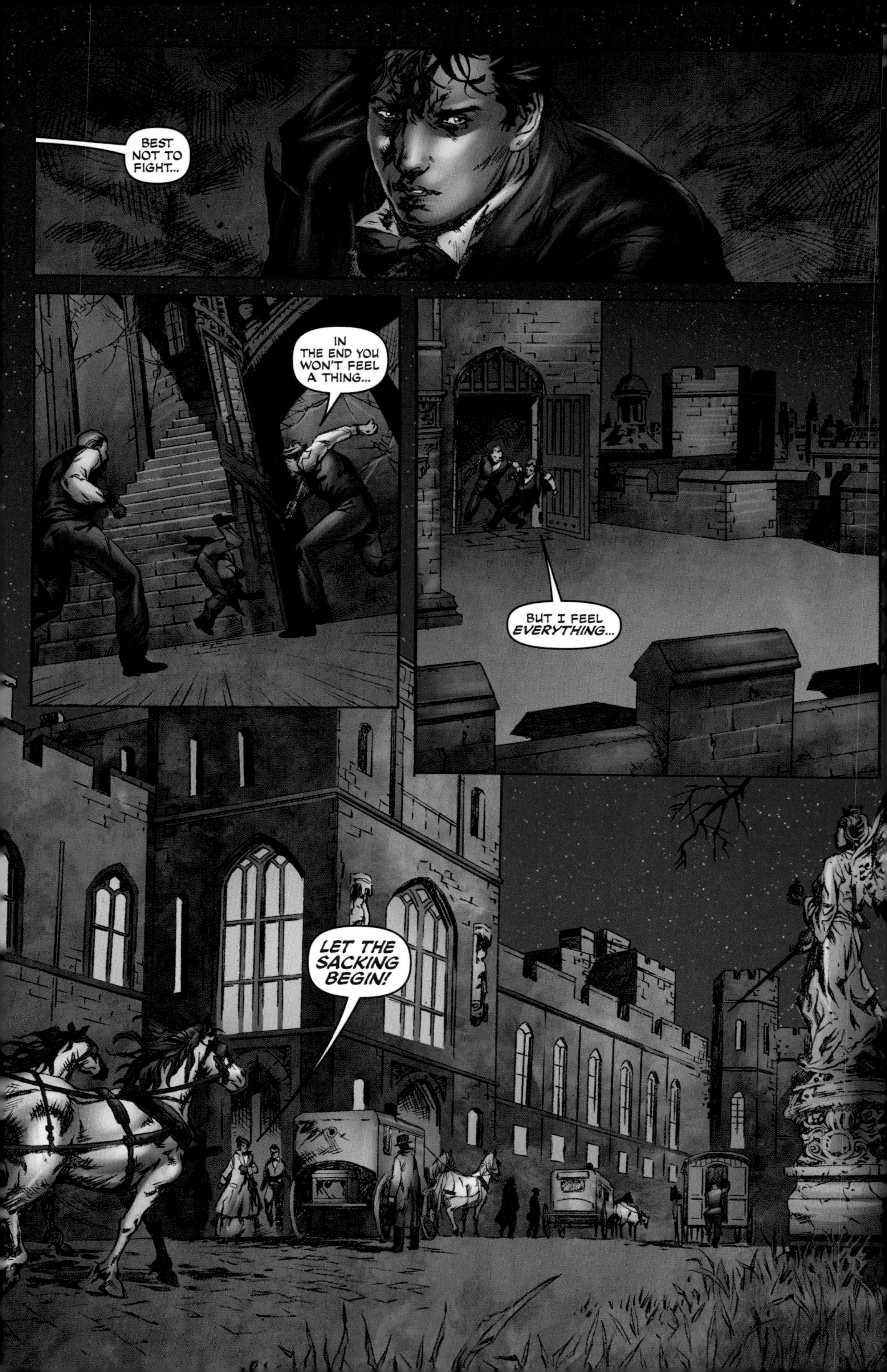
BEST NOT TO FIGHT...
IN THE END YOU WON'T FEEL A THING...
BUT I FEEL *EVERYTHING*...
LET THE SACKING BEGIN!

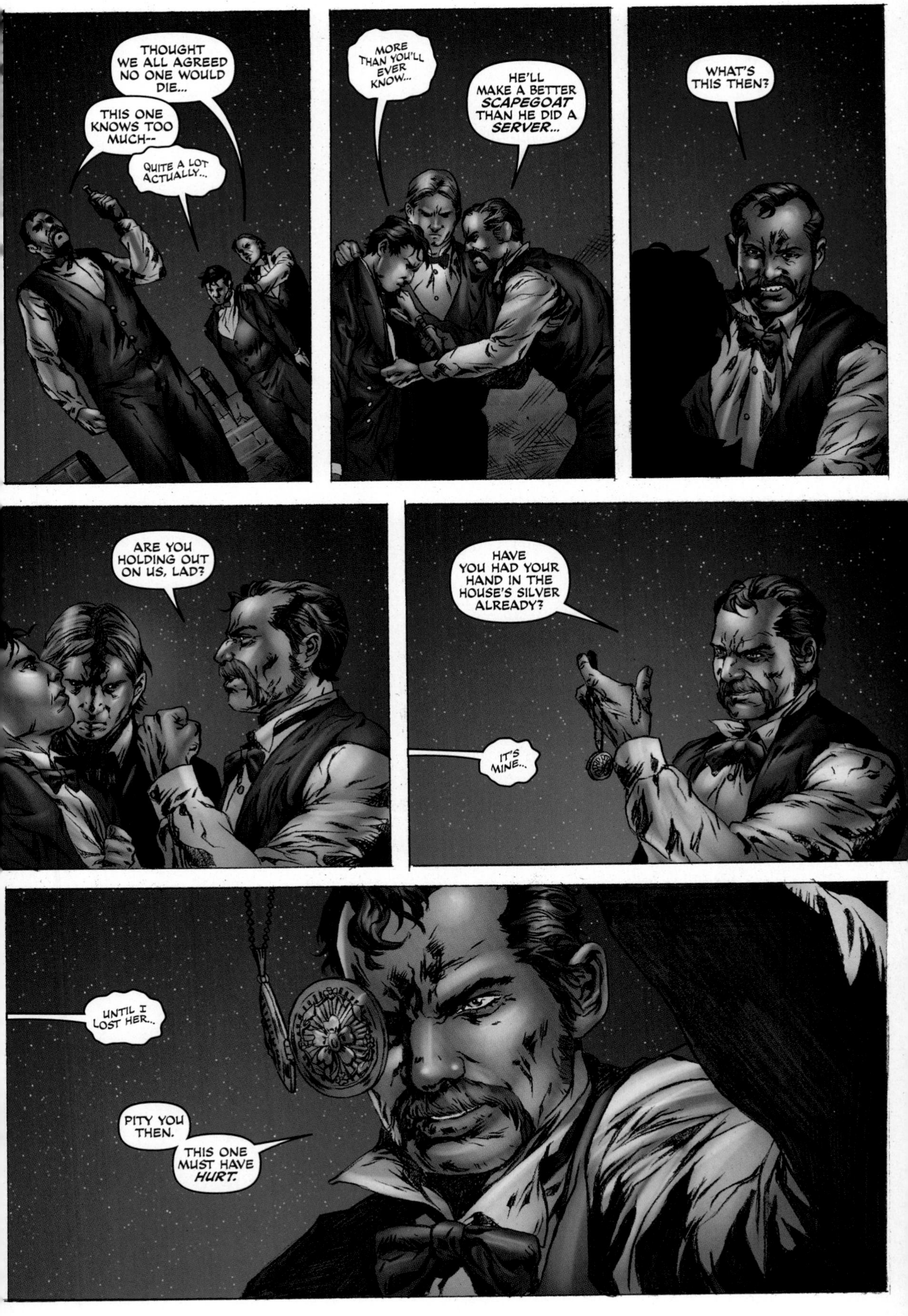
THOUGHT WE ALL AGREED NO ONE WOULD DIE...
THIS ONE KNOWS TOO MUCH--
QUITE A LOT ACTUALLY...
MORE THAN YOU'LL EVER KNOW...
HE'LL MAKE A BETTER *SCAPEGOAT* THAN HE DID A *SERVER*...
WHAT'S THIS THEN?
ARE YOU HOLDING OUT ON US, LAD?
HAVE YOU HAD YOUR HAND IN THE HOUSE'S SILVER ALREADY?
IT'S MINE...
UNTIL I LOST HER...
PITY YOU THEN.
THIS ONE MUST HAVE *HURT.*

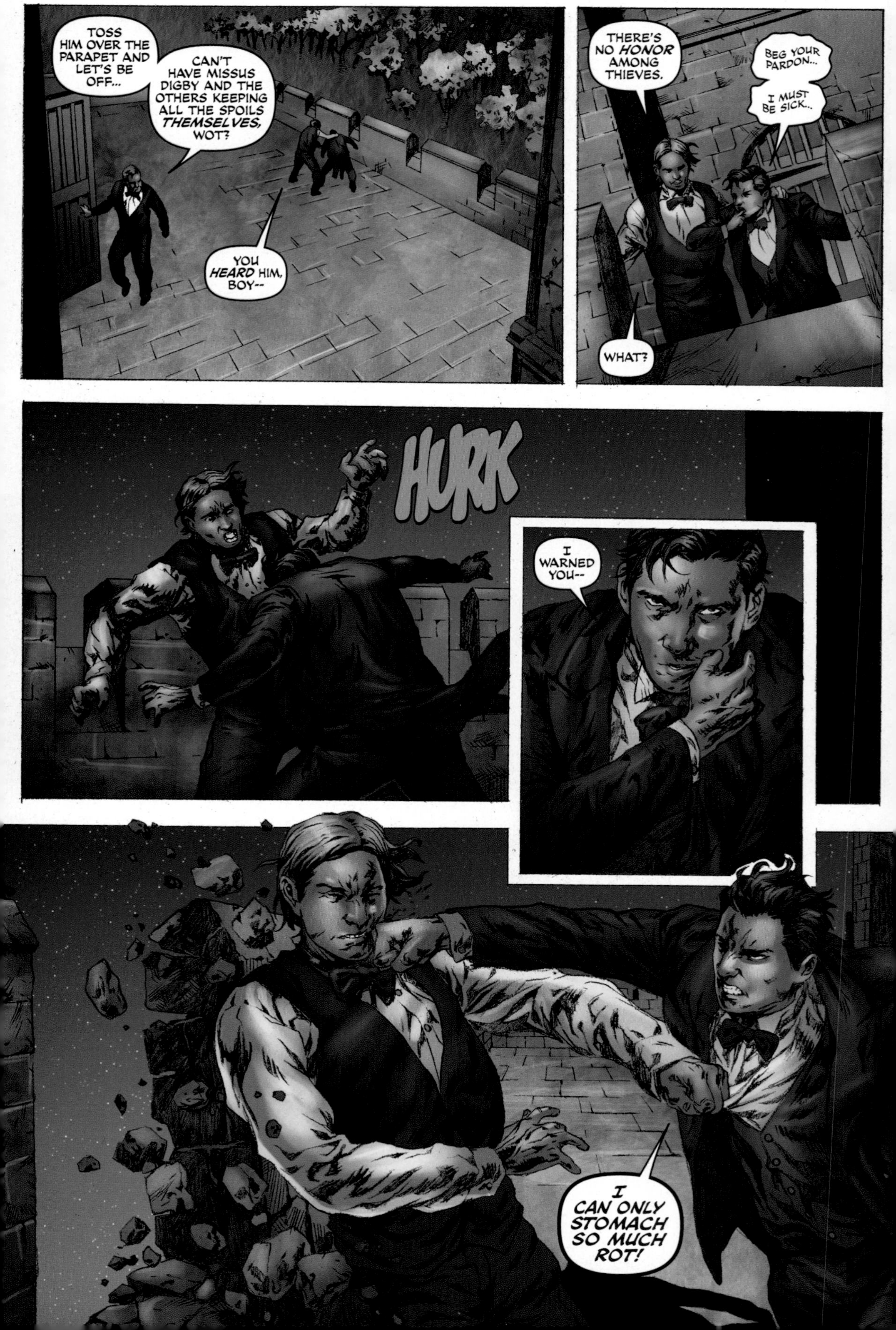
TOSS HIM OVER THE PARAPET AND LET'S BE OFF...
CAN'T HAVE MISSUS DIGBY AND THE OTHERS KEEPING ALL THE SPOILS *THEMSELVES,* WOT?
YOU *HEARD* HIM, BOY--
THERE'S NO *HONOR* AMONG THIEVES.
BEG YOUR PARDON...
I MUST BE SICK..
WHAT?
HURK
I WARNED YOU--
I CAN ONLY STOMACH SO MUCH ROT!

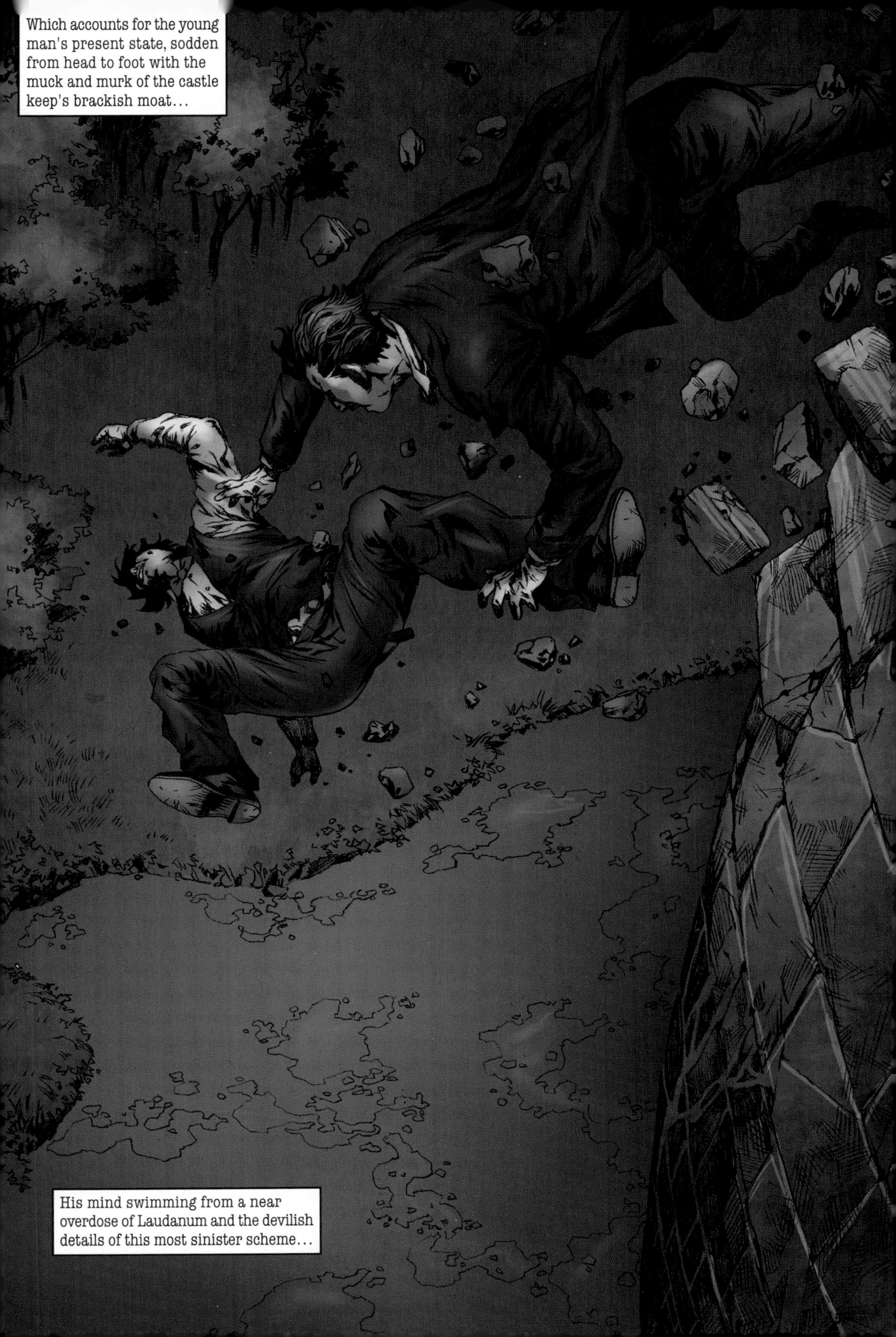
Which accounts for the young man's present state, sodden from head to foot with the muck and murk of the castle keep's brackish moat...
His mind swimming from a near overdose of Laudanum and the devilish details of this most sinister scheme...

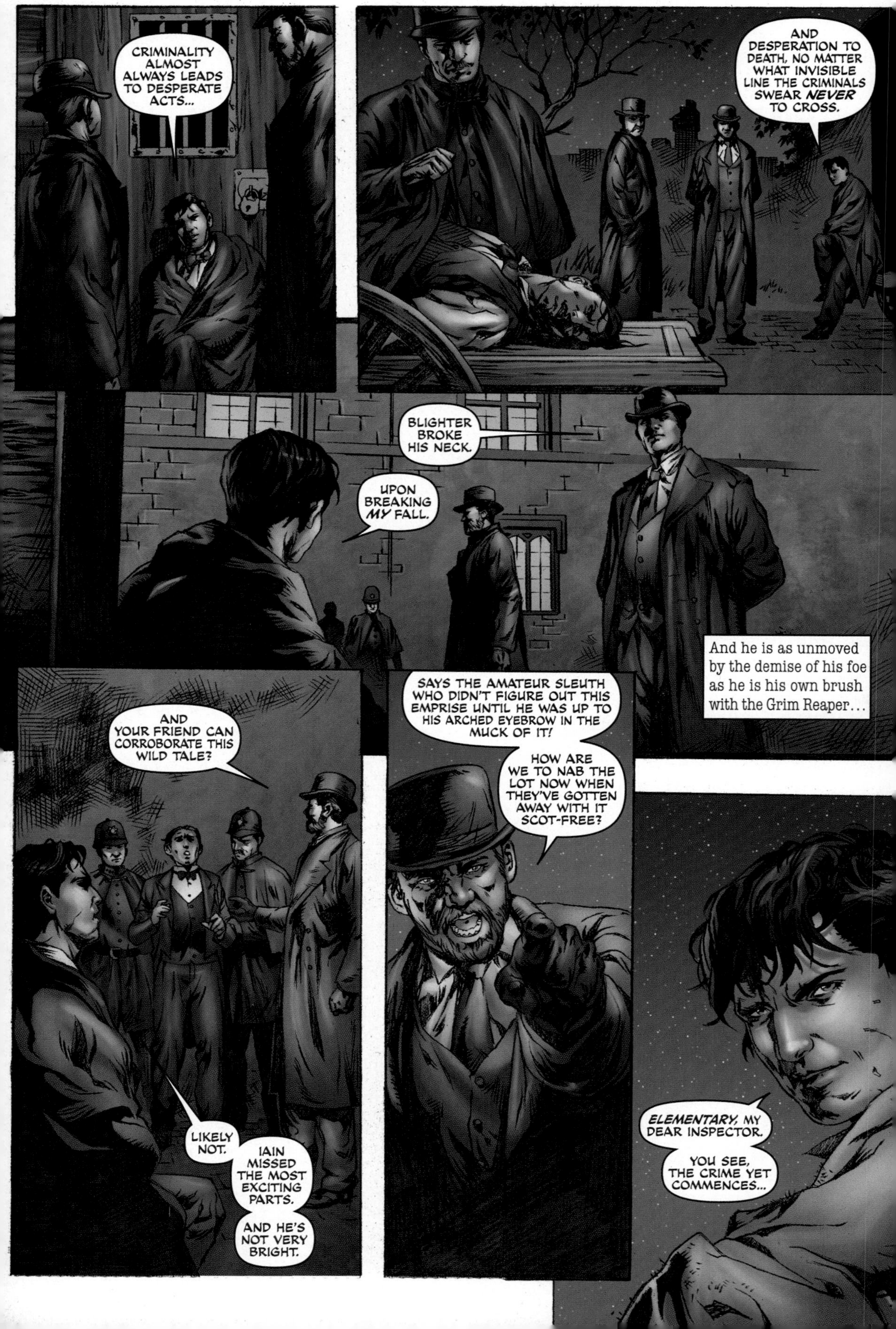
CRIMINALITY ALMOST ALWAYS LEADS TO DESPERATE ACTS...
AND DESPERATION TO DEATH, NO MATTER WHAT INVISIBLE LINE THE CRIMINALS SWEAR NEVER TO CROSS.
BLIGHTER BROKE HIS NECK.
UPON BREAKING MY FALL.
And he is as unmoved by the demise of his foe as he is his own brush with the Grim Reaper...
AND YOUR FRIEND CAN CORROBORATE THIS WILD TALE?
LIKELY NOT.
IAIN MISSED THE MOST EXCITING PARTS.
AND HE'S NOT VERY BRIGHT.
SAYS THE AMATEUR SLEUTH WHO DIDN'T FIGURE OUT THIS EMPRISE UNTIL HE WAS UP TO HIS ARCHED EYEBROW IN THE MUCK OF IT!
HOW ARE WE TO NAB THE LOT NOW WHEN THEY'VE GOTTEN AWAY WITH IT SCOT-FREE?
ELEMENTARY, MY DEAR INSPECTOR.
YOU SEE, THE CRIME YET COMMENCES...

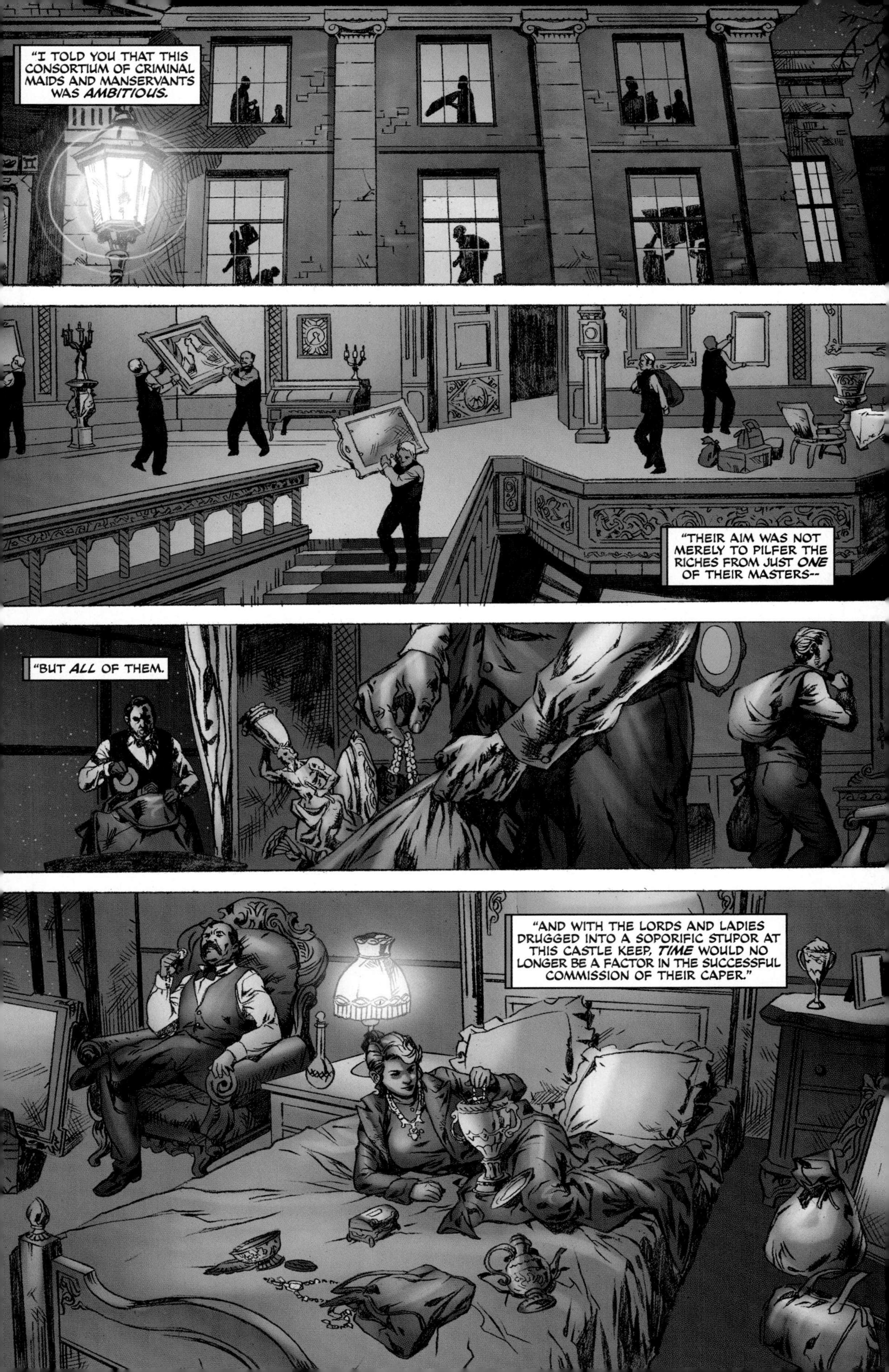
"I TOLD YOU THAT THIS CONSORTIUM OF CRIMINAL MAIDS AND MANSERVANTS WAS *AMBITIOUS.*
"THEIR AIM WAS NOT MERELY TO PILFER THE RICHES FROM JUST *ONE* OF THEIR MASTERS--
"BUT *ALL* OF THEM.
"AND WITH THE LORDS AND LADIES DRUGGED INTO A SOPORIFIC STUPOR AT THIS CASTLE KEEP, *TIME* WOULD NO LONGER BE A FACTOR IN THE SUCCESSFUL COMMISSION OF THEIR CAPER."

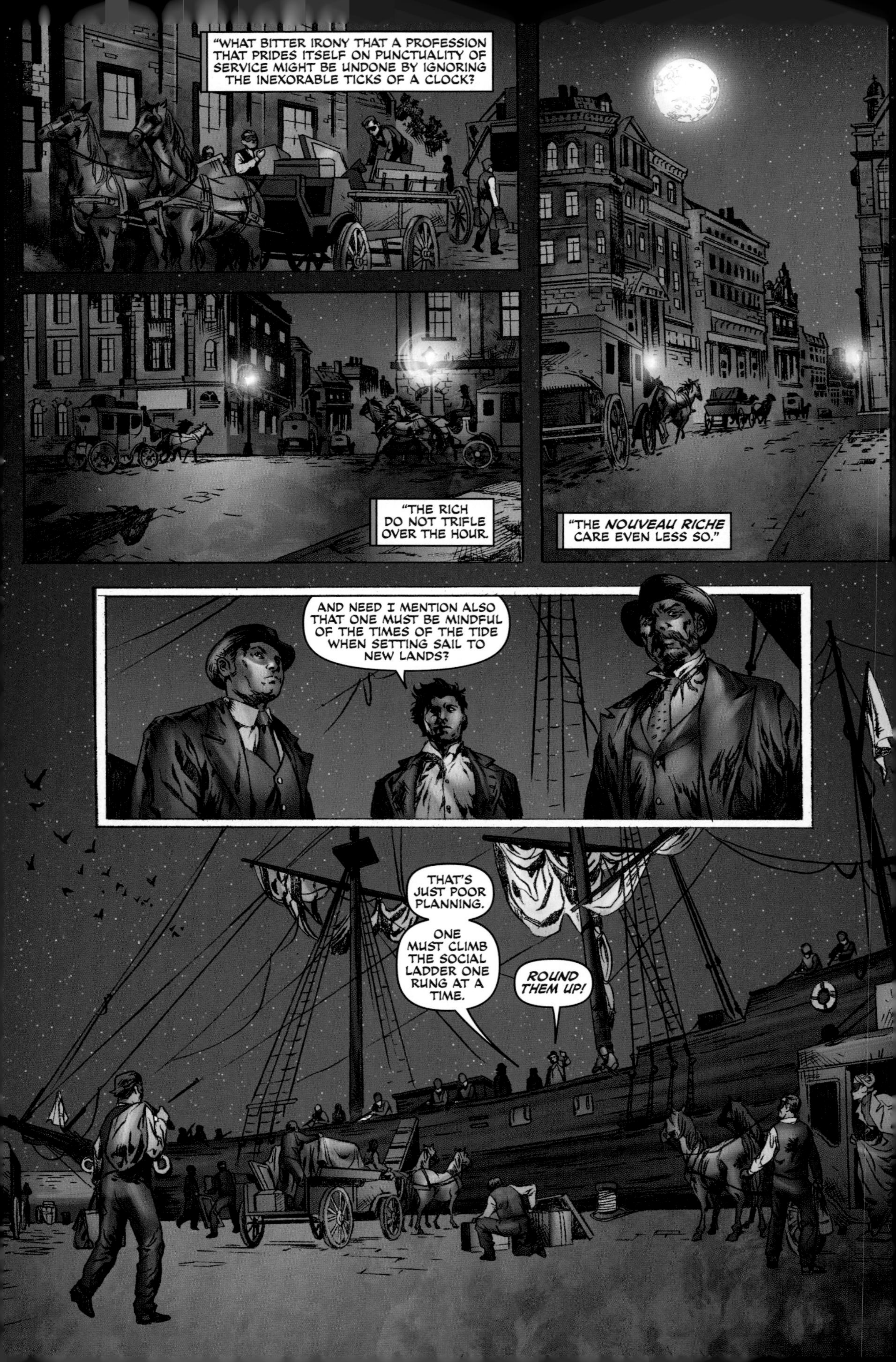
"WHAT BITTER IRONY THAT A PROFESSION THAT PRIDES ITSELF ON PUNCTUALITY OF SERVICE MIGHT BE UNDONE BY IGNORING THE INEXORABLE TICKS OF A CLOCK?
"THE RICH DO NOT TRIFLE OVER THE HOUR.
"THE *NOUVEAU RICHE* CARE EVEN LESS SO."
AND NEED I MENTION ALSO THAT ONE MUST BE MINDFUL OF THE TIMES OF THE TIDE WHEN SETTING SAIL TO NEW LANDS?
THAT'S JUST POOR PLANNING.
ONE MUST CLIMB THE SOCIAL LADDER ONE RUNG AT A TIME.
ROUND THEM UP!

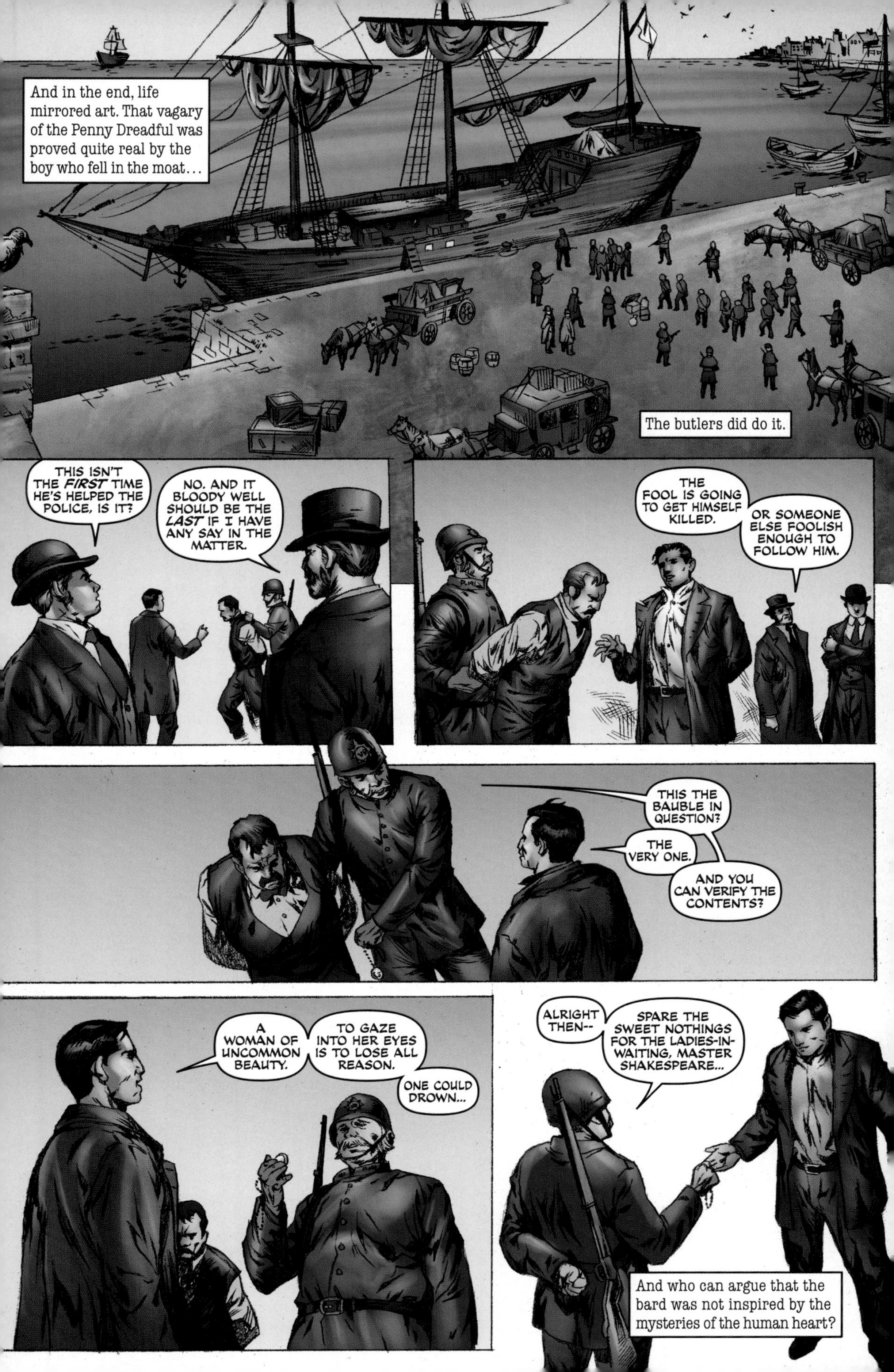
And in the end, life mirrored art. That vagary of the Penny Dreadful was proved quite real by the boy who fell in the moat...
The butlers did do it.
THIS ISN'T THE FIRST TIME HE'S HELPED THE POLICE, IS IT?
NO. AND IT BLOODY WELL SHOULD BE THE LAST IF I HAVE ANY SAY IN THE MATTER.
THE FOOL IS GOING TO GET HIMSELF KILLED.
OR SOMEONE ELSE FOOLISH ENOUGH TO FOLLOW HIM.
THIS THE BAUBLE IN QUESTION?
THE VERY ONE.
AND YOU CAN VERIFY THE CONTENTS?
A WOMAN OF UNCOMMON BEAUTY.
TO GAZE INTO HER EYES IS TO LOSE ALL REASON.
ONE COULD DROWN...
ALRIGHT THEN--
SPARE THE SWEET NOTHINGS FOR THE LADIES-IN-WAITING, MASTER SHAKESPEARE...
And who can argue that the bard was not inspired by the mysteries of the human heart?

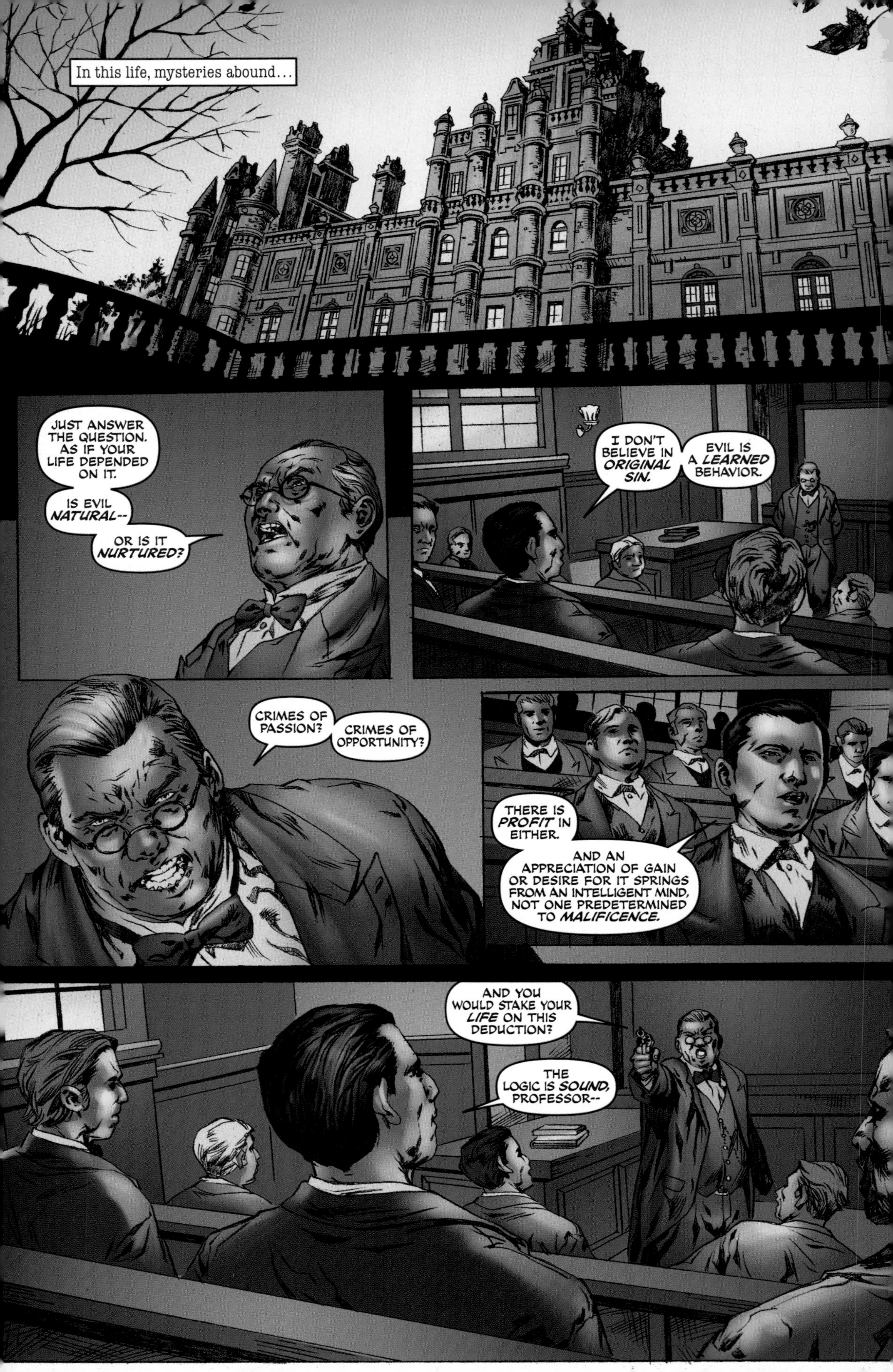
In this life, mysteries abound...
JUST ANSWER THE QUESTION. AS IF YOUR LIFE DEPENDED ON IT.
IS EVIL NATURAL--
OR IS IT NURTURED?
I DON'T BELIEVE IN ORIGINAL SIN.
EVIL IS A LEARNED BEHAVIOR.
CRIMES OF PASSION?
CRIMES OF OPPORTUNITY?
THERE IS PROFIT IN EITHER.
AND AN APPRECIATION OF GAIN OR DESIRE FOR IT SPRINGS FROM AN INTELLIGENT MIND, NOT ONE PREDETERMINED TO MALIFICENCE.
AND YOU WOULD STAKE YOUR LIFE ON THIS DEDUCTION?
THE LOGIC IS SOUND, PROFESSOR--

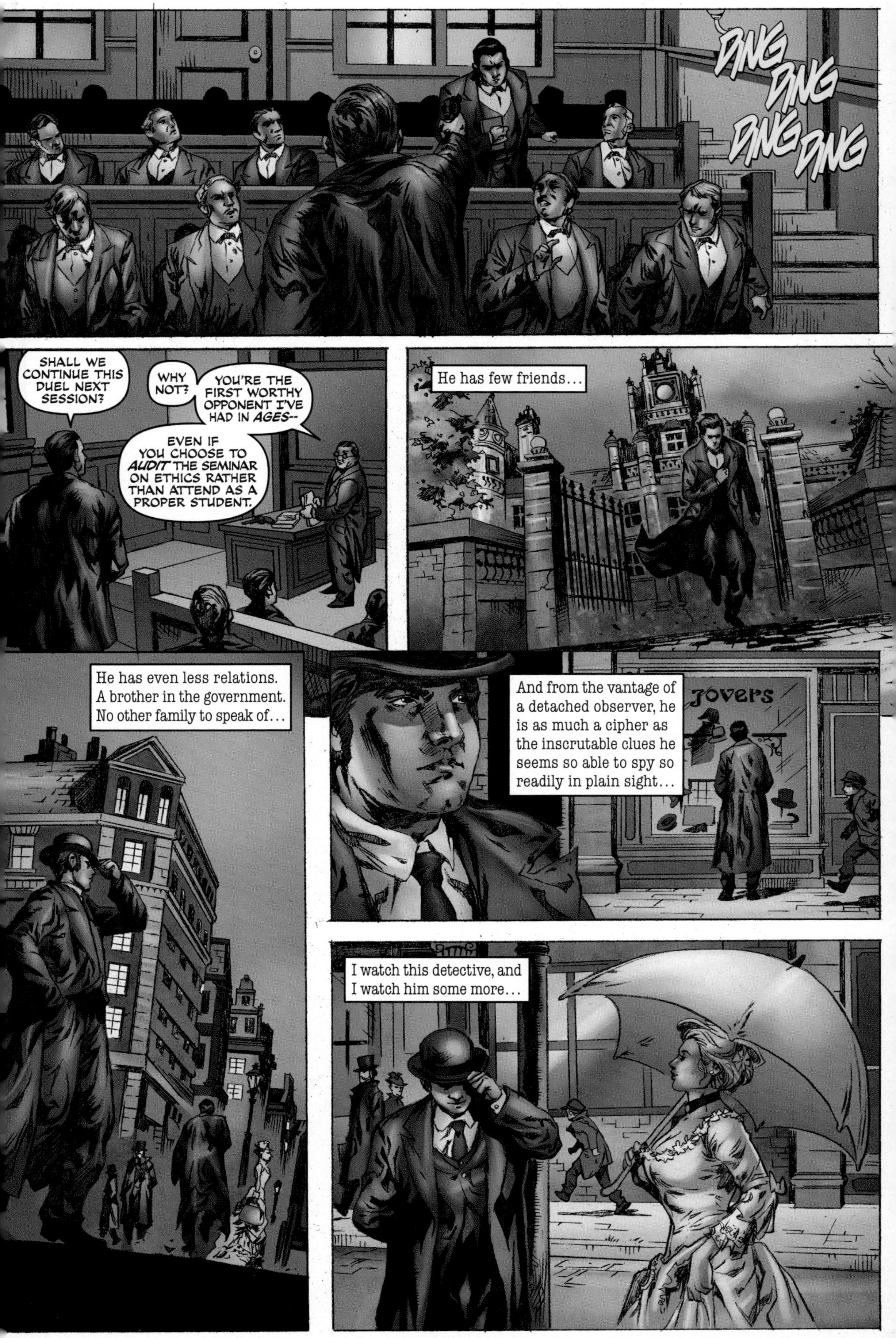
DING DING DING DING
SHALL WE CONTINUE THIS DUEL NEXT SESSION?
WHY NOT?
YOU'RE THE FIRST WORTHY OPPONENT I'VE HAD IN AGES--
EVEN IF YOU CHOOSE TO AUDIT THE SEMINAR ON ETHICS RATHER THAN ATTEND AS A PROPER STUDENT.
He has few friends...
He has even less relations. A brother in the government. No other family to speak of...
And from the vantage of a detached observer, he is as much a cipher as the inscrutable clues he seems so able to spy so readily in plain sight...
JOVERS
I watch this detective, and I watch him some more...

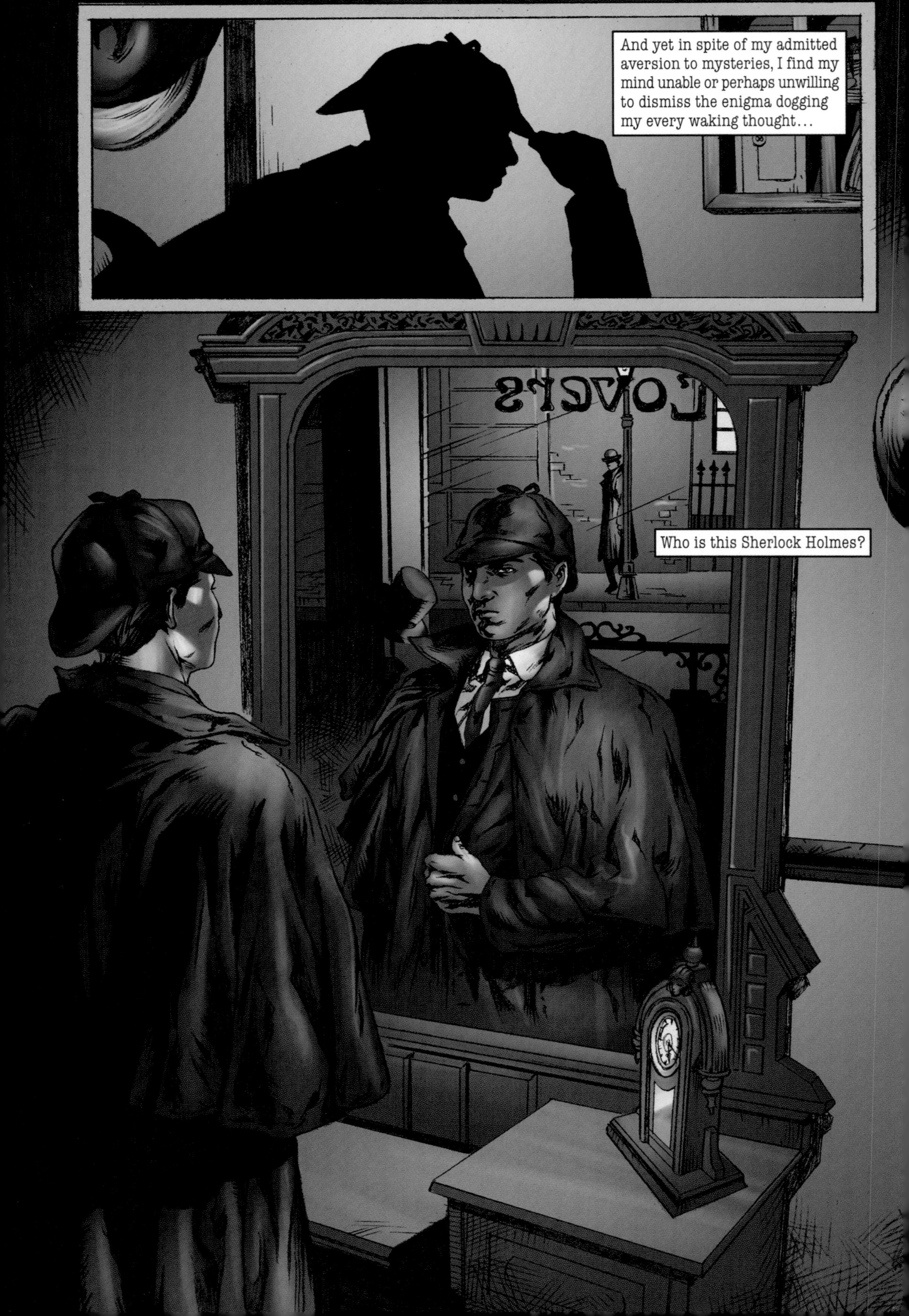
And yet in spite of my admitted aversion to mysteries, I find my mind unable or perhaps unwilling to dismiss the enigma dogging my every waking thought...
Who is this Sherlock Holmes?

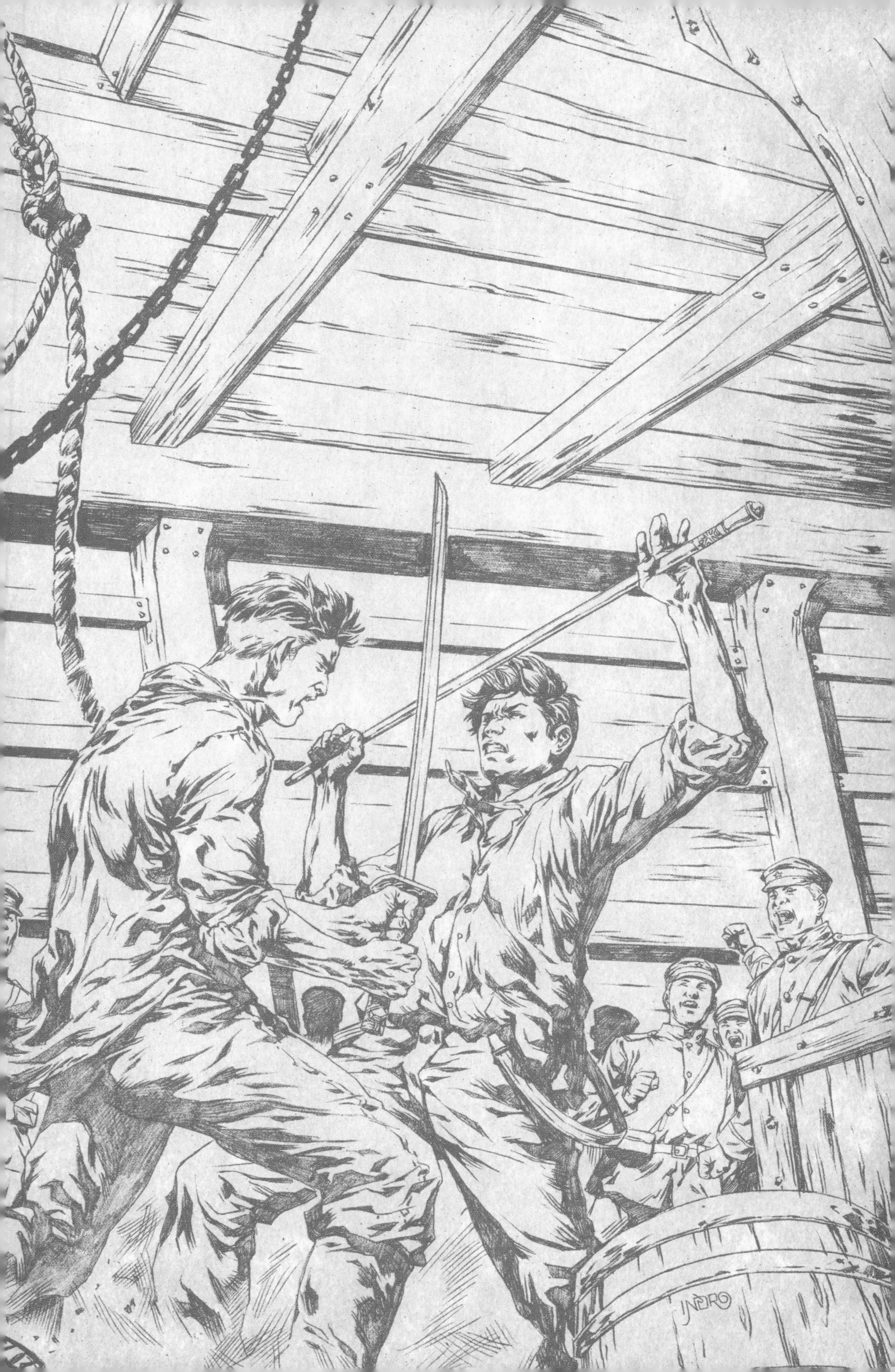
INDRO

Cover by:
FRANCESCO FRANCAVILLA

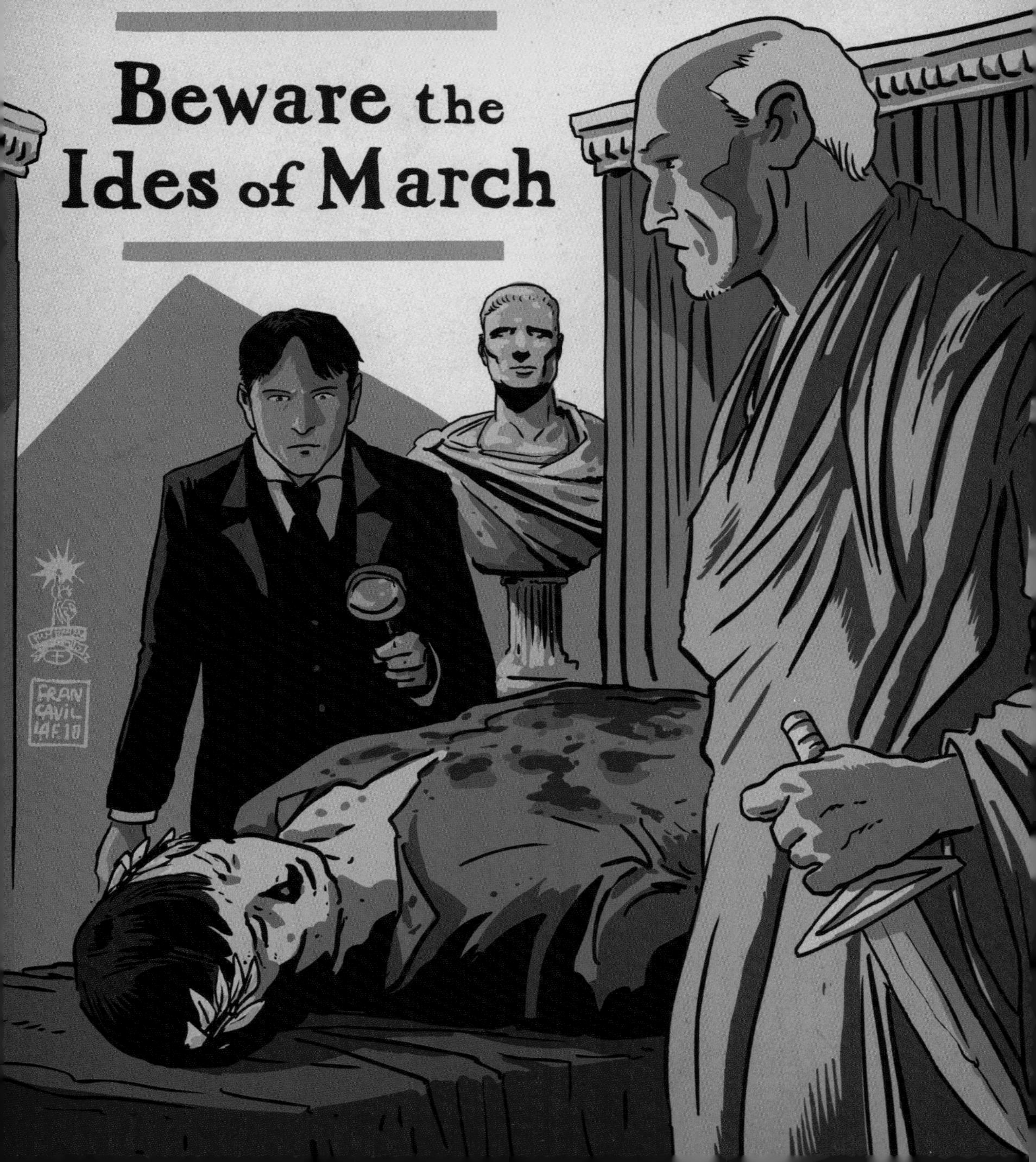
Beware the Ides of March

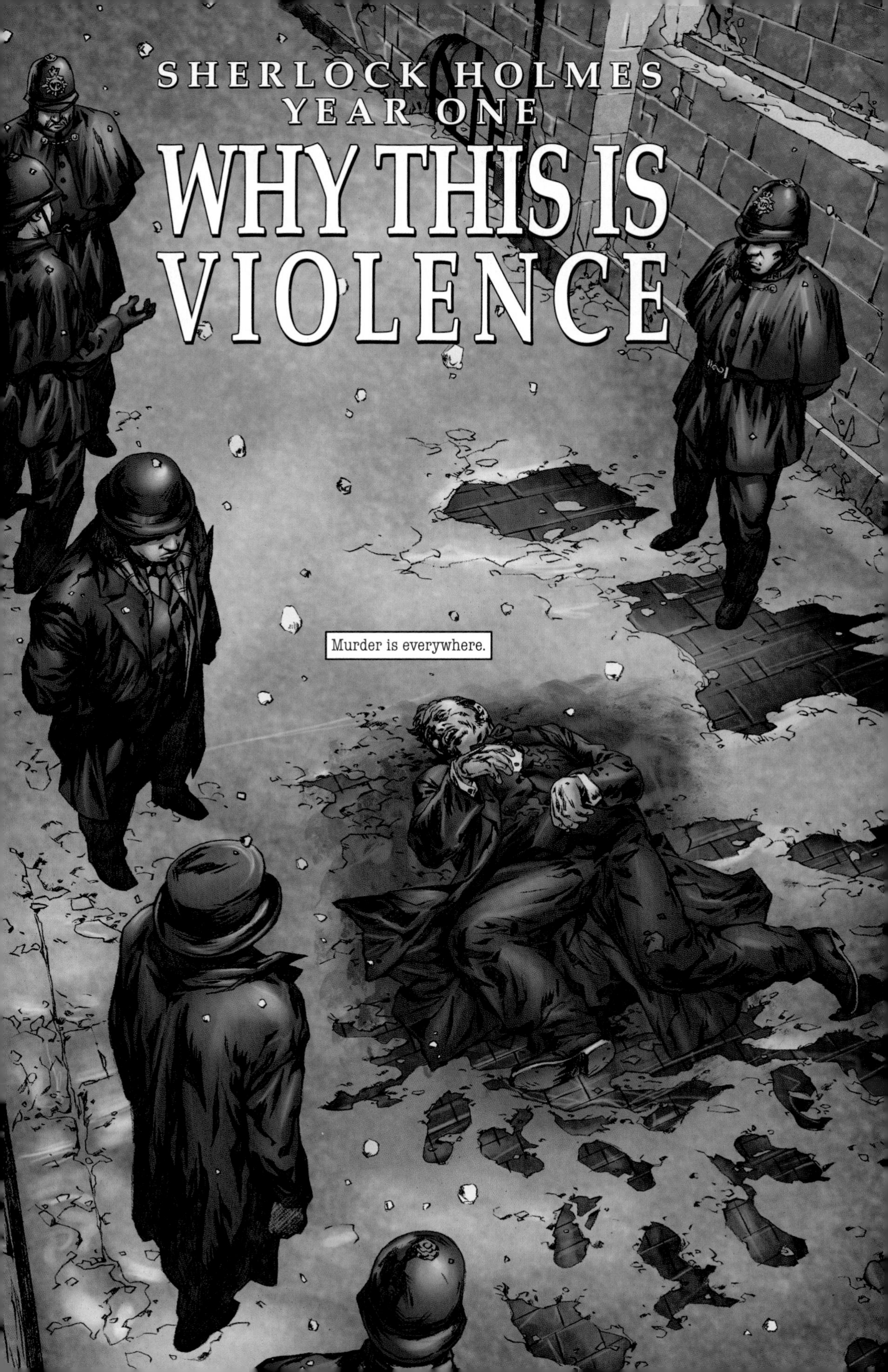
SHERLOCK HOLMES
YEAR ONE
WHY THIS IS VIOLENCE
Murder is everywhere.

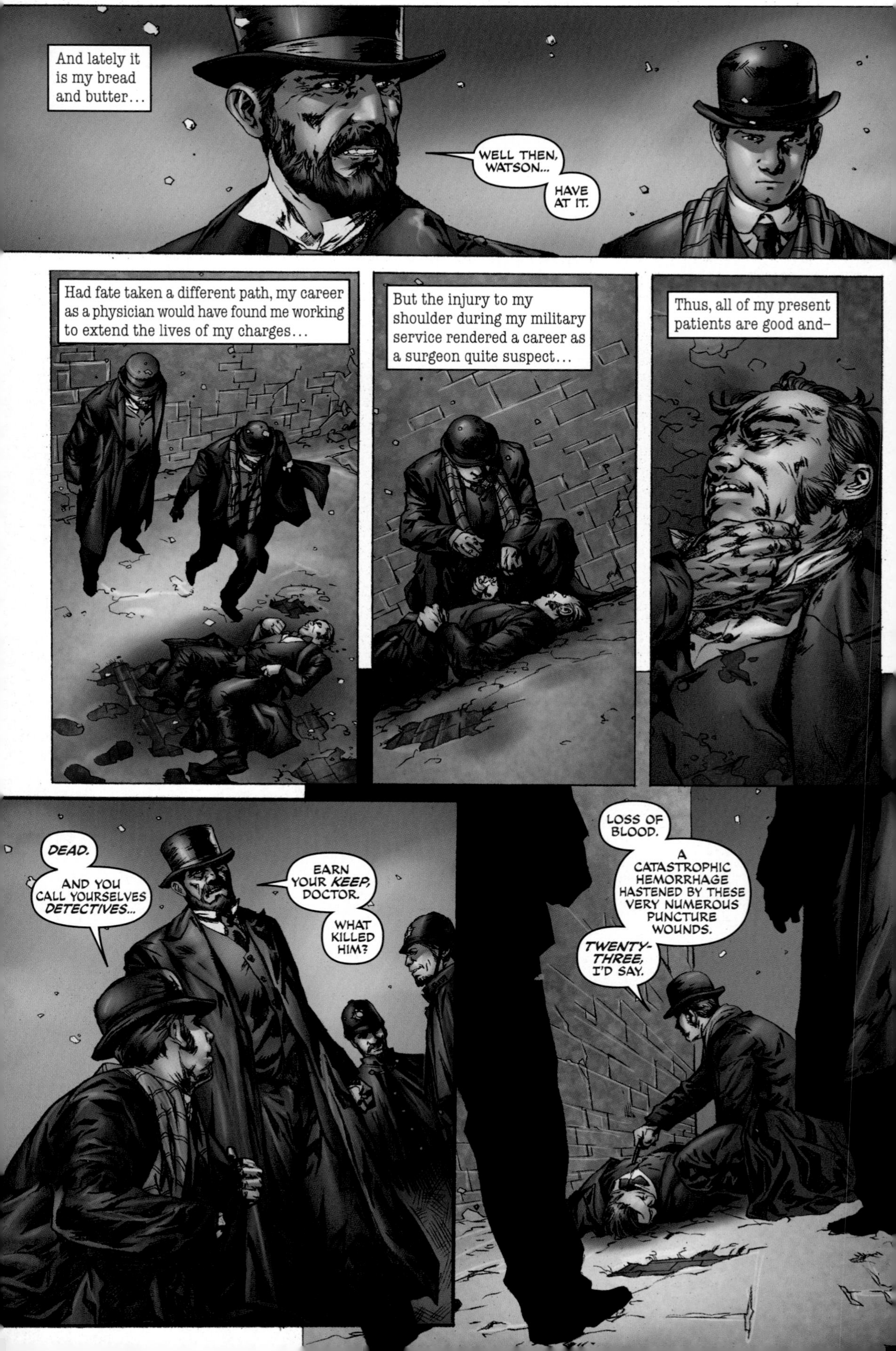
And lately it is my bread and butter...
WELL THEN, WATSON...
HAVE AT IT.
Had fate taken a different path, my career as a physician would have found me working to extend the lives of my charges...
But the injury to my shoulder during my military service rendered a career as a surgeon quite suspect...
Thus, all of my present patients are good and–
DEAD.
AND YOU CALL YOURSELVES DETECTIVES...
EARN YOUR KEEP, DOCTOR.
WHAT KILLED HIM?
LOSS OF BLOOD.
A CATASTROPHIC HEMORRHAGE HASTENED BY THESE VERY NUMEROUS PUNCTURE WOUNDS.
TWENTY-THREE, I'D SAY.

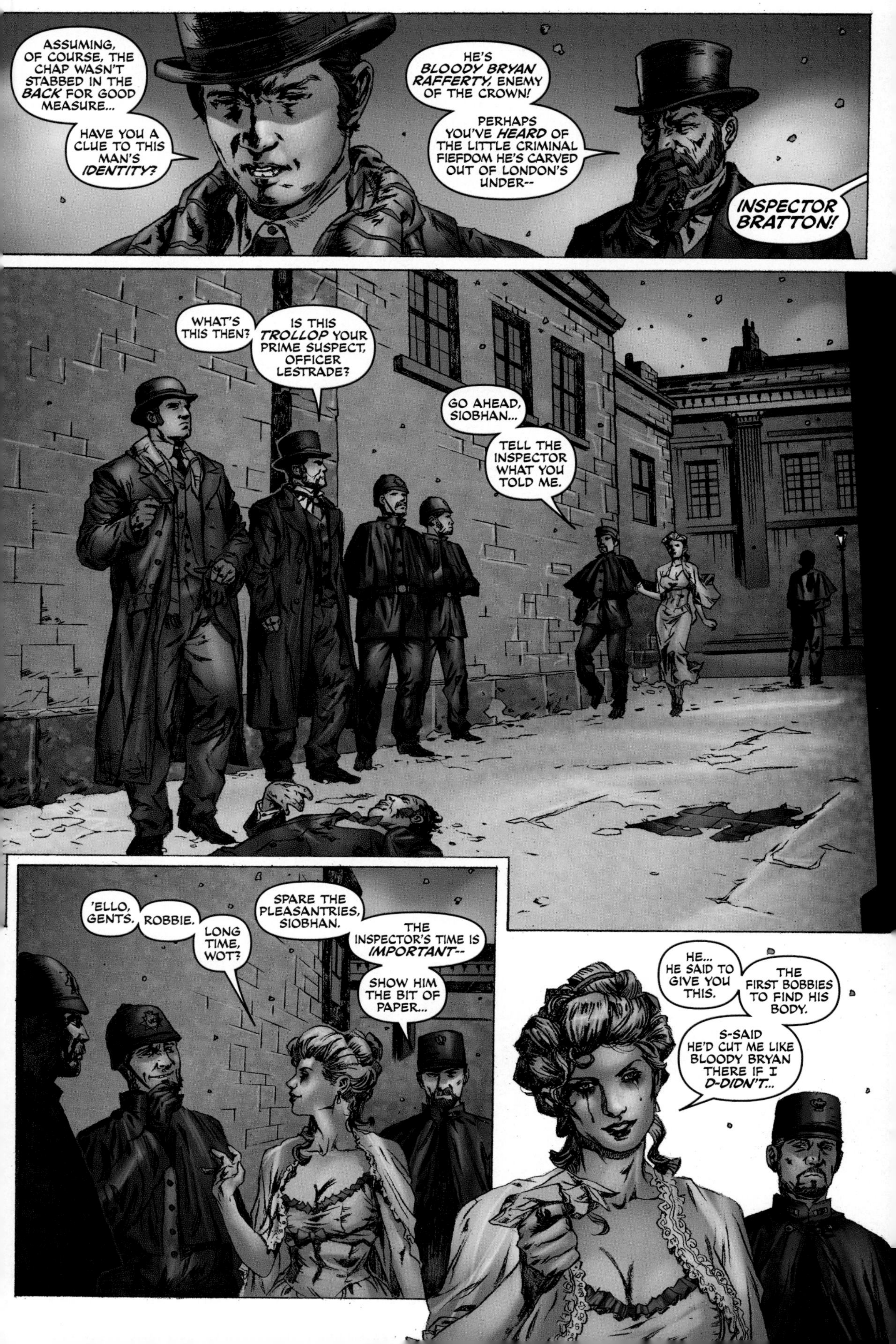
ASSUMING, OF COURSE, THE CHAP WASN'T STABBED IN THE BACK FOR GOOD MEASURE...
HAVE YOU A CLUE TO THIS MAN'S IDENTITY?
HE'S BLOODY BRYAN RAFFERTY, ENEMY OF THE CROWN!
PERHAPS YOU'VE HEARD OF THE LITTLE CRIMINAL FIEFDOM HE'S CARVED OUT OF LONDON'S UNDER--
INSPECTOR BRATTON!
WHAT'S THIS THEN?
IS THIS TROLLOP YOUR PRIME SUSPECT, OFFICER LESTRADE?
GO AHEAD, SIOBHAN...
TELL THE INSPECTOR WHAT YOU TOLD ME.
'ELLO, GENTS.
ROBBIE.
LONG TIME, WOT?
SPARE THE PLEASANTRIES, SIOBHAN.
THE INSPECTOR'S TIME IS IMPORTANT--
SHOW HIM THE BIT OF PAPER...
HE... HE SAID TO GIVE YOU THIS.
THE FIRST BOBBIES TO FIND HIS BODY.
S-SAID HE'D CUT ME LIKE BLOODY BRYAN THERE IF I D-DIDN'T...

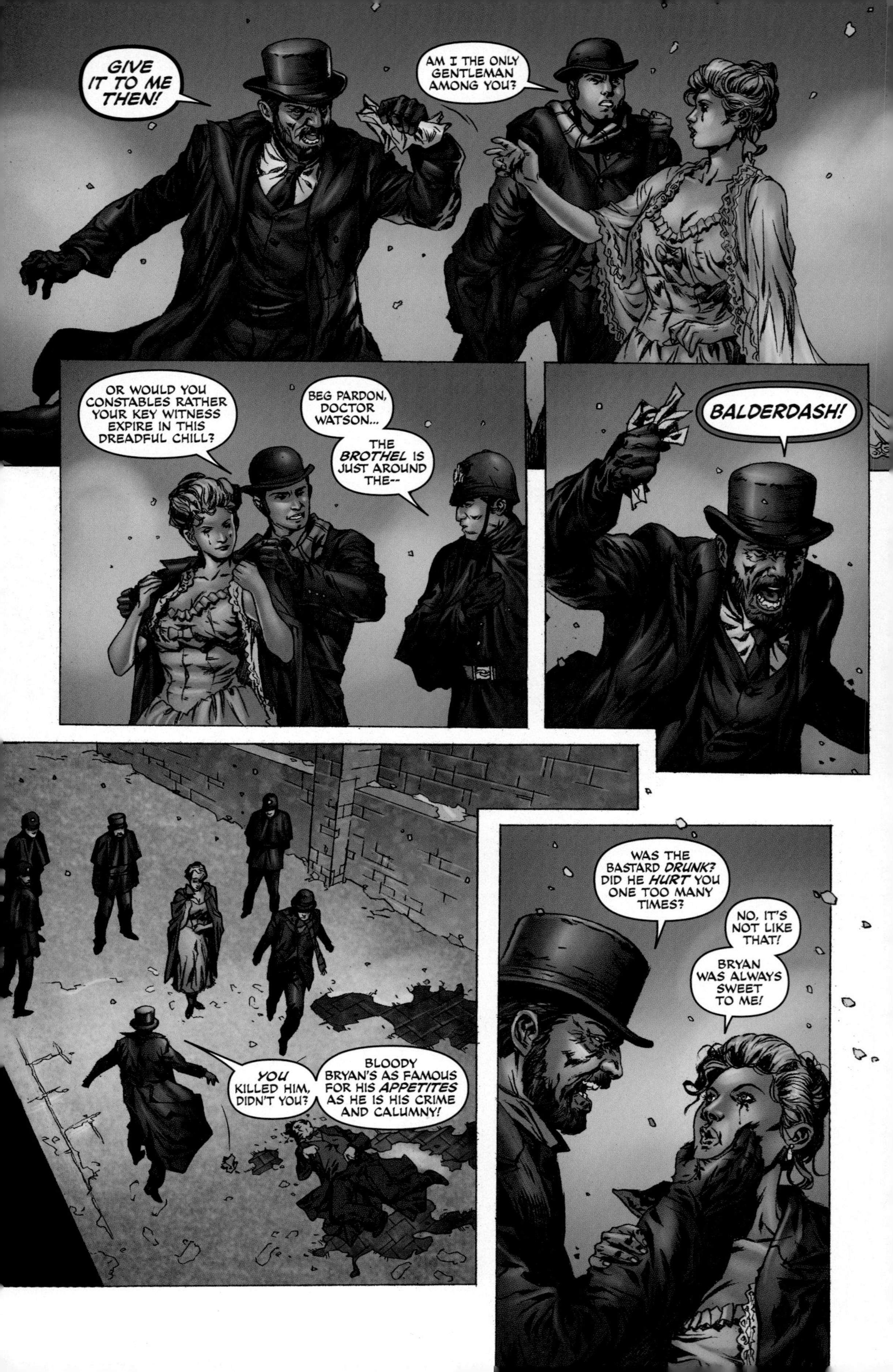
GIVE IT TO ME THEN!
AM I THE ONLY GENTLEMAN AMONG YOU?
OR WOULD YOU CONSTABLES RATHER YOUR KEY WITNESS EXPIRE IN THIS DREADFUL CHILL?
BEG PARDON, DOCTOR WATSON...
THE BROTHEL IS JUST AROUND THE--
BALDERDASH!
YOU KILLED HIM, DIDN'T YOU?
BLOODY BRYAN'S AS FAMOUS FOR HIS APPETITES AS HE IS HIS CRIME AND CALUMNY!
WAS THE BASTARD DRUNK? DID HE HURT YOU ONE TOO MANY TIMES?
NO, IT'S NOT LIKE THAT!
BRYAN WAS ALWAYS SWEET TO ME!

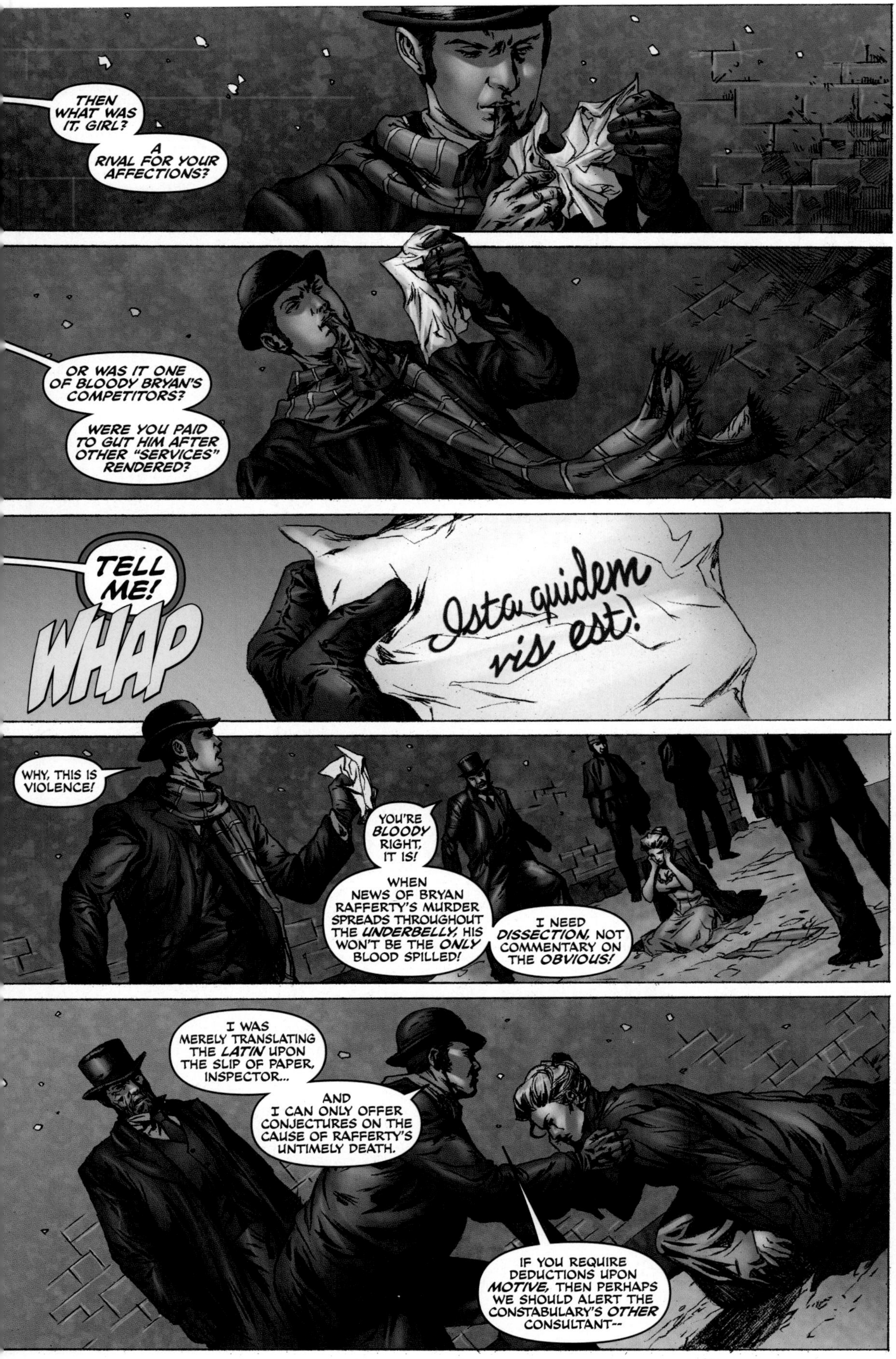
THEN WHAT WAS IT, GIRL?
A RIVAL FOR YOUR AFFECTIONS?
OR WAS IT ONE OF BLOODY BRYAN'S COMPETITORS?
WERE YOU PAID TO GUT HIM AFTER OTHER "SERVICES" RENDERED?
TELL ME!
WHAP
Ista quidem vis est!
WHY, THIS IS VIOLENCE!
YOU'RE BLOODY RIGHT, IT IS!
WHEN NEWS OF BRYAN RAFFERTY'S MURDER SPREADS THROUGHOUT THE UNDERBELLY, HIS WON'T BE THE ONLY BLOOD SPILLED!
I NEED DISSECTION, NOT COMMENTARY ON THE OBVIOUS!
I WAS MERELY TRANSLATING THE LATIN UPON THE SLIP OF PAPER, INSPECTOR...
AND I CAN ONLY OFFER CONJECTURES ON THE CAUSE OF RAFFERTY'S UNTIMELY DEATH.
IF YOU REQUIRE DEDUCTIONS UPON MOTIVE, THEN PERHAPS WE SHOULD ALERT THE CONSTABULARY'S OTHER CONSULTANT--

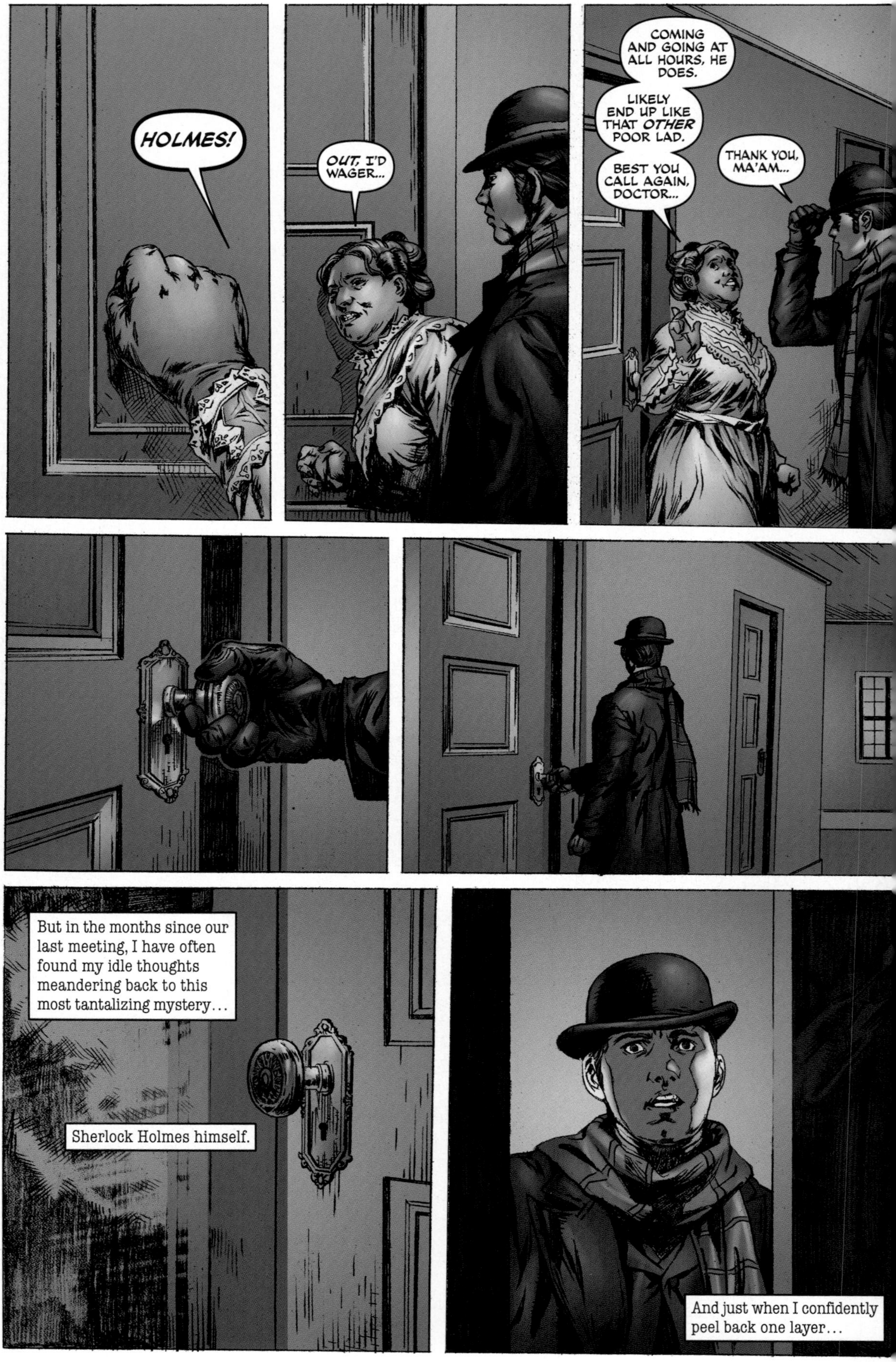
HOLMES!
OUT, I'D WAGER...
COMING AND GOING AT ALL HOURS, HE DOES.
LIKELY END UP LIKE THAT OTHER POOR LAD.
BEST YOU CALL AGAIN, DOCTOR...
THANK YOU, MA'AM...
But in the months since our last meeting, I have often found my idle thoughts meandering back to this most tantalizing mystery...
Sherlock Holmes himself.
And just when I confidently peel back one layer...

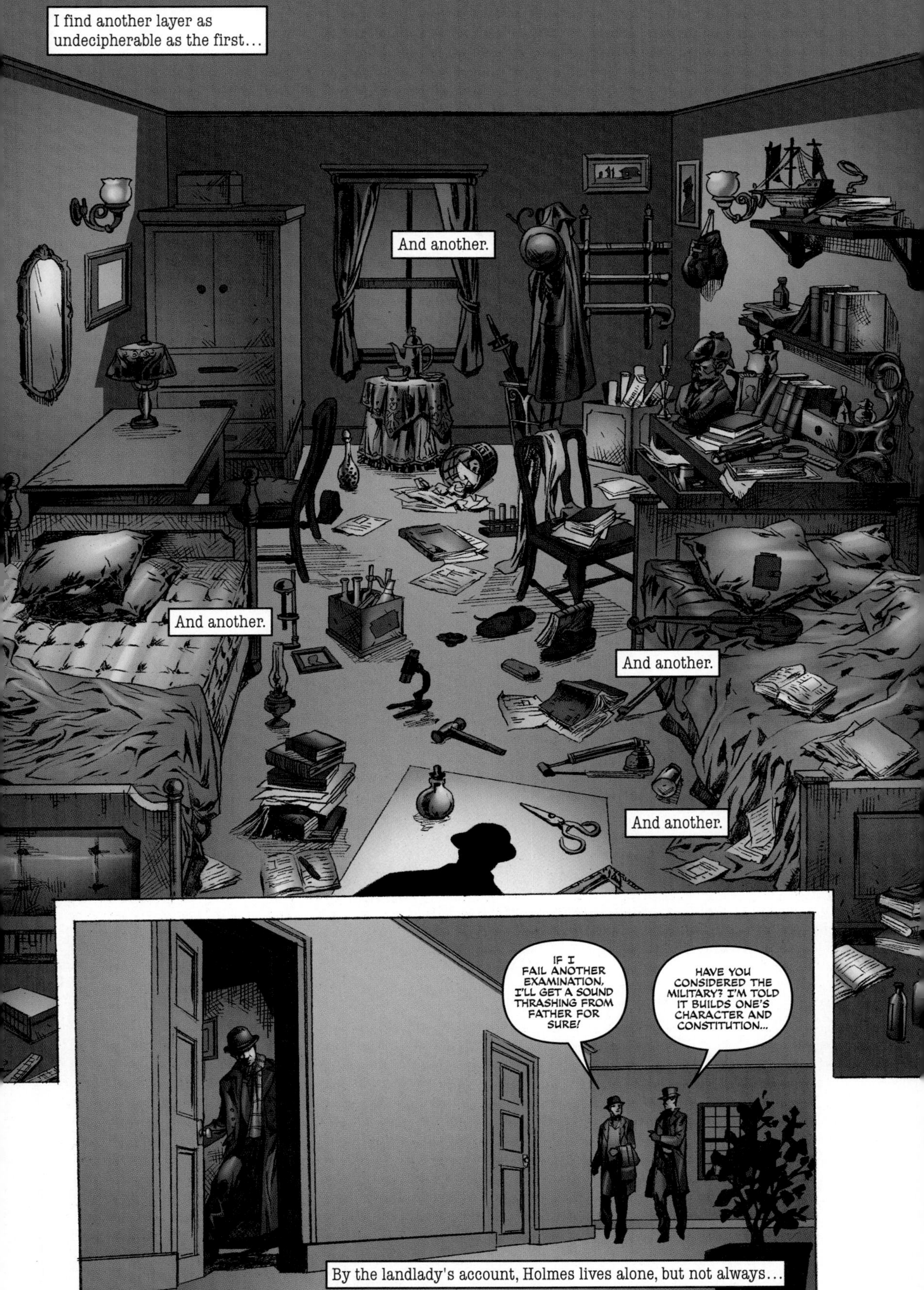
I find another layer as undecipherable as the first...
And another.
And another.
And another.
And another.
IF I FAIL ANOTHER EXAMINATION, I'LL GET A SOUND THRASHING FROM FATHER FOR SURE!
HAVE YOU CONSIDERED THE MILITARY? I'M TOLD IT BUILDS ONE'S CHARACTER AND CONSTITUTION...
By the landlady's account, Holmes lives alone, but not always...

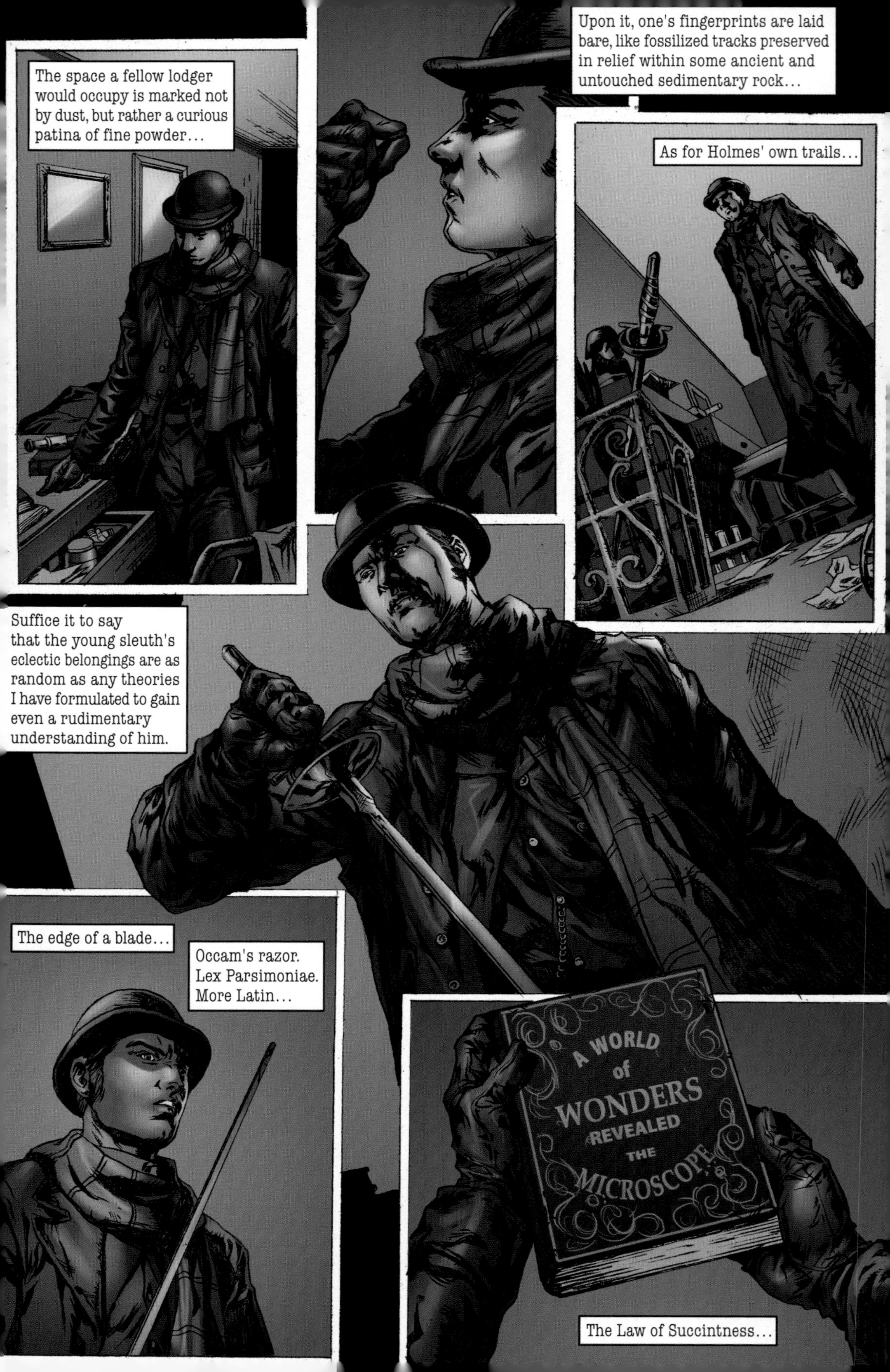
The space a fellow lodger would occupy is marked not by dust, but rather a curious patina of fine powder...
Upon it, one's fingerprints are laid bare, like fossilized tracks preserved in relief within some ancient and untouched sedimentary rock...
As for Holmes' own trails...
Suffice it to say that the young sleuth's eclectic belongings are as random as any theories I have formulated to gain even a rudimentary understanding of him.
The edge of a blade...
Occam's razor. Lex Parsimoniae. More Latin...
A WORLD of WONDERS REVEALED THE MICROSCOPE
The Law of Succintness...

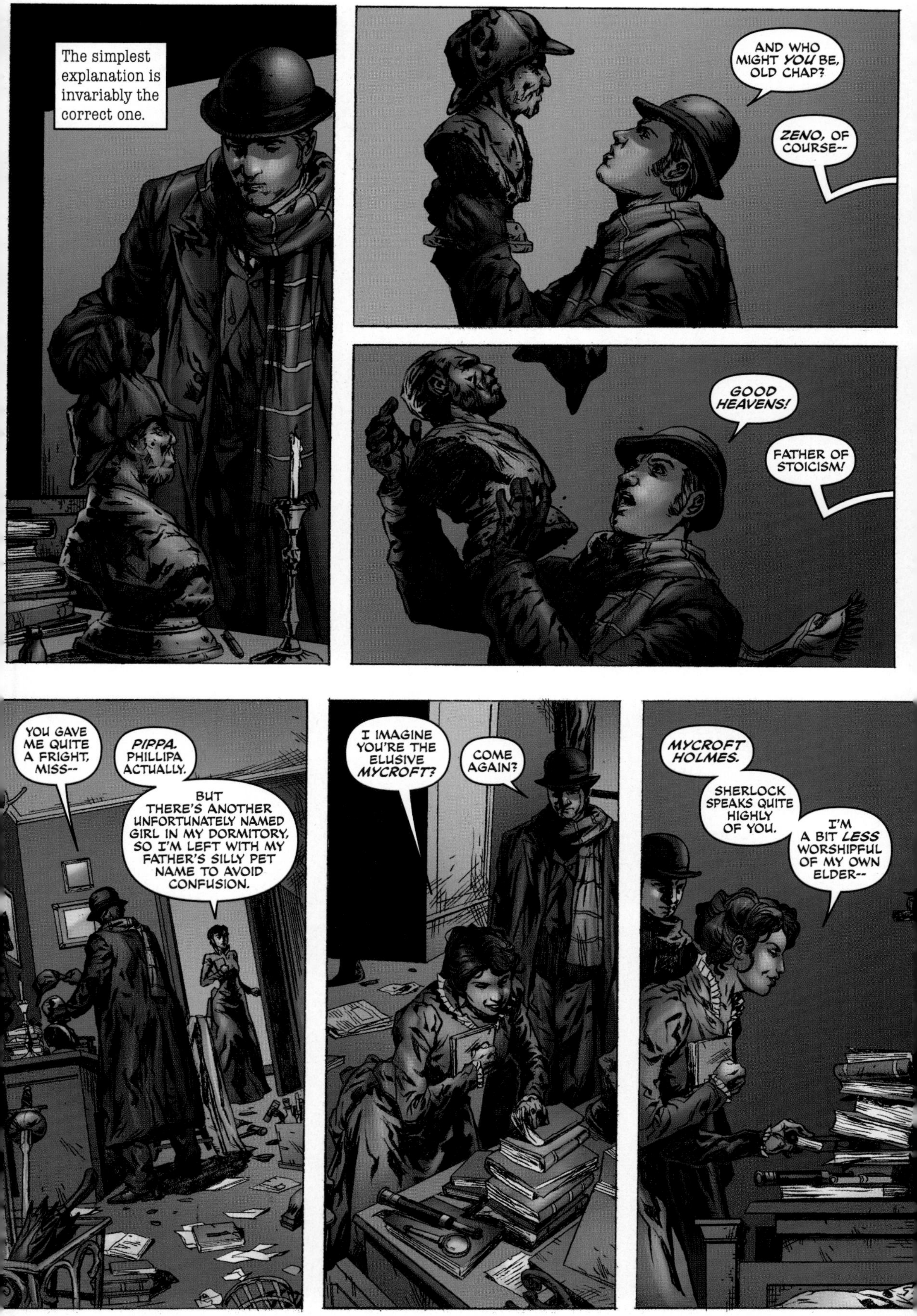
The simplest explanation is invariably the correct one.
AND WHO MIGHT *YOU* BE, OLD CHAP?
ZENO, OF COURSE--
GOOD HEAVENS!
FATHER OF STOICISM!
YOU GAVE ME QUITE A FRIGHT, MISS--
PIPPA. PHILLIPA ACTUALLY.
BUT THERE'S ANOTHER UNFORTUNATELY NAMED GIRL IN MY DORMITORY, SO I'M LEFT WITH MY FATHER'S SILLY PET NAME TO AVOID CONFUSION.
I IMAGINE YOU'RE THE ELUSIVE *MYCROFT?*
COME AGAIN?
MYCROFT HOLMES.
SHERLOCK SPEAKS QUITE HIGHLY OF YOU.
I'M A BIT *LESS* WORSHIPFUL OF MY OWN ELDER--

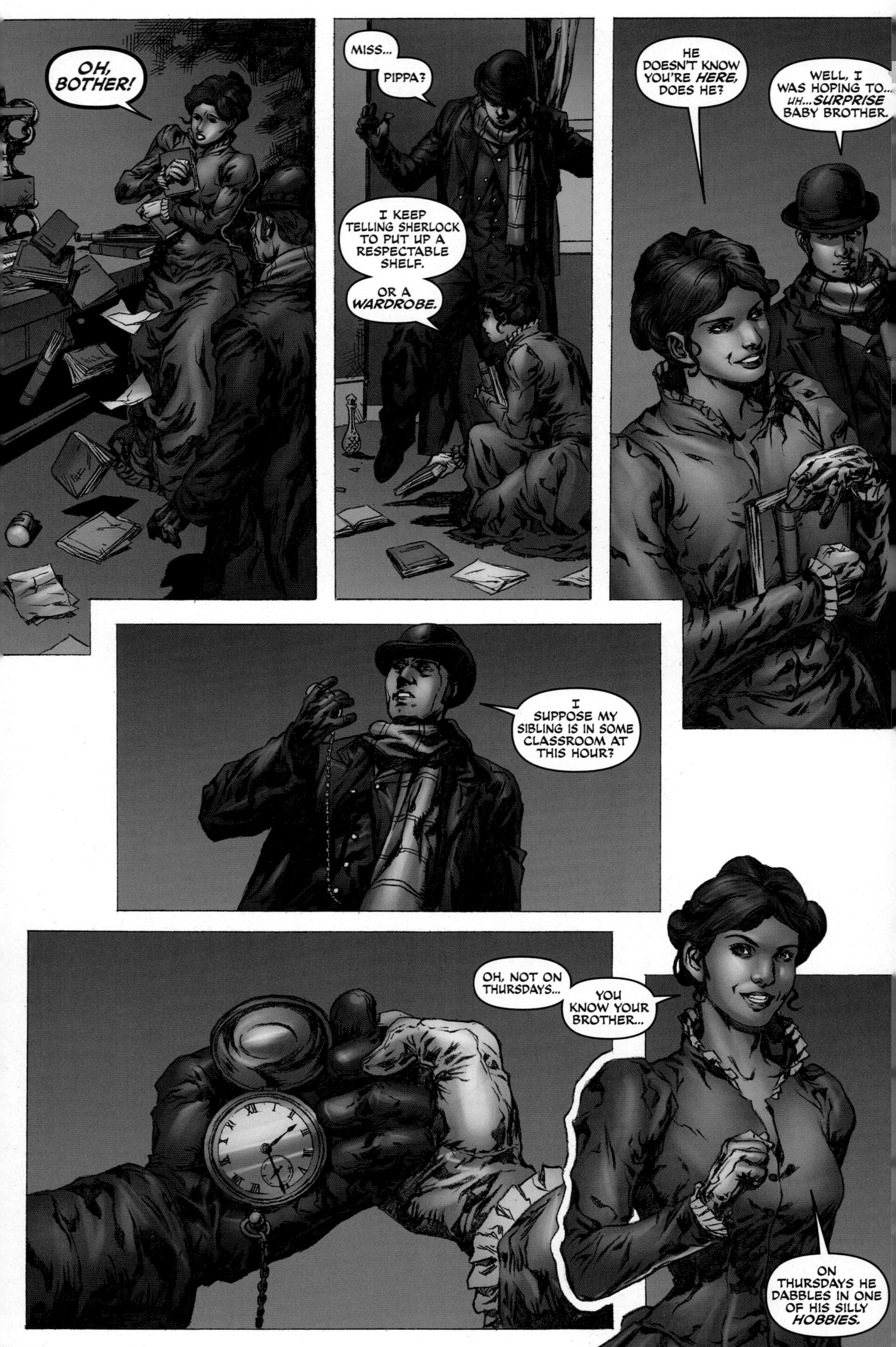
OH, BOTHER!
MISS...
PIPPA?
I KEEP TELLING SHERLOCK TO PUT UP A RESPECTABLE SHELF.
OR A WARDROBE.
HE DOESN'T KNOW YOU'RE HERE, DOES HE?
WELL, I WAS HOPING TO... UH...SURPRISE BABY BROTHER.
I SUPPOSE MY SIBLING IS IN SOME CLASSROOM AT THIS HOUR?
OH, NOT ON THURSDAYS...
YOU KNOW YOUR BROTHER...
ON THURSDAYS HE DABBLES IN ONE OF HIS SILLY HOBBIES.

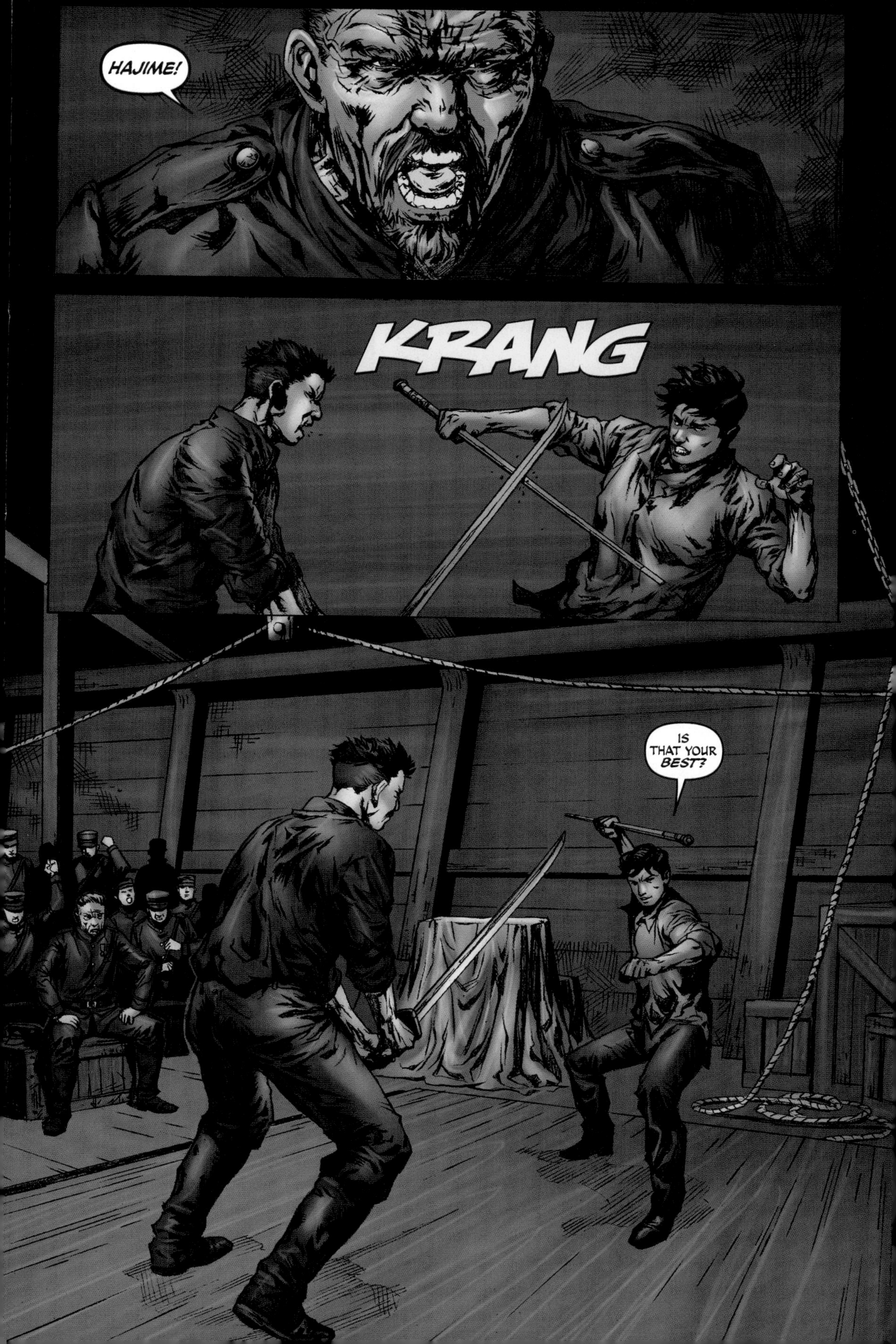
HAJIME!
KRANG
IS THAT YOUR BEST?

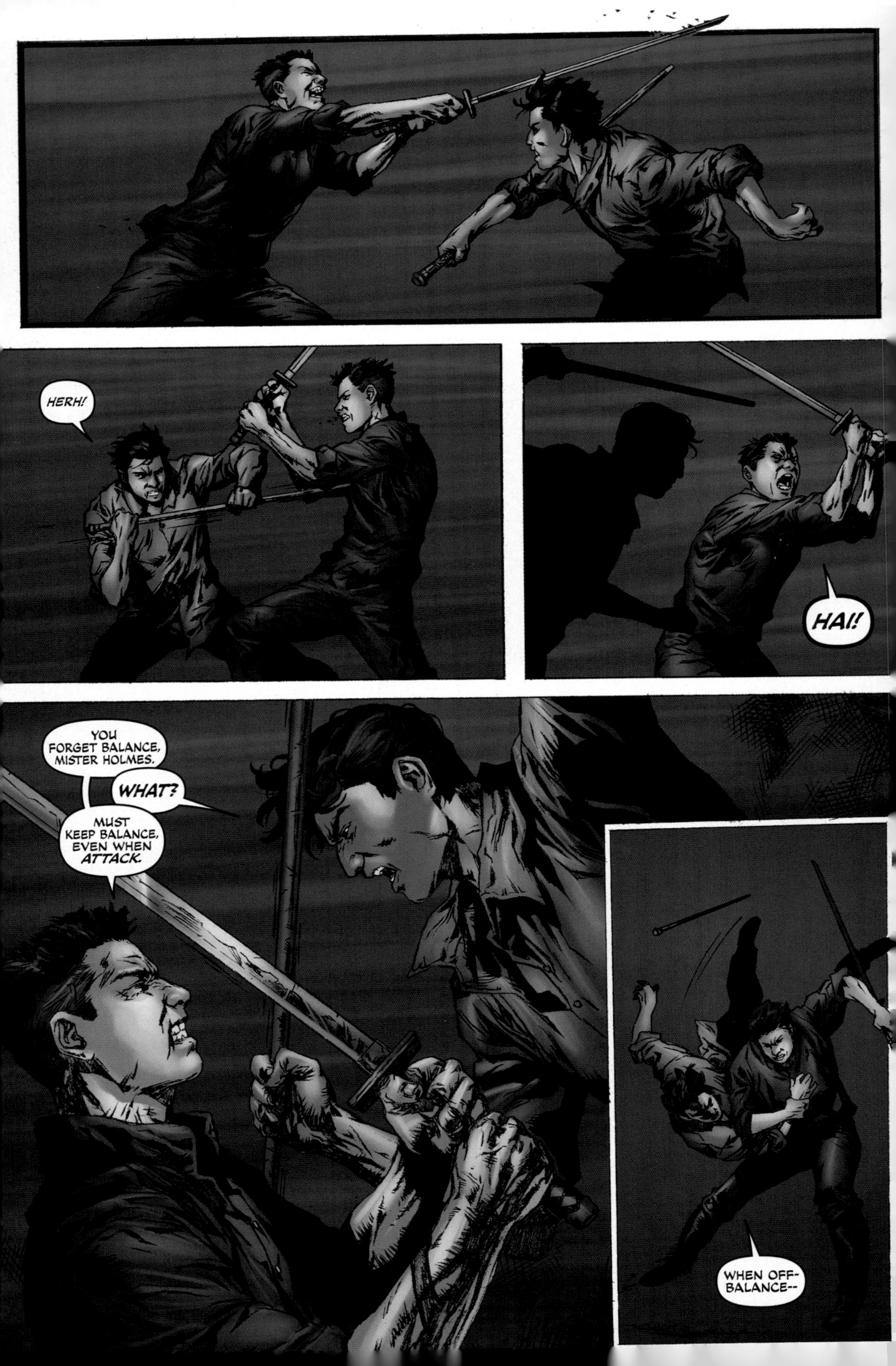
HERH!
HAI!
YOU FORGET BALANCE, MISTER HOLMES.
WHAT?
MUST KEEP BALANCE, EVEN WHEN ATTACK.
WHEN OFF-BALANCE--

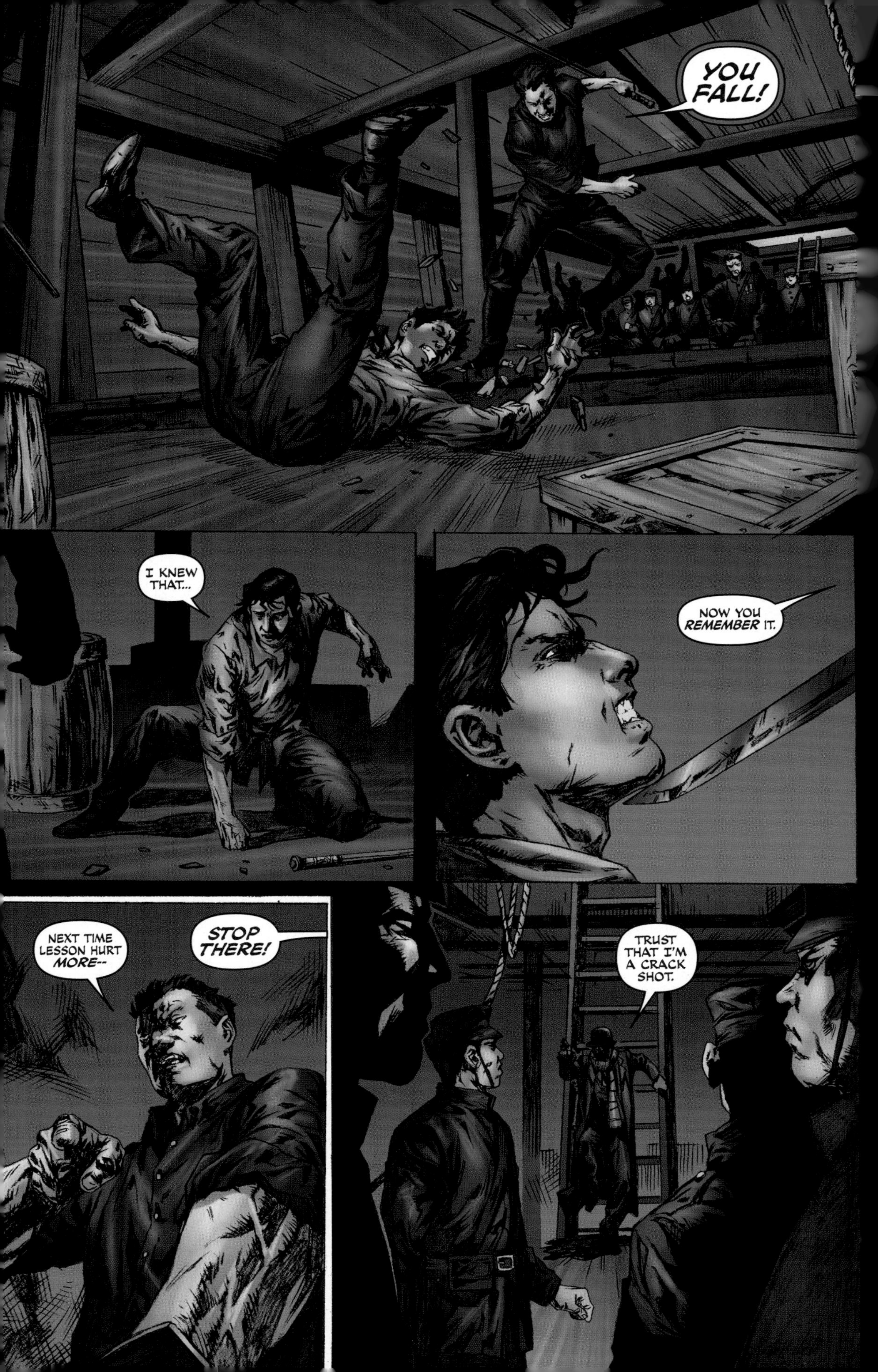
YOU FALL!
I KNEW THAT...
NOW YOU REMEMBER IT.
NEXT TIME LESSON HURT MORE--
STOP THERE!
TRUST THAT I'M A CRACK SHOT.

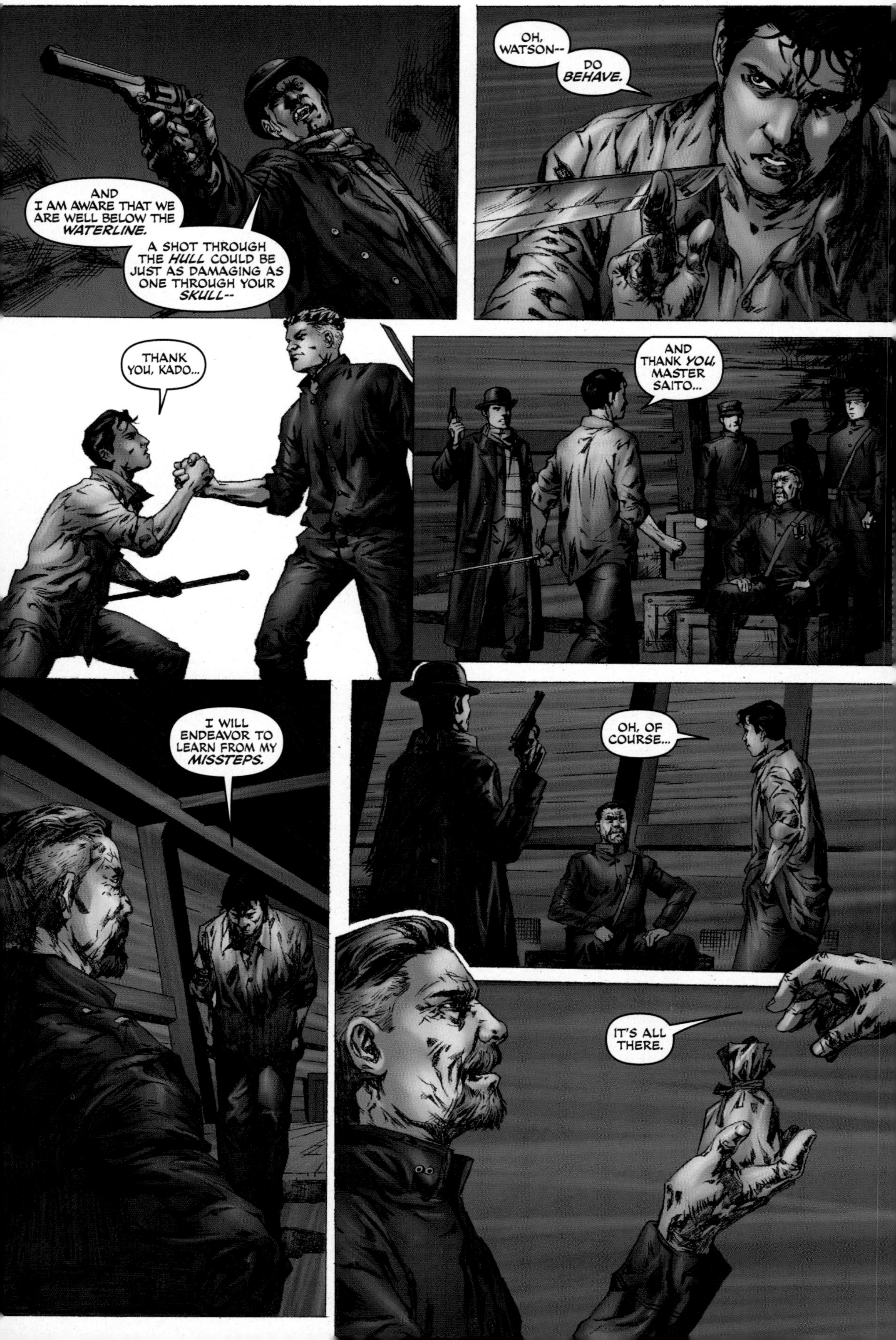
AND I AM AWARE THAT WE ARE WELL BELOW THE WATERLINE.
A SHOT THROUGH THE HULL COULD BE JUST AS DAMAGING AS ONE THROUGH YOUR SKULL--
OH, WATSON--
DO BEHAVE.
THANK YOU, KADO...
AND THANK YOU, MASTER SAITO...
I WILL ENDEAVOR TO LEARN FROM MY MISSTEPS.
OH, OF COURSE...
IT'S ALL THERE.

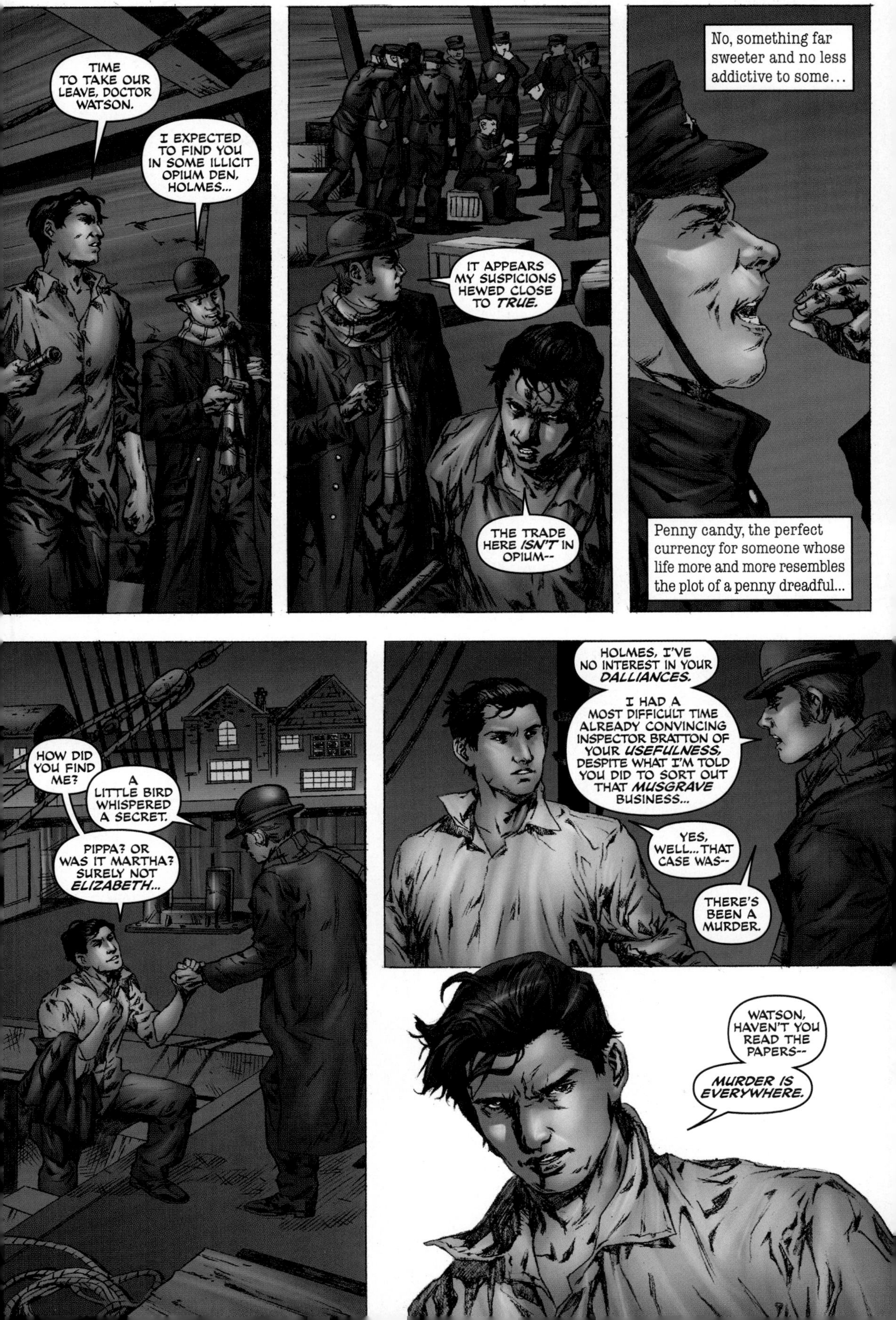
TIME TO TAKE OUR LEAVE, DOCTOR WATSON.
I EXPECTED TO FIND YOU IN SOME ILLICIT OPIUM DEN, HOLMES...
IT APPEARS MY SUSPICIONS HEWED CLOSE TO *TRUE.*
THE TRADE HERE *ISN'T* IN OPIUM--
No, something far sweeter and no less addictive to some...
Penny candy, the perfect currency for someone whose life more and more resembles the plot of a penny dreadful...
HOW DID YOU FIND ME?
A LITTLE BIRD WHISPERED A SECRET.
PIPPA? OR WAS IT MARTHA? SURELY NOT *ELIZABETH*...
HOLMES, I'VE NO INTEREST IN YOUR *DALLIANCES.*
I HAD A MOST DIFFICULT TIME ALREADY CONVINCING INSPECTOR BRATTON OF YOUR *USEFULNESS,* DESPITE WHAT I'M TOLD YOU DID TO SORT OUT THAT *MUSGRAVE* BUSINESS...
YES, WELL...THAT CASE WAS--
THERE'S BEEN A MURDER.
WATSON, HAVEN'T YOU READ THE PAPERS--
MURDER IS EVERYWHERE.

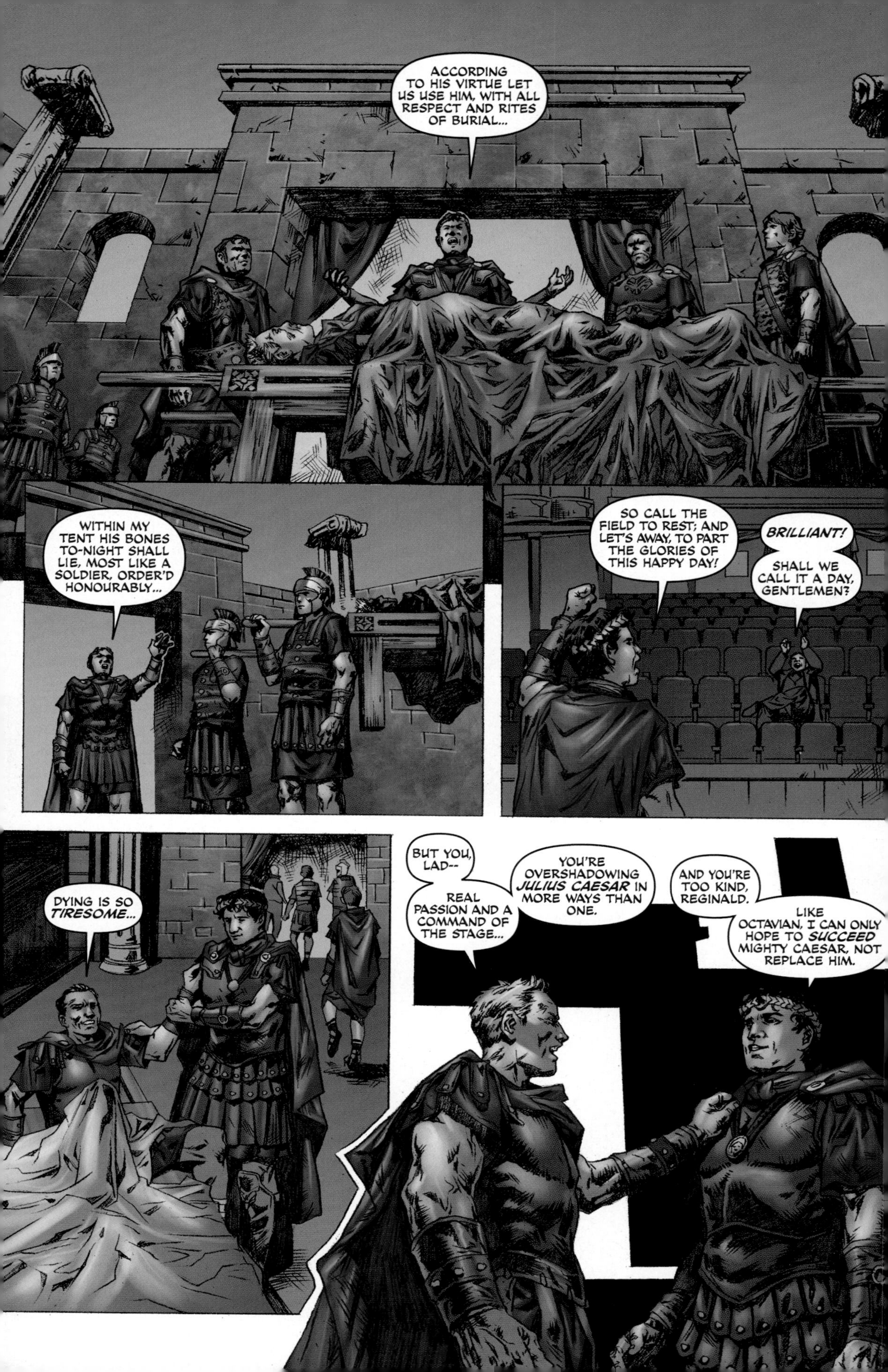
ACCORDING TO HIS VIRTUE LET US USE HIM, WITH ALL RESPECT AND RITES OF BURIAL...
WITHIN MY TENT HIS BONES TO-NIGHT SHALL LIE, MOST LIKE A SOLDIER, ORDER'D HONOURABLY...
SO CALL THE FIELD TO REST; AND LET'S AWAY, TO PART THE GLORIES OF THIS HAPPY DAY!
BRILLIANT!
SHALL WE CALL IT A DAY, GENTLEMEN?
DYING IS SO TIRESOME...
BUT YOU, LAD--
REAL PASSION AND A COMMAND OF THE STAGE...
YOU'RE OVERSHADOWING JULIUS CAESAR IN MORE WAYS THAN ONE.
AND YOU'RE TOO KIND, REGINALD.
LIKE OCTAVIAN, I CAN ONLY HOPE TO SUCCEED MIGHTY CAESAR, NOT REPLACE HIM.

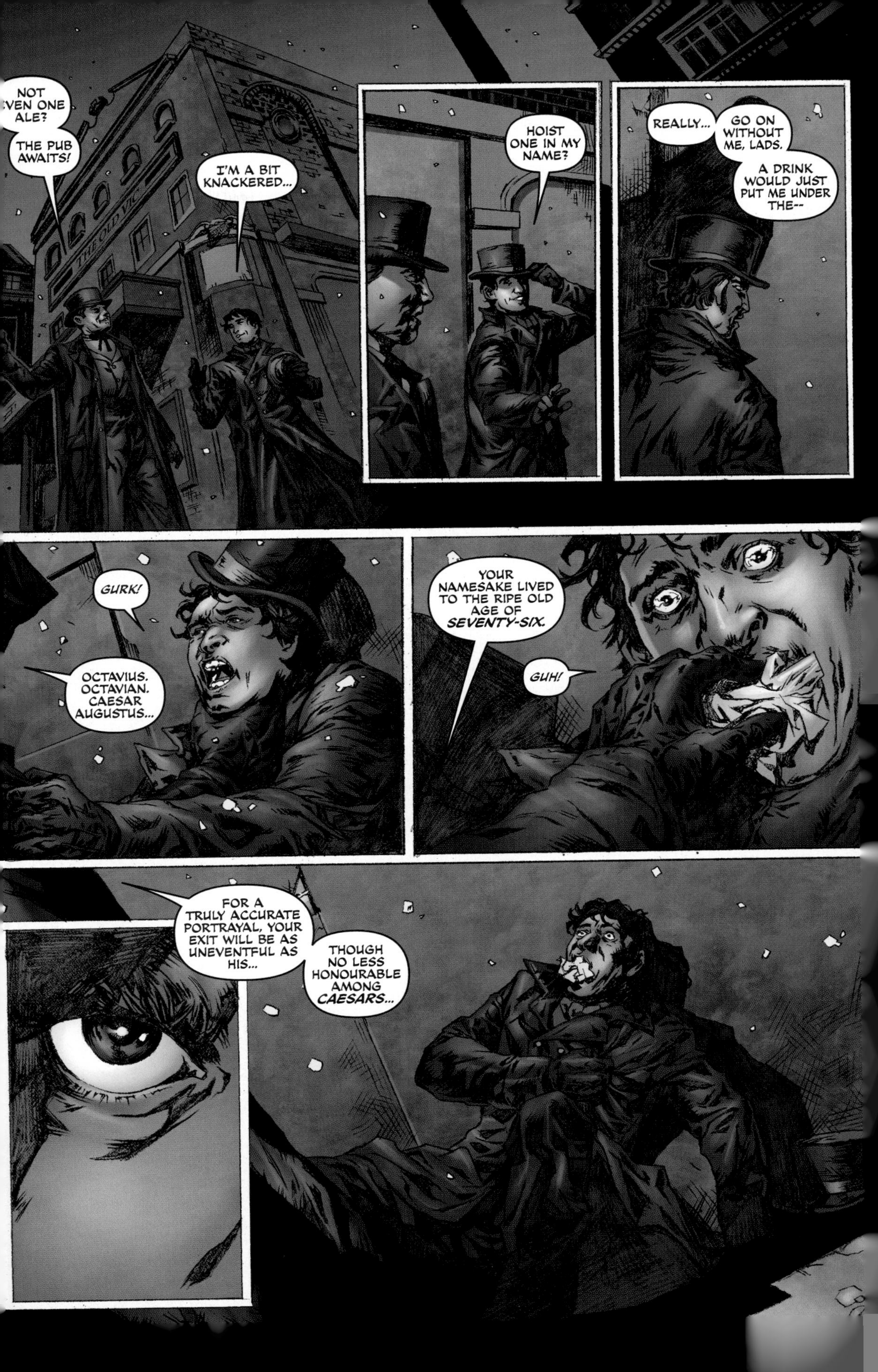
NOT
EVEN ONE ALE?
THE PUB AWAITS!
I'M A BIT KNACKERED...
HOIST ONE IN MY NAME?
REALLY...
GO ON WITHOUT ME, LADS.
A DRINK WOULD JUST PUT ME UNDER THE--
GURK!
OCTAVIUS. OCTAVIAN. CAESAR AUGUSTUS...
YOUR NAMESAKE LIVED TO THE RIPE OLD AGE OF SEVENTY-SIX.
GUH!
FOR A TRULY ACCURATE PORTRAYAL, YOUR EXIT WILL BE AS UNEVENTFUL AS HIS...
THOUGH NO LESS HONOURABLE AMONG CAESARS...

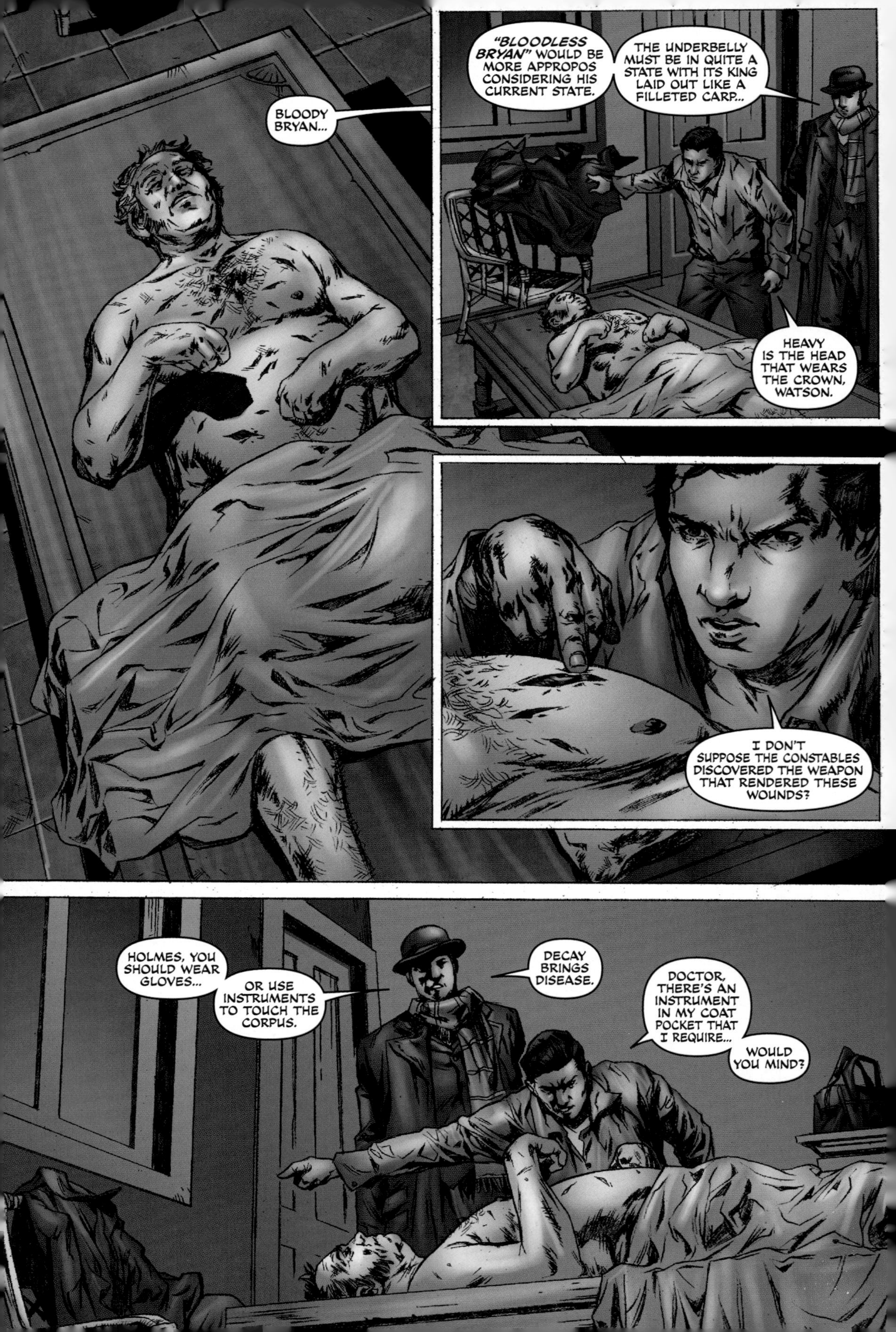
BLOODY BRYAN...
"BLOODLESS BRYAN" WOULD BE MORE APPROPOS CONSIDERING HIS CURRENT STATE.
THE UNDERBELLY MUST BE IN QUITE A STATE WITH ITS KING LAID OUT LIKE A FILLETED CARP...
HEAVY IS THE HEAD THAT WEARS THE CROWN, WATSON.
I DON'T SUPPOSE THE CONSTABLES DISCOVERED THE WEAPON THAT RENDERED THESE WOUNDS?
HOLMES, YOU SHOULD WEAR GLOVES...
OR USE INSTRUMENTS TO TOUCH THE CORPUS.
DECAY BRINGS DISEASE.
DOCTOR, THERE'S AN INSTRUMENT IN MY COAT POCKET THAT I REQUIRE...
WOULD YOU MIND?

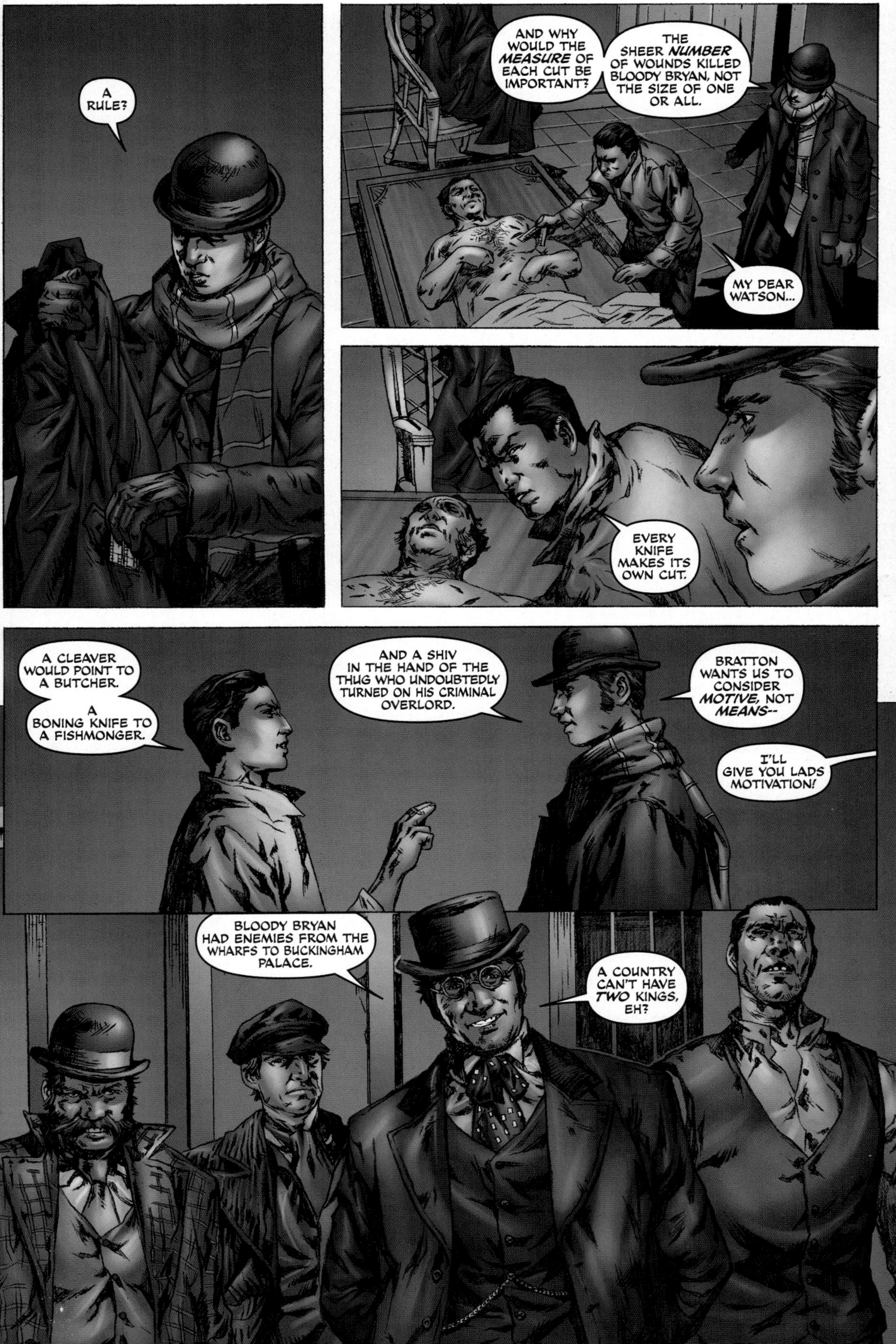
A RULE?
AND WHY WOULD THE *MEASURE* OF EACH CUT BE IMPORTANT?
THE SHEER *NUMBER* OF WOUNDS KILLED BLOODY BRYAN, NOT THE SIZE OF ONE OR ALL.
MY DEAR WATSON...
EVERY KNIFE MAKES ITS OWN CUT.
A CLEAVER WOULD POINT TO A BUTCHER.
A BONING KNIFE TO A FISHMONGER.
AND A SHIV IN THE HAND OF THE THUG WHO UNDOUBTEDLY TURNED ON HIS CRIMINAL OVERLORD.
BRATTON WANTS US TO CONSIDER *MOTIVE*, NOT *MEANS*--
I'LL GIVE YOU LADS MOTIVATION!
BLOODY BRYAN HAD ENEMIES FROM THE WHARFS TO BUCKINGHAM PALACE.
A COUNTRY CAN'T HAVE *TWO* KINGS, EH?

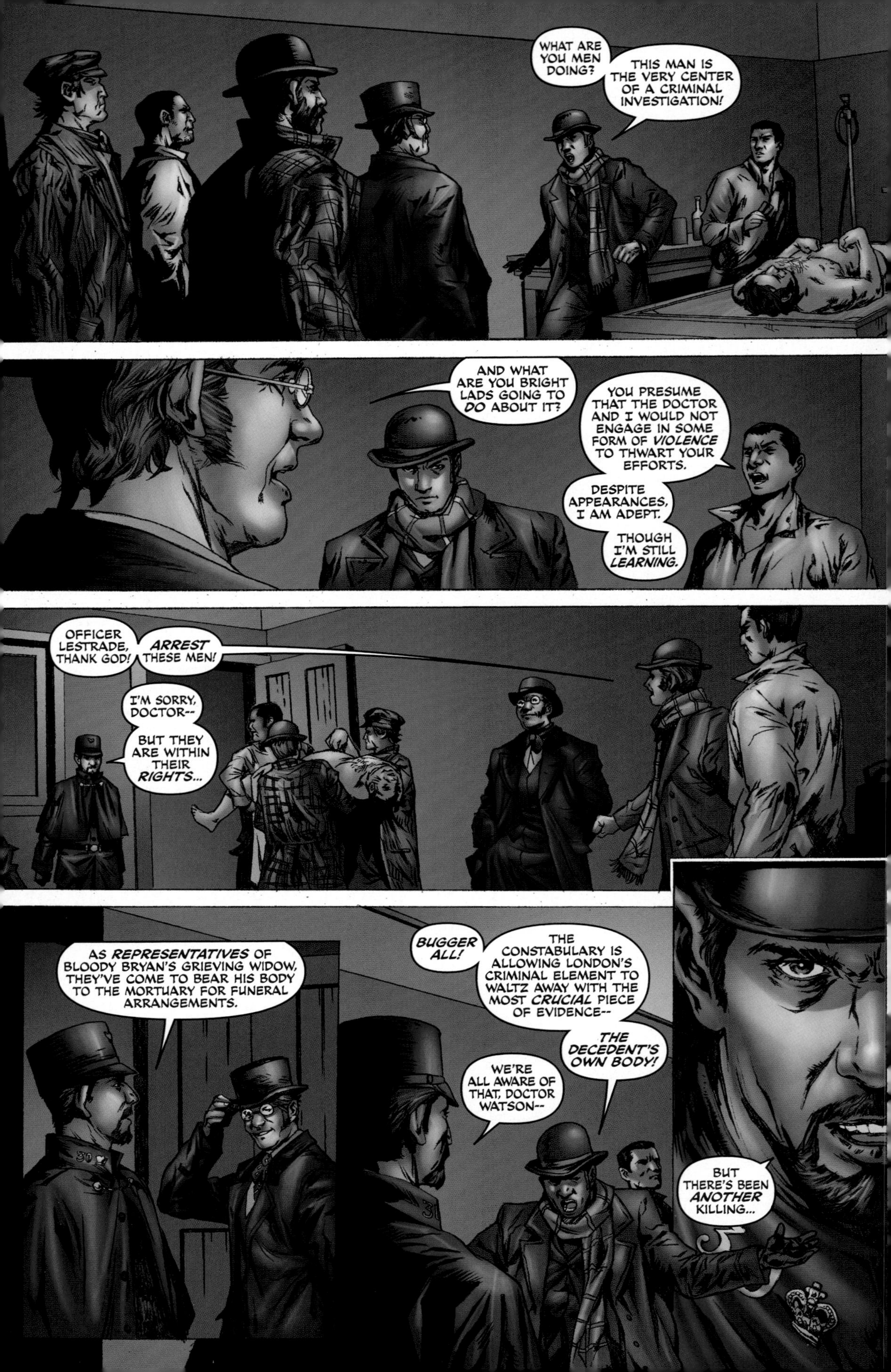
WHAT ARE YOU MEN DOING?
THIS MAN IS THE VERY CENTER OF A CRIMINAL INVESTIGATION!
AND WHAT ARE YOU BRIGHT LADS GOING TO DO ABOUT IT?
YOU PRESUME THAT THE DOCTOR AND I WOULD NOT ENGAGE IN SOME FORM OF VIOLENCE TO THWART YOUR EFFORTS.
DESPITE APPEARANCES, I AM ADEPT.
THOUGH I'M STILL LEARNING.
OFFICER LESTRADE, THANK GOD!
ARREST THESE MEN!
I'M SORRY, DOCTOR--
BUT THEY ARE WITHIN THEIR RIGHTS...
AS REPRESENTATIVES OF BLOODY BRYAN'S GRIEVING WIDOW, THEY'VE COME TO BEAR HIS BODY TO THE MORTUARY FOR FUNERAL ARRANGEMENTS.
BUGGER ALL!
THE CONSTABULARY IS ALLOWING LONDON'S CRIMINAL ELEMENT TO WALTZ AWAY WITH THE MOST CRUCIAL PIECE OF EVIDENCE--
THE DECEDENT'S OWN BODY!
WE'RE ALL AWARE OF THAT, DOCTOR WATSON--
BUT THERE'S BEEN ANOTHER KILLING...

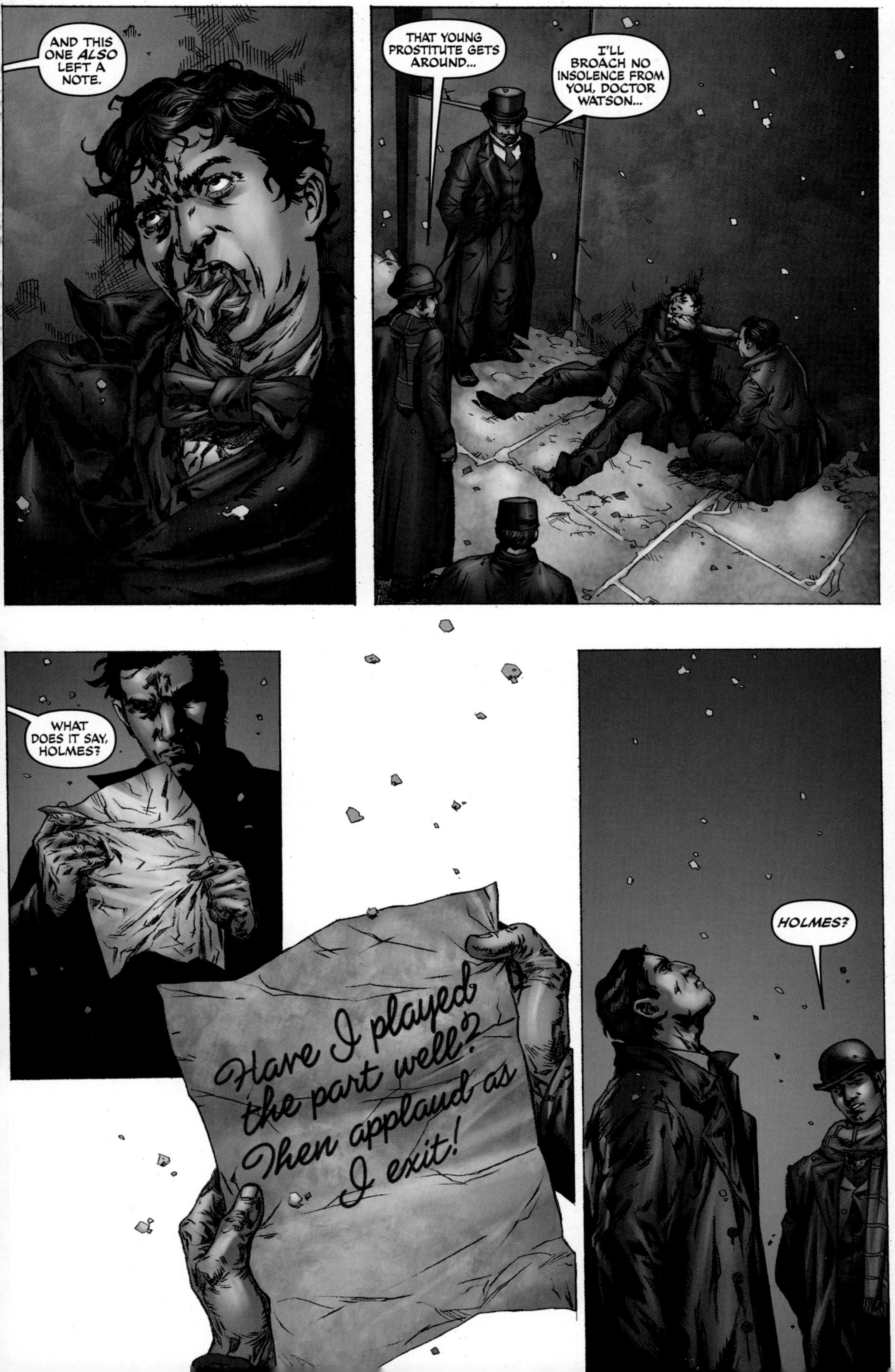
AND THIS ONE ALSO LEFT A NOTE.
THAT YOUNG PROSTITUTE GETS AROUND...
I'LL BROACH NO INSOLENCE FROM YOU, DOCTOR WATSON...
WHAT DOES IT SAY, HOLMES?
Have I played the part well? Then applaud as I exit!
HOLMES?

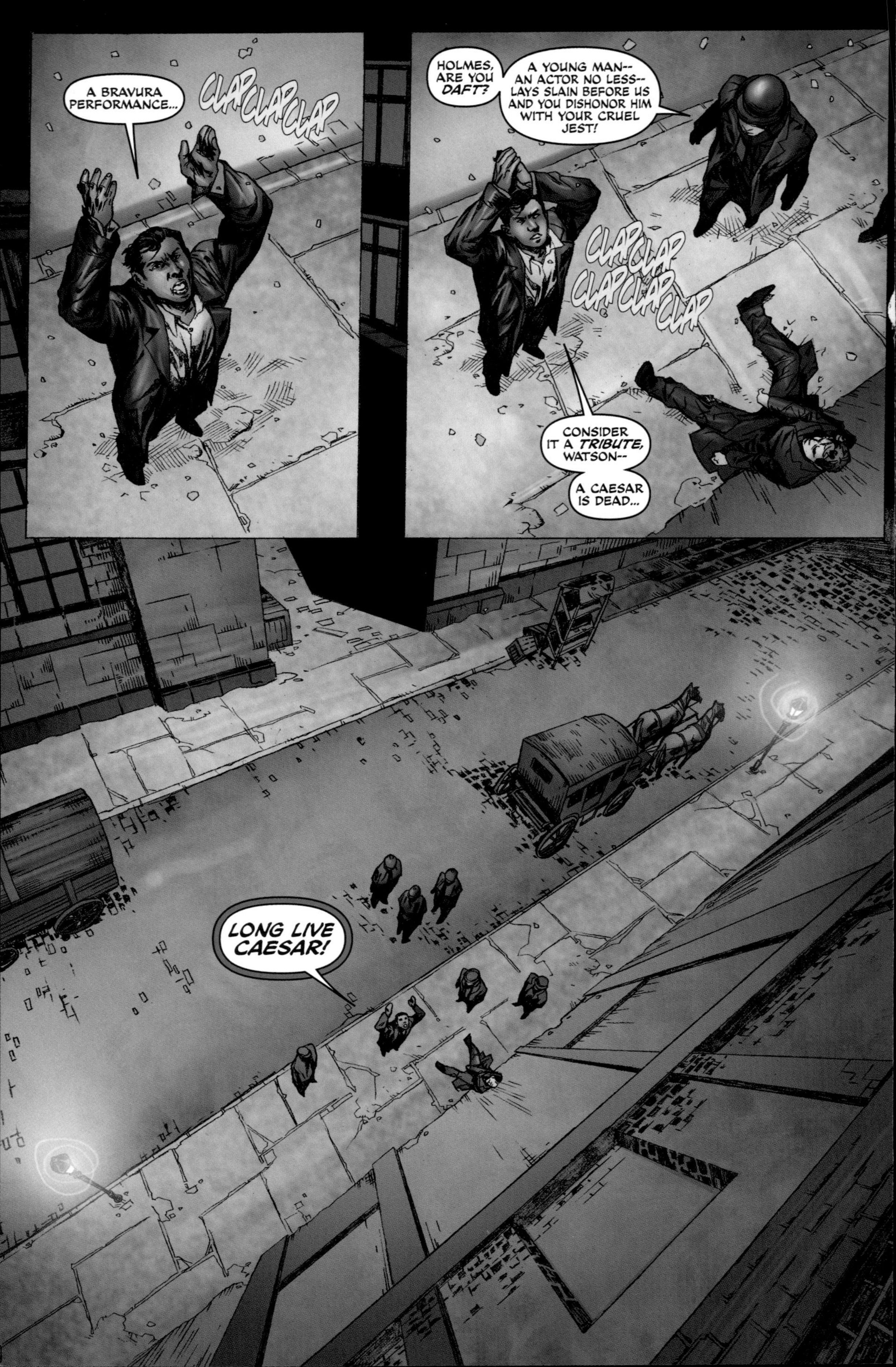
A BRAVURA PERFORMANCE...
CLAP CLAP CLAP
HOLMES, ARE YOU *DAFT?*
A YOUNG MAN-- AN ACTOR NO LESS-- LAYS SLAIN BEFORE US AND YOU DISHONOR HIM WITH YOUR CRUEL JEST!
CLAP CLAP CLAP CLAP CLAP
CONSIDER IT A *TRIBUTE,* WATSON--
A CAESAR IS DEAD...
LONG LIVE CAESAR!

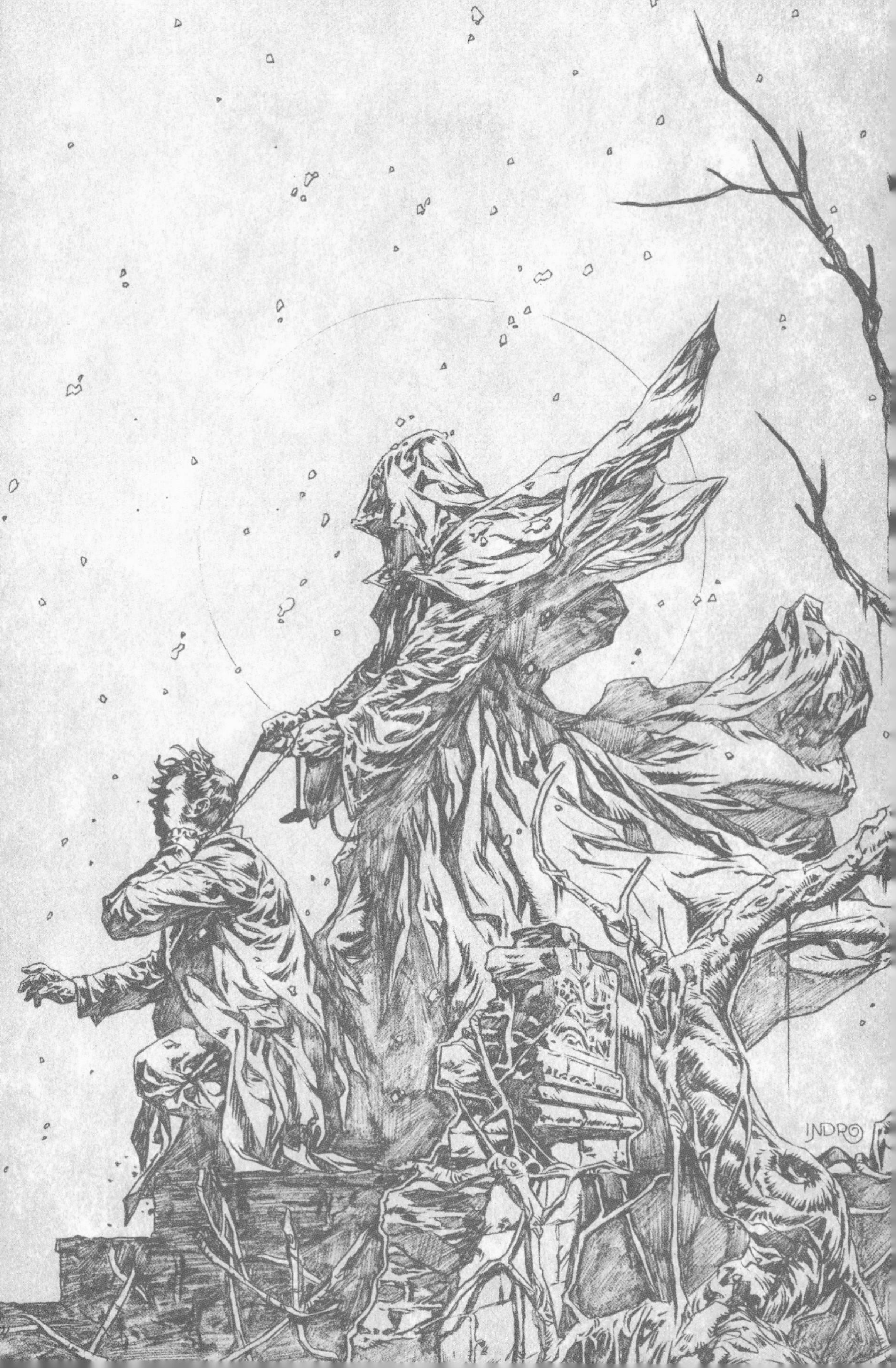
INDRO

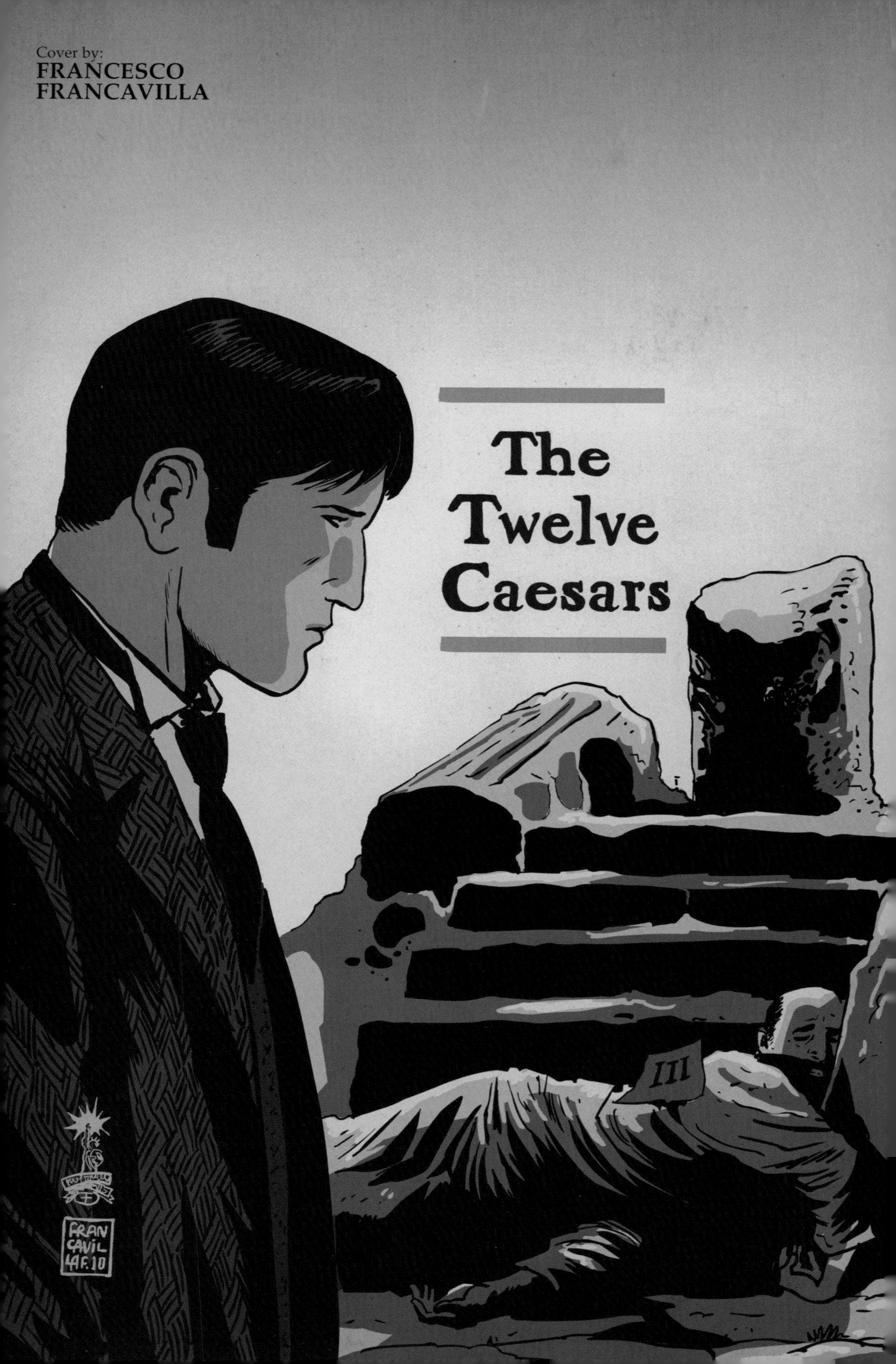
Cover by:
FRANCESCO
FRANCAVILLA
The
Twelve
Caesars
III
FRAN
CAVIL
LA F. 10

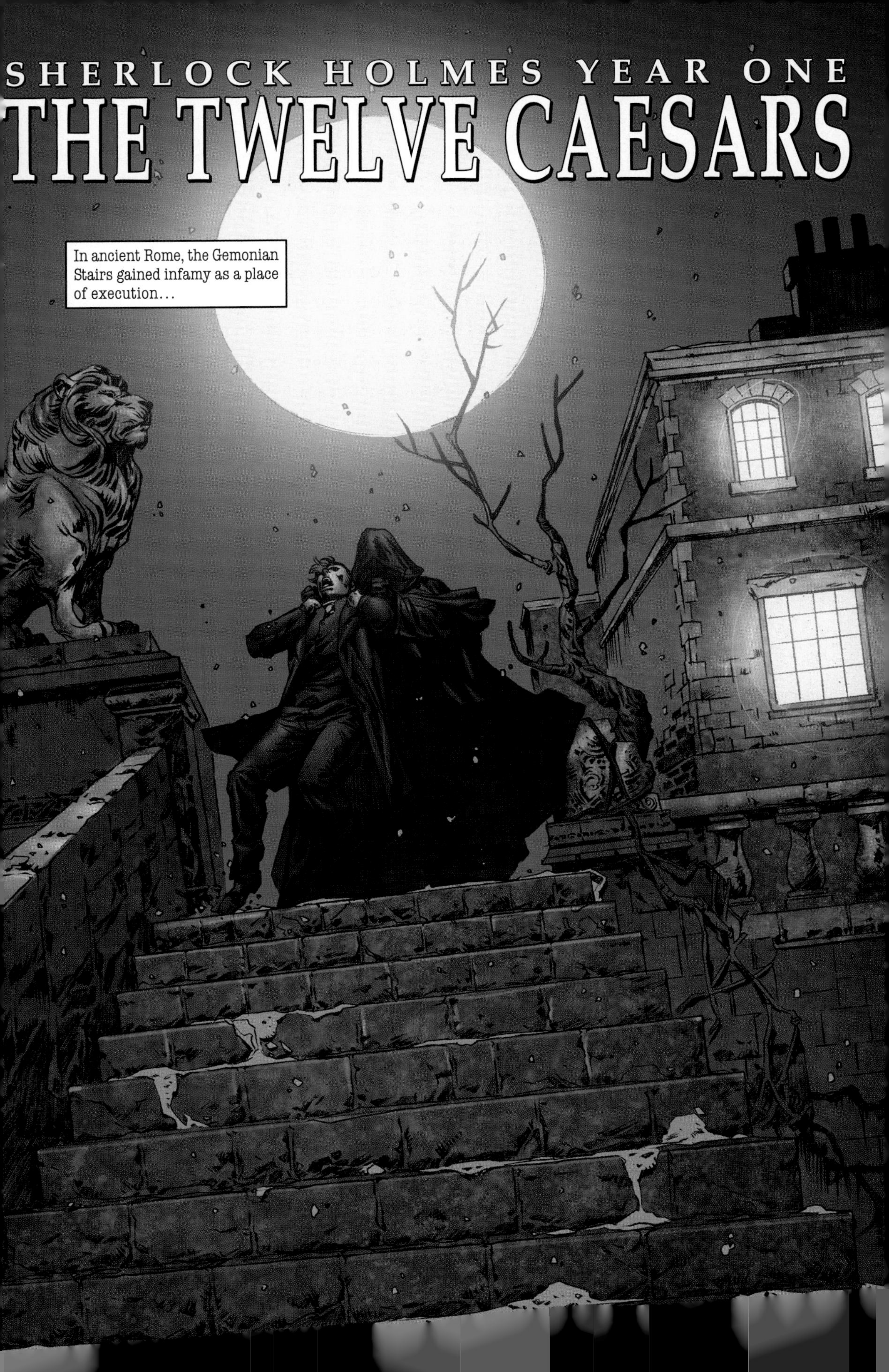
SHERLOCK HOLMES YEAR ONE
THE TWELVE CAESARS
In ancient Rome, the Gemonian Stairs gained infamy as a place of execution...

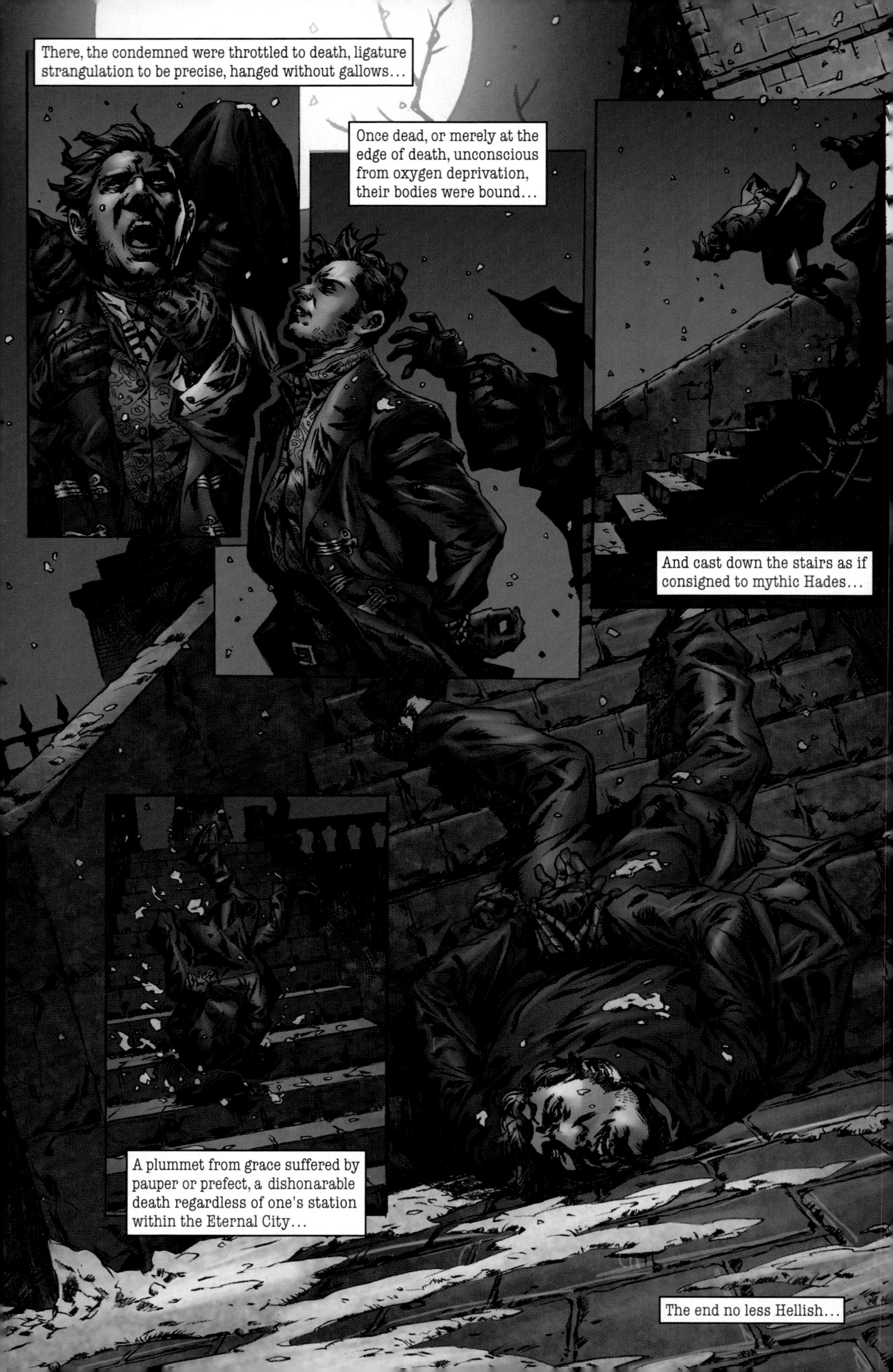
There, the condemned were throttled to death, ligature strangulation to be precise, hanged without gallows...
Once dead, or merely at the edge of death, unconscious from oxygen deprivation, their bodies were bound...
And cast down the stairs as if consigned to mythic Hades...
A plummet from grace suffered by pauper or prefect, a dishonarable death regardless of one's station within the Eternal City...
The end no less Hellish...

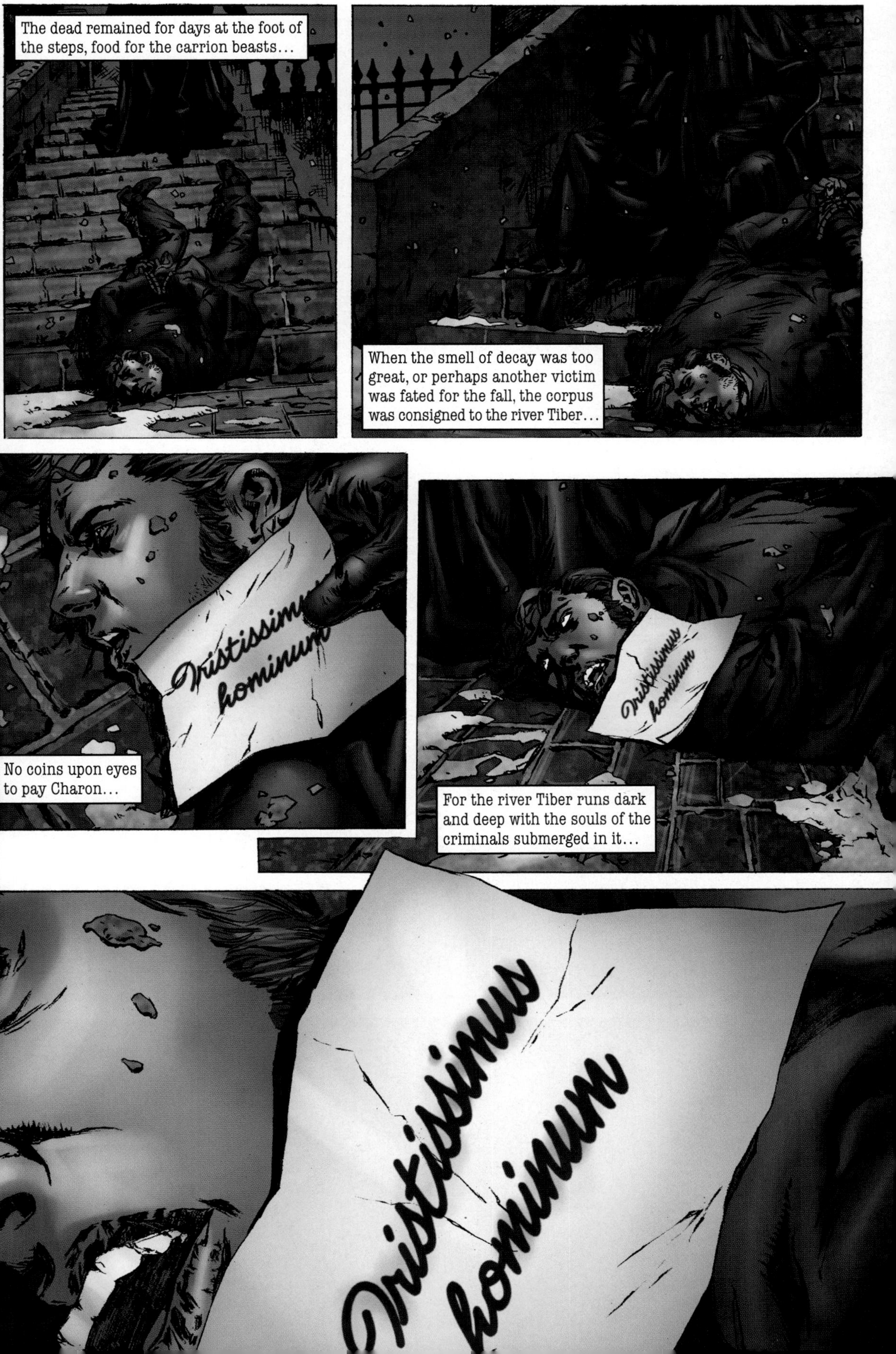
The dead remained for days at the foot of the steps, food for the carrion beasts...
When the smell of decay was too great, or perhaps another victim was fated for the fall, the corpus was consigned to the river Tiber...
Tristissimus hominum
No coins upon eyes to pay Charon...
Tristissimus hominum
For the river Tiber runs dark and deep with the souls of the criminals submerged in it...
Tristissimus hominum

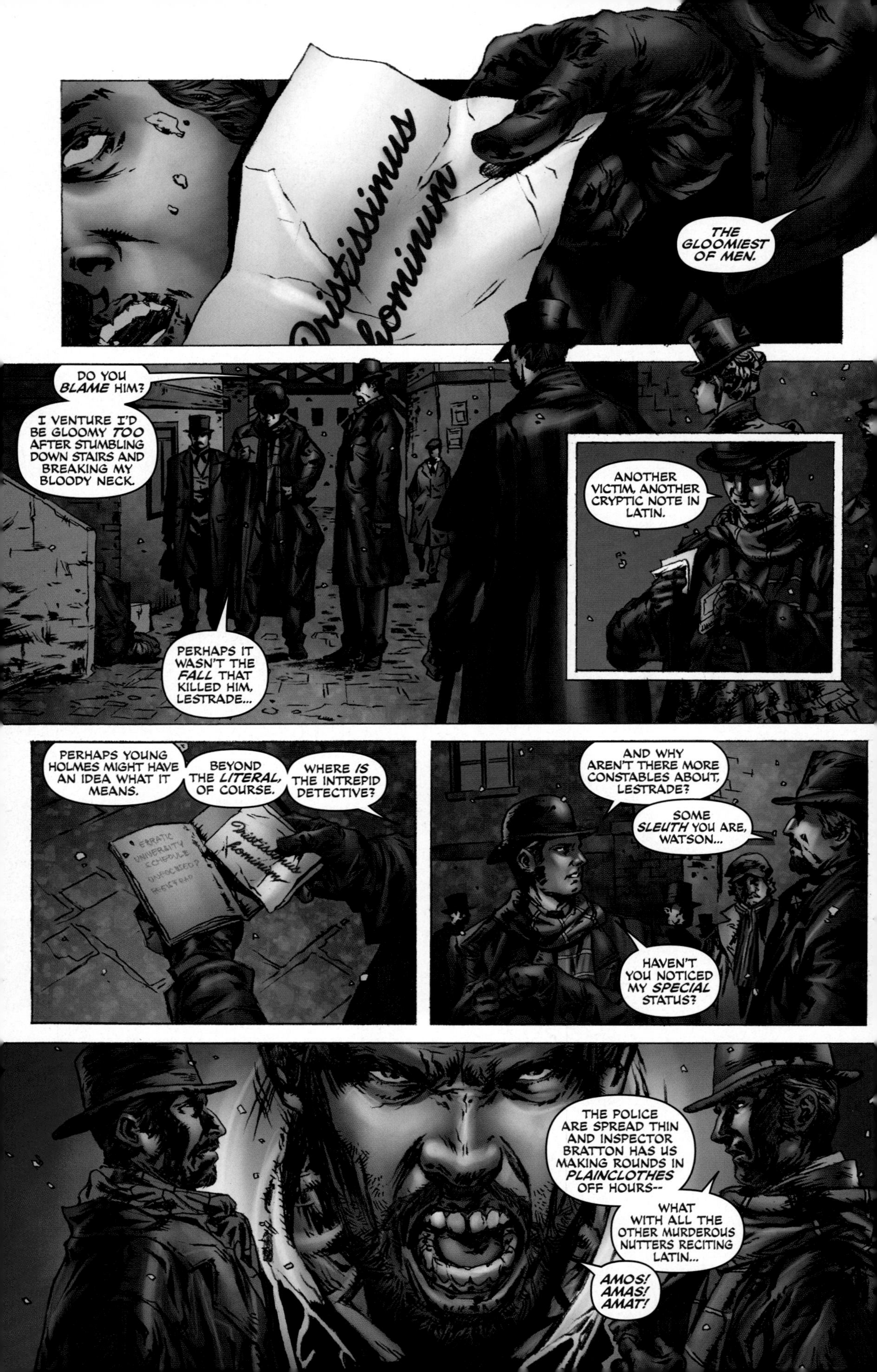
Tristissimus hominum
THE GLOOMIEST OF MEN.
DO YOU BLAME HIM?
I VENTURE I'D BE GLOOMY TOO AFTER STUMBLING DOWN STAIRS AND BREAKING MY BLOODY NECK.
ANOTHER VICTIM, ANOTHER CRYPTIC NOTE IN LATIN.
PERHAPS IT WASN'T THE FALL THAT KILLED HIM, LESTRADE...
PERHAPS YOUNG HOLMES MIGHT HAVE AN IDEA WHAT IT MEANS.
BEYOND THE LITERAL, OF COURSE.
WHERE IS THE INTREPID DETECTIVE?
AND WHY AREN'T THERE MORE CONSTABLES ABOUT, LESTRADE?
SOME SLEUTH YOU ARE, WATSON...
HAVEN'T YOU NOTICED MY SPECIAL STATUS?
THE POLICE ARE SPREAD THIN AND INSPECTOR BRATTON HAS US MAKING ROUNDS IN PLAINCLOTHES OFF HOURS--
WHAT WITH ALL THE OTHER MURDEROUS NUTTERS RECITING LATIN...
AMOS! AMAS! AMAT!

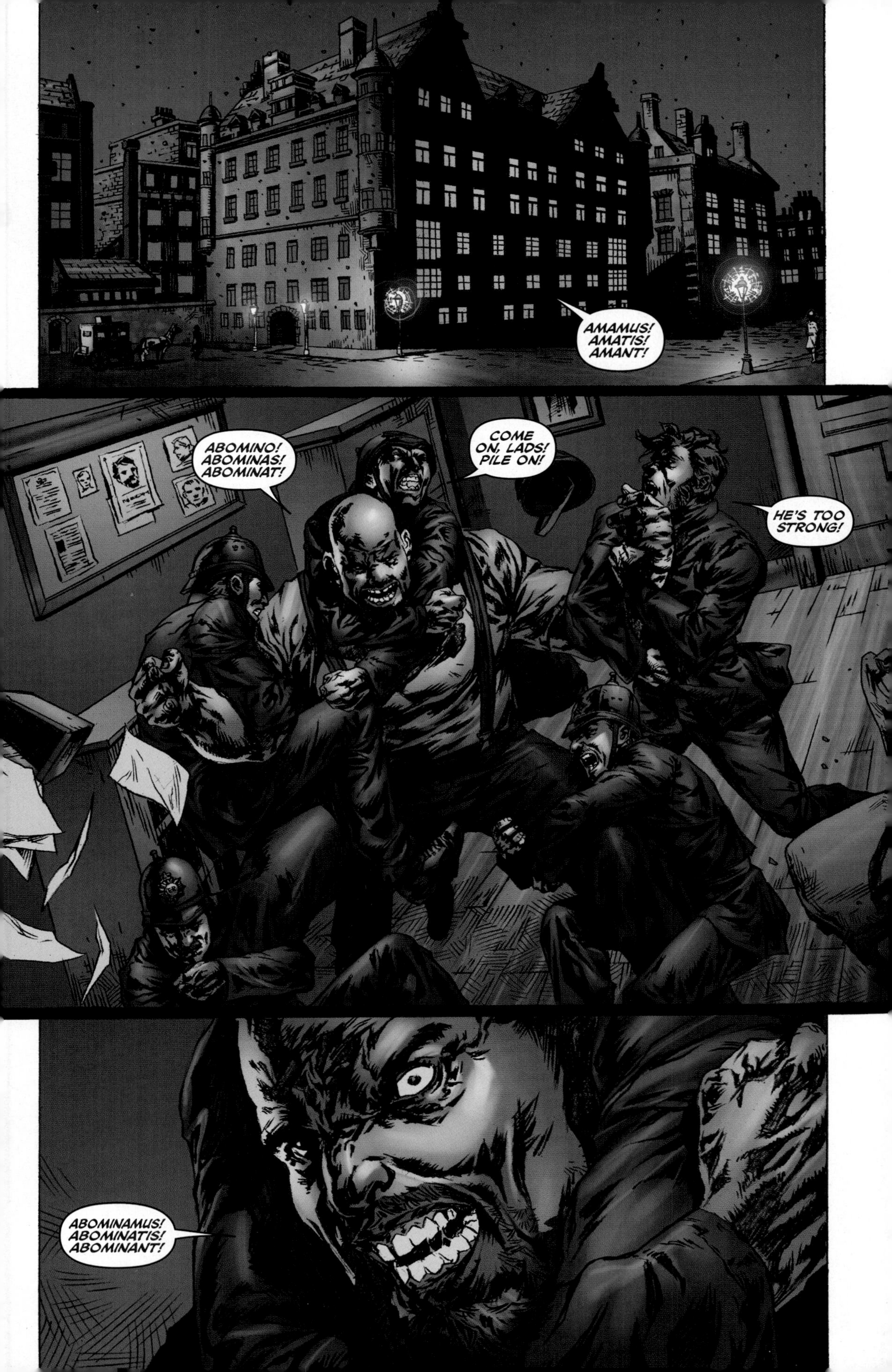
AMAMUS! AMATIS! AMANT!
ABOMINO! ABOMINAS! ABOMINAT!
COME ON, LADS! PILE ON!
HE'S TOO STRONG!
ABOMINAMUS! ABOMINATIS! ABOMINANT!

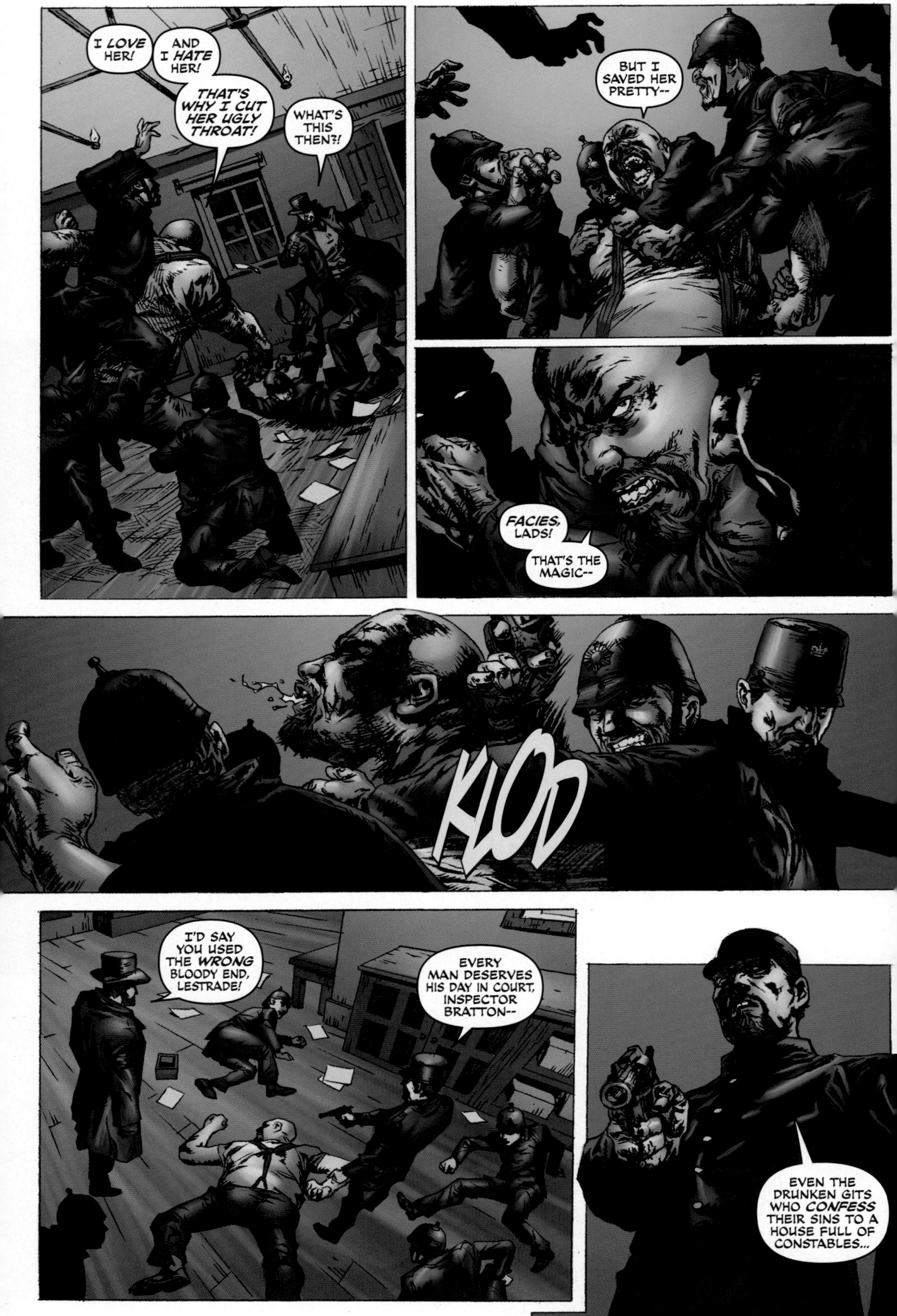
I LOVE HER!
AND I HATE HER!
THAT'S WHY I CUT HER UGLY THROAT!
WHAT'S THIS THEN?!
BUT I SAVED HER PRETTY--
FACIES, LADS!
THAT'S THE MAGIC--
KLOD
I'D SAY YOU USED THE WRONG BLOODY END, LESTRADE!
EVERY MAN DESERVES HIS DAY IN COURT, INSPECTOR BRATTON--
EVEN THE DRUNKEN GITS WHO CONFESS THEIR SINS TO A HOUSE FULL OF CONSTABLES...

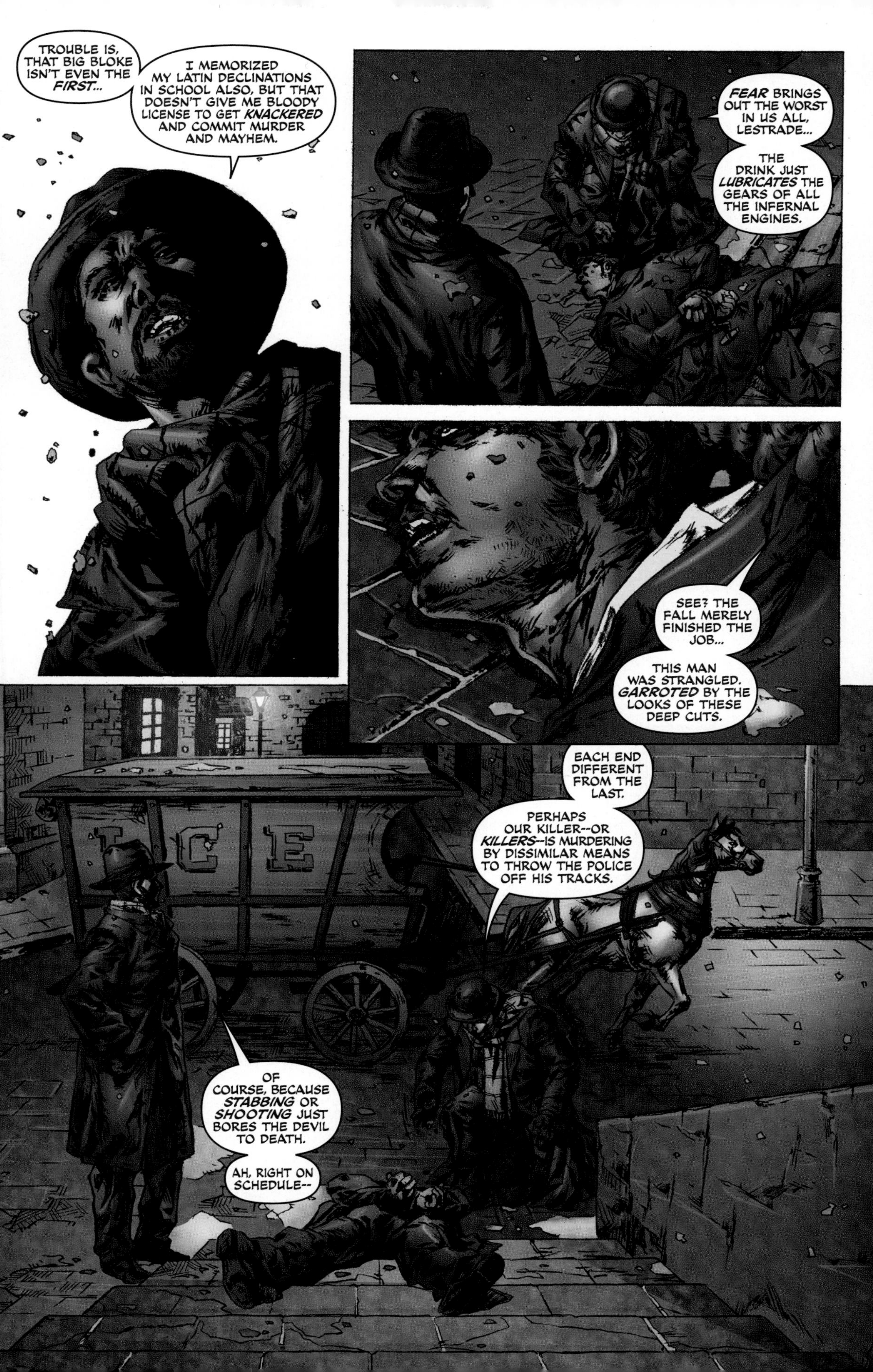
TROUBLE IS, THAT BIG BLOKE ISN'T EVEN THE *FIRST*...
I MEMORIZED MY LATIN DECLINATIONS IN SCHOOL ALSO, BUT THAT DOESN'T GIVE ME BLOODY LICENSE TO GET *KNACKERED* AND COMMIT MURDER AND MAYHEM.
FEAR BRINGS OUT THE WORST IN US ALL, LESTRADE...
THE DRINK JUST *LUBRICATES* THE GEARS OF ALL THE INFERNAL ENGINES.
SEE? THE FALL MERELY FINISHED THE JOB...
THIS MAN WAS STRANGLED. *GARROTED* BY THE LOOKS OF THESE DEEP CUTS.
ICE
EACH END DIFFERENT FROM THE LAST.
PERHAPS OUR KILLER--OR *KILLERS*--IS MURDERING BY DISSIMILAR MEANS TO THROW THE POLICE OFF HIS TRACKS.
OF COURSE, BECAUSE *STABBING* OR *SHOOTING* JUST BORES THE DEVIL TO DEATH.
AH, RIGHT ON SCHEDULE--

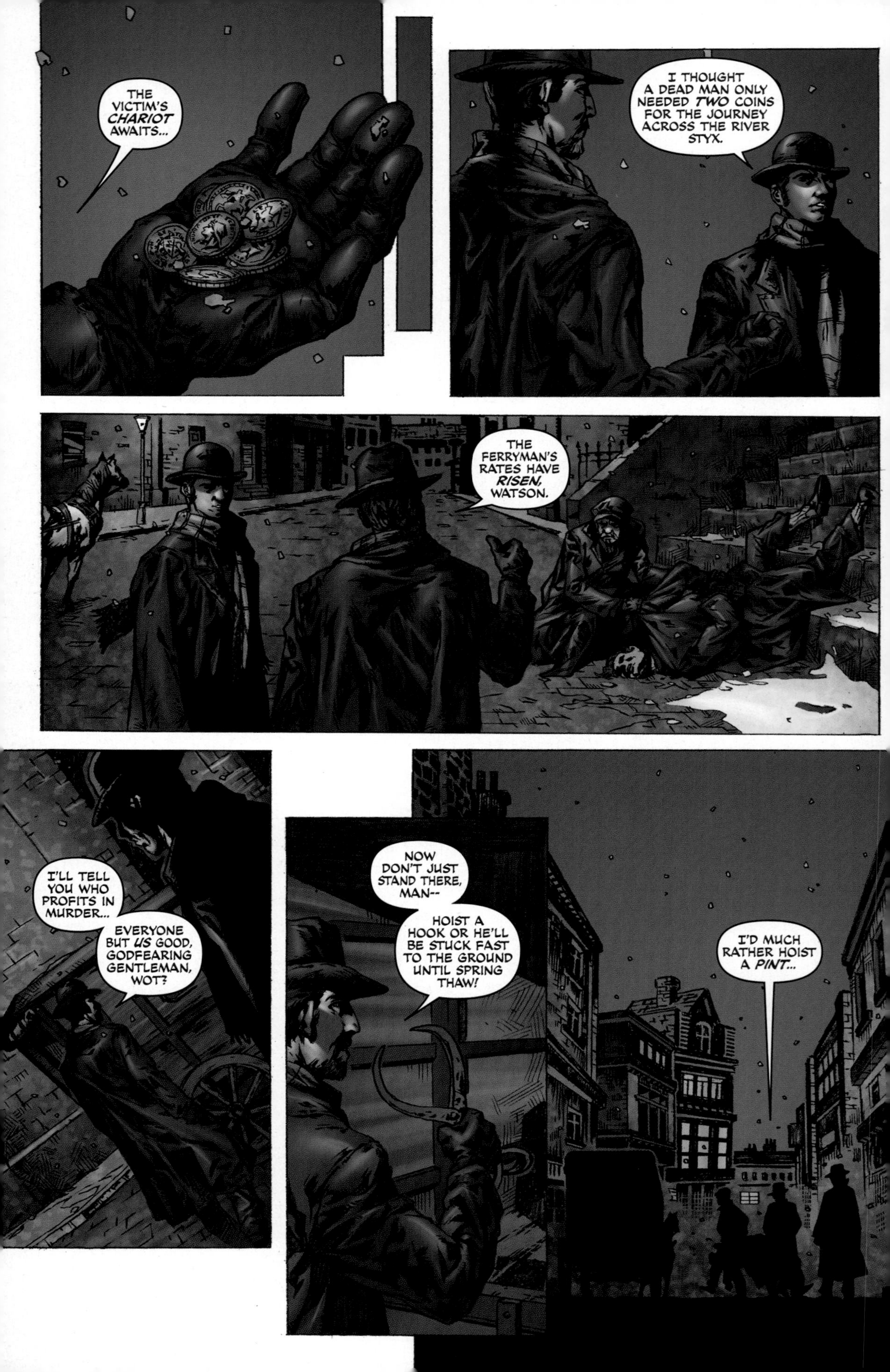
THE VICTIM'S *CHARIOT* AWAITS...
I THOUGHT A DEAD MAN ONLY NEEDED *TWO* COINS FOR THE JOURNEY ACROSS THE RIVER STYX.
THE FERRYMAN'S RATES HAVE *RISEN,* WATSON.
I'LL TELL YOU WHO PROFITS IN MURDER...
EVERYONE BUT *US* GOOD, GODFEARING GENTLEMAN, WOT?
NOW DON'T JUST STAND THERE, MAN--
HOIST A HOOK OR HE'LL BE STUCK FAST TO THE GROUND UNTIL SPRING THAW!
I'D MUCH RATHER HOIST A *PINT*...

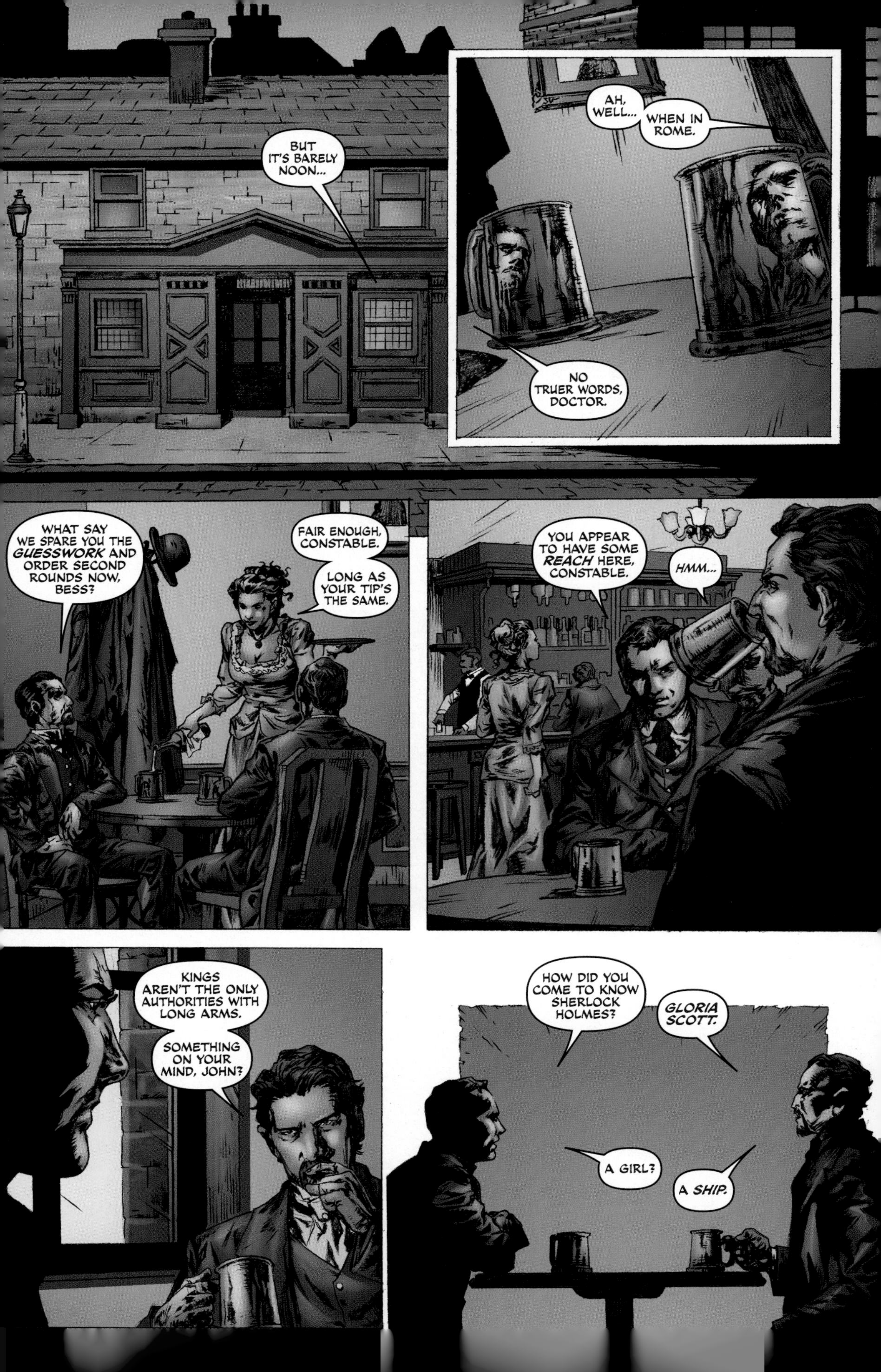
BUT IT'S BARELY NOON...
AH, WELL...
WHEN IN ROME.
NO TRUER WORDS, DOCTOR.
WHAT SAY WE SPARE YOU THE *GUESSWORK* AND ORDER SECOND ROUNDS NOW, BESS?
FAIR ENOUGH, CONSTABLE.
LONG AS YOUR TIP'S THE SAME.
YOU APPEAR TO HAVE SOME *REACH* HERE, CONSTABLE.
HMM...
KINGS AREN'T THE ONLY AUTHORITIES WITH LONG ARMS.
SOMETHING ON YOUR MIND, JOHN?
HOW DID YOU COME TO KNOW SHERLOCK HOLMES?
GLORIA SCOTT.
A GIRL?
A *SHIP.*

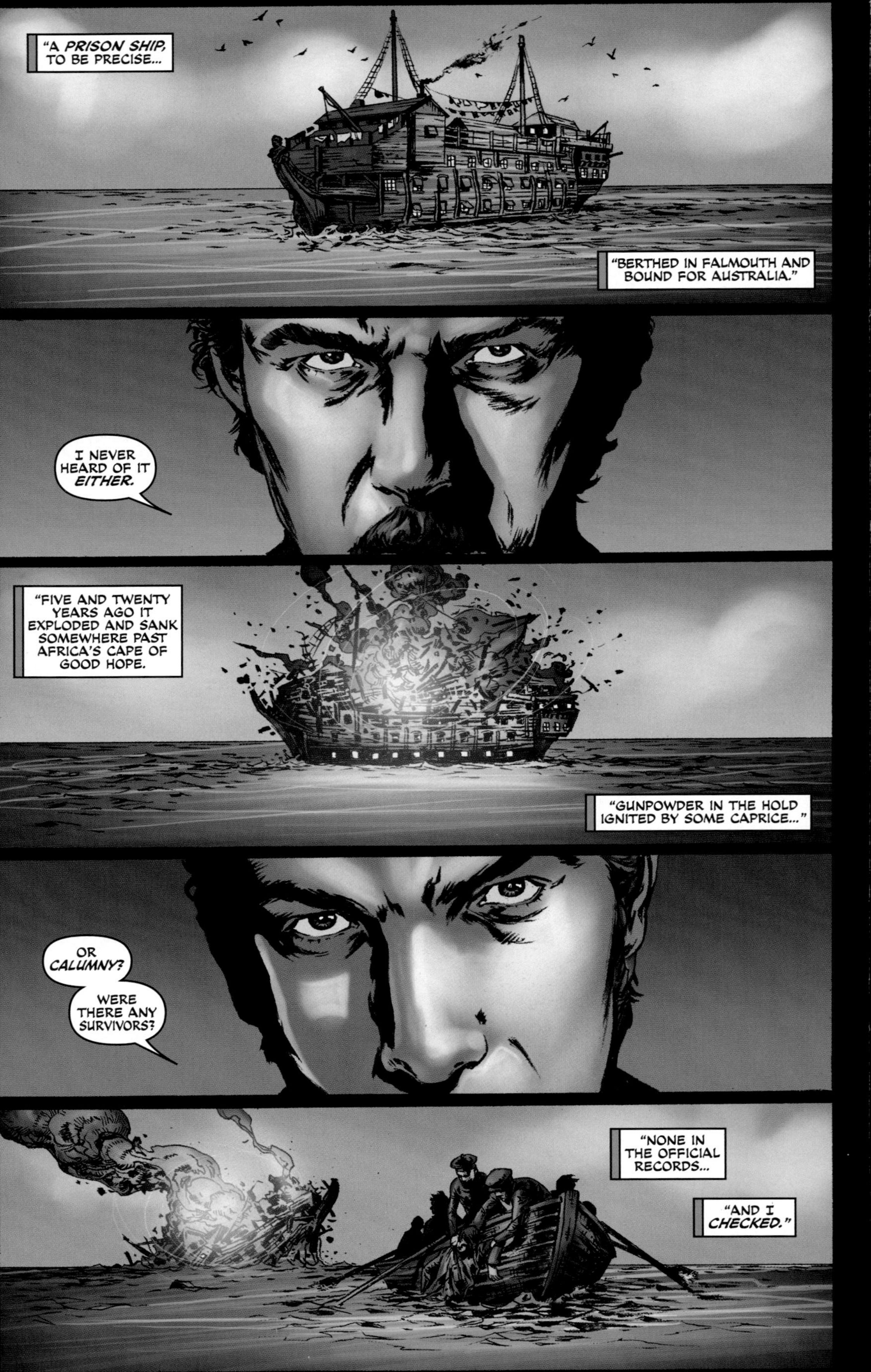
"A *PRISON SHIP,* TO BE PRECISE...
"BERTHED IN FALMOUTH AND BOUND FOR AUSTRALIA."
I NEVER HEARD OF IT *EITHER.*
"FIVE AND TWENTY YEARS AGO IT EXPLODED AND SANK SOMEWHERE PAST AFRICA'S CAPE OF GOOD HOPE.
"GUNPOWDER IN THE HOLD IGNITED BY SOME CAPRICE..."
OR *CALUMNY?*
WERE THERE ANY SURVIVORS?
"NONE IN THE OFFICIAL RECORDS...
"AND I *CHECKED.*"

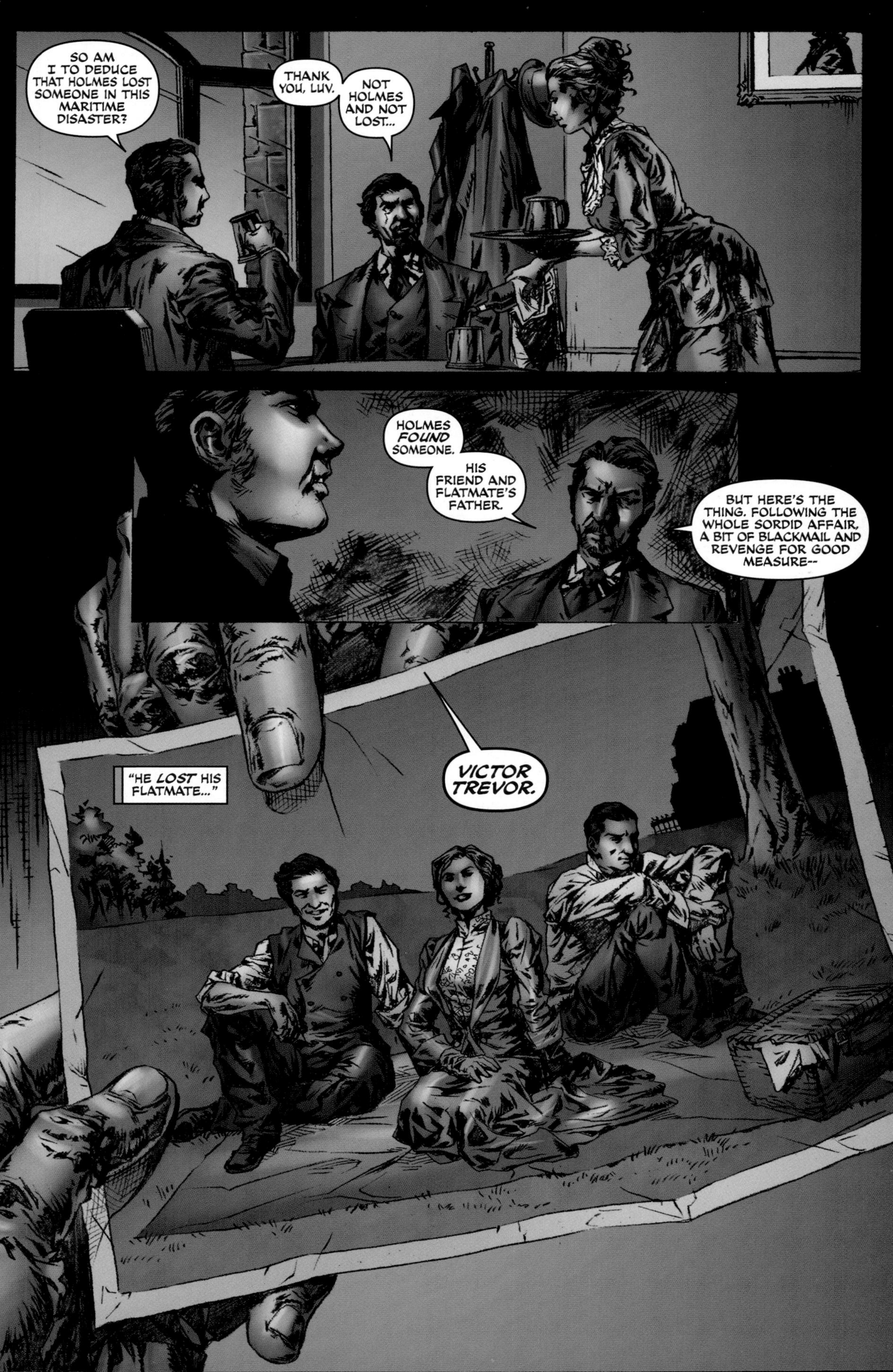
SO AM I TO DEDUCE THAT HOLMES LOST SOMEONE IN THIS MARITIME DISASTER?
THANK YOU, LUV.
NOT HOLMES AND NOT LOST...
HOLMES *FOUND* SOMEONE.
HIS FRIEND AND FLATMATE'S FATHER.
BUT HERE'S THE THING. FOLLOWING THE WHOLE SORDID AFFAIR, A BIT OF BLACKMAIL AND REVENGE FOR GOOD MEASURE--
VICTOR TREVOR.
"HE *LOST* HIS FLATMATE..."

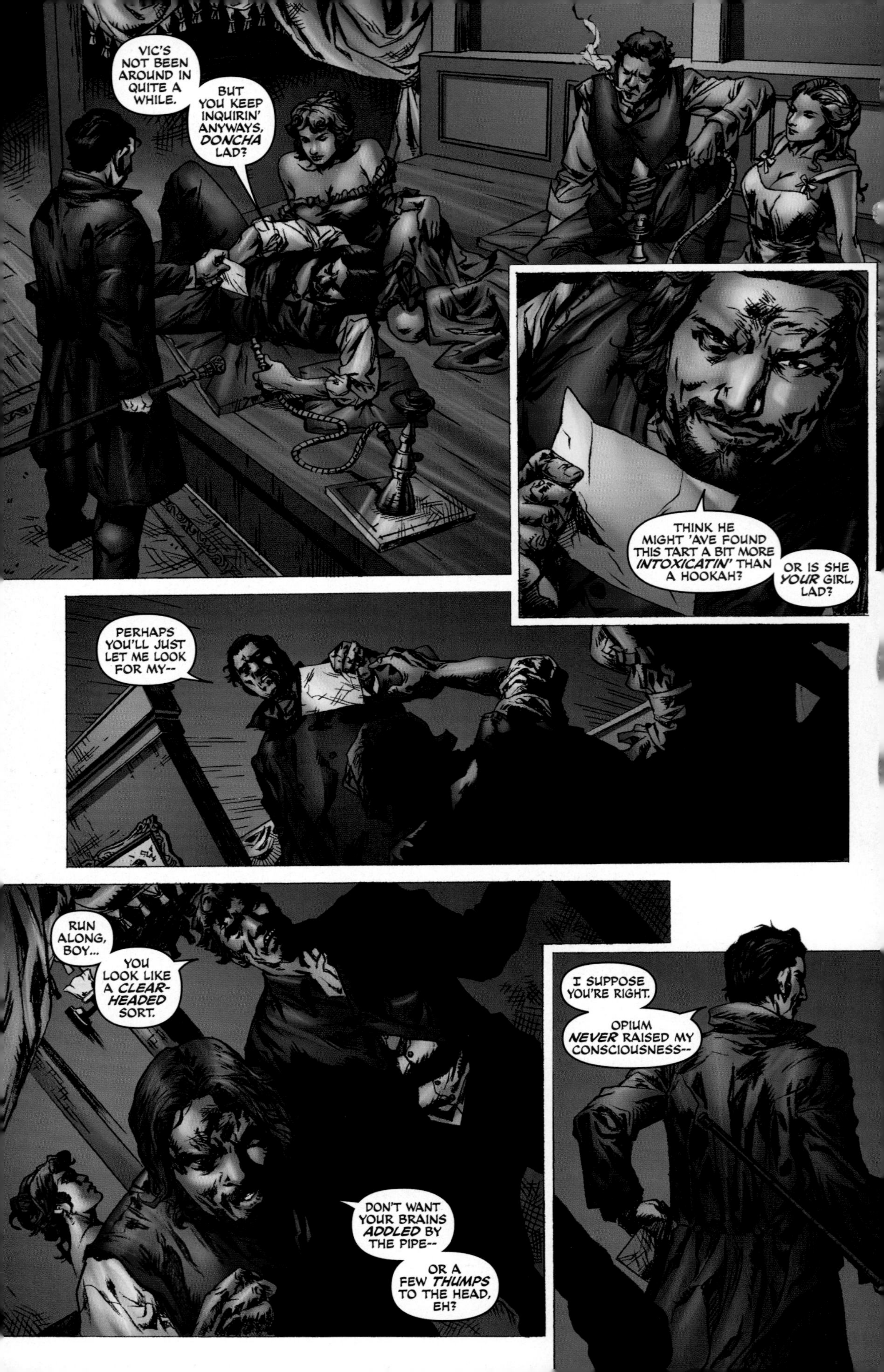
VIC'S NOT BEEN AROUND IN QUITE A WHILE.
BUT YOU KEEP INQUIRIN' ANYWAYS, DONCHA LAD?
THINK HE MIGHT 'AVE FOUND THIS TART A BIT MORE INTOXICATIN' THAN A HOOKAH?
OR IS SHE YOUR GIRL, LAD?
PERHAPS YOU'LL JUST LET ME LOOK FOR MY--
RUN ALONG, BOY...
YOU LOOK LIKE A CLEAR-HEADED SORT.
DON'T WANT YOUR BRAINS ADDLED BY THE PIPE--
OR A FEW THUMPS TO THE HEAD, EH?
I SUPPOSE YOU'RE RIGHT.
OPIUM NEVER RAISED MY CONSCIOUSNESS--

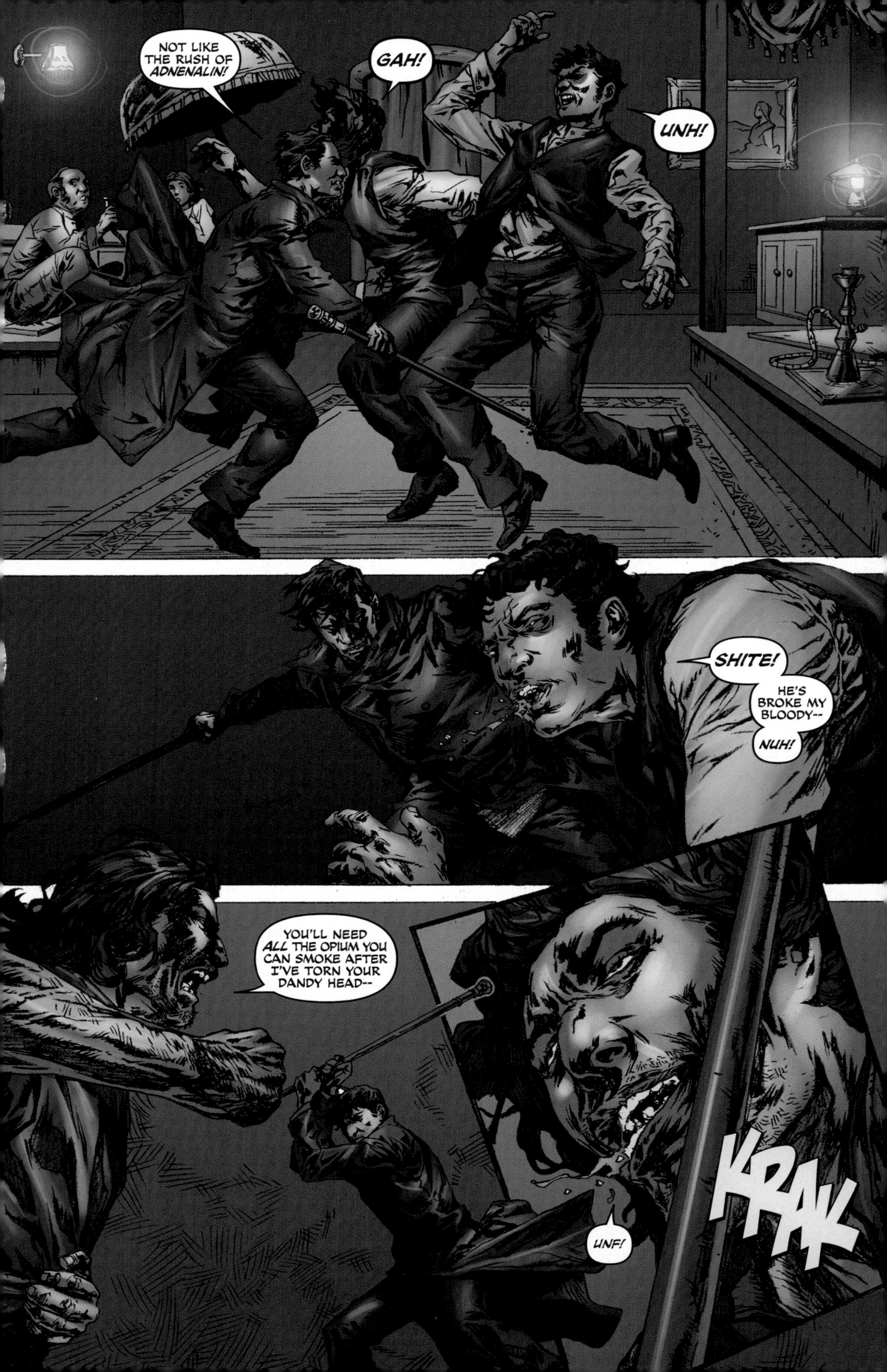
NOT LIKE THE RUSH OF *ADNENALIN!*
GAH!
UNH!
SHITE!
HE'S BROKE MY BLOODY--
NUH!
YOU'LL NEED *ALL* THE OPIUM YOU CAN SMOKE AFTER I'VE TORN YOUR DANDY HEAD--
KRAK
UNF!

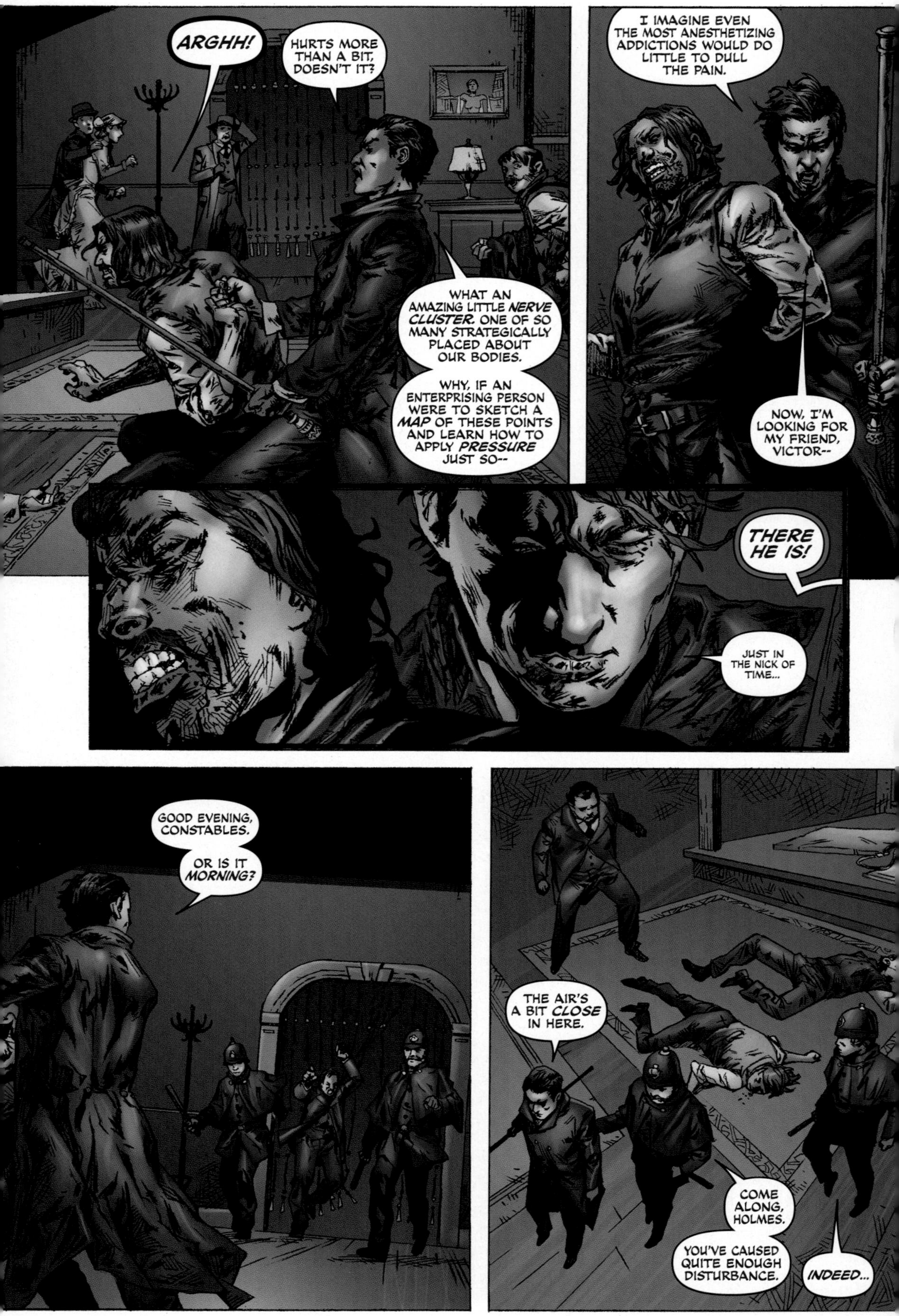
ARGHH!
HURTS MORE THAN A BIT, DOESN'T IT?
WHAT AN AMAZING LITTLE NERVE CLUSTER. ONE OF SO MANY STRATEGICALLY PLACED ABOUT OUR BODIES.
WHY, IF AN ENTERPRISING PERSON WERE TO SKETCH A MAP OF THESE POINTS AND LEARN HOW TO APPLY PRESSURE JUST SO--
I IMAGINE EVEN THE MOST ANESTHETIZING ADDICTIONS WOULD DO LITTLE TO DULL THE PAIN.
NOW, I'M LOOKING FOR MY FRIEND, VICTOR--
THERE HE IS!
JUST IN THE NICK OF TIME...
GOOD EVENING, CONSTABLES.
OR IS IT MORNING?
THE AIR'S A BIT CLOSE IN HERE.
COME ALONG, HOLMES.
YOU'VE CAUSED QUITE ENOUGH DISTURBANCE.
INDEED...

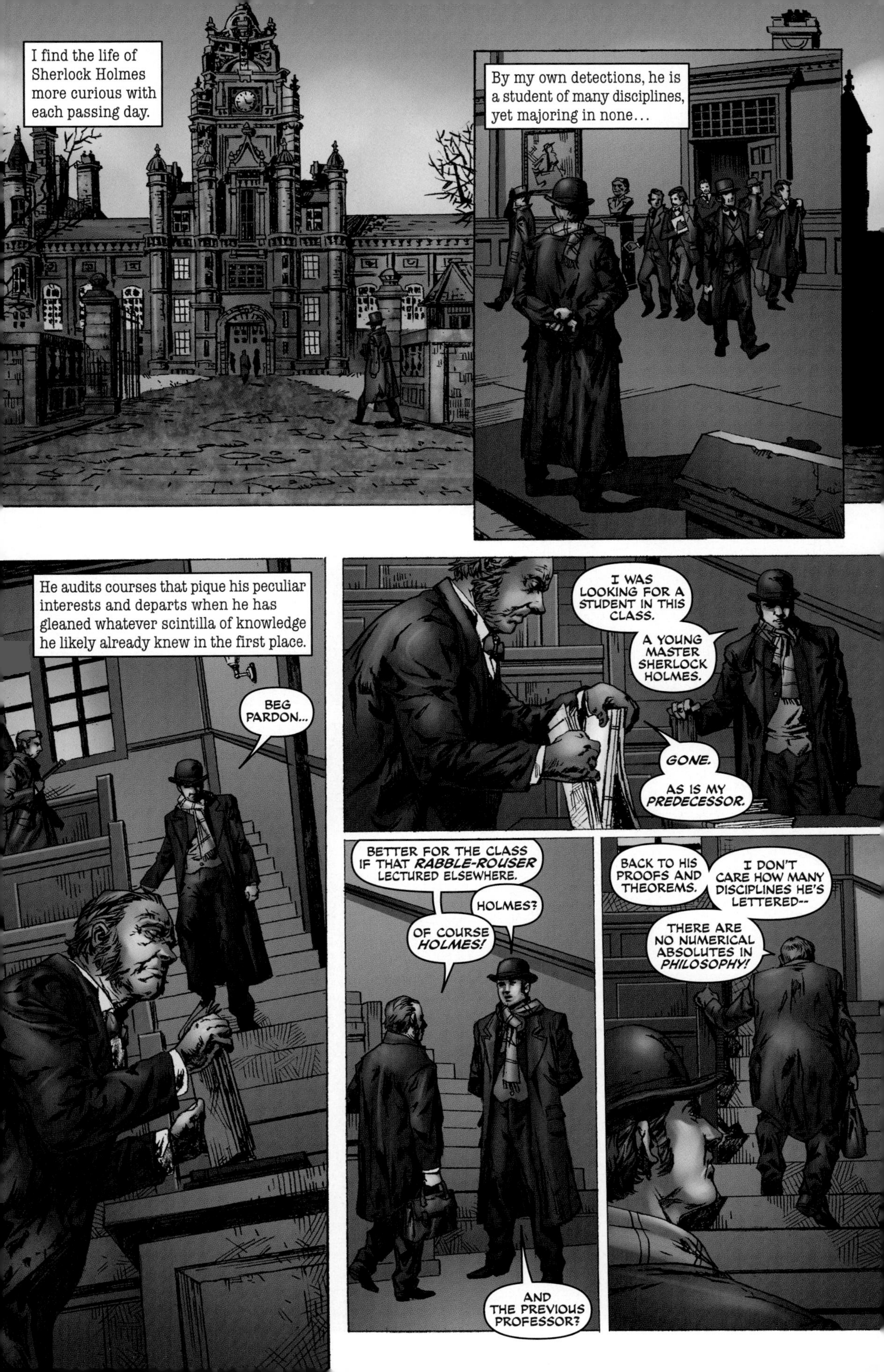
I find the life of Sherlock Holmes more curious with each passing day.
By my own detections, he is a student of many disciplines, yet majoring in none...
He audits courses that pique his peculiar interests and departs when he has gleaned whatever scintilla of knowledge he likely already knew in the first place.
BEG PARDON...
I WAS LOOKING FOR A STUDENT IN THIS CLASS.
A YOUNG MASTER SHERLOCK HOLMES.
GONE.
AS IS MY PREDECESSOR.
BETTER FOR THE CLASS IF THAT RABBLE-ROUSER LECTURED ELSEWHERE.
HOLMES?
OF COURSE HOLMES!
AND THE PREVIOUS PROFESSOR?
BACK TO HIS PROOFS AND THEOREMS.
I DON'T CARE HOW MANY DISCIPLINES HE'S LETTERED--
THERE ARE NO NUMERICAL ABSOLUTES IN PHILOSOPHY!

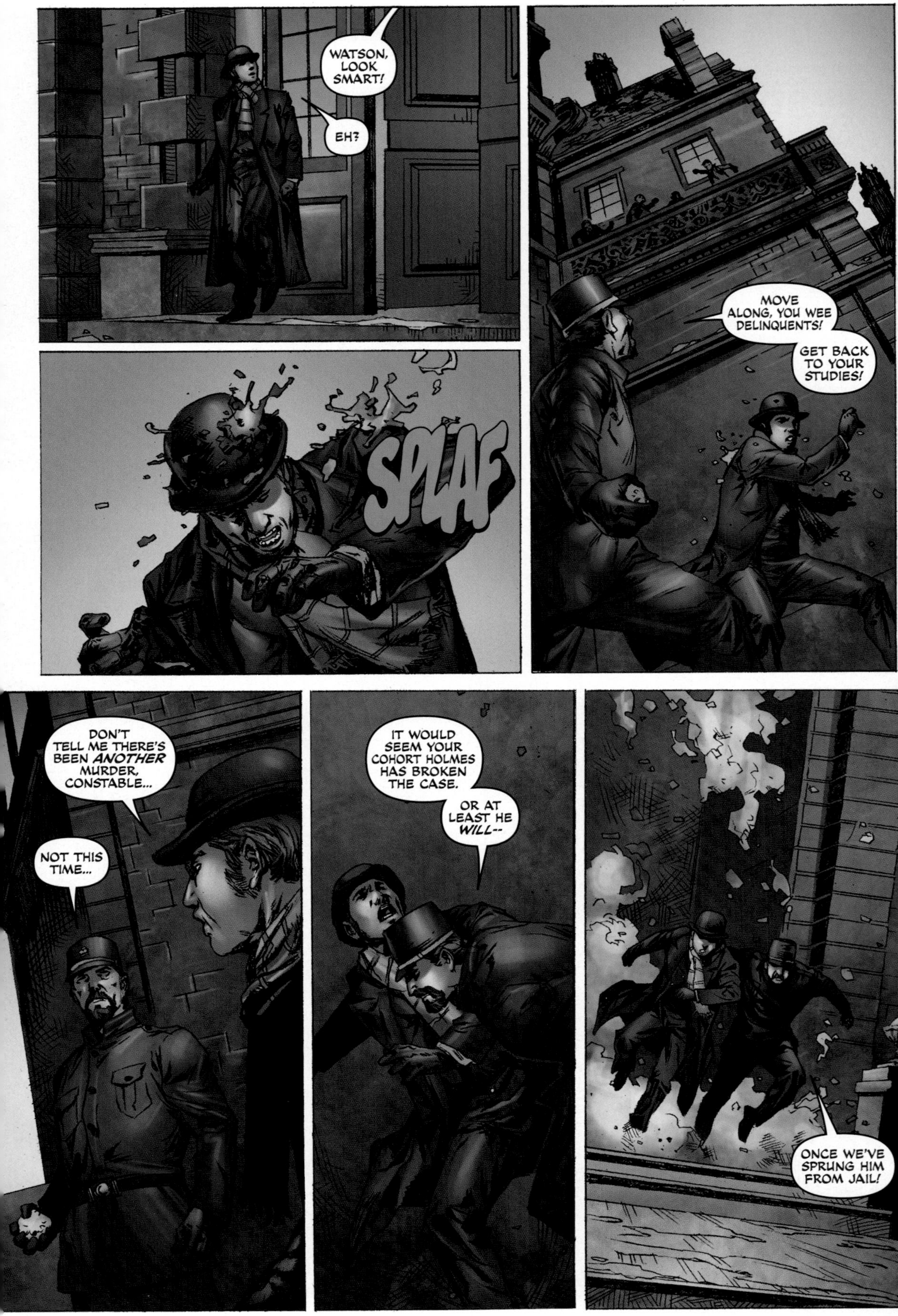
WATSON, LOOK SMART!
EH?
SPLAF
MOVE ALONG, YOU WEE DELINQUENTS!
GET BACK TO YOUR STUDIES!
DON'T TELL ME THERE'S BEEN *ANOTHER* MURDER, CONSTABLE...
NOT THIS TIME...
IT WOULD SEEM YOUR COHORT HOLMES HAS BROKEN THE CASE.
OR AT LEAST HE *WILL*--
ONCE WE'VE SPRUNG HIM FROM JAIL!

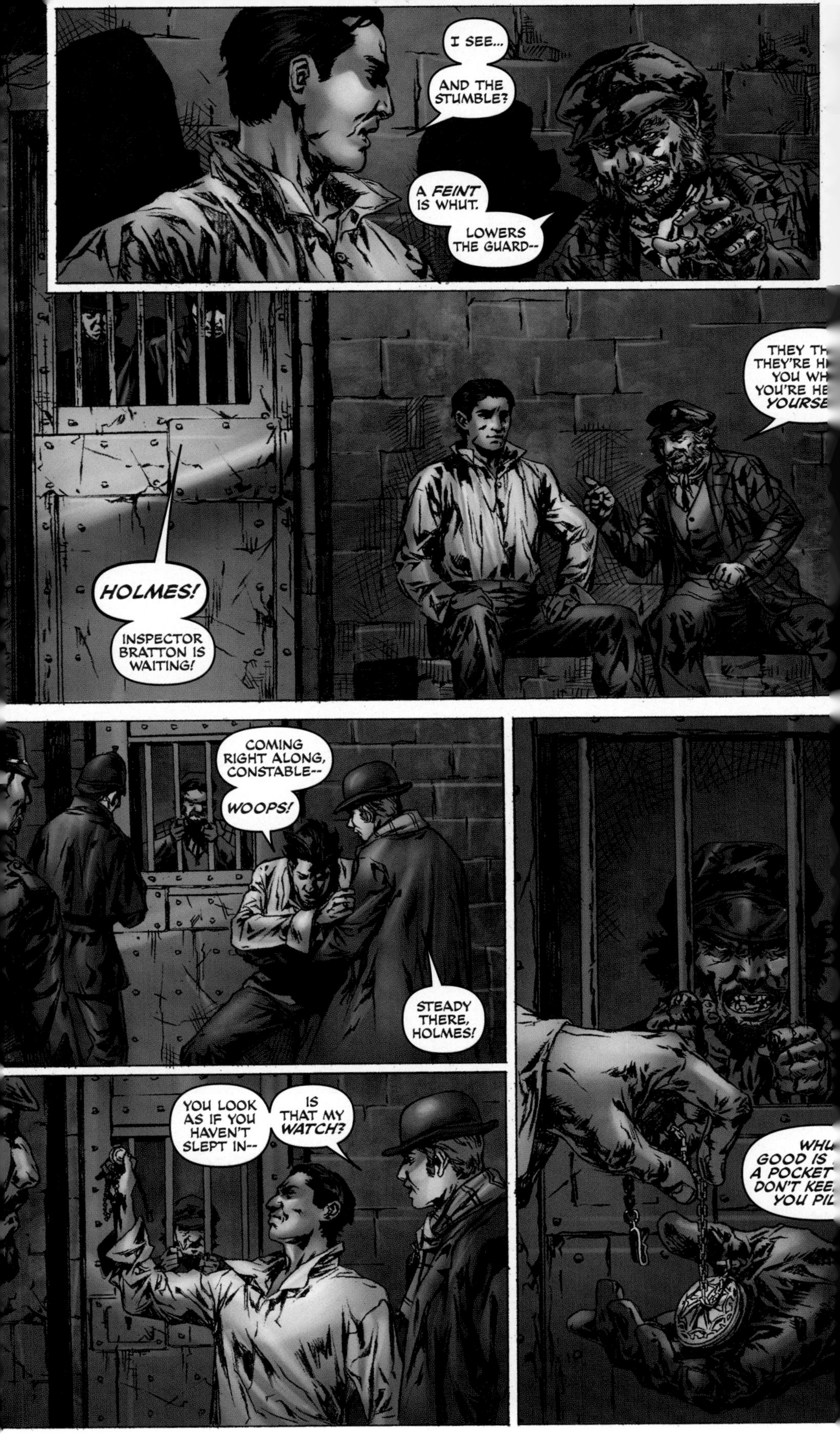

I SEE...
AND THE STUMBLE?
A *FEINT* IS WHUT.
LOWERS THE GUARD--
THEY TH
THEY'RE HE
YOU WH
YOU'RE HE
YOURSE
HOLMES!
INSPECTOR BRATTON IS WAITING!
COMING RIGHT ALONG, CONSTABLE--
WOOPS!
STEADY THERE, HOLMES!
YOU LOOK AS IF YOU HAVEN'T SLEPT IN--
IS THAT MY *WATCH?*
WHU
GOOD IS
A POCKET
DON'T KEE
YOU PIL

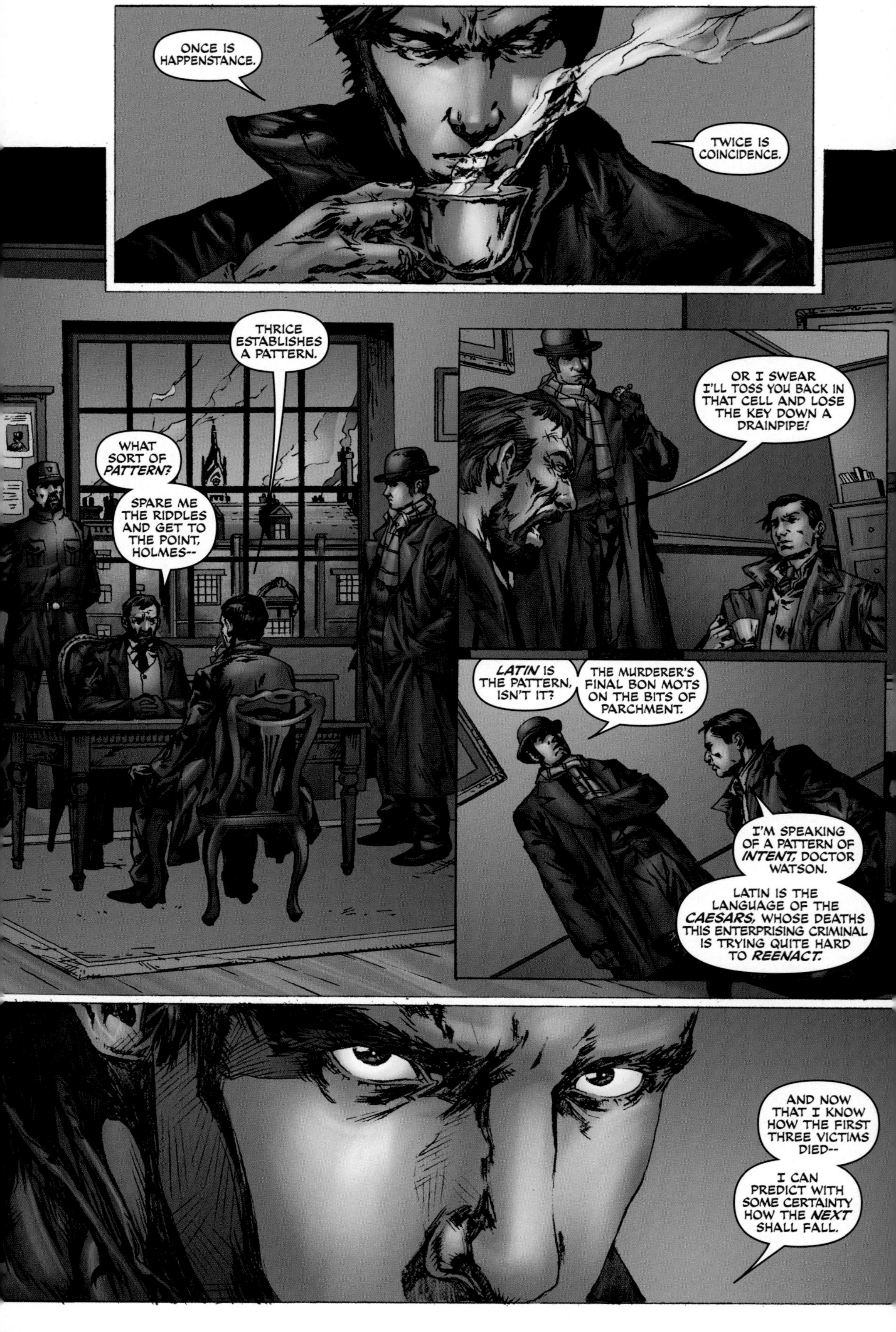
ONCE IS HAPPENSTANCE.
TWICE IS COINCIDENCE.
THRICE ESTABLISHES A PATTERN.
WHAT SORT OF *PATTERN?*
SPARE ME THE RIDDLES AND GET TO THE POINT, HOLMES--
OR I SWEAR I'LL TOSS YOU BACK IN THAT CELL AND LOSE THE KEY DOWN A DRAINPIPE!
LATIN IS THE PATTERN, ISN'T IT?
THE MURDERER'S FINAL BON MOTS ON THE BITS OF PARCHMENT.
I'M SPEAKING OF A PATTERN OF *INTENT,* DOCTOR WATSON.
LATIN IS THE LANGUAGE OF THE *CAESARS,* WHOSE DEATHS THIS ENTERPRISING CRIMINAL IS TRYING QUITE HARD TO *REENACT.*
AND NOW THAT I KNOW HOW THE FIRST THREE VICTIMS DIED--
I CAN PREDICT WITH SOME CERTAINTY HOW THE *NEXT* SHALL FALL.

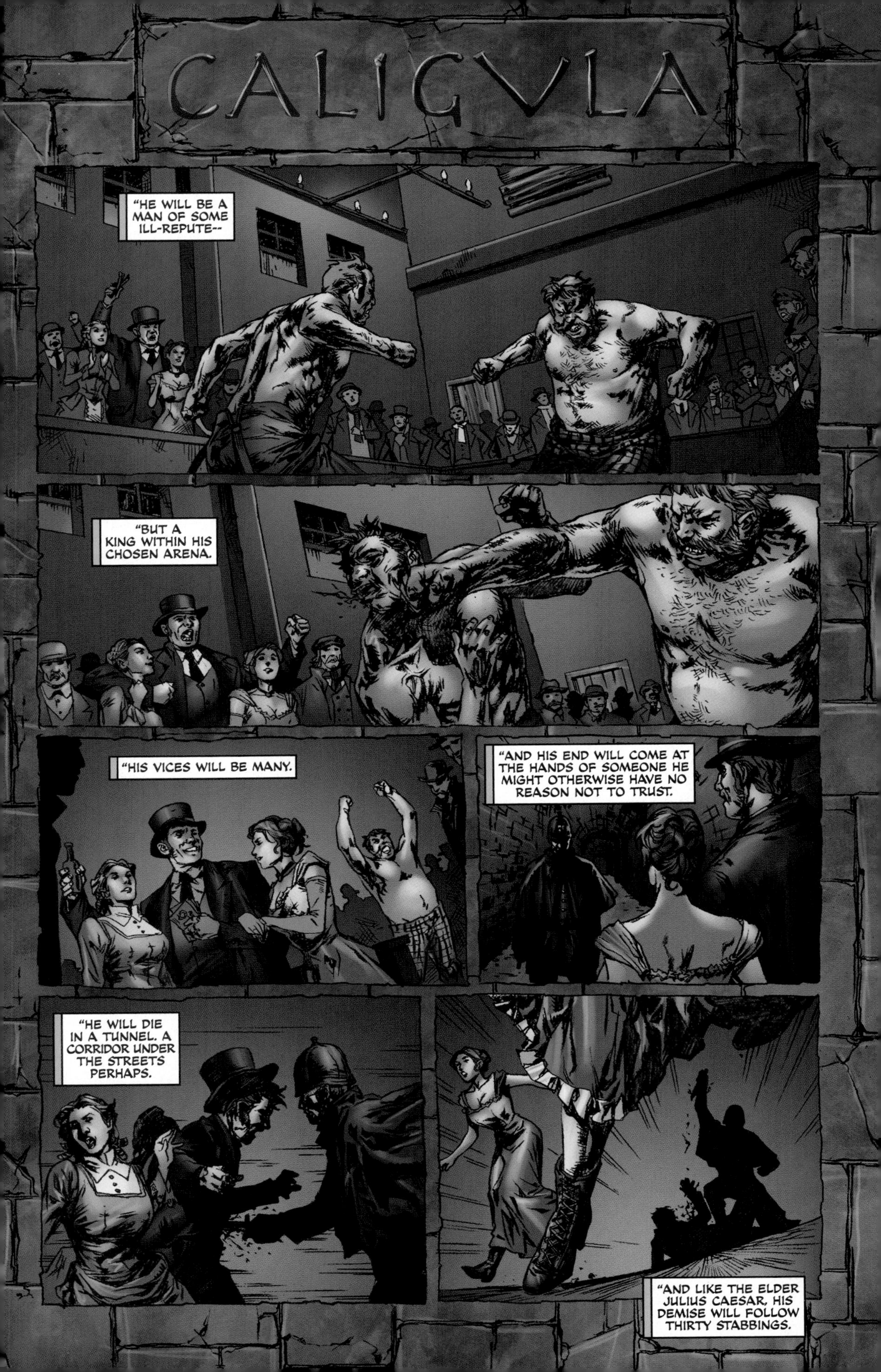
CALIGVLA
"HE WILL BE A MAN OF SOME ILL-REPUTE--
"BUT A KING WITHIN HIS CHOSEN ARENA.
"HIS VICES WILL BE MANY.
"AND HIS END WILL COME AT THE HANDS OF SOMEONE HE MIGHT OTHERWISE HAVE NO REASON NOT TO TRUST.
"HE WILL DIE IN A TUNNEL. A CORRIDOR UNDER THE STREETS PERHAPS.
"AND LIKE THE ELDER JULIUS CAESAR, HIS DEMISE WILL FOLLOW THIRTY STABBINGS.

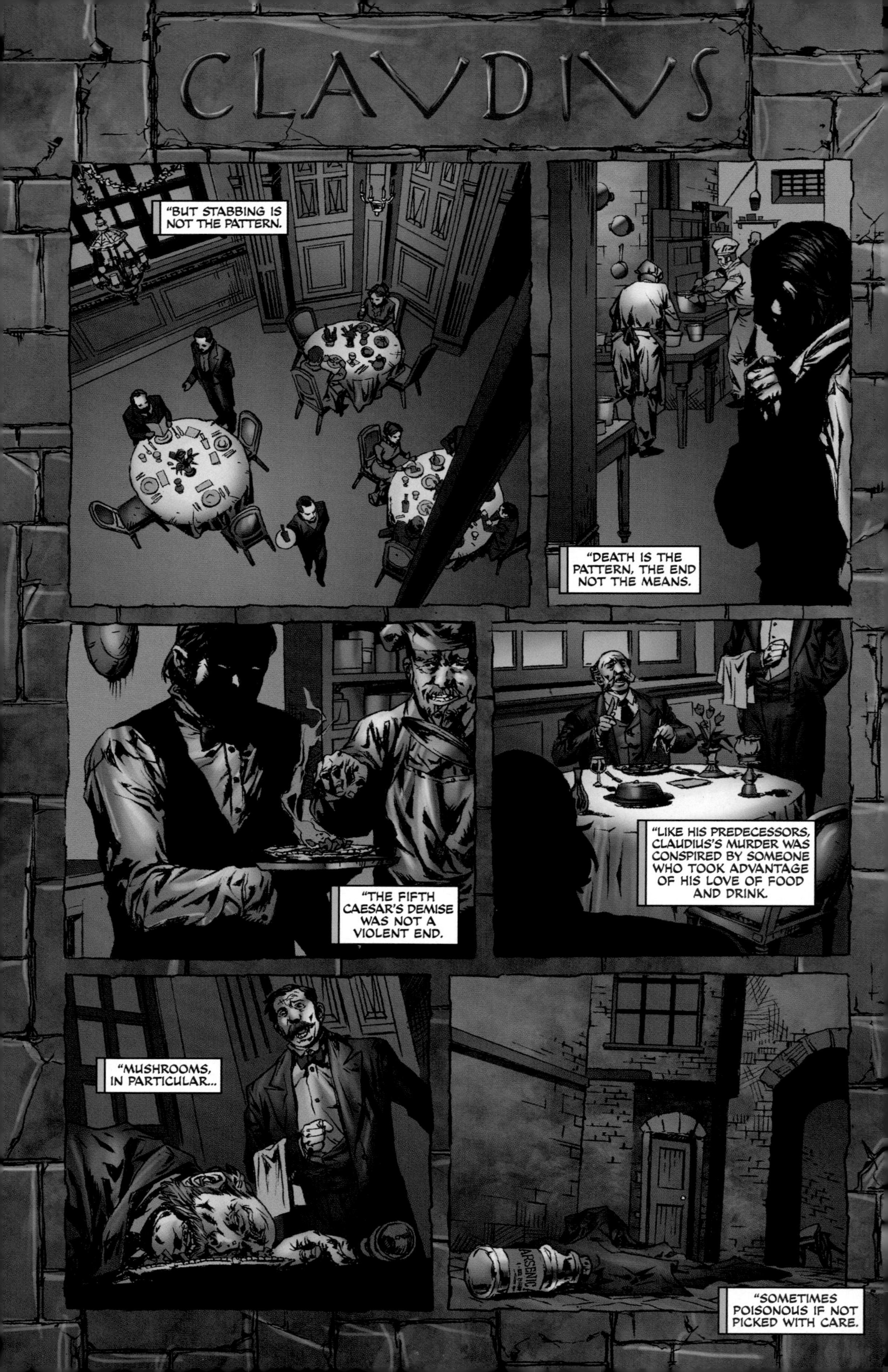
CLAVDIVS
"BUT STABBING IS NOT THE PATTERN.
"DEATH IS THE PATTERN, THE END NOT THE MEANS.
"THE FIFTH CAESAR'S DEMISE WAS NOT A VIOLENT END.
"LIKE HIS PREDECESSORS, CLAUDIUS'S MURDER WAS CONSPIRED BY SOMEONE WHO TOOK ADVANTAGE OF HIS LOVE OF FOOD AND DRINK.
"MUSHROOMS, IN PARTICULAR...
ARSENIC
"SOMETIMES POISONOUS IF NOT PICKED WITH CARE.

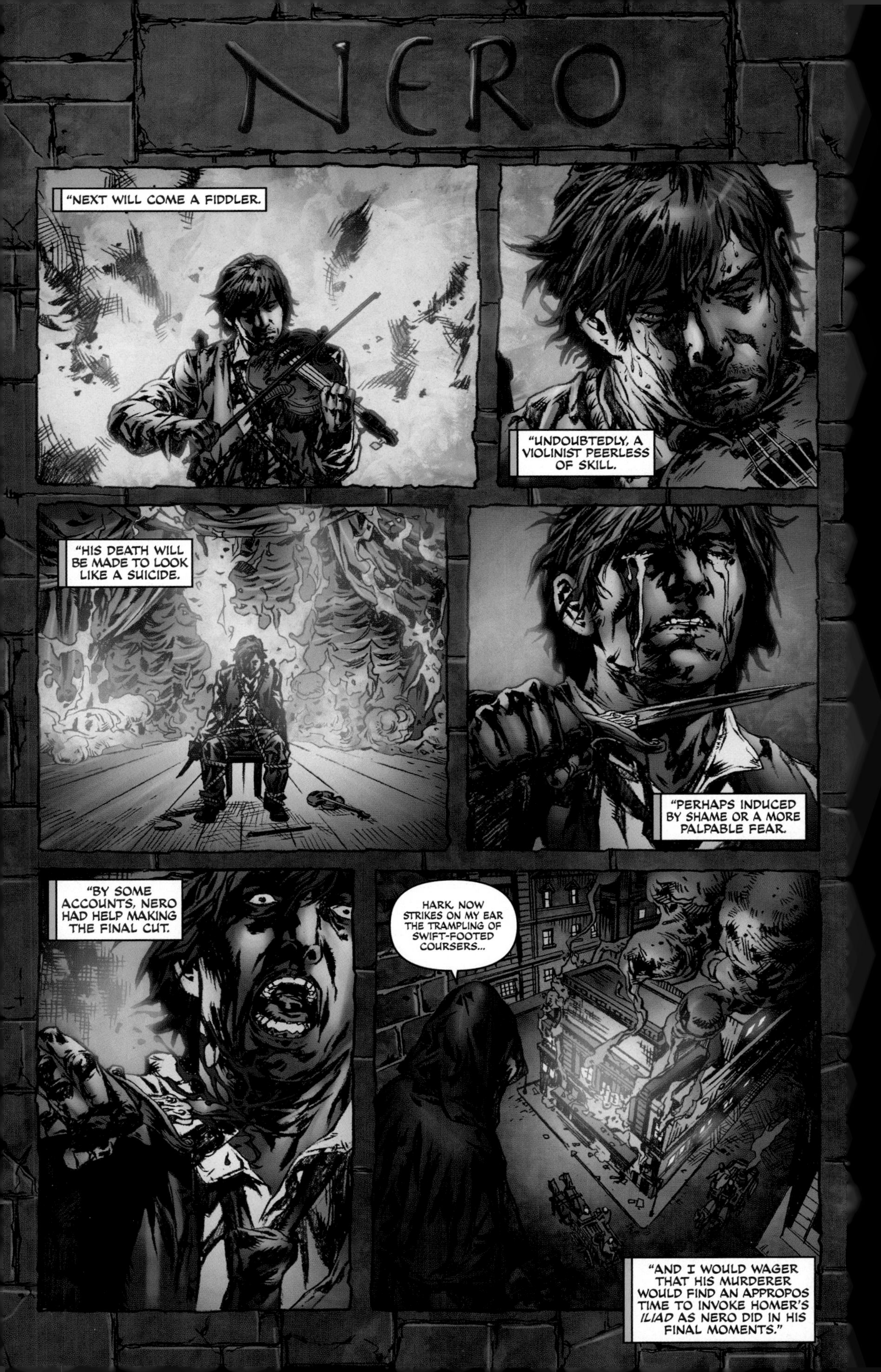
NERO
"NEXT WILL COME A FIDDLER.
"UNDOUBTEDLY, A VIOLINIST PEERLESS OF SKILL.
"HIS DEATH WILL BE MADE TO LOOK LIKE A SUICIDE.
"PERHAPS INDUCED BY SHAME OR A MORE PALPABLE FEAR.
"BY SOME ACCOUNTS, NERO HAD HELP MAKING THE FINAL CUT.
HARK, NOW STRIKES ON MY EAR THE TRAMPLING OF SWIFT-FOOTED COURSERS...
"AND I WOULD WAGER THAT HIS MURDERER WOULD FIND AN APPROPOS TIME TO INVOKE HOMER'S *ILIAD* AS NERO DID IN HIS FINAL MOMENTS."

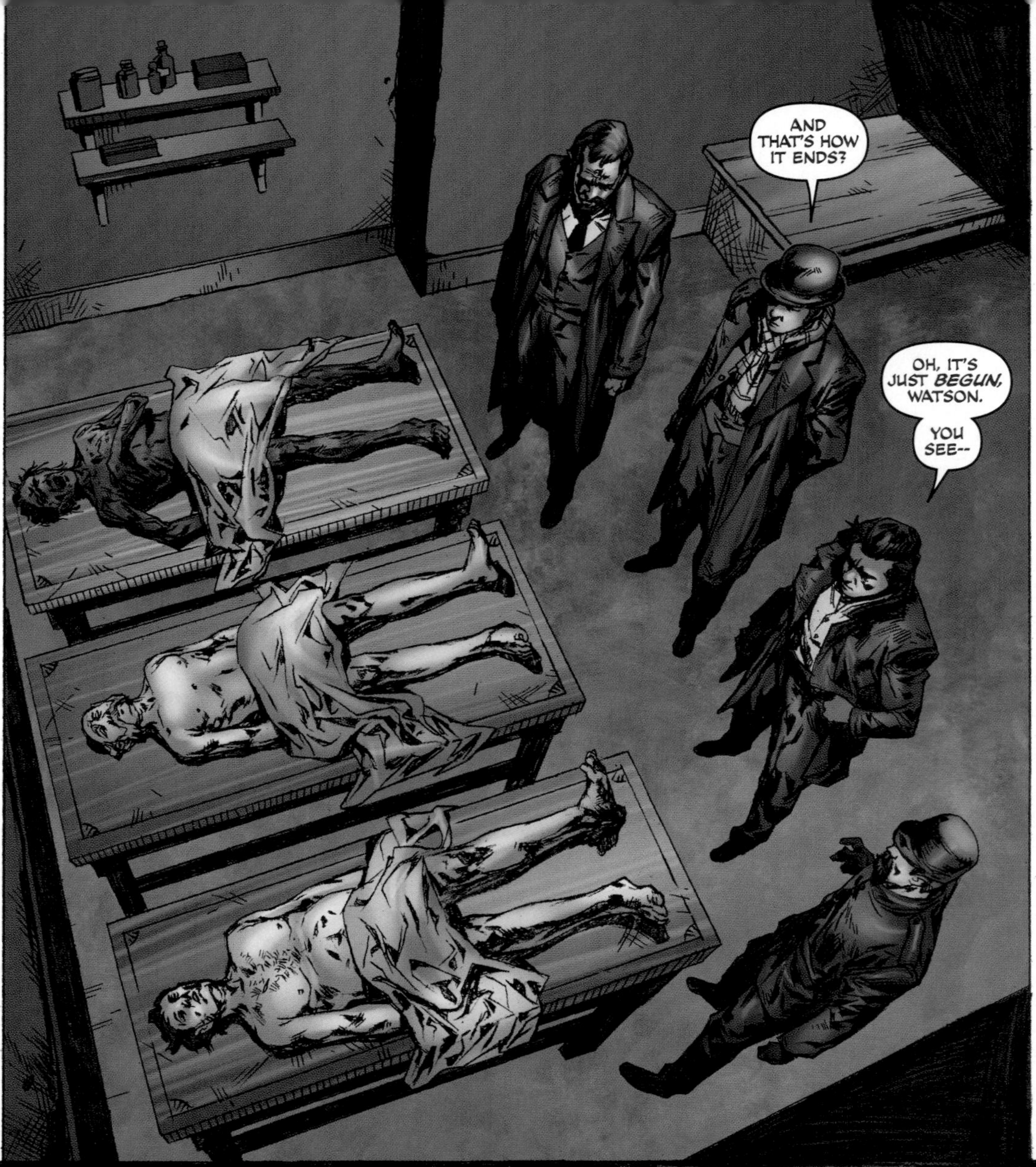
AND THAT'S HOW IT ENDS?
OH, IT'S JUST *BEGUN,* WATSON.
YOU SEE--

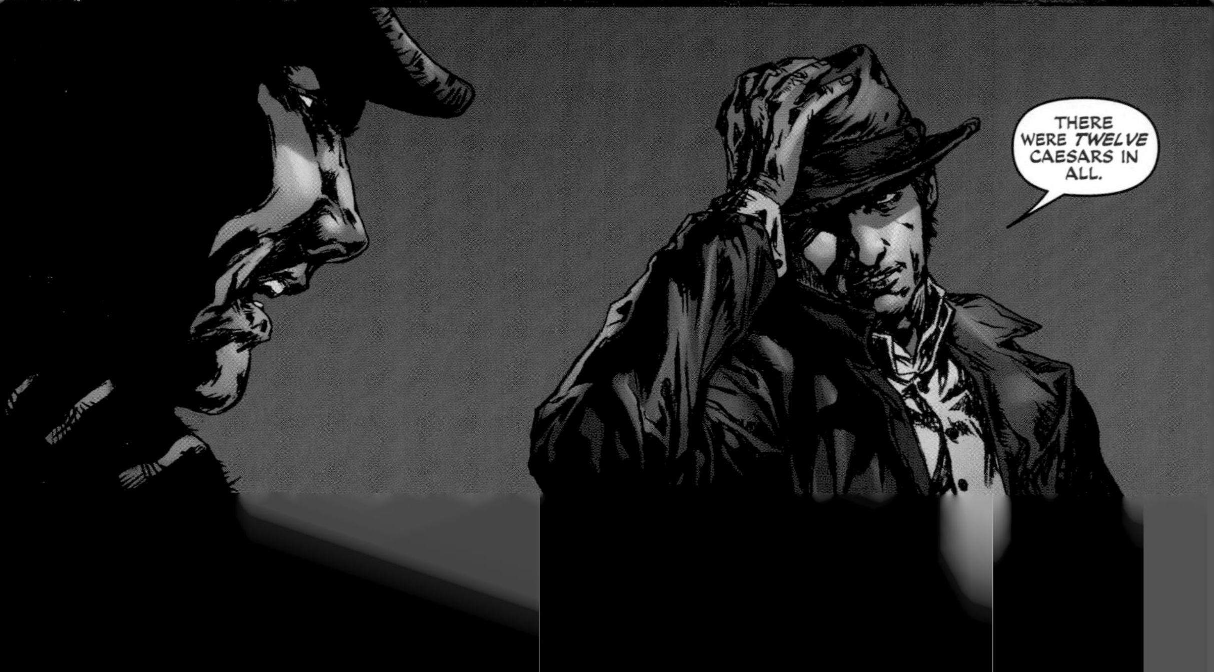
THERE WERE *TWELVE* CAESARS IN ALL.

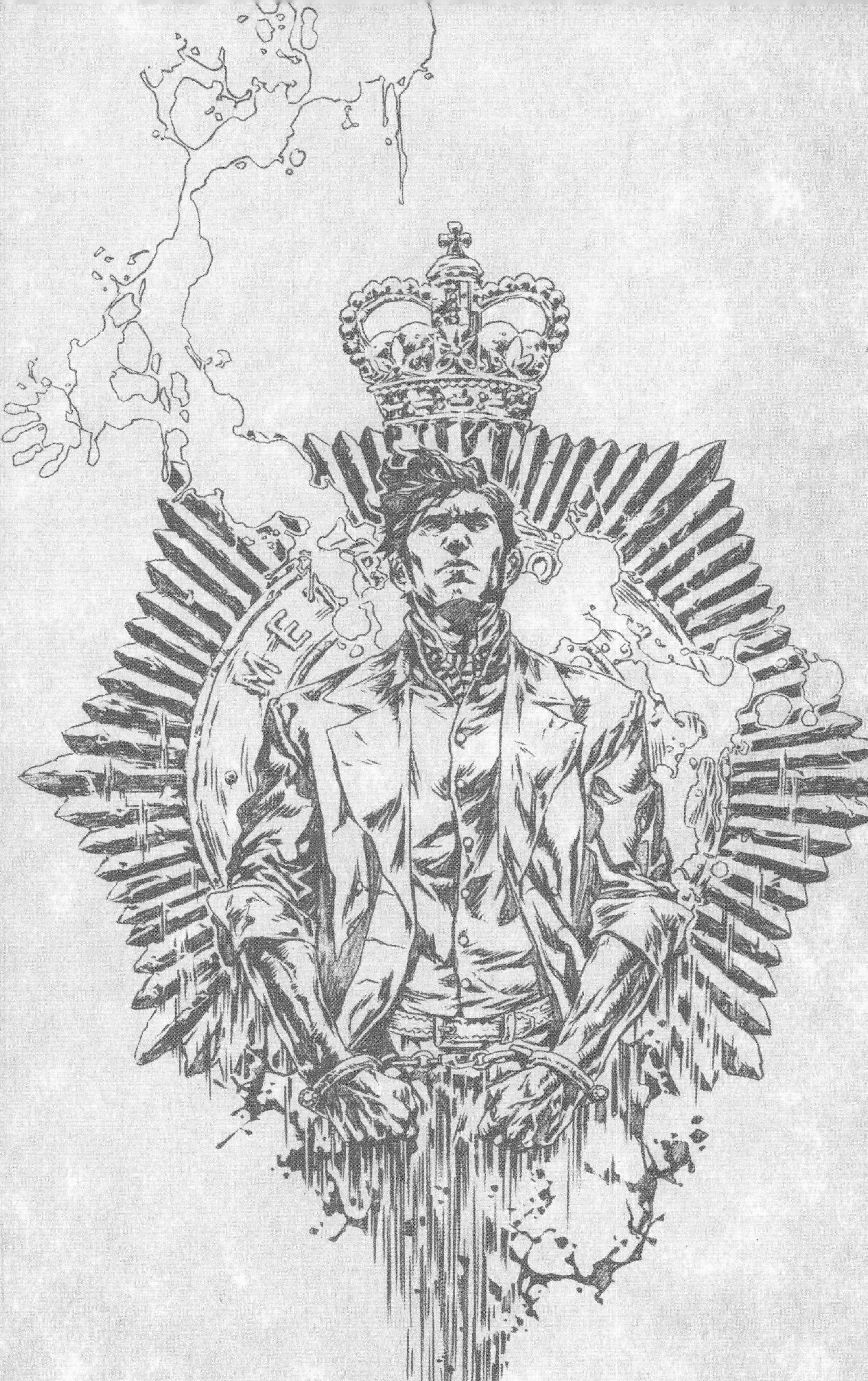

Cover by:
FRANCESCO
FRANCAVILLA

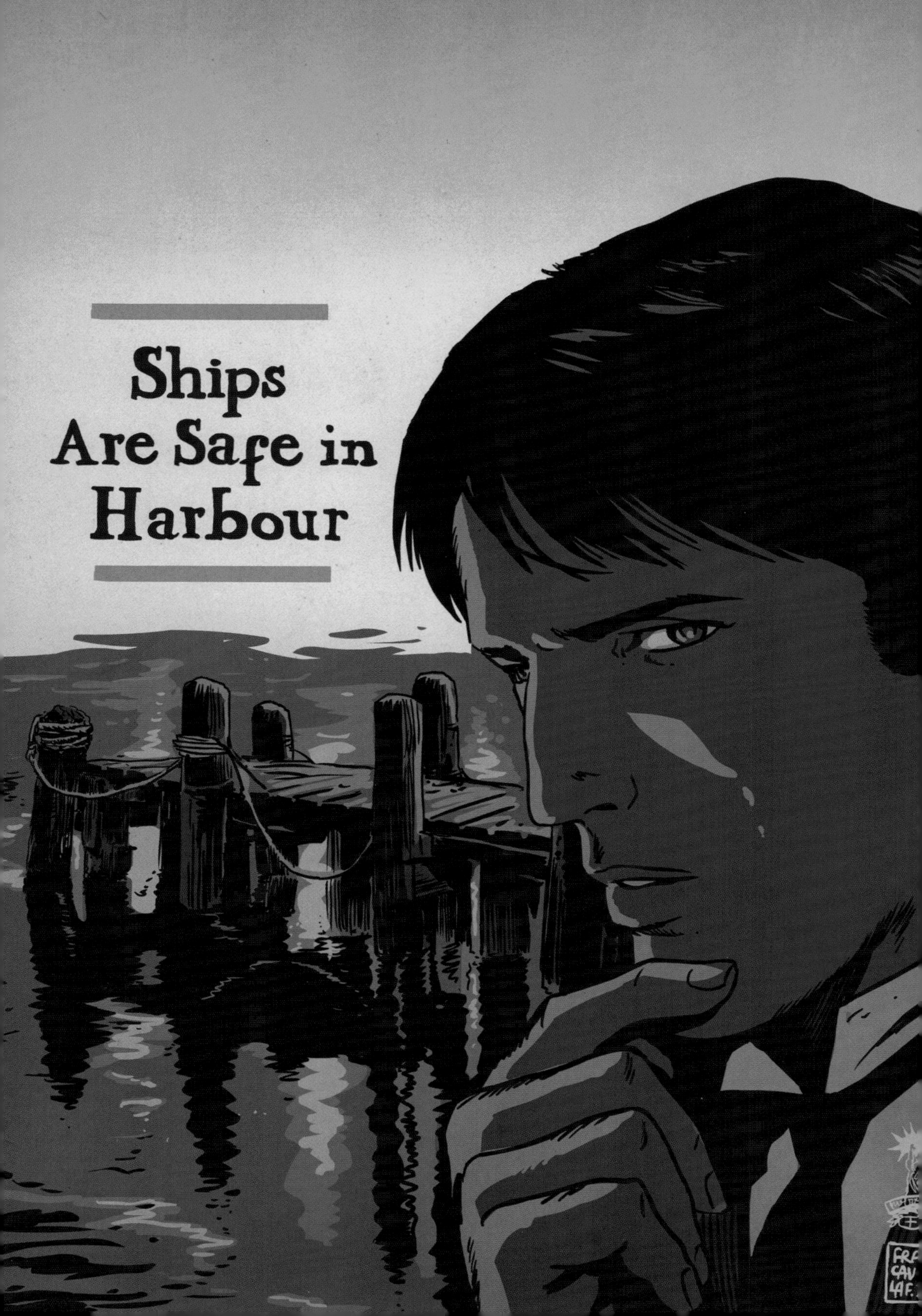
Ships
Are Safe in
Harbour

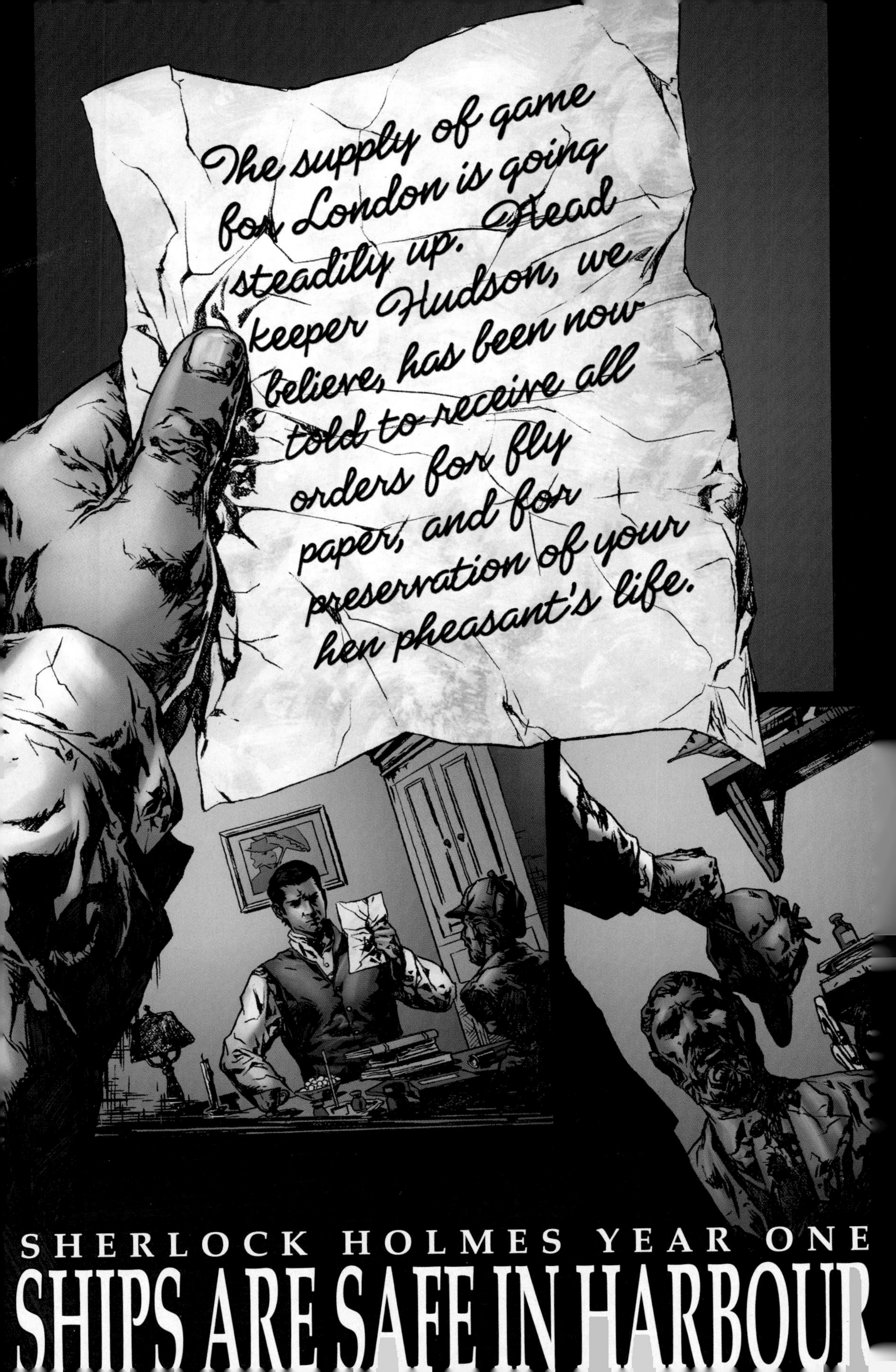
The supply of game for London is going steadily up. Head keeper Hudson, we believe, has been now told to receive all orders for fly paper, and for preservation of your hen pheasant's life.
SHERLOCK HOLMES YEAR ONE
SHIPS ARE SAFE IN HARBOUR

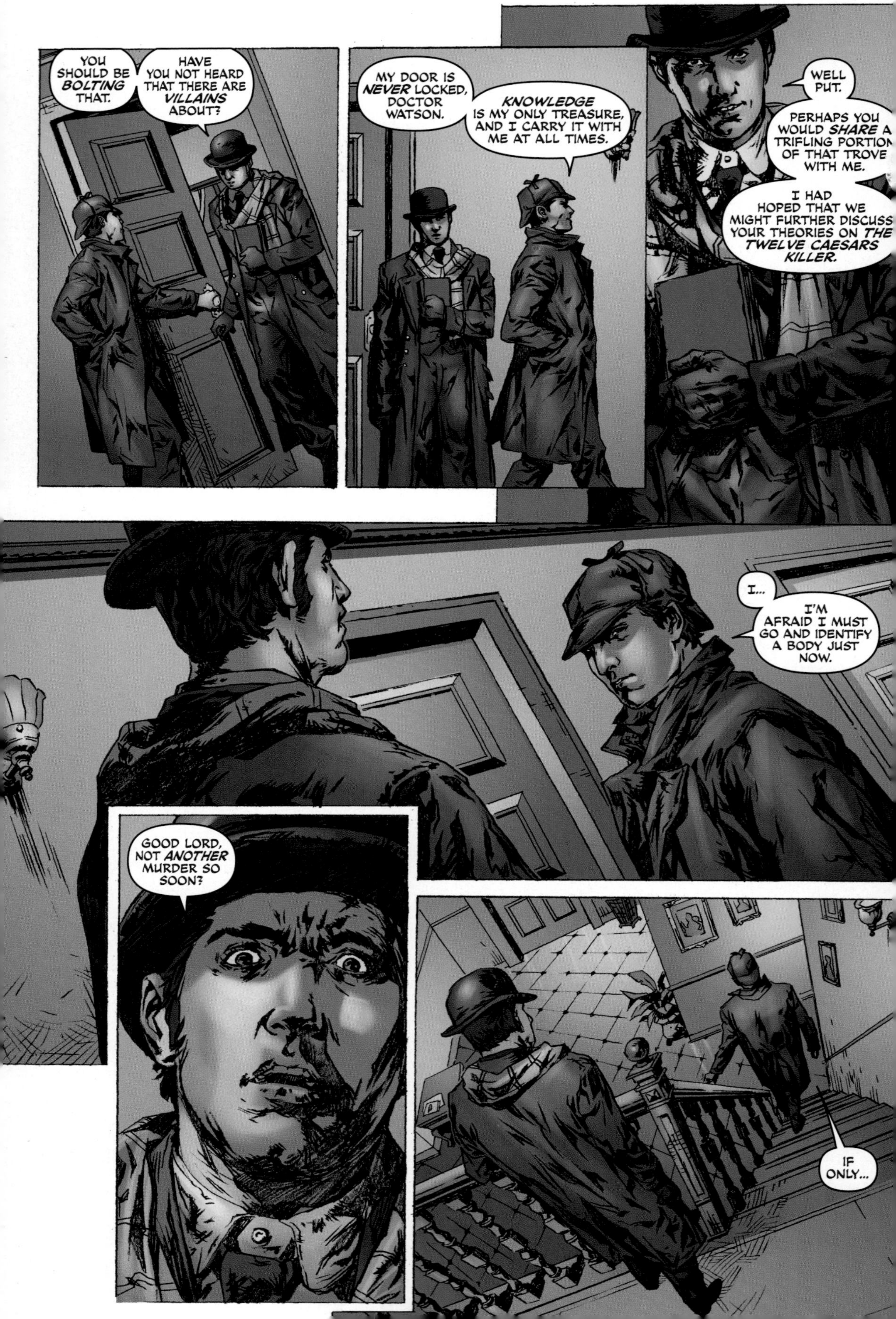
YOU SHOULD BE *BOLTING* THAT.
HAVE YOU NOT HEARD THAT THERE ARE *VILLAINS* ABOUT?
MY DOOR IS *NEVER* LOCKED, DOCTOR WATSON.
KNOWLEDGE IS MY ONLY TREASURE, AND I CARRY IT WITH ME AT ALL TIMES.
WELL PUT.
PERHAPS YOU WOULD *SHARE* A TRIFLING PORTION OF THAT TROVE WITH ME.
I HAD HOPED THAT WE MIGHT FURTHER DISCUSS YOUR THEORIES ON *THE TWELVE CAESARS KILLER.*
I...
I'M AFRAID I MUST GO AND IDENTIFY A BODY JUST NOW.
GOOD LORD, NOT *ANOTHER* MURDER SO SOON?
IF ONLY...

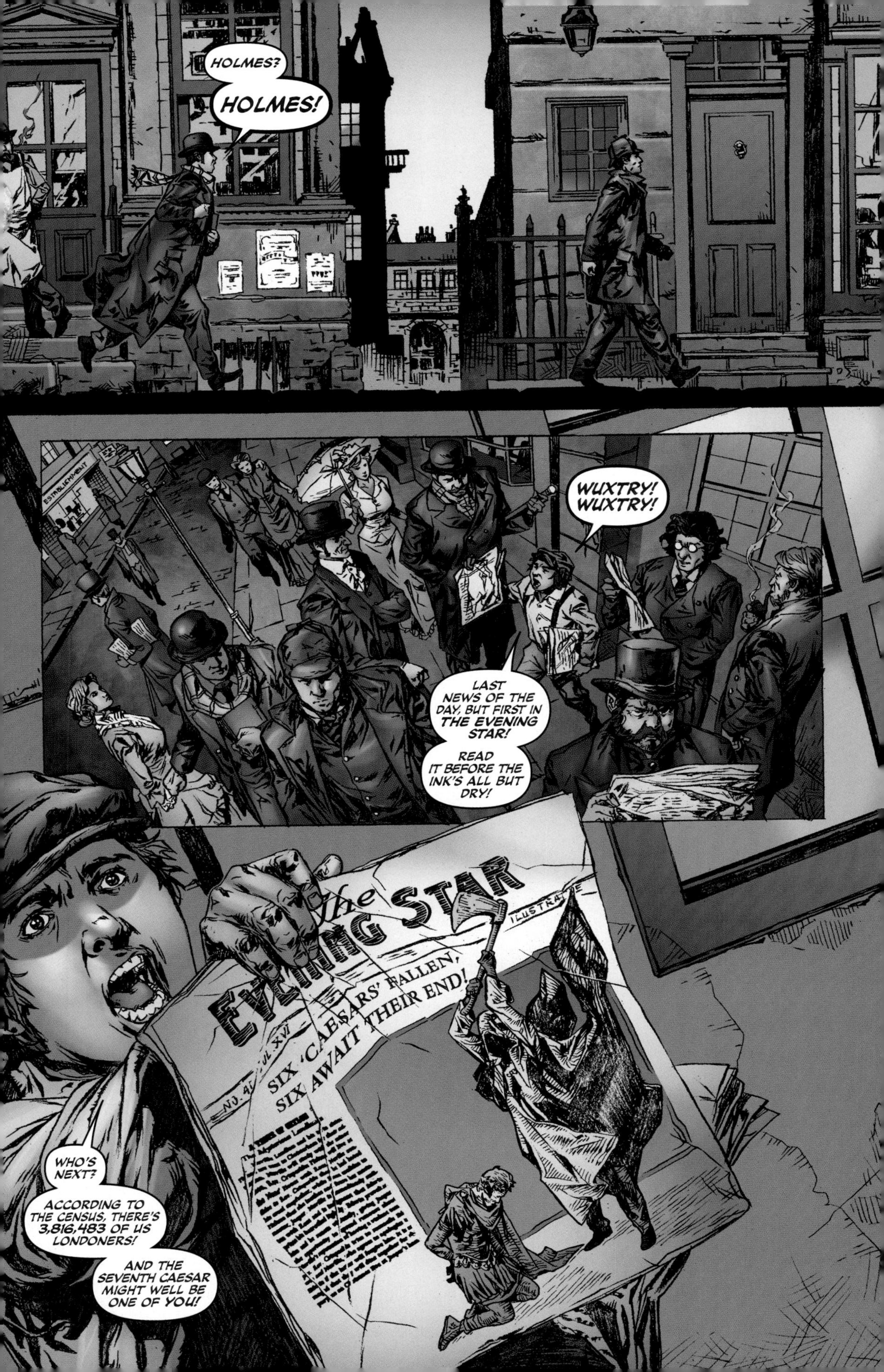
HOLMES?
HOLMES!
WUXTRY! WUXTRY!
LAST NEWS OF THE DAY, BUT FIRST IN THE EVENING STAR!
READ IT BEFORE THE INK'S ALL BUT DRY!
The EVENING STAR
SIX 'CAESARS' FALLEN, SIX AWAIT THEIR END!
WHO'S NEXT?
ACCORDING TO THE CENSUS, THERE'S 3,816,483 OF US LONDONERS!
AND THE SEVENTH CAESAR MIGHT WELL BE ONE OF YOU!

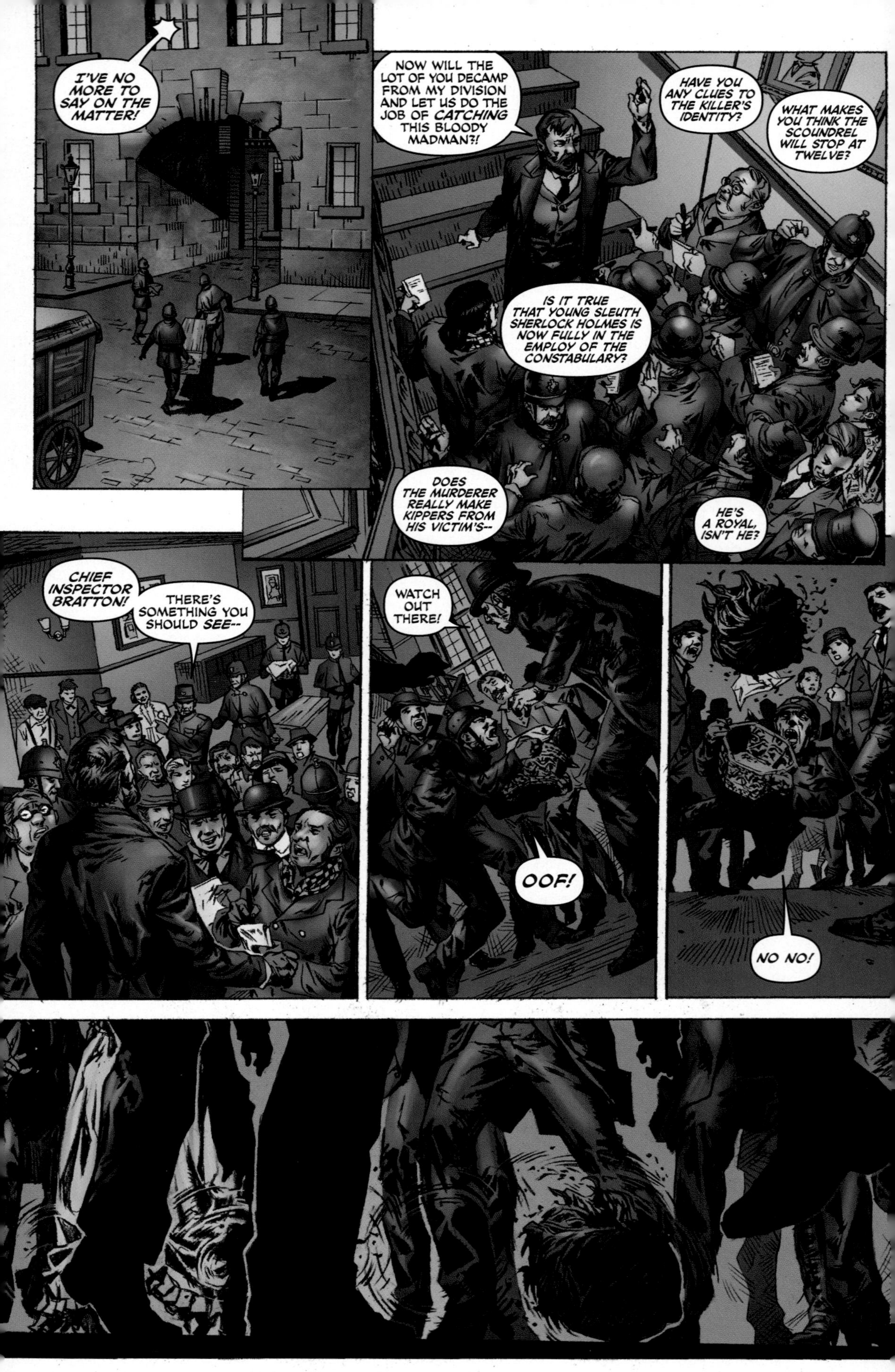
I'VE NO MORE TO SAY ON THE MATTER!
NOW WILL THE LOT OF YOU DECAMP FROM MY DIVISION AND LET US DO THE JOB OF CATCHING THIS BLOODY MADMAN?!
HAVE YOU ANY CLUES TO THE KILLER'S IDENTITY?
WHAT MAKES YOU THINK THE SCOUNDREL WILL STOP AT TWELVE?
IS IT TRUE THAT YOUNG SLEUTH SHERLOCK HOLMES IS NOW FULLY IN THE EMPLOY OF THE CONSTABULARY?
DOES THE MURDERER REALLY MAKE KIPPERS FROM HIS VICTIM'S--
HE'S A ROYAL, ISN'T HE?
CHIEF INSPECTOR BRATTON!
THERE'S SOMETHING YOU SHOULD SEE--
WATCH OUT THERE!
OOF!
NO NO!

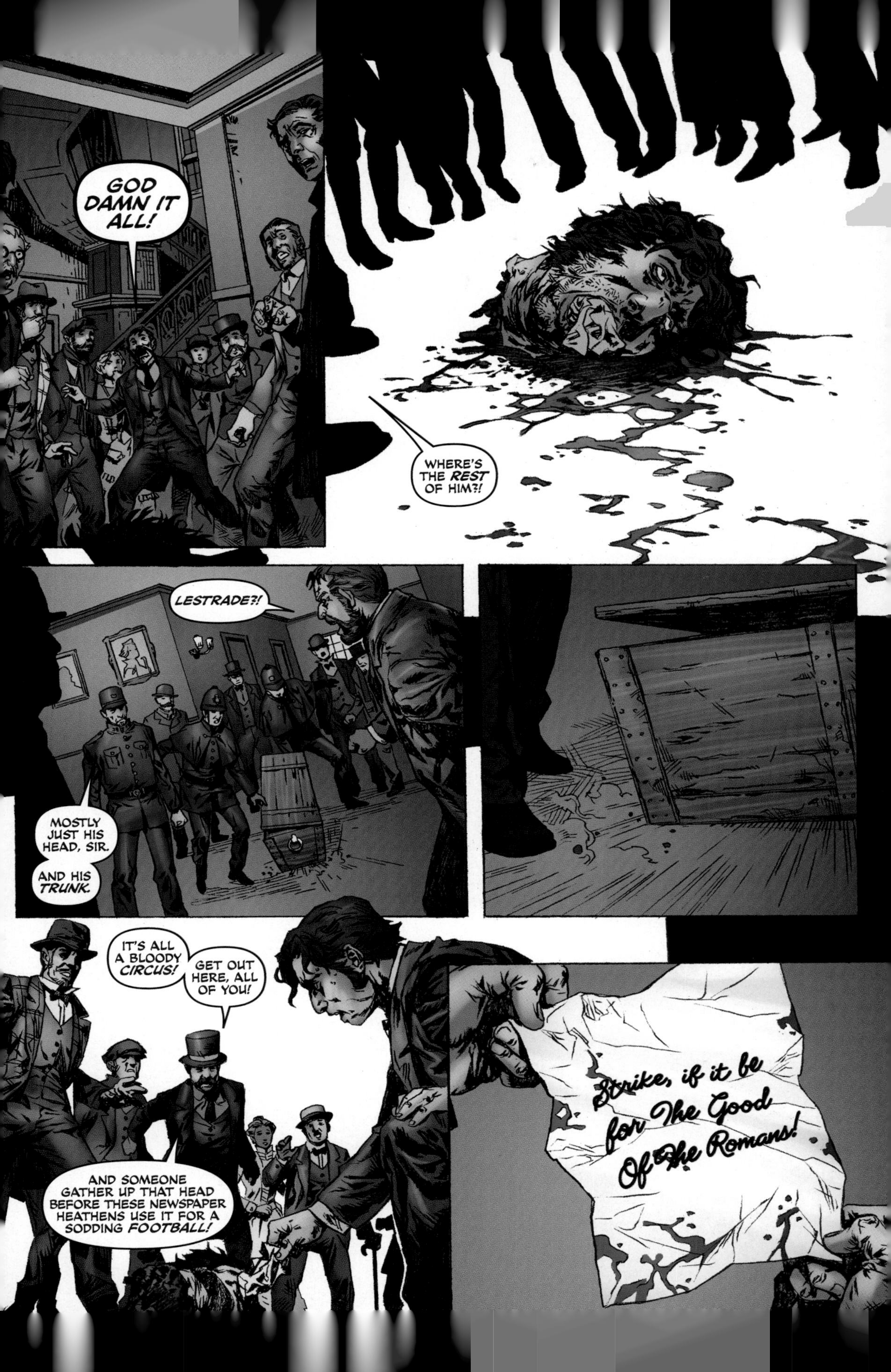
GOD DAMN IT ALL!
WHERE'S THE REST OF HIM?!
LESTRADE?!
MOSTLY JUST HIS HEAD, SIR.
AND HIS TRUNK.
IT'S ALL A BLOODY CIRCUS!
GET OUT HERE, ALL OF YOU!
AND SOMEONE GATHER UP THAT HEAD BEFORE THESE NEWSPAPER HEATHENS USE IT FOR A SODDING FOOTBALL!
Strike, if it be for The Good Of the Romans!

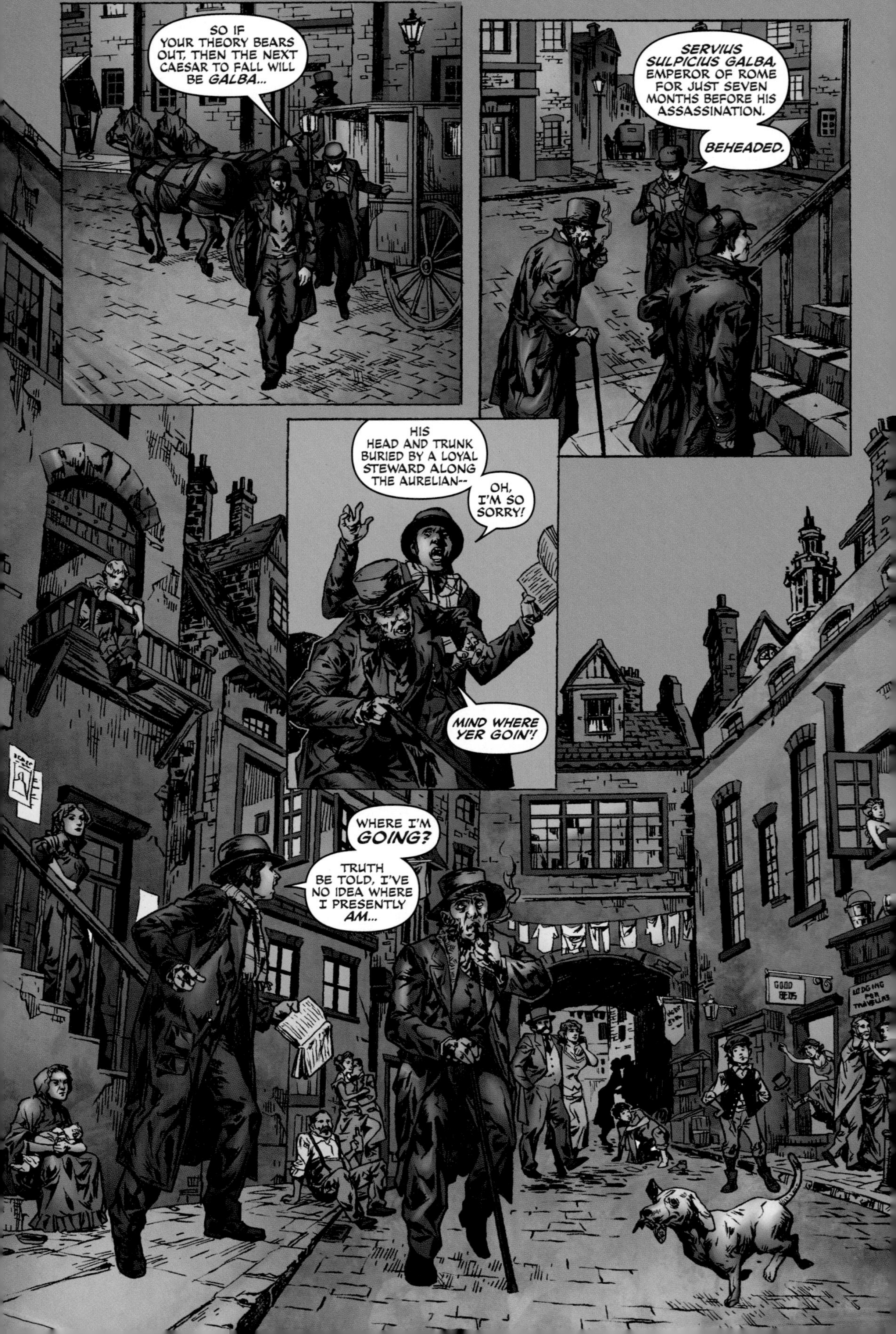
SO IF YOUR THEORY BEARS OUT, THEN THE NEXT CAESAR TO FALL WILL BE *GALBA*...
SERVIUS SULPICIUS GALBA, EMPEROR OF ROME FOR JUST SEVEN MONTHS BEFORE HIS ASSASSINATION.
BEHEADED.
HIS HEAD AND TRUNK BURIED BY A LOYAL STEWARD ALONG THE AURELIAN--
OH, I'M SO SORRY!
MIND WHERE YER GOIN'!
WHERE I'M *GOING?*
TRUTH BE TOLD, I'VE NO IDEA WHERE I PRESENTLY *AM*...
GOOD BEDS

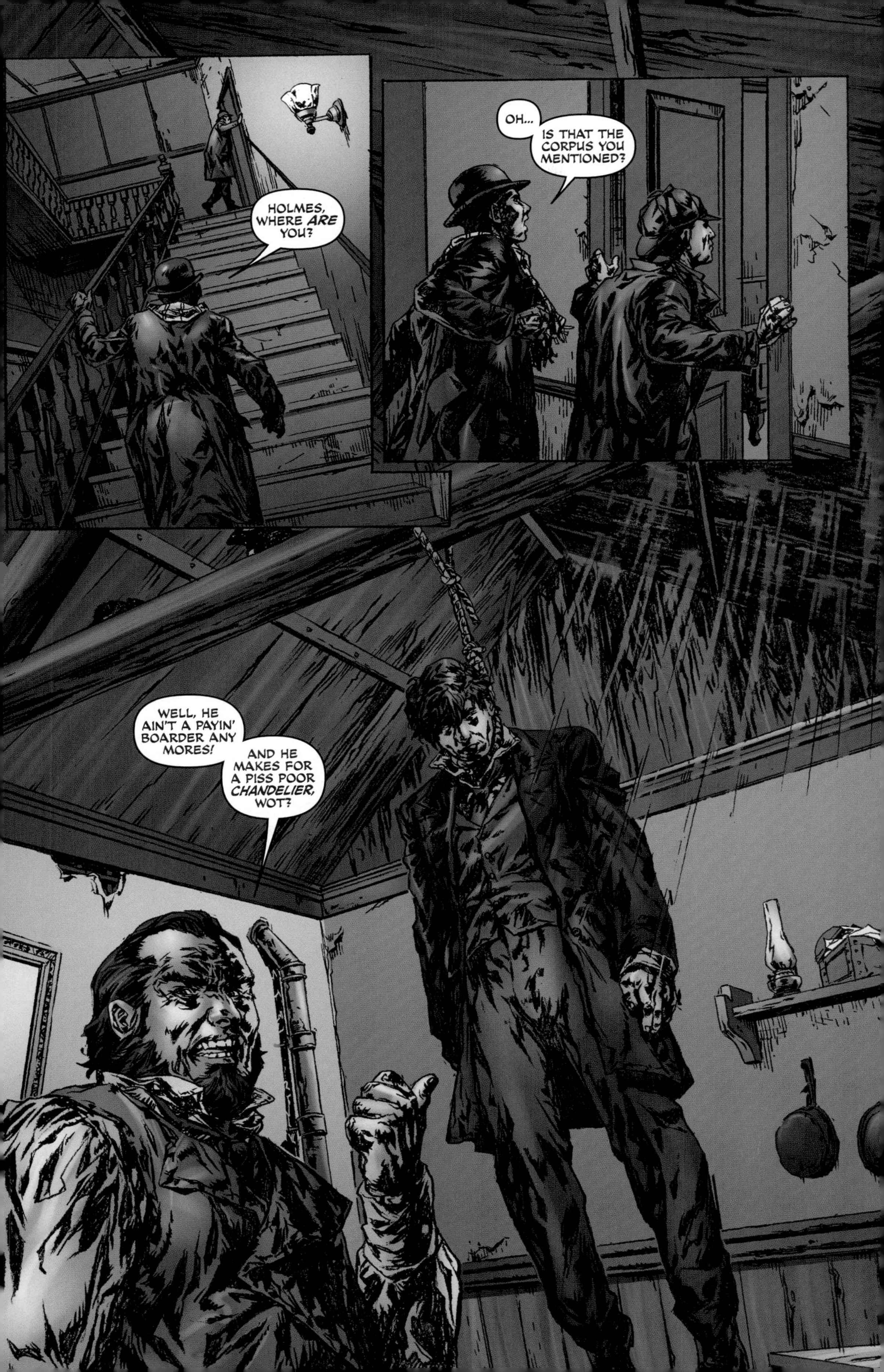
HOLMES, WHERE *ARE* YOU?
OH...
IS THAT THE CORPUS YOU MENTIONED?
WELL, HE AIN'T A PAYIN' BOARDER ANY MORES!
AND HE MAKES FOR A PISS POOR *CHANDELIER*, WOT?

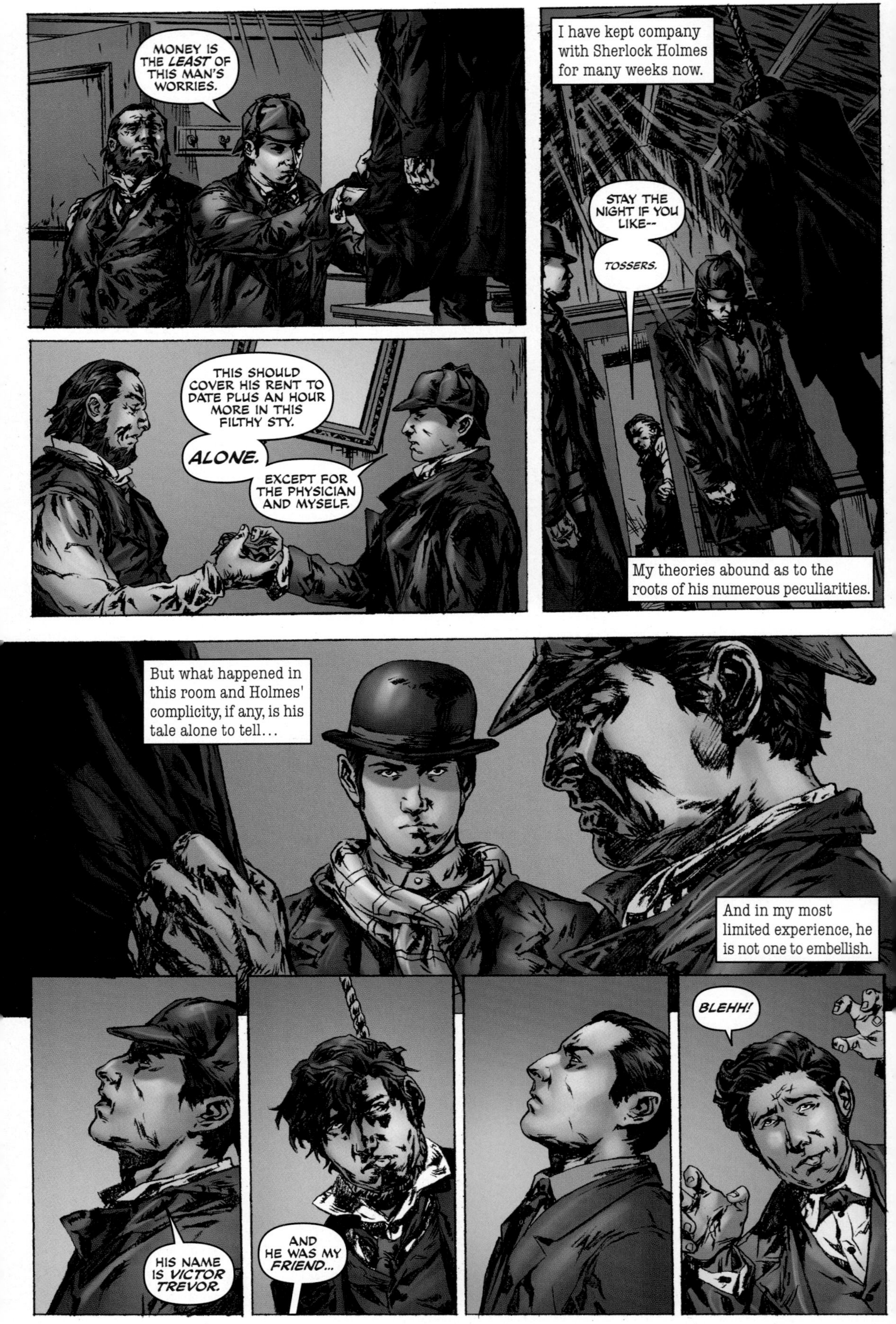
MONEY IS THE *LEAST* OF THIS MAN'S WORRIES.
THIS SHOULD COVER HIS RENT TO DATE PLUS AN HOUR MORE IN THIS FILTHY STY.
ALONE.
EXCEPT FOR THE PHYSICIAN AND MYSELF.
I have kept company with Sherlock Holmes for many weeks now.
STAY THE NIGHT IF YOU LIKE--
TOSSERS.
My theories abound as to the roots of his numerous peculiarities.
But what happened in this room and Holmes' complicity, if any, is his tale alone to tell...
And in my most limited experience, he is not one to embellish.
HIS NAME IS *VICTOR TREVOR.*
AND HE WAS MY *FRIEND...*
BLEHH!

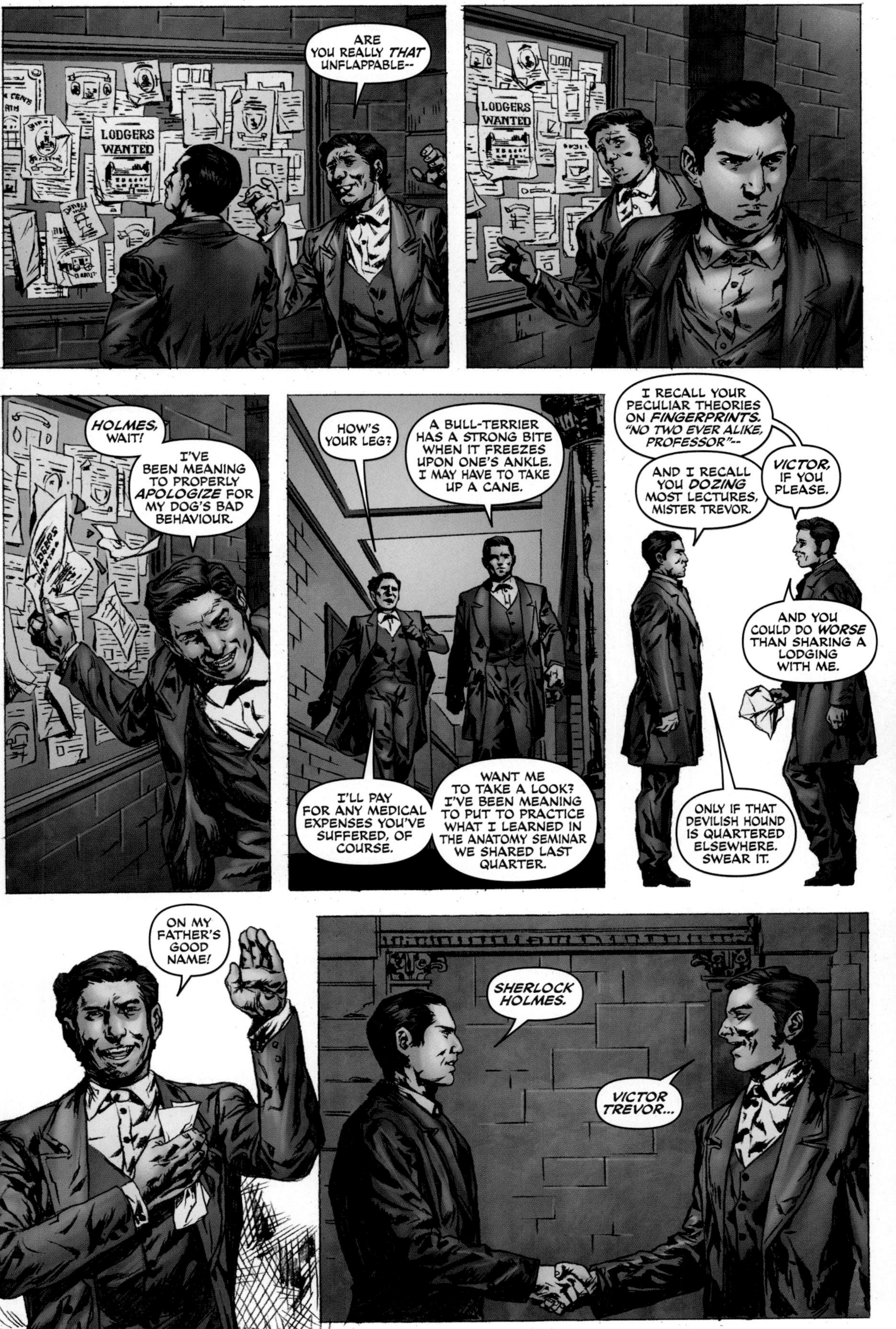
LODGERS WANTED
ARE YOU REALLY *THAT* UNFLAPPABLE--
LODGERS WANTED
HOLMES, WAIT!
I'VE BEEN MEANING TO PROPERLY *APOLOGIZE* FOR MY DOG'S BAD BEHAVIOUR.
HOW'S YOUR LEG?
A BULL-TERRIER HAS A STRONG BITE WHEN IT FREEZES UPON ONE'S ANKLE. I MAY HAVE TO TAKE UP A CANE.
I'LL PAY FOR ANY MEDICAL EXPENSES YOU'VE SUFFERED, OF COURSE.
WANT ME TO TAKE A LOOK? I'VE BEEN MEANING TO PUT TO PRACTICE WHAT I LEARNED IN THE ANATOMY SEMINAR WE SHARED LAST QUARTER.
I RECALL YOUR PECULIAR THEORIES ON *FINGERPRINTS.* *"NO TWO EVER ALIKE, PROFESSOR"--*
AND I RECALL YOU *DOZING* MOST LECTURES, MISTER TREVOR.
VICTOR, IF YOU PLEASE.
AND YOU COULD DO *WORSE* THAN SHARING A LODGING WITH ME.
ONLY IF THAT DEVILISH HOUND IS QUARTERED ELSEWHERE. SWEAR IT.
ON MY FATHER'S GOOD NAME!
SHERLOCK HOLMES.
VICTOR TREVOR...

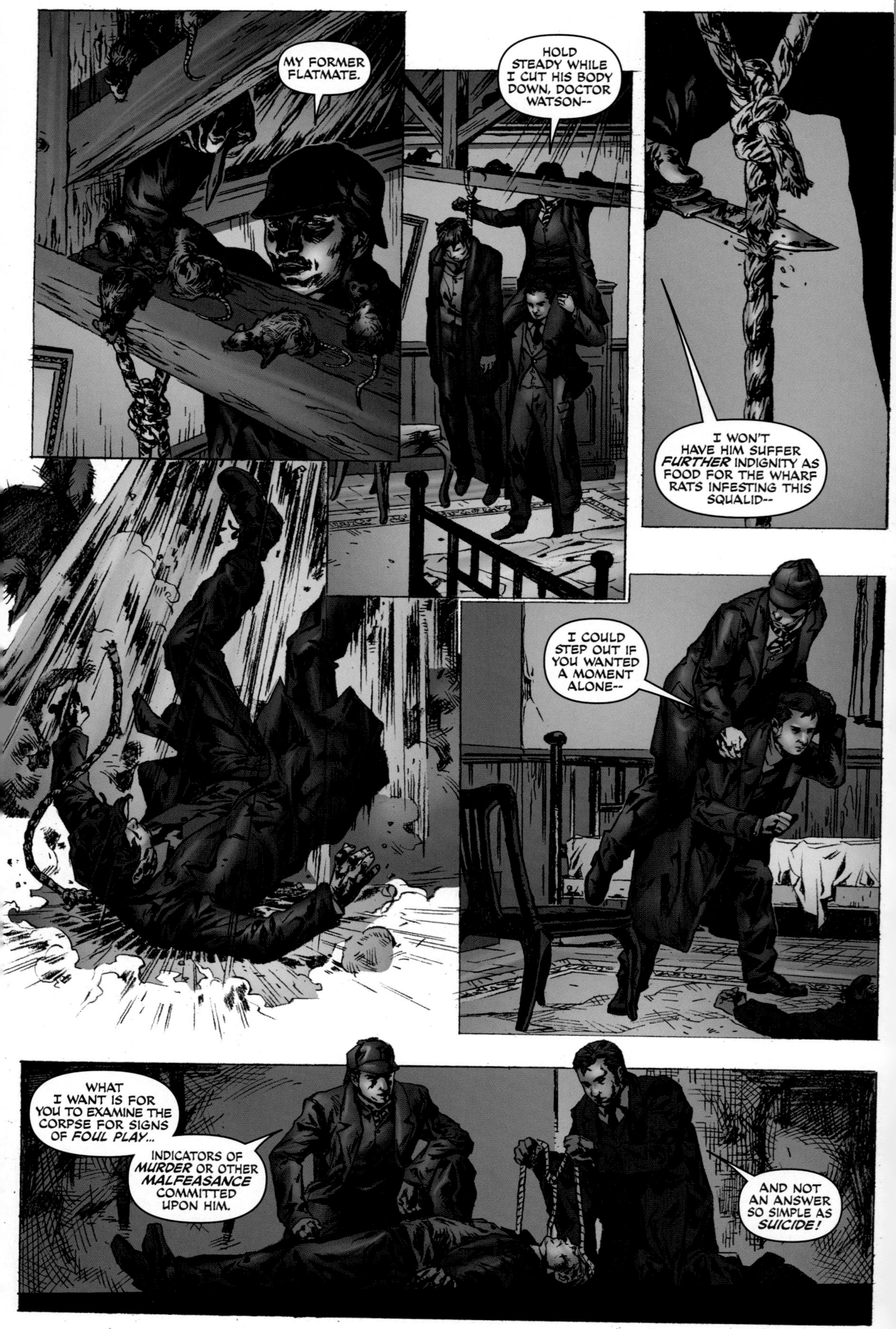
MY FORMER FLATMATE.
HOLD STEADY WHILE I CUT HIS BODY DOWN, DOCTOR WATSON--
I WON'T HAVE HIM SUFFER *FURTHER* INDIGNITY AS FOOD FOR THE WHARF RATS INFESTING THIS SQUALID--
I COULD STEP OUT IF YOU WANTED A MOMENT ALONE--
WHAT I WANT IS FOR YOU TO EXAMINE THE CORPSE FOR SIGNS OF *FOUL PLAY*...
INDICATORS OF *MURDER* OR OTHER *MALFEASANCE* COMMITTED UPON HIM.
AND NOT AN ANSWER SO SIMPLE AS *SUICIDE!*

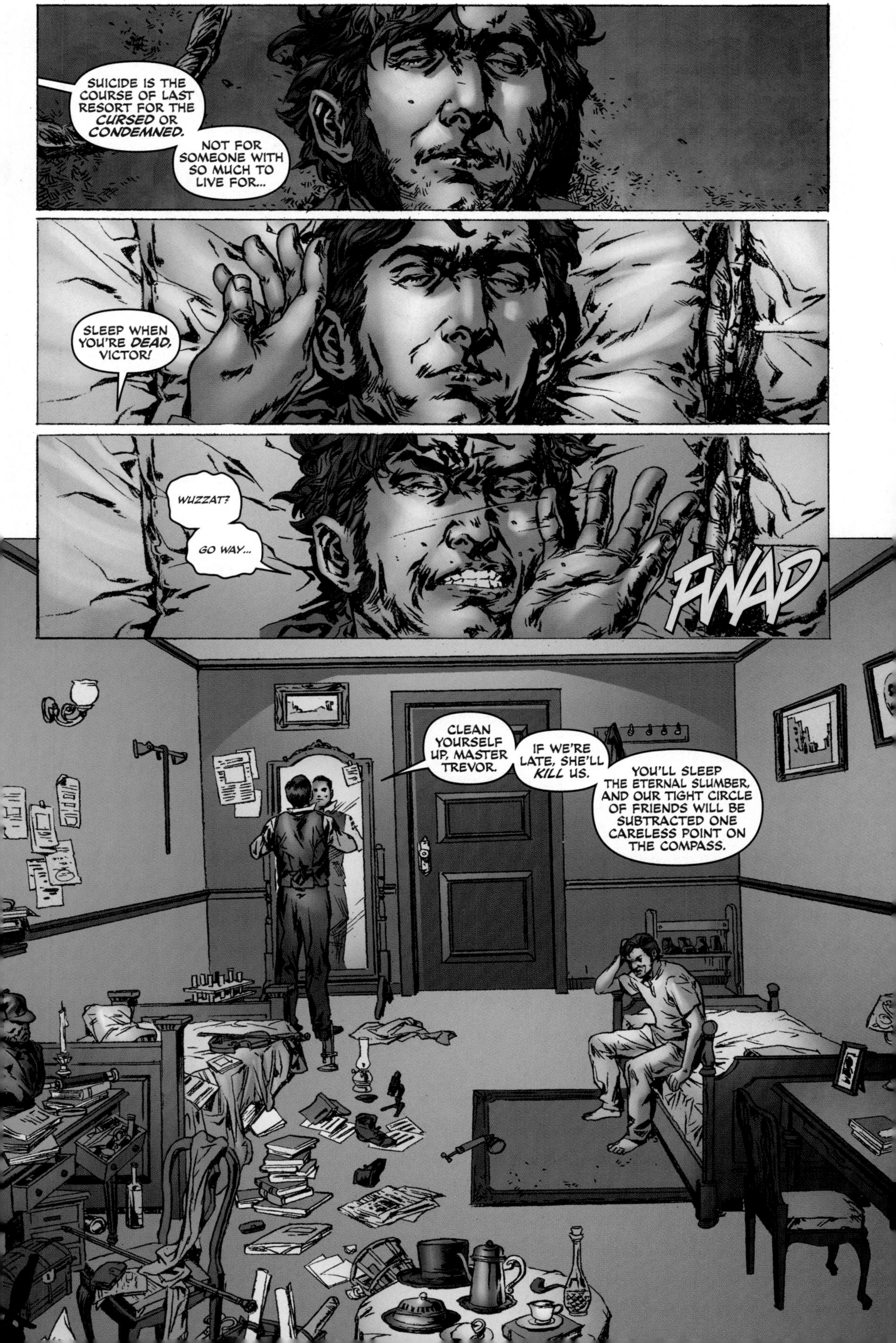
SUICIDE IS THE COURSE OF LAST RESORT FOR THE *CURSED* OR *CONDEMNED.*
NOT FOR SOMEONE WITH SO MUCH TO LIVE FOR...
SLEEP WHEN YOU'RE *DEAD,* VICTOR!
WUZZAT?
GO WAY...
FWAP
CLEAN YOURSELF UP, MASTER TREVOR.
IF WE'RE LATE, SHE'LL *KILL* US.
YOU'LL SLEEP THE ETERNAL SLUMBER, AND OUR TIGHT CIRCLE OF FRIENDS WILL BE SUBTRACTED ONE CARELESS POINT ON THE COMPASS.

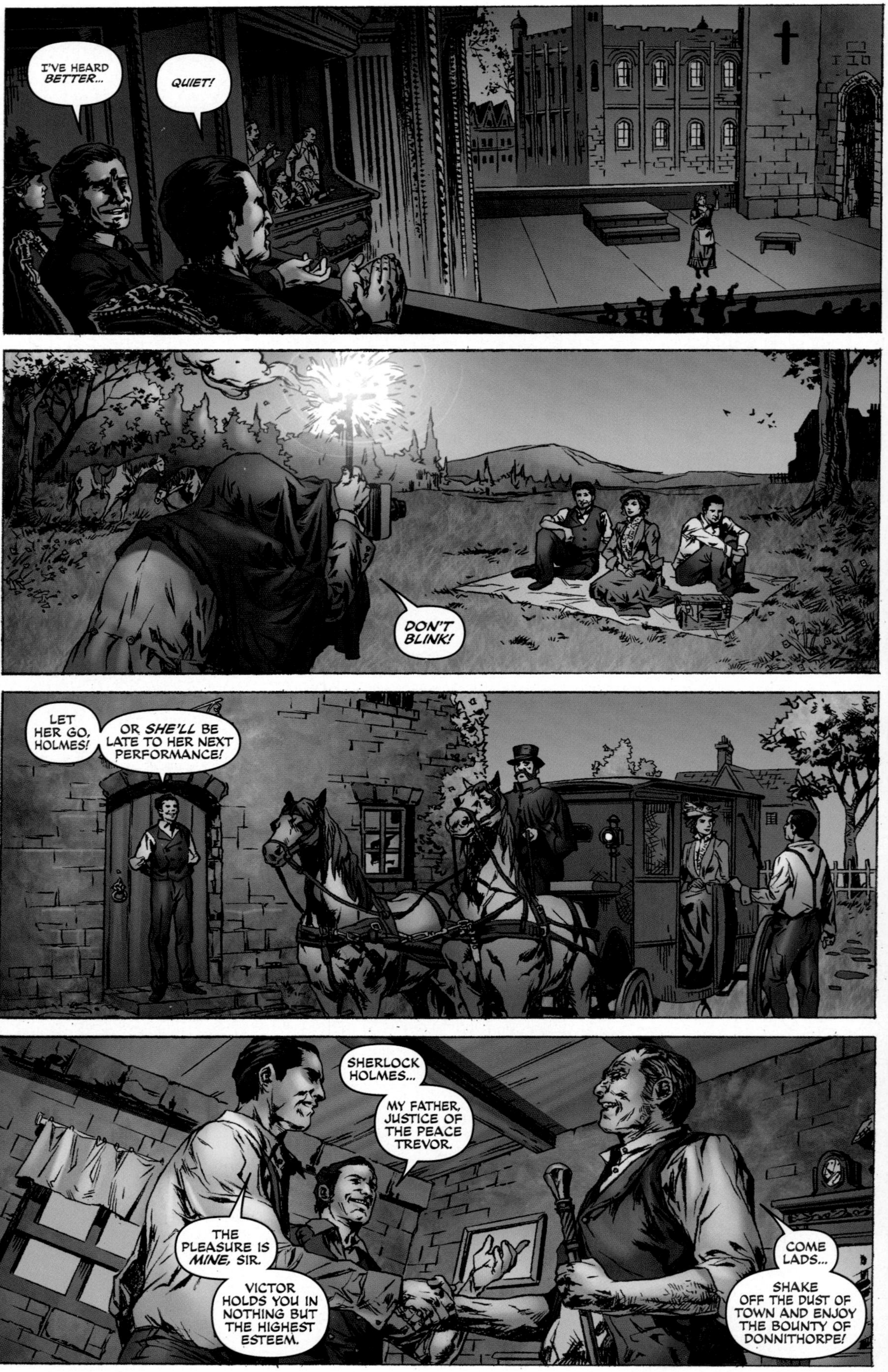

I'VE HEARD BETTER...
QUIET!
DON'T BLINK!
LET HER GO, HOLMES!
OR SHE'LL BE LATE TO HER NEXT PERFORMANCE!
SHERLOCK HOLMES...
MY FATHER, JUSTICE OF THE PEACE TREVOR.
THE PLEASURE IS MINE, SIR.
VICTOR HOLDS YOU IN NOTHING BUT THE HIGHEST ESTEEM.
COME LADS...
SHAKE OFF THE DUST OF TOWN AND ENJOY THE BOUNTY OF DONNITHORPE!

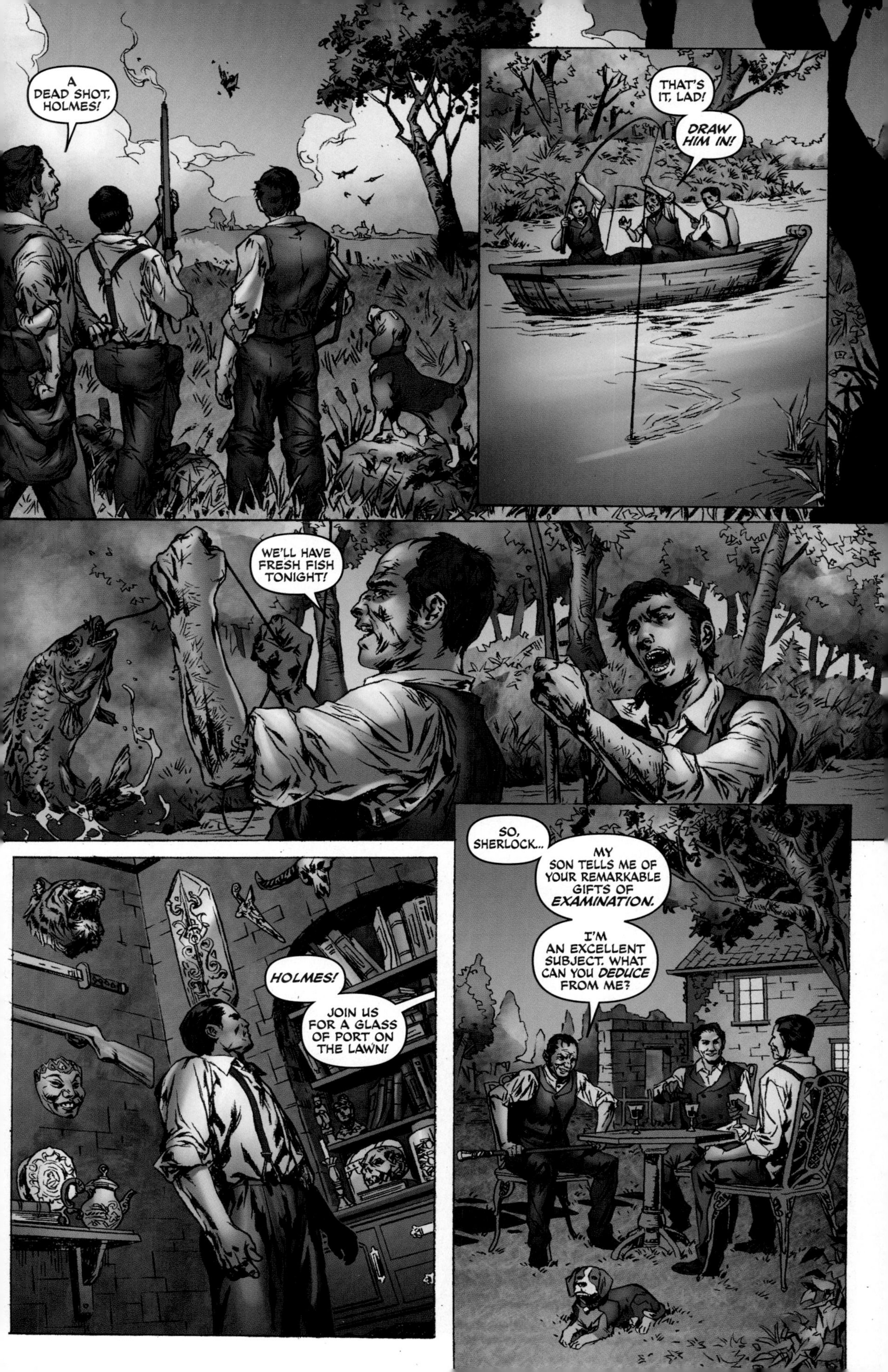
A DEAD SHOT, HOLMES!
THAT'S IT, LAD!
DRAW HIM IN!
WE'LL HAVE FRESH FISH TONIGHT!
HOLMES!
JOIN US FOR A GLASS OF PORT ON THE LAWN!
SO, SHERLOCK...
MY SON TELLS ME OF YOUR REMARKABLE GIFTS OF EXAMINATION.
I'M AN EXCELLENT SUBJECT. WHAT CAN YOU DEDUCE FROM ME?

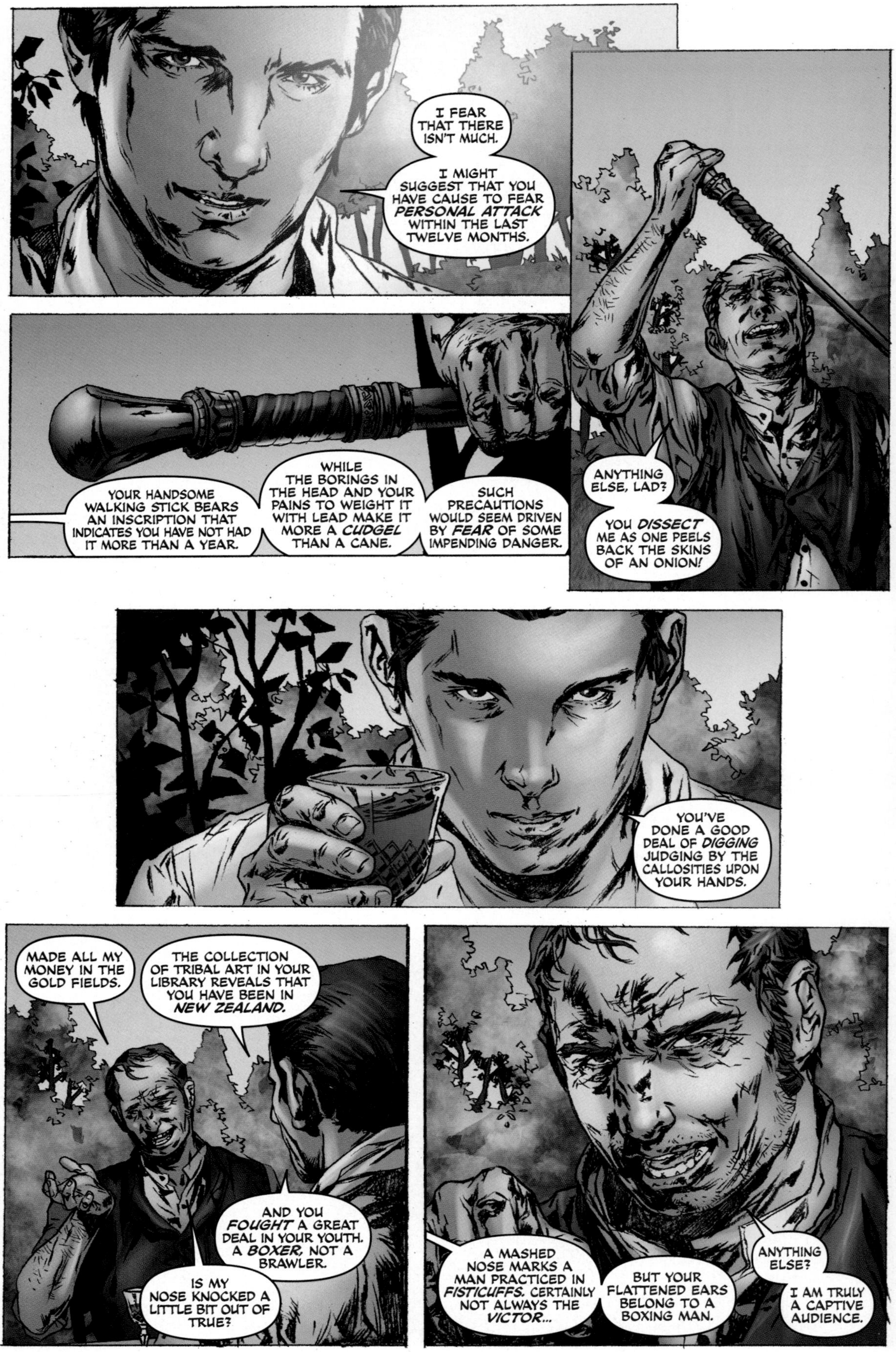
I FEAR THAT THERE ISN'T MUCH.
I MIGHT SUGGEST THAT YOU HAVE CAUSE TO FEAR PERSONAL ATTACK WITHIN THE LAST TWELVE MONTHS.
YOUR HANDSOME WALKING STICK BEARS AN INSCRIPTION THAT INDICATES YOU HAVE NOT HAD IT MORE THAN A YEAR.
WHILE THE BORINGS IN THE HEAD AND YOUR PAINS TO WEIGHT IT WITH LEAD MAKE IT MORE A CUDGEL THAN A CANE.
SUCH PRECAUTIONS WOULD SEEM DRIVEN BY FEAR OF SOME IMPENDING DANGER.
ANYTHING ELSE, LAD?
YOU DISSECT ME AS ONE PEELS BACK THE SKINS OF AN ONION!
YOU'VE DONE A GOOD DEAL OF DIGGING JUDGING BY THE CALLOSITIES UPON YOUR HANDS.
MADE ALL MY MONEY IN THE GOLD FIELDS.
THE COLLECTION OF TRIBAL ART IN YOUR LIBRARY REVEALS THAT YOU HAVE BEEN IN NEW ZEALAND.
AND YOU FOUGHT A GREAT DEAL IN YOUR YOUTH. A BOXER, NOT A BRAWLER.
IS MY NOSE KNOCKED A LITTLE BIT OUT OF TRUE?
A MASHED NOSE MARKS A MAN PRACTICED IN FISTICUFFS. CERTAINLY NOT ALWAYS THE VICTOR...
BUT YOUR FLATTENED EARS BELONG TO A BOXING MAN.
ANYTHING ELSE?
I AM TRULY A CAPTIVE AUDIENCE.

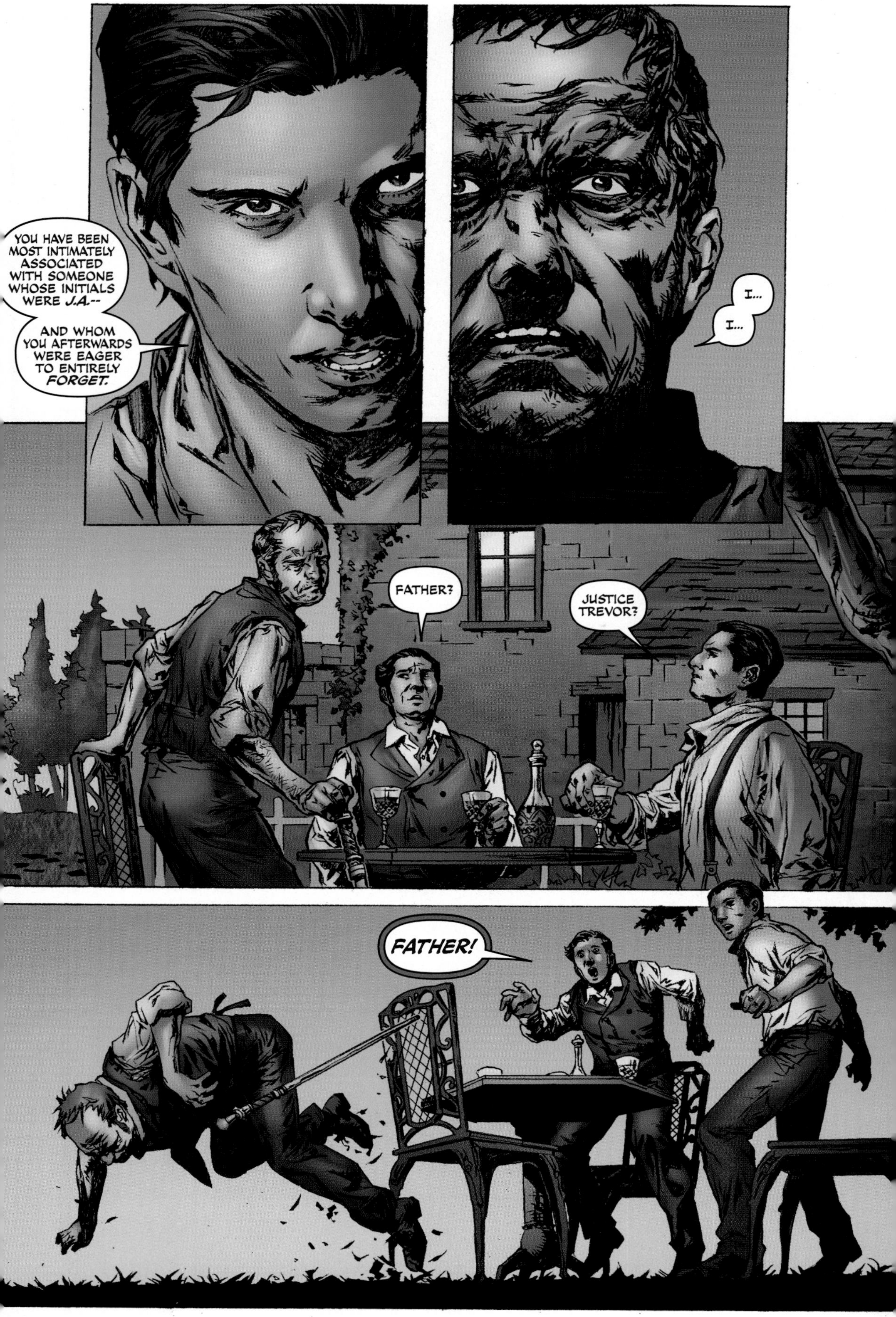
YOU HAVE BEEN MOST INTIMATELY ASSOCIATED WITH SOMEONE WHOSE INITIALS WERE J.A.--
AND WHOM YOU AFTERWARDS WERE EAGER TO ENTIRELY FORGET.
I...
I...
FATHER?
JUSTICE TREVOR?
FATHER!

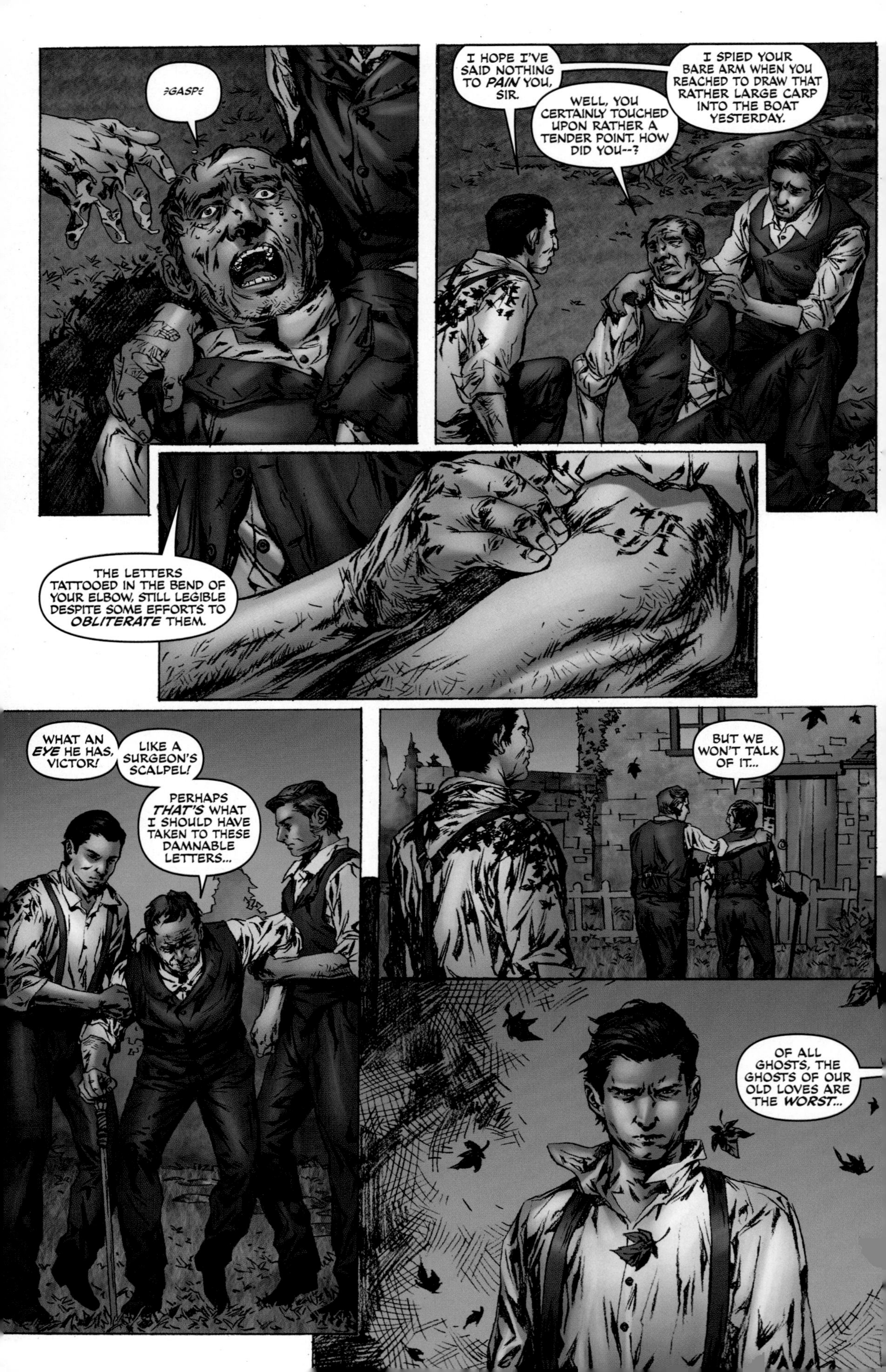

GASP
I HOPE I'VE SAID NOTHING TO *PAIN* YOU, SIR.
WELL, YOU CERTAINLY TOUCHED UPON RATHER A TENDER POINT. HOW DID YOU--?
I SPIED YOUR BARE ARM WHEN YOU REACHED TO DRAW THAT RATHER LARGE CARP INTO THE BOAT YESTERDAY.
THE LETTERS TATTOOED IN THE BEND OF YOUR ELBOW, STILL LEGIBLE DESPITE SOME EFFORTS TO *OBLITERATE* THEM.
WHAT AN *EYE* HE HAS, VICTOR!
LIKE A SURGEON'S SCALPEL!
PERHAPS *THAT'S* WHAT I SHOULD HAVE TAKEN TO THESE DAMNABLE LETTERS...
BUT WE WON'T TALK OF IT...
OF ALL GHOSTS, THE GHOSTS OF OUR OLD LOVES ARE THE *WORST*...

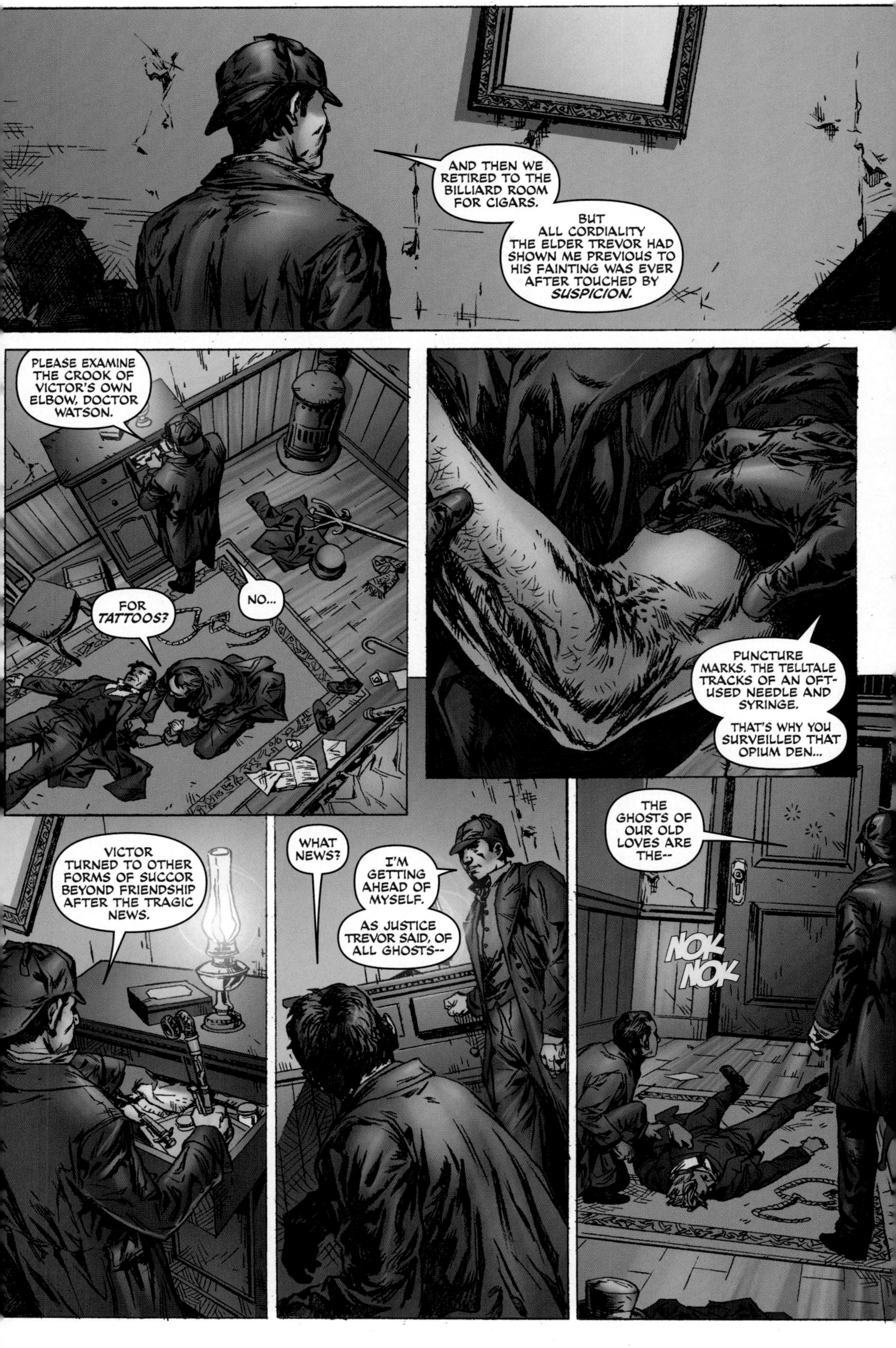
AND THEN WE RETIRED TO THE BILLIARD ROOM FOR CIGARS.
BUT ALL CORDIALITY THE ELDER TREVOR HAD SHOWN ME PREVIOUS TO HIS FAINTING WAS EVER AFTER TOUCHED BY *SUSPICION.*
PLEASE EXAMINE THE CROOK OF VICTOR'S OWN ELBOW, DOCTOR WATSON.
FOR *TATTOOS?*
NO...
PUNCTURE MARKS. THE TELLTALE TRACKS OF AN OFT-USED NEEDLE AND SYRINGE.
THAT'S WHY YOU SURVEILLED THAT OPIUM DEN...
VICTOR TURNED TO OTHER FORMS OF SUCCOR BEYOND FRIENDSHIP AFTER THE TRAGIC NEWS.
WHAT NEWS?
I'M GETTING AHEAD OF MYSELF.
AS JUSTICE TREVOR SAID, OF ALL GHOSTS--
THE GHOSTS OF OUR OLD LOVES ARE THE--
NOK NOK

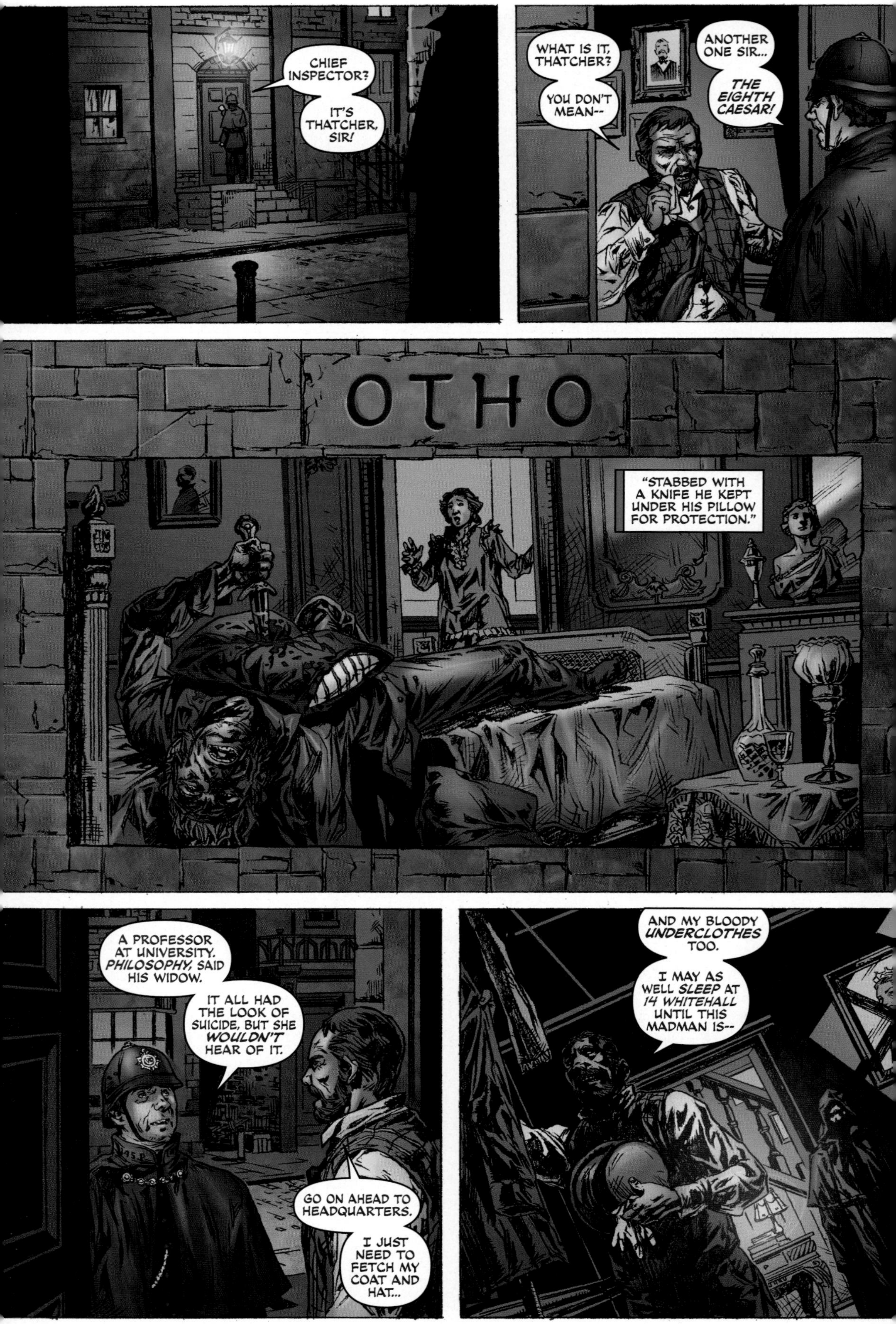
CHIEF INSPECTOR?
IT'S THATCHER, SIR!
WHAT IS IT, THATCHER?
YOU DON'T MEAN--
ANOTHER ONE SIR...
THE EIGHTH CAESAR!
OTHO
"STABBED WITH A KNIFE HE KEPT UNDER HIS PILLOW FOR PROTECTION."
A PROFESSOR AT UNIVERSITY. *PHILOSOPHY,* SAID HIS WIDOW.
IT ALL HAD THE LOOK OF SUICIDE, BUT SHE *WOULDN'T* HEAR OF IT.
GO ON AHEAD TO HEADQUARTERS.
I JUST NEED TO FETCH MY COAT AND HAT...
AND MY BLOODY *UNDERCLOTHES* TOO.
I MAY AS WELL *SLEEP* AT *14 WHITEHALL* UNTIL THIS MADMAN IS--

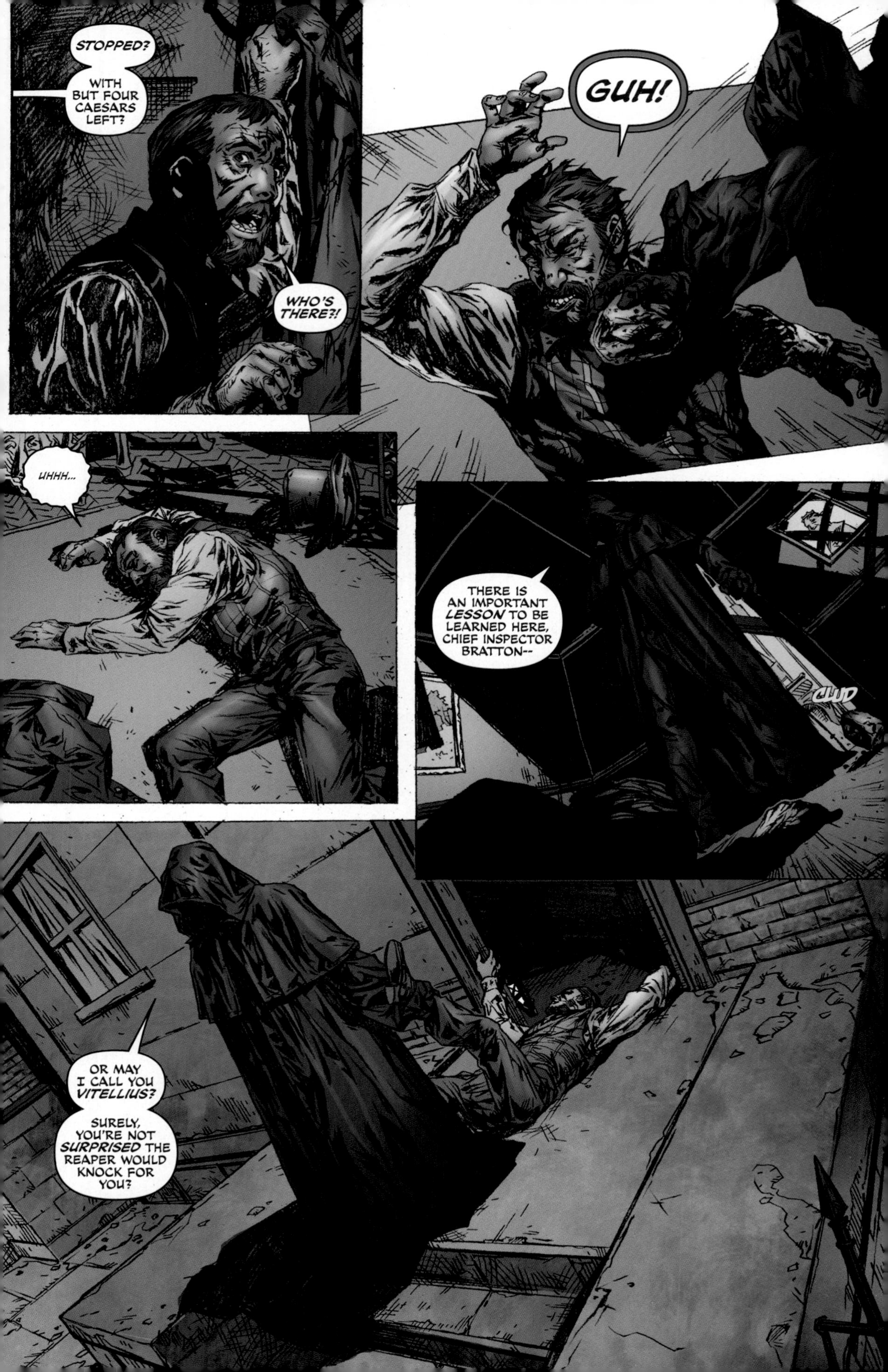
STOPPED?
WITH BUT FOUR CAESARS LEFT?
WHO'S THERE?!
GUH!
UHHH...
THERE IS AN IMPORTANT LESSON TO BE LEARNED HERE, CHIEF INSPECTOR BRATTON--
CLUD
OR MAY I CALL YOU VITELLIUS?
SURELY, YOU'RE NOT SURPRISED THE REAPER WOULD KNOCK FOR YOU?

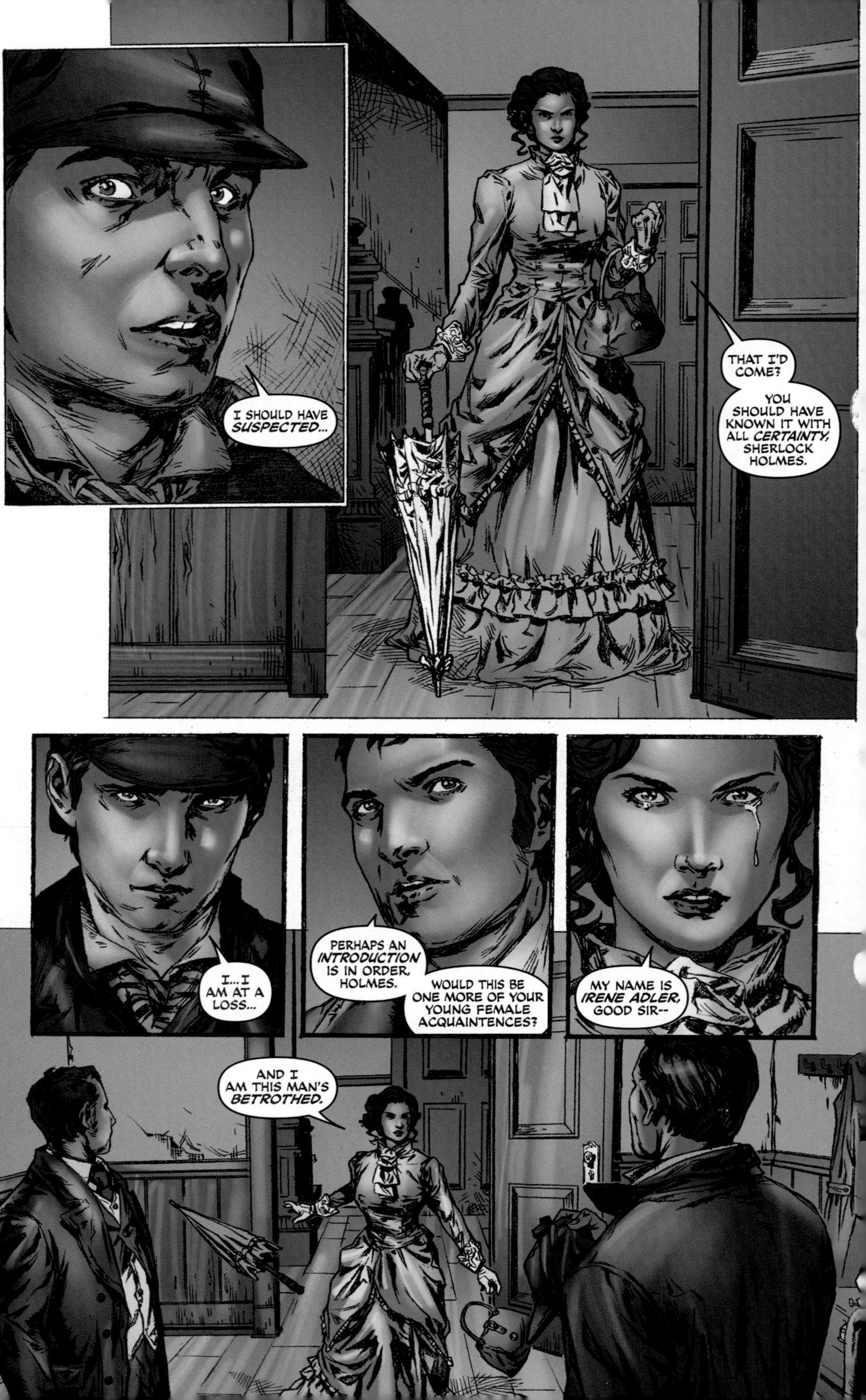
I SHOULD HAVE *SUSPECTED*...
THAT I'D COME?
YOU SHOULD HAVE KNOWN IT WITH ALL *CERTAINTY,* SHERLOCK HOLMES.
I... I AM AT A LOSS...
PERHAPS AN *INTRODUCTION* IS IN ORDER, HOLMES.
WOULD THIS BE ONE MORE OF YOUR YOUNG FEMALE ACQUAINTENCES?
MY NAME IS *IRENE ADLER,* GOOD SIR--
AND I AM THIS MAN'S *BETROTHED.*

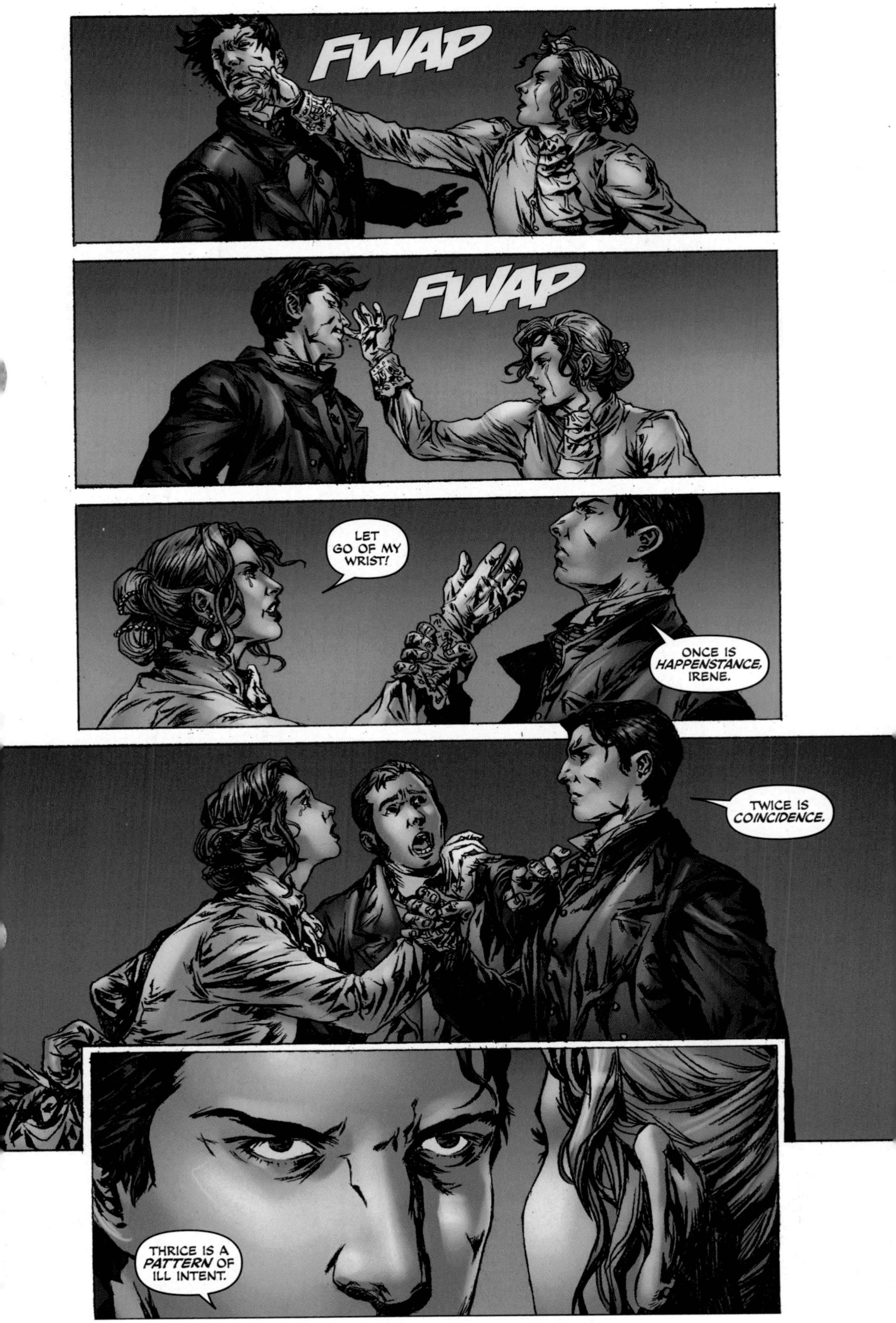
FWAP
FWAP
LET GO OF MY WRIST!
ONCE IS *HAPPENSTANCE,* IRENE.
TWICE IS *COINCIDENCE.*
THRICE IS A *PATTERN* OF ILL INTENT.

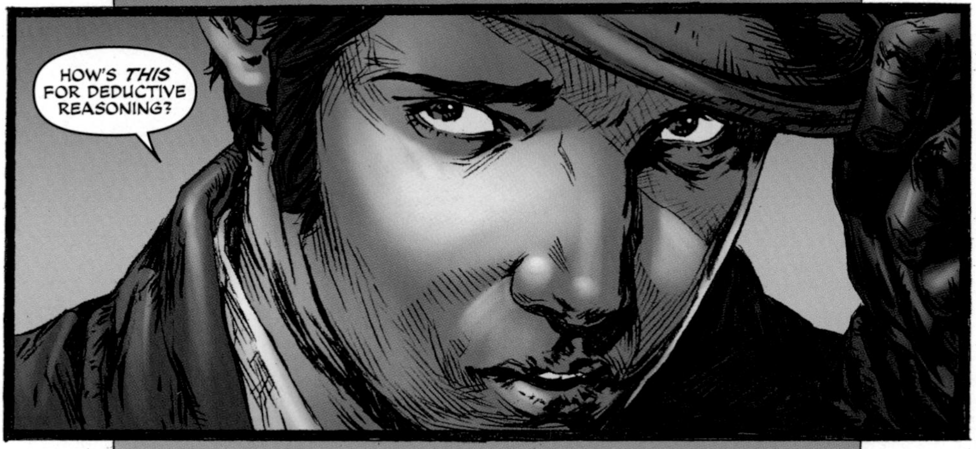
HOW'S *THIS* FOR DEDUCTIVE REASONING?

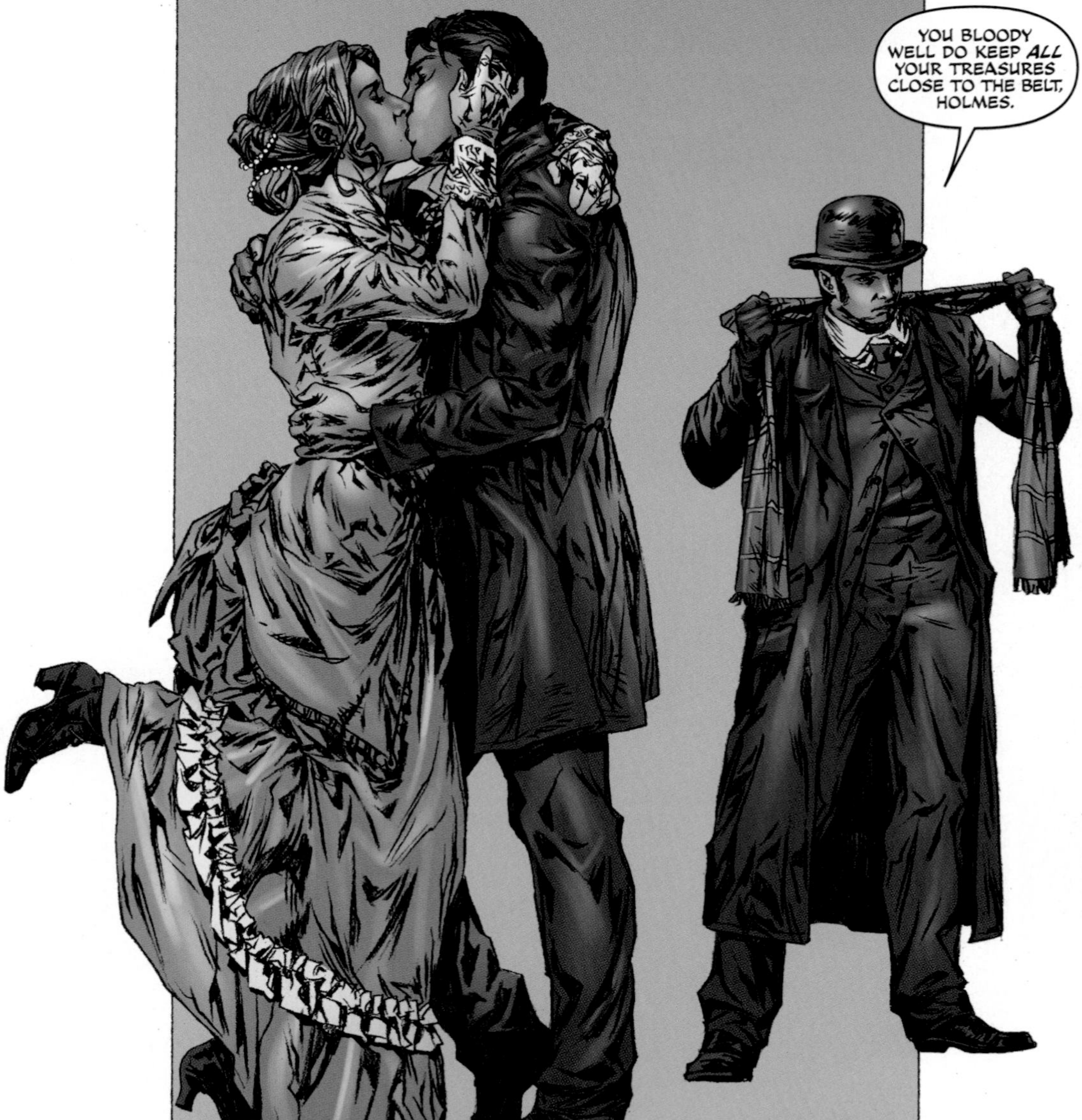
YOU BLOODY WELL DO KEEP *ALL* YOUR TREASURES CLOSE TO THE BELT, HOLMES.

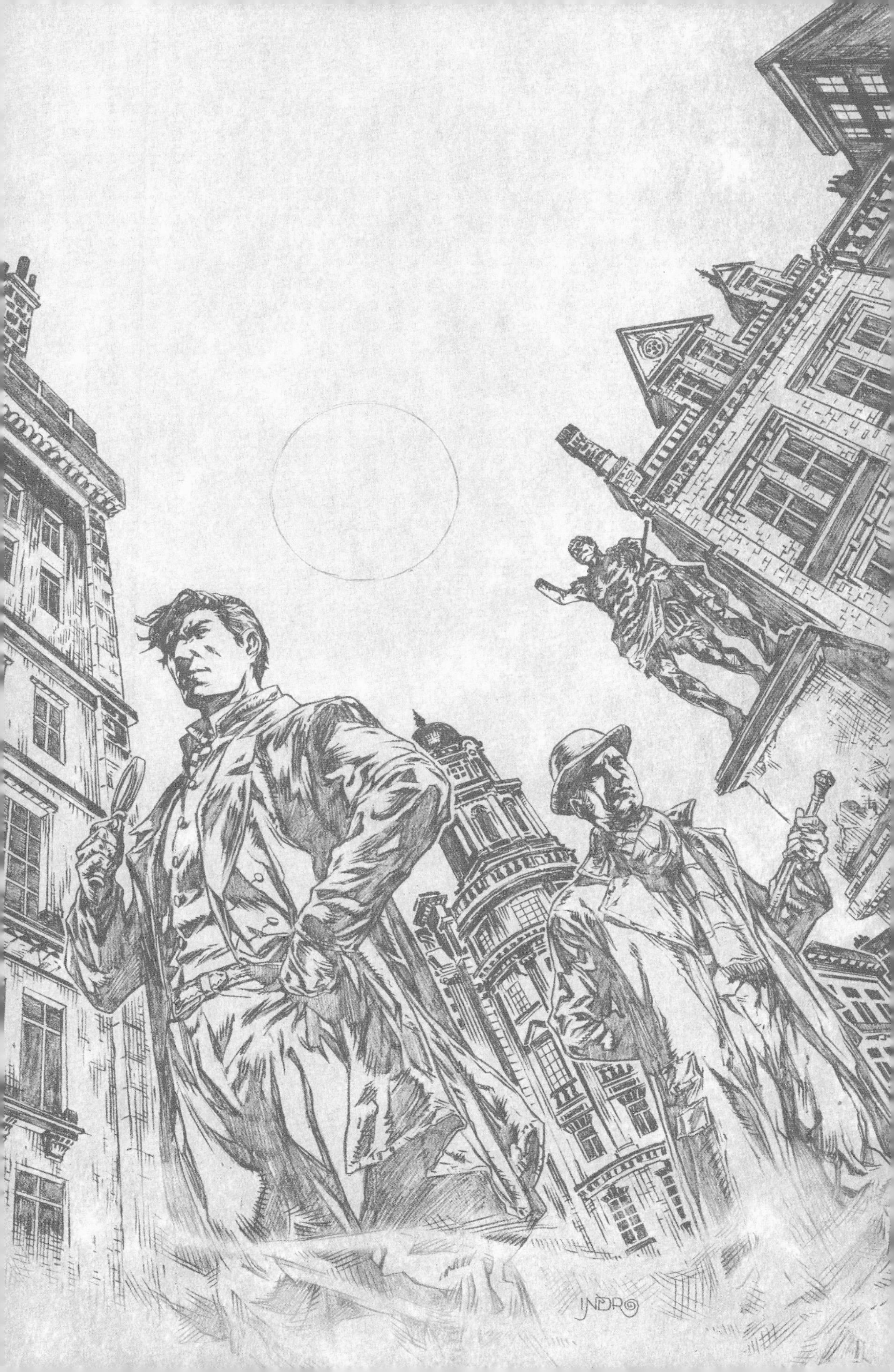

Cover by:
FRANCESCO FRANCAVILLA

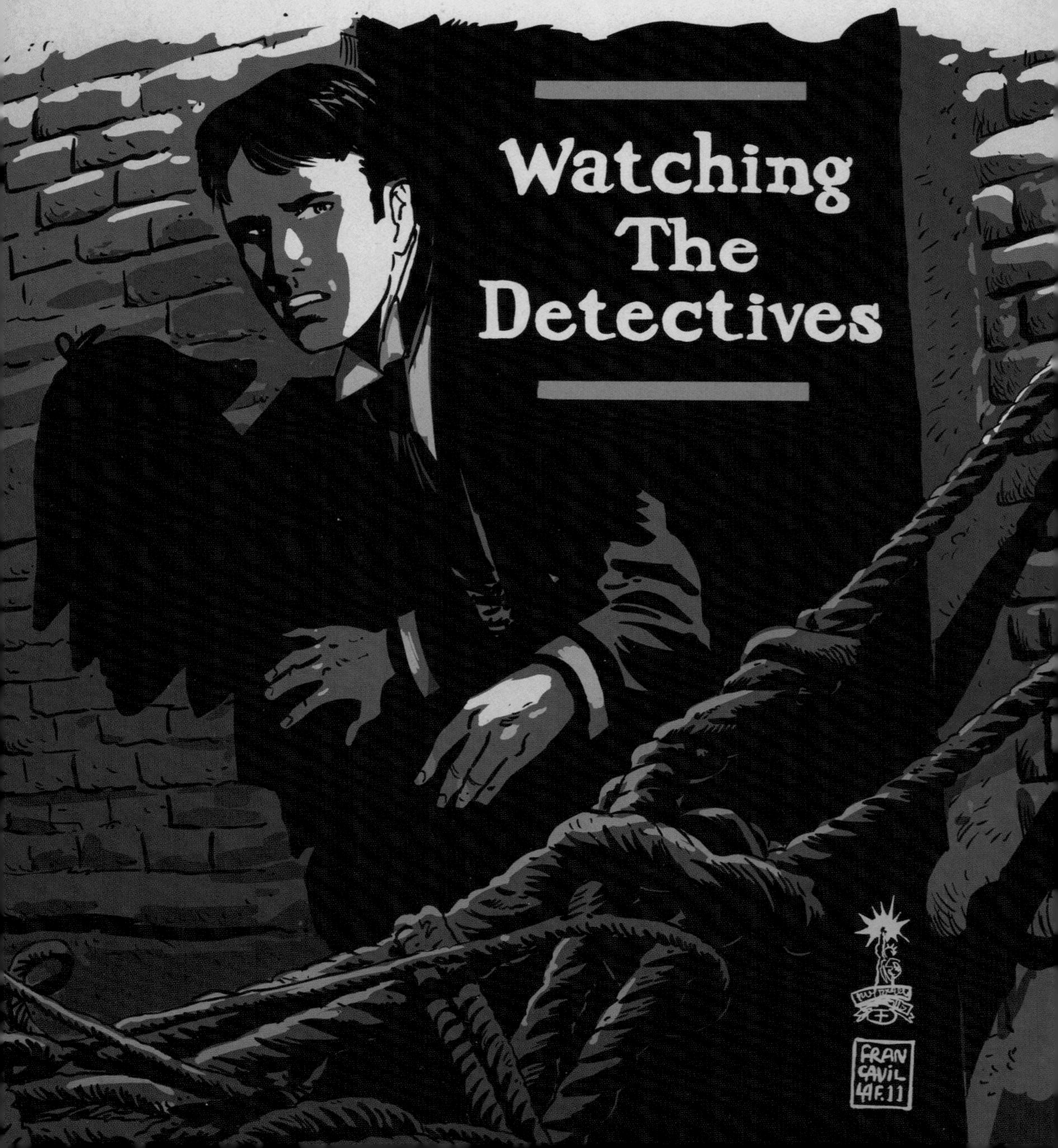
Watching
The
Detectives
FRAN
CAVIL
LA F.11

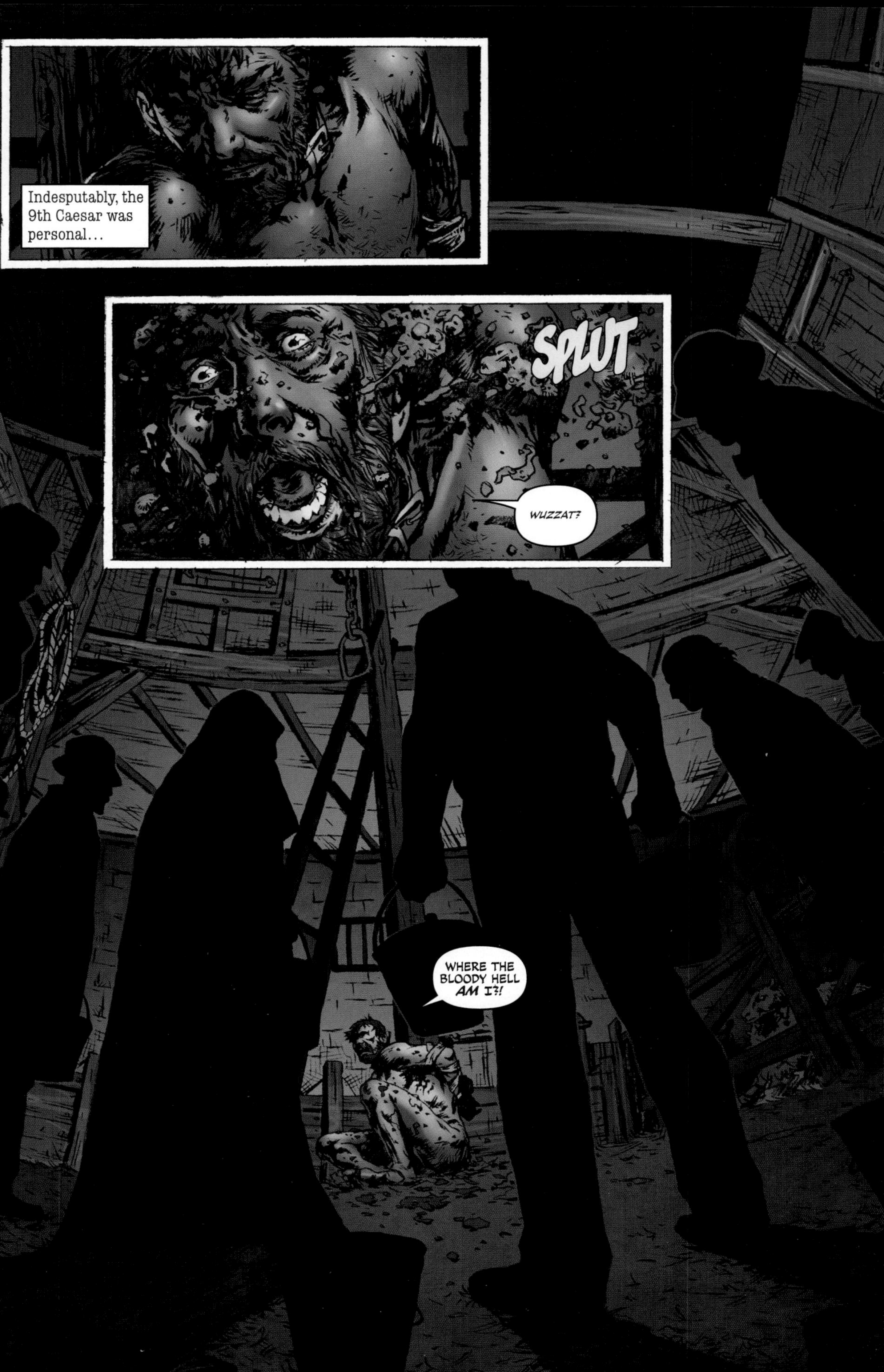
Indesputably, the
9th Caesar was
personal...
SPLUT
WUZZAT?
WHERE THE
BLOODY HELL
AM I?!

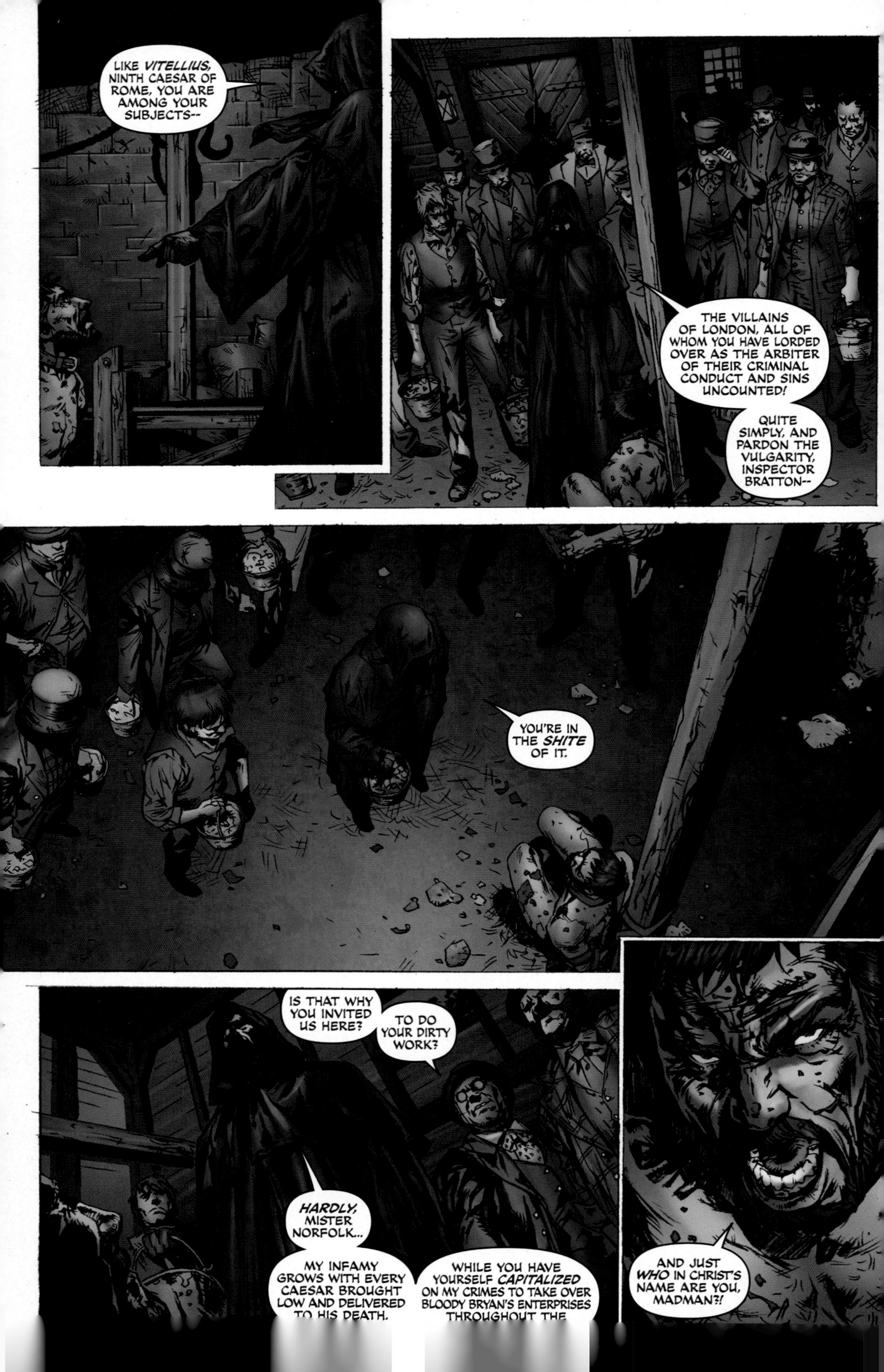
LIKE VITELLIUS, NINTH CAESAR OF ROME, YOU ARE AMONG YOUR SUBJECTS--
THE VILLAINS OF LONDON, ALL OF WHOM YOU HAVE LORDED OVER AS THE ARBITER OF THEIR CRIMINAL CONDUCT AND SINS UNCOUNTED!
QUITE SIMPLY, AND PARDON THE VULGARITY, INSPECTOR BRATTON--
YOU'RE IN THE SHITE OF IT.
IS THAT WHY YOU INVITED US HERE?
TO DO YOUR DIRTY WORK?
HARDLY, MISTER NORFOLK...
MY INFAMY GROWS WITH EVERY CAESAR BROUGHT LOW AND DELIVERED TO HIS DEATH.
WHILE YOU HAVE YOURSELF CAPITALIZED ON MY CRIMES TO TAKE OVER BLOODY BRYAN'S ENTERPRISES THROUGHOUT THE
AND JUST WHO IN CHRIST'S NAME ARE YOU, MADMAN?!

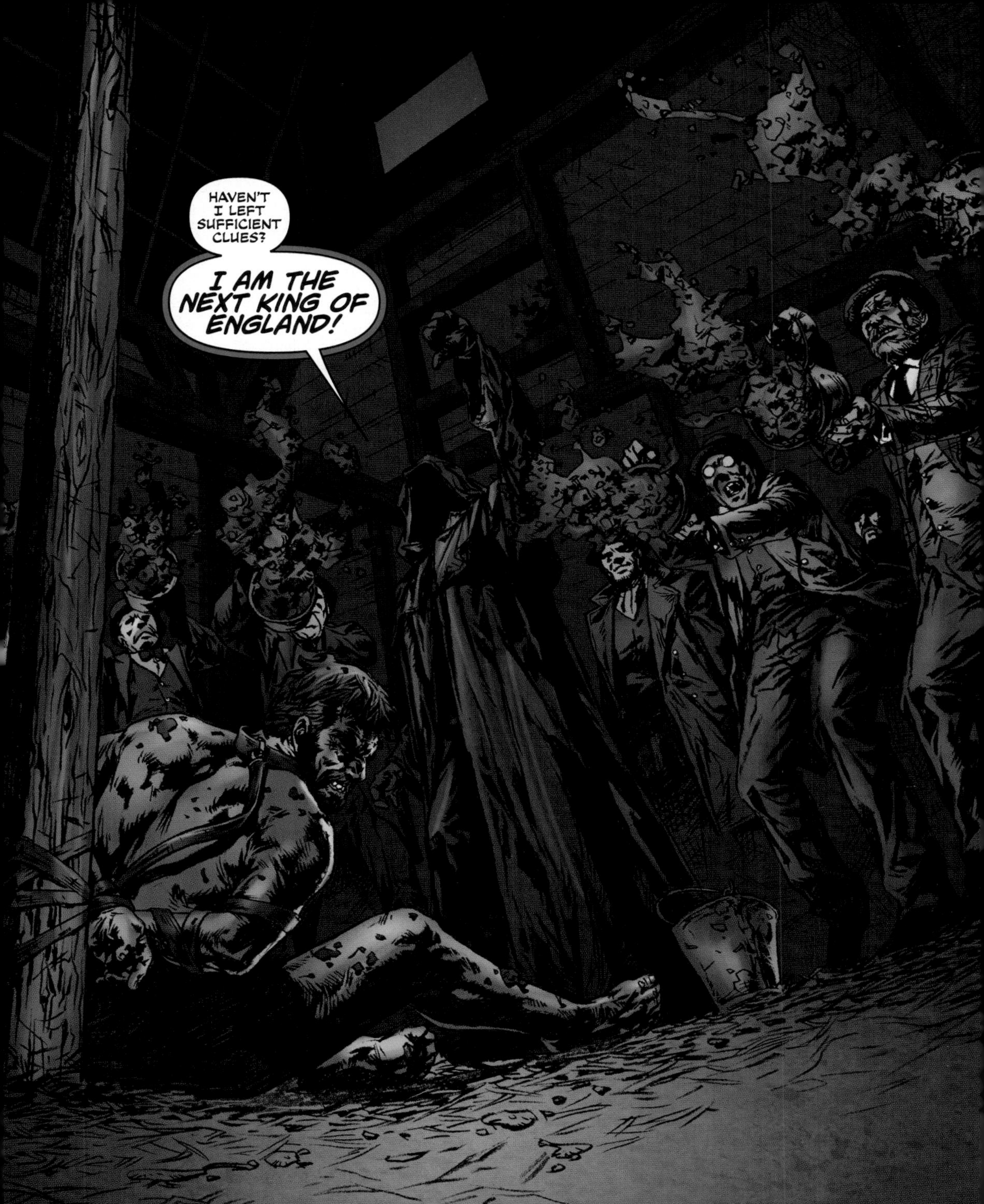
HAVEN'T I LEFT SUFFICIENT CLUES?
I AM THE NEXT KING OF ENGLAND!

SHERLOCK HOLMES YEAR ONE

CUI BONO?

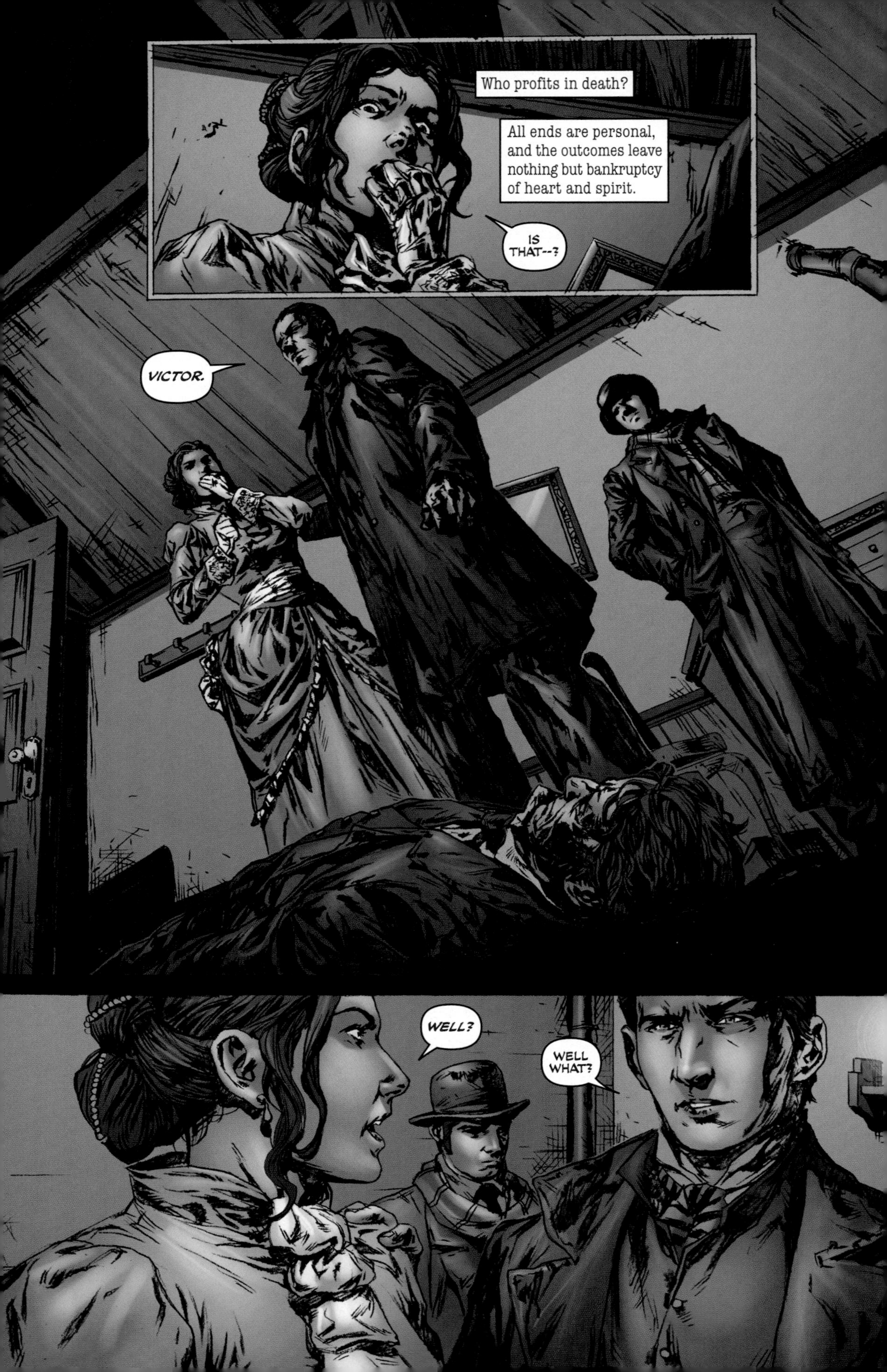
Who profits in death?
All ends are personal, and the outcomes leave nothing but bankruptcy of heart and spirit.
IS THAT--?
VICTOR.
WELL?
WELL WHAT?

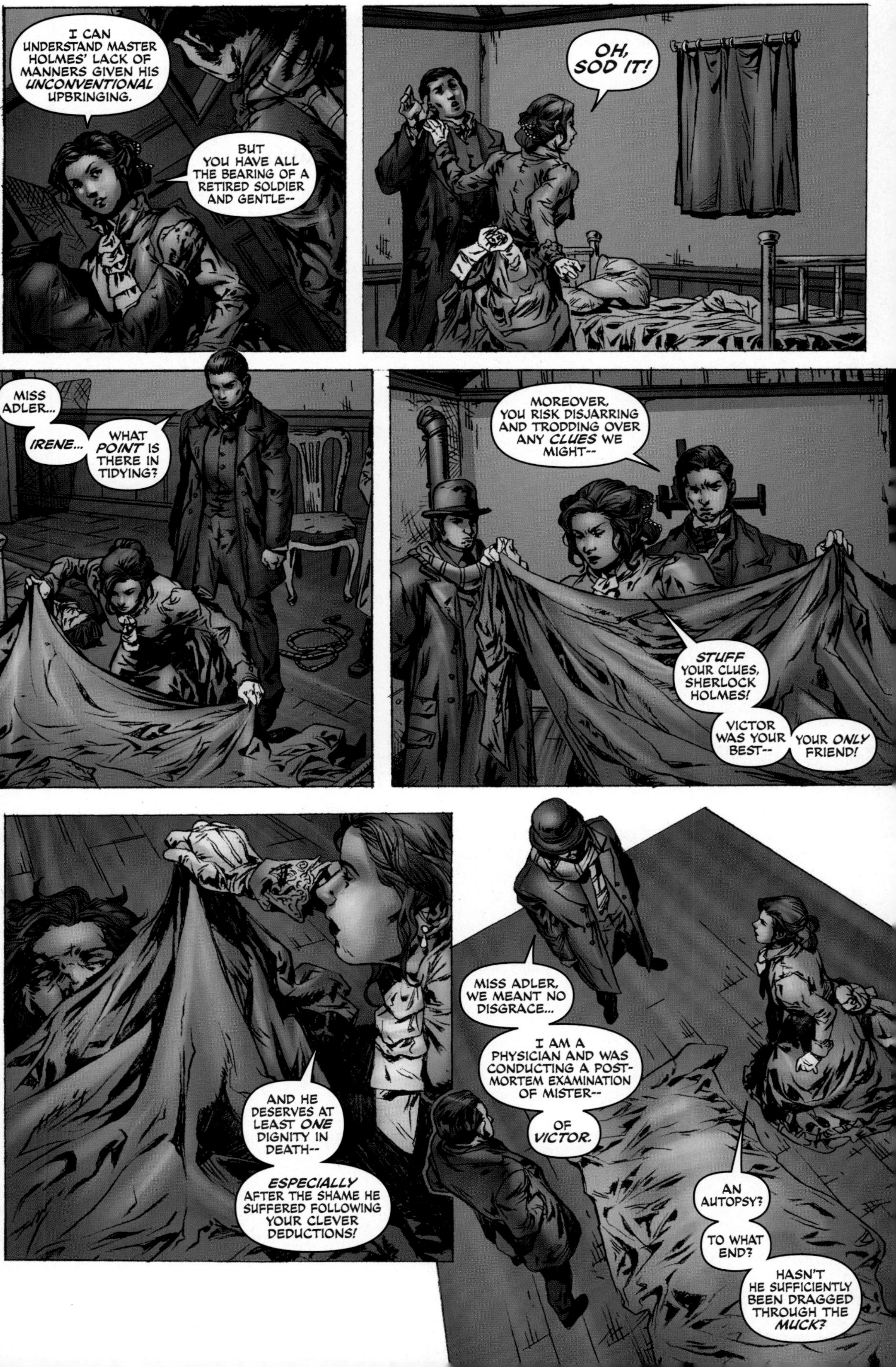

I CAN UNDERSTAND MASTER HOLMES' LACK OF MANNERS GIVEN HIS *UNCONVENTIONAL* UPBRINGING.
BUT YOU HAVE ALL THE BEARING OF A RETIRED SOLDIER AND GENTLE--
OH, SOD IT!
MISS ADLER...
IRENE...
WHAT *POINT* IS THERE IN TIDYING?
MOREOVER, YOU RISK DISJARRING AND TRODDING OVER ANY *CLUES* WE MIGHT--
STUFF YOUR CLUES, SHERLOCK HOLMES!
VICTOR WAS YOUR BEST--
YOUR *ONLY* FRIEND!
AND HE DESERVES AT LEAST *ONE* DIGNITY IN DEATH--
ESPECIALLY AFTER THE SHAME HE SUFFERED FOLLOWING YOUR CLEVER DEDUCTIONS!
MISS ADLER, WE MEANT NO DISGRACE...
I AM A PHYSICIAN AND WAS CONDUCTING A POST-MORTEM EXAMINATION OF MISTER--
OF *VICTOR*.
AN AUTOPSY?
TO WHAT END?
HASN'T HE SUFFICIENTLY BEEN DRAGGED THROUGH THE *MUCK*?

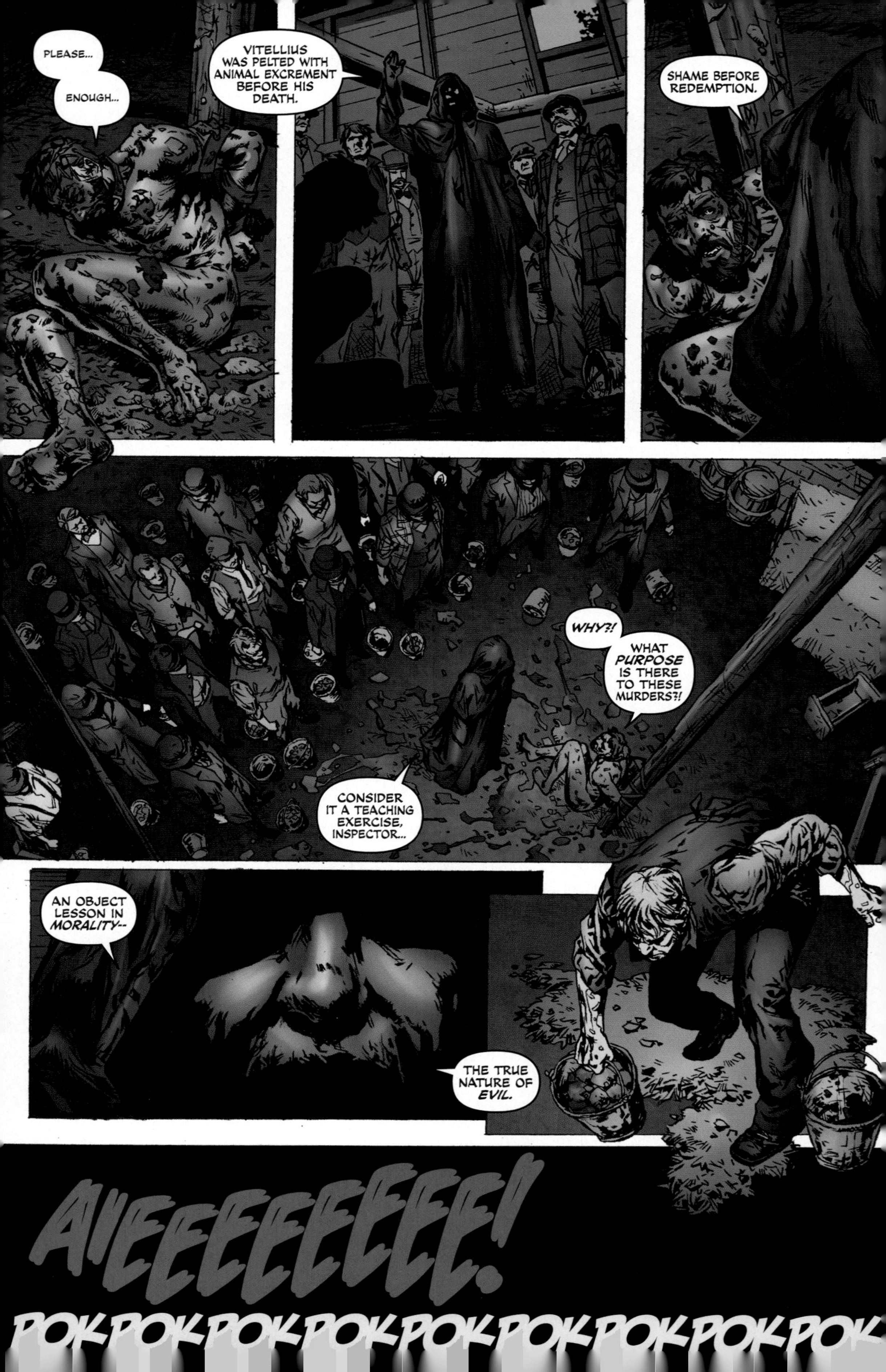
PLEASE...
ENOUGH...
VITELLIUS WAS PELTED WITH ANIMAL EXCREMENT BEFORE HIS DEATH.
SHAME BEFORE REDEMPTION.
WHY?!
WHAT *PURPOSE* IS THERE TO THESE MURDERS?!
CONSIDER IT A TEACHING EXERCISE, INSPECTOR...
AN OBJECT LESSON IN *MORALITY*--
THE TRUE NATURE OF *EVIL.*
AIEEEEEEEE!
POKPOKPOKPOKPOKPOKPOKPOKPOK

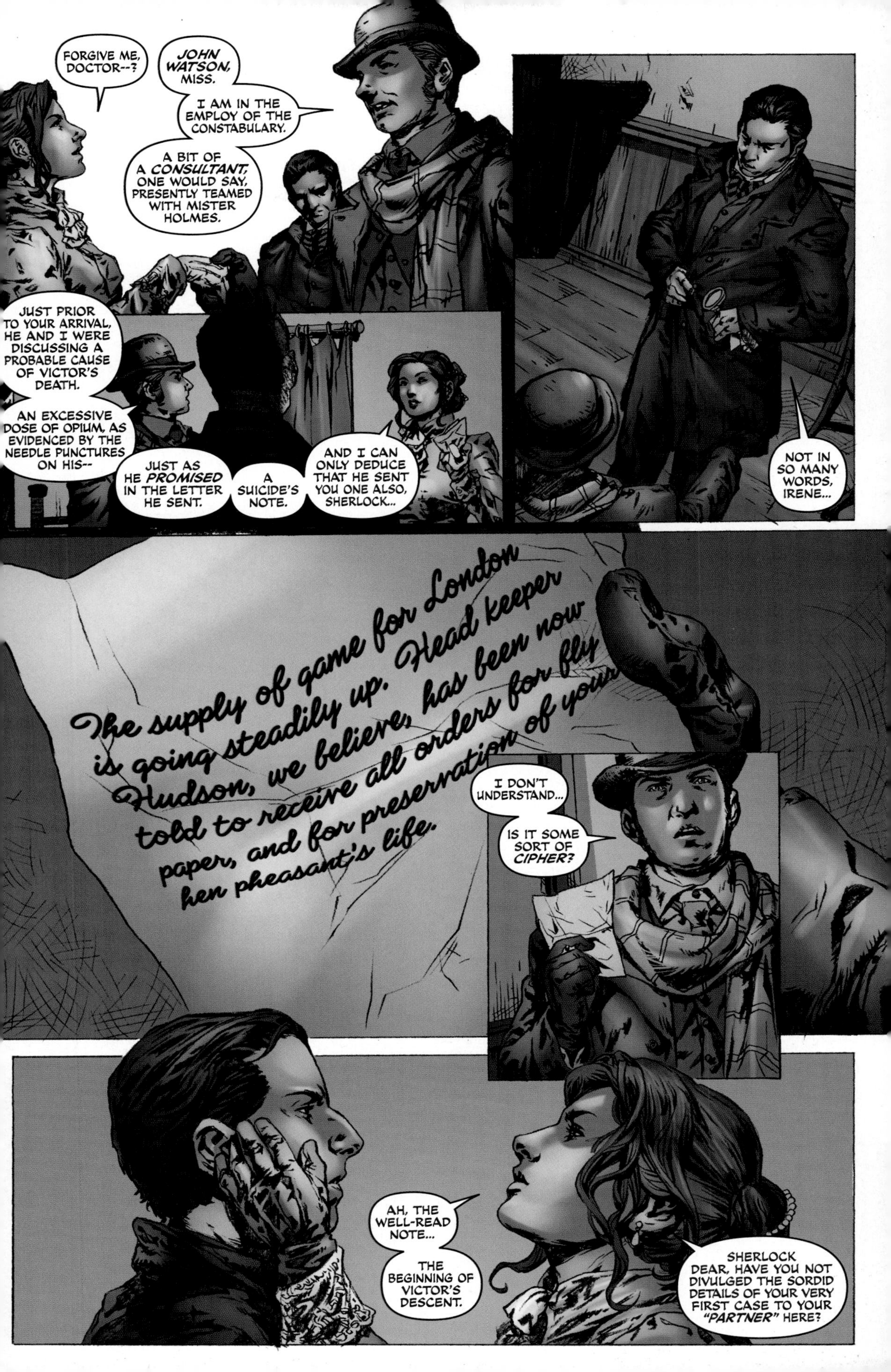
FORGIVE ME, DOCTOR--?
JOHN WATSON, MISS.
I AM IN THE EMPLOY OF THE CONSTABULARY.
A BIT OF A CONSULTANT, ONE WOULD SAY, PRESENTLY TEAMED WITH MISTER HOLMES.
JUST PRIOR TO YOUR ARRIVAL, HE AND I WERE DISCUSSING A PROBABLE CAUSE OF VICTOR'S DEATH.
AN EXCESSIVE DOSE OF OPIUM, AS EVIDENCED BY THE NEEDLE PUNCTURES ON HIS--
JUST AS HE PROMISED IN THE LETTER HE SENT.
A SUICIDE'S NOTE.
AND I CAN ONLY DEDUCE THAT HE SENT YOU ONE ALSO, SHERLOCK...
NOT IN SO MANY WORDS, IRENE...
The supply of game for London is going steadily up. Head keeper Hudson, we believe, has been now told to receive all orders for fly paper, and for preservation of your hen pheasant's life.
I DON'T UNDERSTAND...
IS IT SOME SORT OF CIPHER?
AH, THE WELL-READ NOTE...
THE BEGINNING OF VICTOR'S DESCENT.
SHERLOCK DEAR, HAVE YOU NOT DIVULGED THE SORDID DETAILS OF YOUR VERY FIRST CASE TO YOUR "PARTNER" HERE?

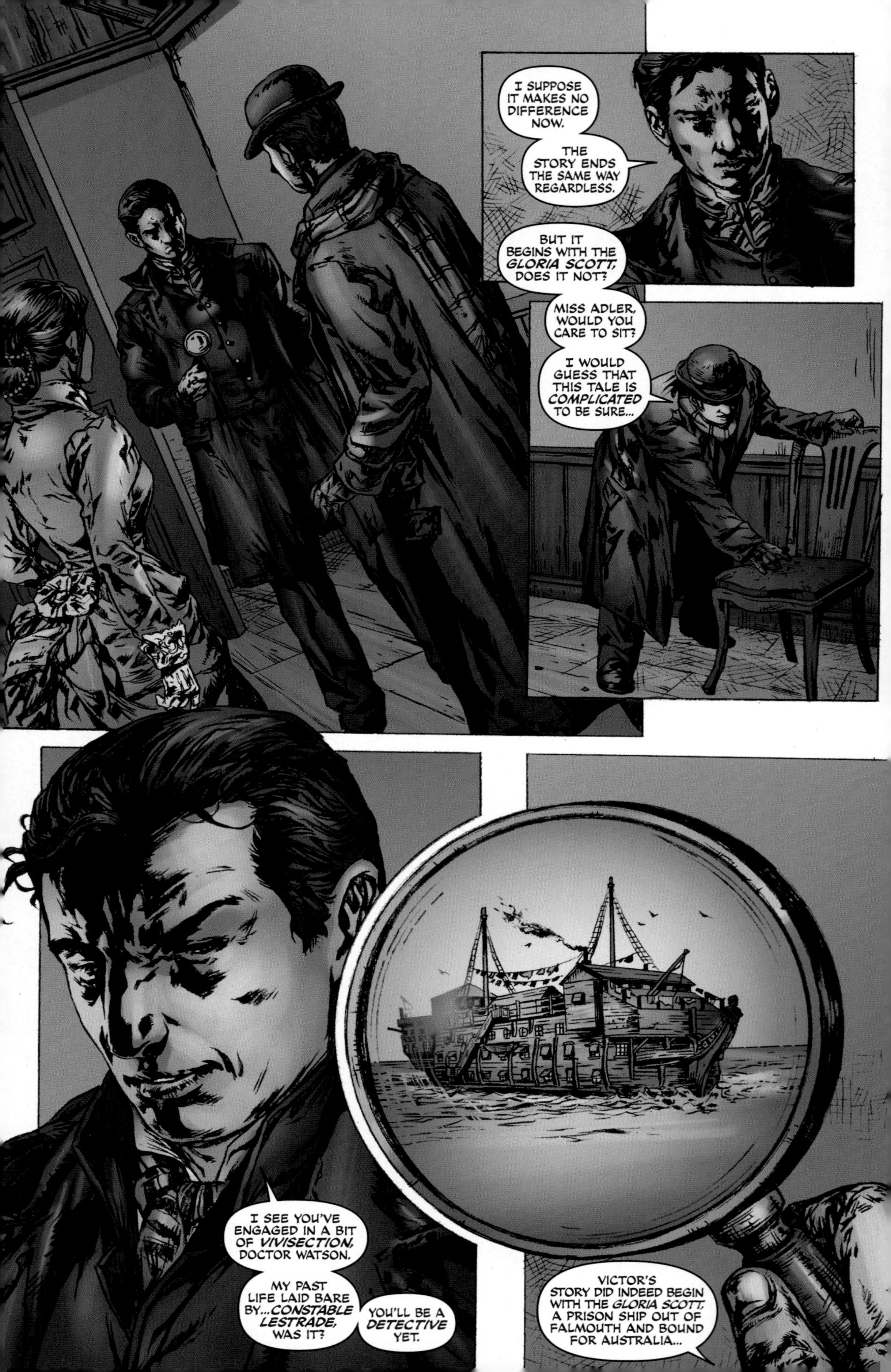

I SUPPOSE IT MAKES NO DIFFERENCE NOW.
THE STORY ENDS THE SAME WAY REGARDLESS.
BUT IT BEGINS WITH THE *GLORIA SCOTT,* DOES IT NOT?
MISS ADLER, WOULD YOU CARE TO SIT?
I WOULD GUESS THAT THIS TALE IS *COMPLICATED* TO BE SURE...
I SEE YOU'VE ENGAGED IN A BIT OF *VIVISECTION,* DOCTOR WATSON.
MY PAST LIFE LAID BARE BY...*CONSTABLE LESTRADE,* WAS IT?
YOU'LL BE A *DETECTIVE* YET.
VICTOR'S STORY DID INDEED BEGIN WITH THE *GLORIA SCOTT,* A PRISON SHIP OUT OF FALMOUTH AND BOUND FOR AUSTRALIA...

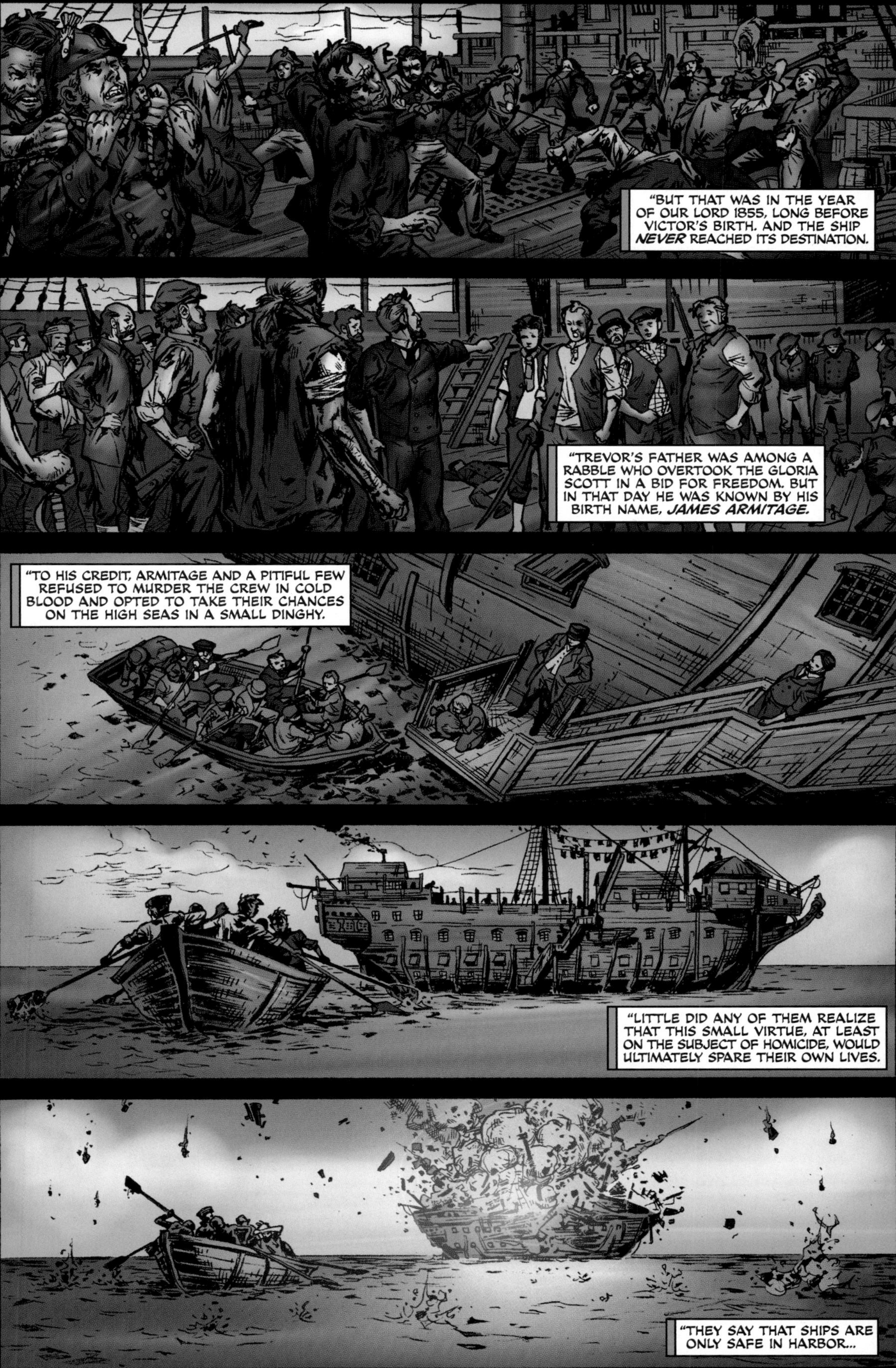
"BUT THAT WAS IN THE YEAR OF OUR LORD 1855, LONG BEFORE VICTOR'S BIRTH. AND THE SHIP *NEVER* REACHED ITS DESTINATION.
"TREVOR'S FATHER WAS AMONG A RABBLE WHO OVERTOOK THE GLORIA SCOTT IN A BID FOR FREEDOM. BUT IN THAT DAY HE WAS KNOWN BY HIS BIRTH NAME, *JAMES ARMITAGE.*
"TO HIS CREDIT, ARMITAGE AND A PITIFUL FEW REFUSED TO MURDER THE CREW IN COLD BLOOD AND OPTED TO TAKE THEIR CHANCES ON THE HIGH SEAS IN A SMALL DINGHY.
"LITTLE DID ANY OF THEM REALIZE THAT THIS SMALL VIRTUE, AT LEAST ON THE SUBJECT OF HOMICIDE, WOULD ULTIMATELY SPARE THEIR OWN LIVES.
"THEY SAY THAT SHIPS ARE ONLY SAFE IN HARBOR...

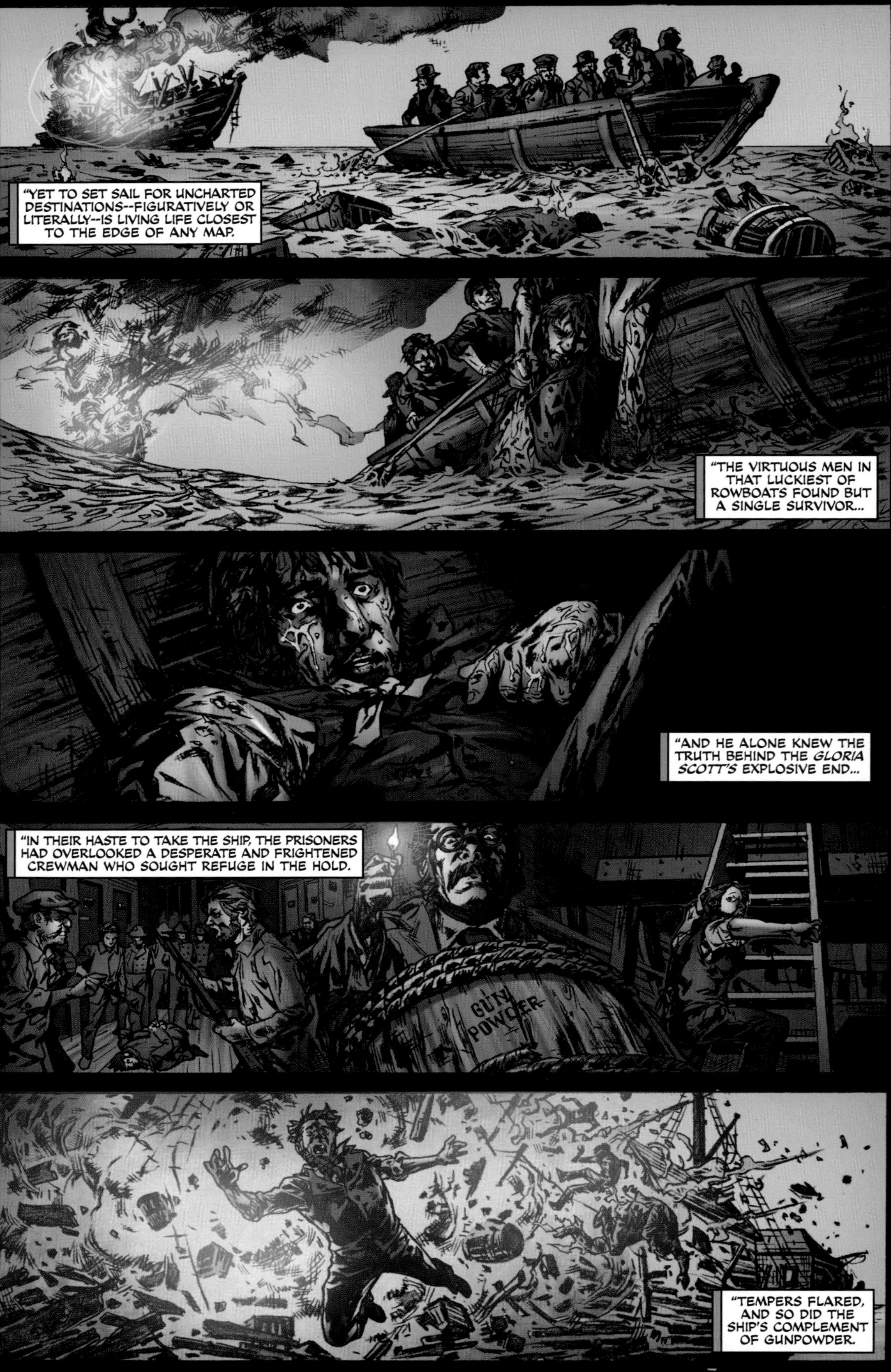
"YET TO SET SAIL FOR UNCHARTED DESTINATIONS--FIGURATIVELY OR LITERALLY--IS LIVING LIFE CLOSEST TO THE EDGE OF ANY MAP.
"THE VIRTUOUS MEN IN THAT LUCKIEST OF ROWBOATS FOUND BUT A SINGLE SURVIVOR...
"AND HE ALONE KNEW THE TRUTH BEHIND THE *GLORIA SCOTT'S* EXPLOSIVE END...
"IN THEIR HASTE TO TAKE THE SHIP, THE PRISONERS HAD OVERLOOKED A DESPERATE AND FRIGHTENED CREWMAN WHO SOUGHT REFUGE IN THE HOLD.
GUN POWDER
"TEMPERS FLARED, AND SO DID THE SHIP'S COMPLEMENT OF GUNPOWDER.

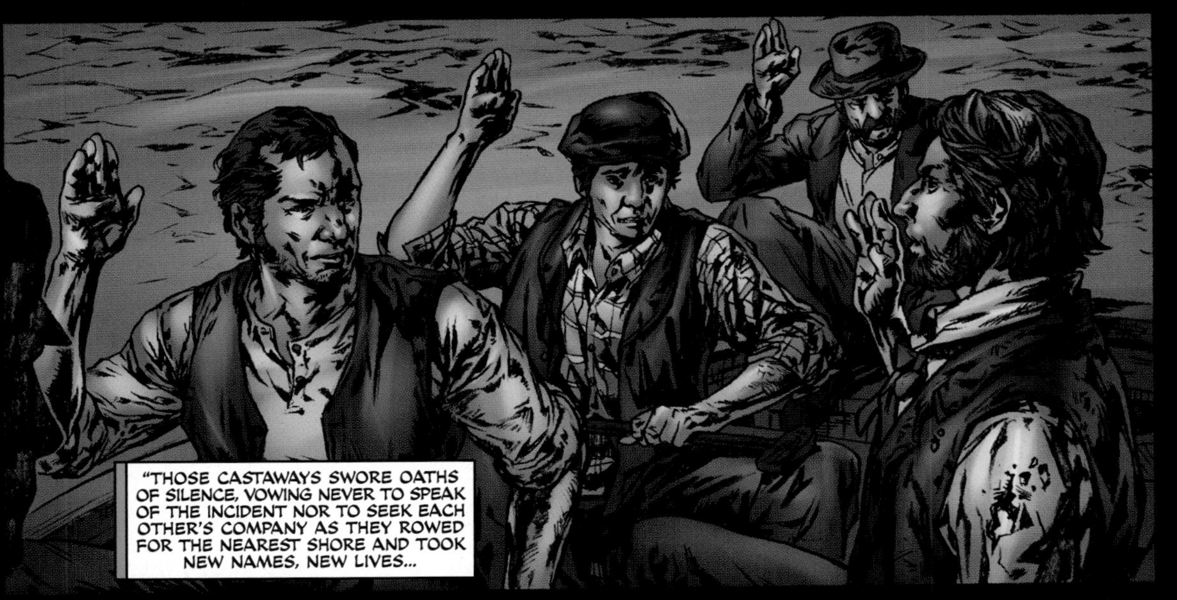
"THOSE CASTAWAYS SWORE OATHS OF SILENCE, VOWING NEVER TO SPEAK OF THE INCIDENT NOR TO SEEK EACH OTHER'S COMPANY AS THEY ROWED FOR THE NEAREST SHORE AND TOOK NEW NAMES, NEW LIVES...

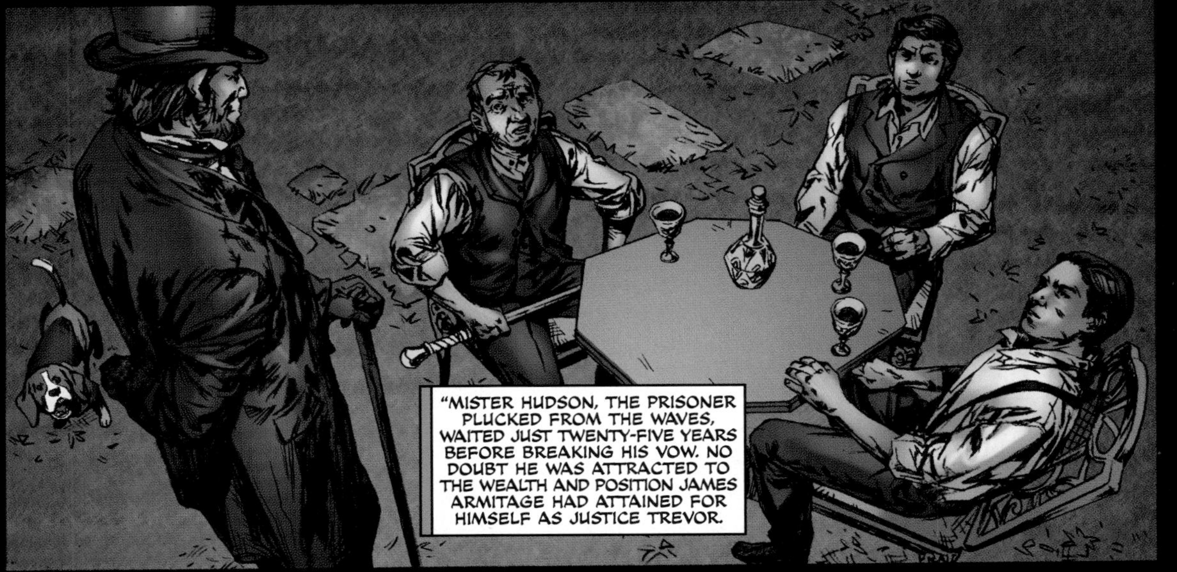
"MISTER HUDSON, THE PRISONER PLUCKED FROM THE WAVES, WAITED JUST TWENTY-FIVE YEARS BEFORE BREAKING HIS VOW. NO DOUBT HE WAS ATTRACTED TO THE WEALTH AND POSITION JAMES ARMITAGE HAD ATTAINED FOR HIMSELF AS JUSTICE TREVOR.

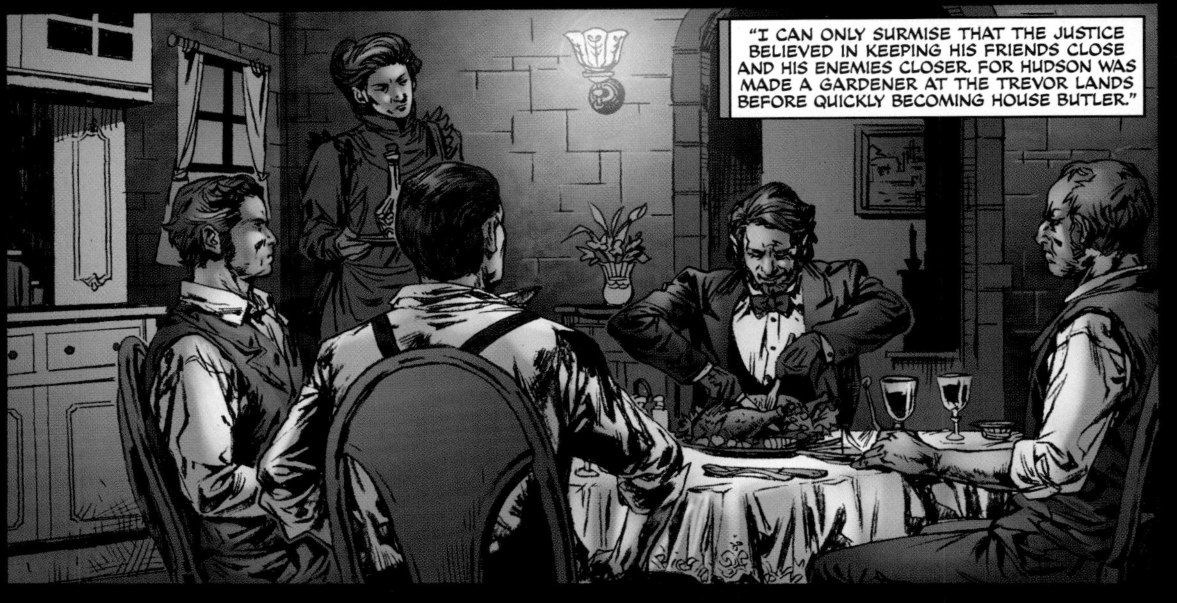
"I CAN ONLY SURMISE THAT THE JUSTICE BELIEVED IN KEEPING HIS FRIENDS CLOSE AND HIS ENEMIES CLOSER. FOR HUDSON WAS MADE A GARDENER AT THE TREVOR LANDS BEFORE QUICKLY BECOMING HOUSE BUTLER."

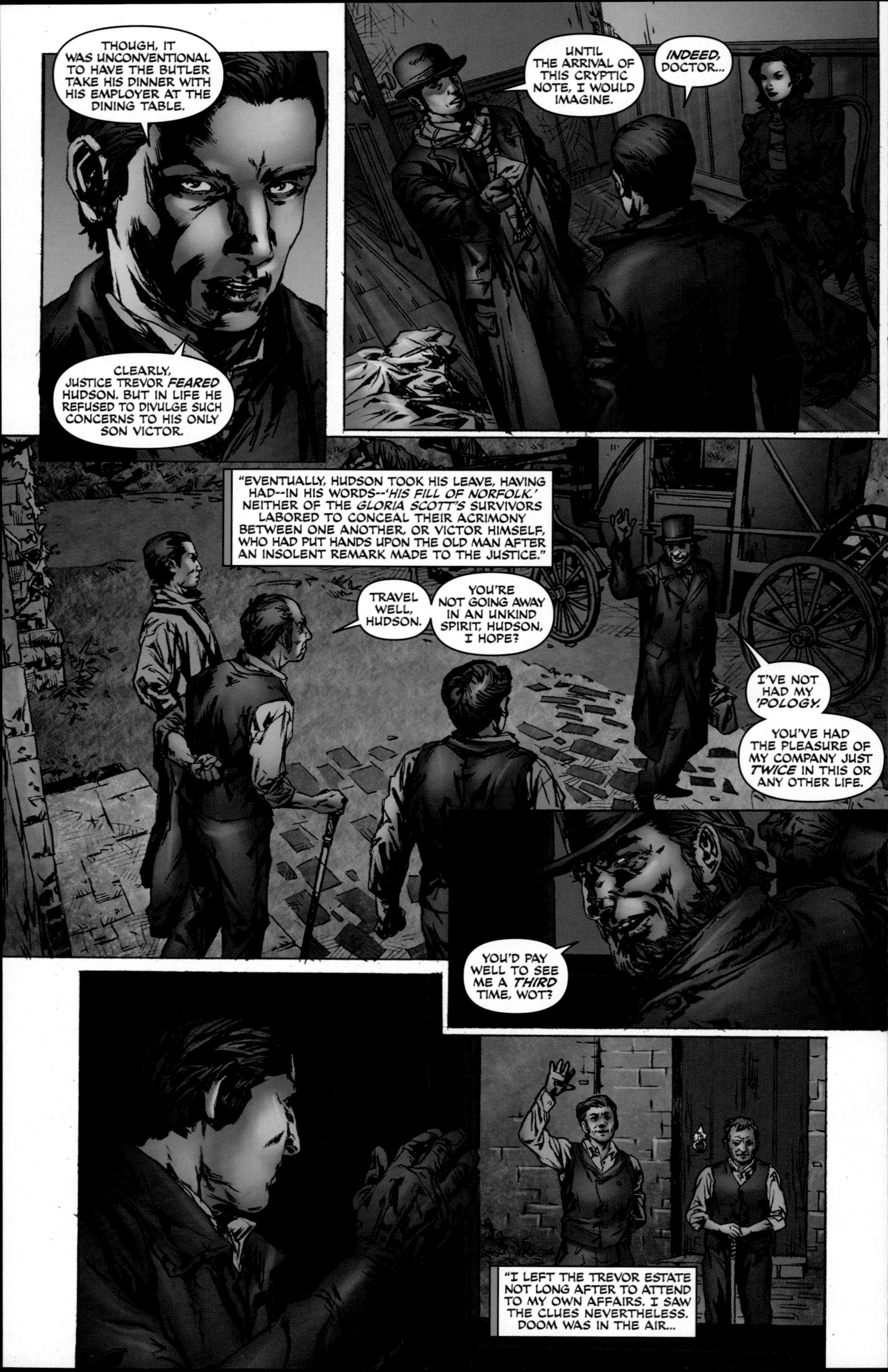
THOUGH, IT WAS UNCONVENTIONAL TO HAVE THE BUTLER TAKE HIS DINNER WITH HIS EMPLOYER AT THE DINING TABLE.
CLEARLY, JUSTICE TREVOR *FEARED* HUDSON. BUT IN LIFE HE REFUSED TO DIVULGE SUCH CONCERNS TO HIS ONLY SON VICTOR.
UNTIL THE ARRIVAL OF THIS CRYPTIC NOTE, I WOULD IMAGINE.
INDEED, DOCTOR...
"EVENTUALLY, HUDSON TOOK HIS LEAVE, HAVING HAD--IN HIS WORDS--*'HIS FILL OF NORFOLK.'* NEITHER OF THE *GLORIA SCOTT'S* SURVIVORS LABORED TO CONCEAL THEIR ACRIMONY BETWEEN ONE ANOTHER, OR VICTOR HIMSELF, WHO HAD PUT HANDS UPON THE OLD MAN AFTER AN INSOLENT REMARK MADE TO THE JUSTICE."
TRAVEL WELL, HUDSON.
YOU'RE NOT GOING AWAY IN AN UNKIND SPIRIT, HUDSON, I HOPE?
I'VE NOT HAD MY *'POLOGY.*
YOU'VE HAD THE PLEASURE OF MY COMPANY JUST *TWICE* IN THIS OR ANY OTHER LIFE.
YOU'D PAY WELL TO SEE ME A *THIRD* TIME, WOT?
"I LEFT THE TREVOR ESTATE NOT LONG AFTER TO ATTEND TO MY OWN AFFAIRS. I SAW THE CLUES NEVERTHELESS. DOOM WAS IN THE AIR...

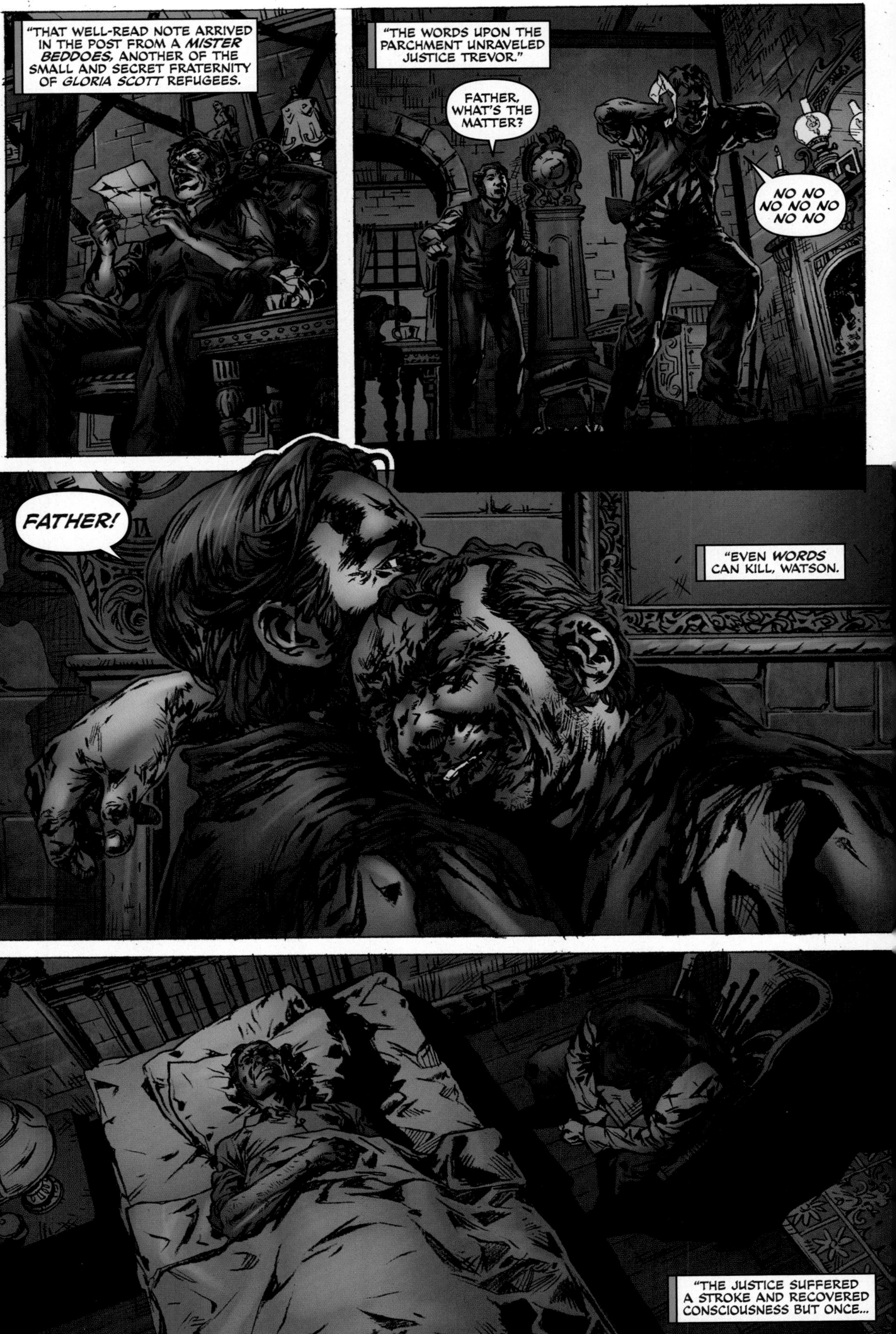
"THAT WELL-READ NOTE ARRIVED IN THE POST FROM A *MISTER BEDDOES*, ANOTHER OF THE SMALL AND SECRET FRATERNITY OF *GLORIA SCOTT* REFUGEES.
"THE WORDS UPON THE PARCHMENT UNRAVELED JUSTICE TREVOR."
FATHER, WHAT'S THE MATTER?
NO NO NO NO NO NO NO
FATHER!
"EVEN *WORDS* CAN KILL, WATSON.
"THE JUSTICE SUFFERED A STROKE AND RECOVERED CONSCIOUSNESS BUT ONCE...

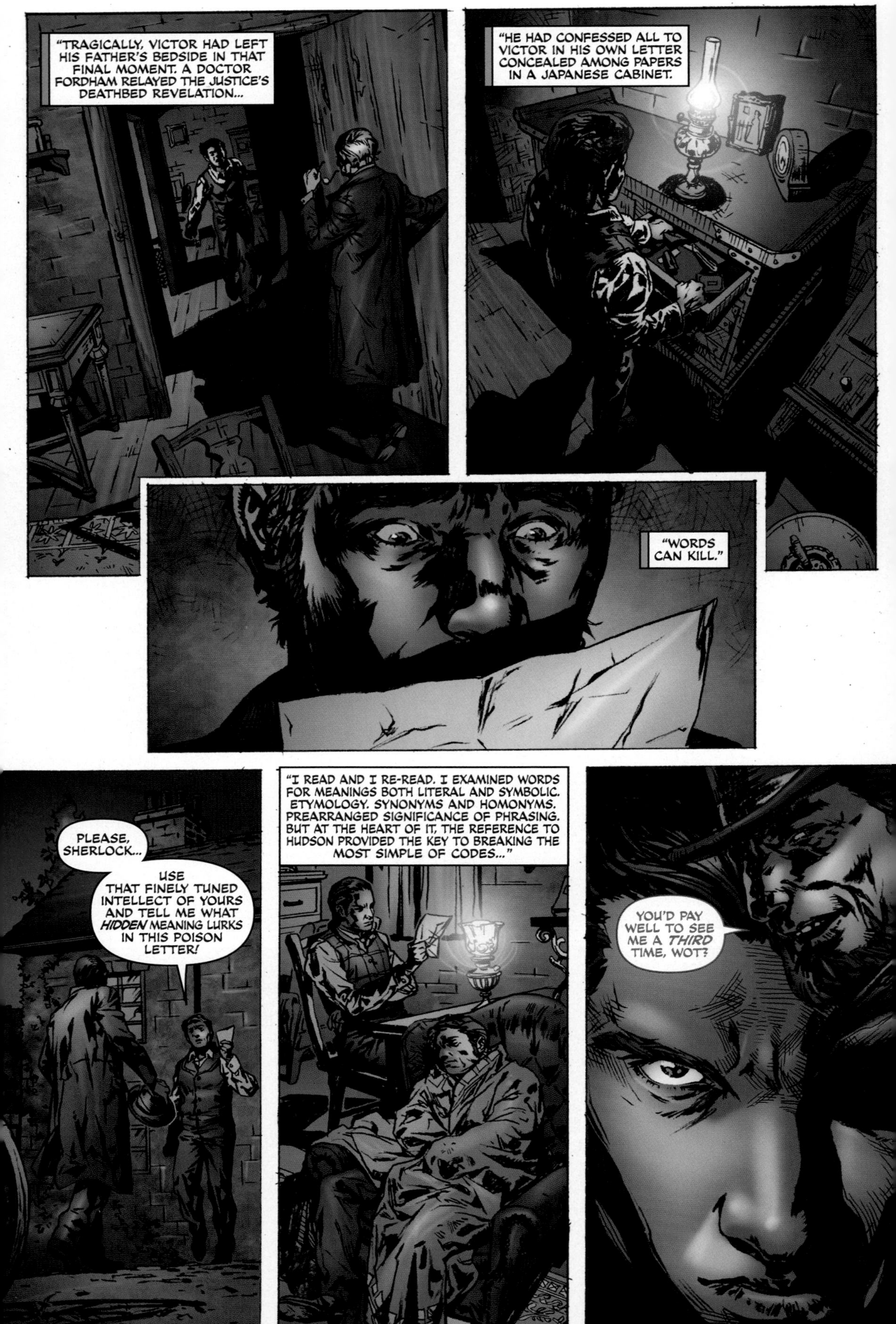
"TRAGICALLY, VICTOR HAD LEFT HIS FATHER'S BEDSIDE IN THAT FINAL MOMENT. A DOCTOR FORDHAM RELAYED THE JUSTICE'S DEATHBED REVELATION...
"HE HAD CONFESSED ALL TO VICTOR IN HIS OWN LETTER CONCEALED AMONG PAPERS IN A JAPANESE CABINET.
"WORDS CAN KILL."
PLEASE, SHERLOCK...
USE THAT FINELY TUNED INTELLECT OF YOURS AND TELL ME WHAT *HIDDEN* MEANING LURKS IN THIS POISON LETTER!
"I READ AND I RE-READ. I EXAMINED WORDS FOR MEANINGS BOTH LITERAL AND SYMBOLIC. ETYMOLOGY. SYNONYMS AND HOMONYMS. PREARRANGED SIGNIFICANCE OF PHRASING. BUT AT THE HEART OF IT, THE REFERENCE TO HUDSON PROVIDED THE KEY TO BREAKING THE MOST SIMPLE OF CODES..."
YOU'D PAY WELL TO SEE ME A *THIRD* TIME, WOT?

ONCE IS HAPPENSTANCE.

TWICE IS COINCIDENCE.

THRICE IS A PATTERN OF ILL INTENT.

"HUDSON DID INDEED CALL UPON BEDDOES, LIKELY TO RECRUIT HIS FELLOW SURVIVOR IN A SCHEME TO BLACKMAIL JUSTICE TREVOR FOR HAVING THE TEMERITY TO PROSPER IN THE YEARS SINCE THE *GLORIA SCOTT* EXPLODED AND SANK BENEATH THE SOUTH PACIFIC WAVES.

"BUT BEDDOES WAS AMONG THE SMALL RETINUE THAT LEFT THE SHIP RATHER THAN MURDER THE CAPTURED CREW. DESPITE THE WELL-WORN MAXIM, PERHAPS THERE IS HONOR AMONG THIEVES.

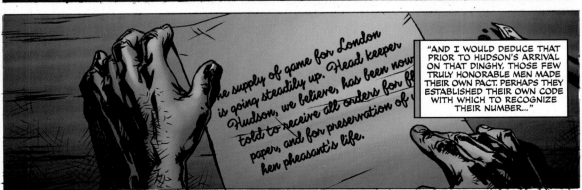

he supply of game for London is going steadily up. Head keeper Hudson, we believe, has been now told to receive all orders for fl paper, and for preservation of hen pheasant's life.

"AND I WOULD DEDUCE THAT PRIOR TO HUDSON'S ARRIVAL ON THAT DINGHY, THOSE FEW TRULY HONORABLE MEN MADE THEIR OWN PACT. PERHAPS THEY ESTABLISHED THEIR OWN CODE WITH WHICH TO RECOGNIZE THEIR NUMBER..."

THE NUMBER *THREE!*

THE MESSAGE IS IN EVERY *THIRD* WORD!

The supply of game for London is going steadily up. Head keeper Hudson, we believe, has been now told to receive all

FLY FOR YOUR LIFE.

BUT HE DIDN'T, DID HE?

I BELIEVE JUSTICE TREVOR WAS RELUCTANT TO GIVE UP THE *LEGITIMATE* LIFE HE HAD WORKED SO HARD TO ACHIEVE AFTER FATE HAD OFFERED A MEANS TO ERADICATE HIS PAST SINS.

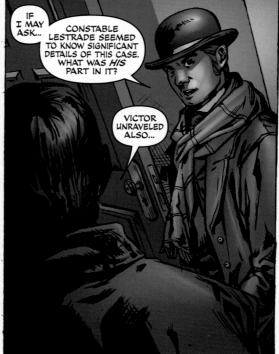

IF I MAY ASK...

CONSTABLE LESTRADE SEEMED TO KNOW SIGNIFICANT DETAILS OF THIS CASE. WHAT WAS *HIS* PART IN IT?

VICTOR UNRAVELED ALSO...

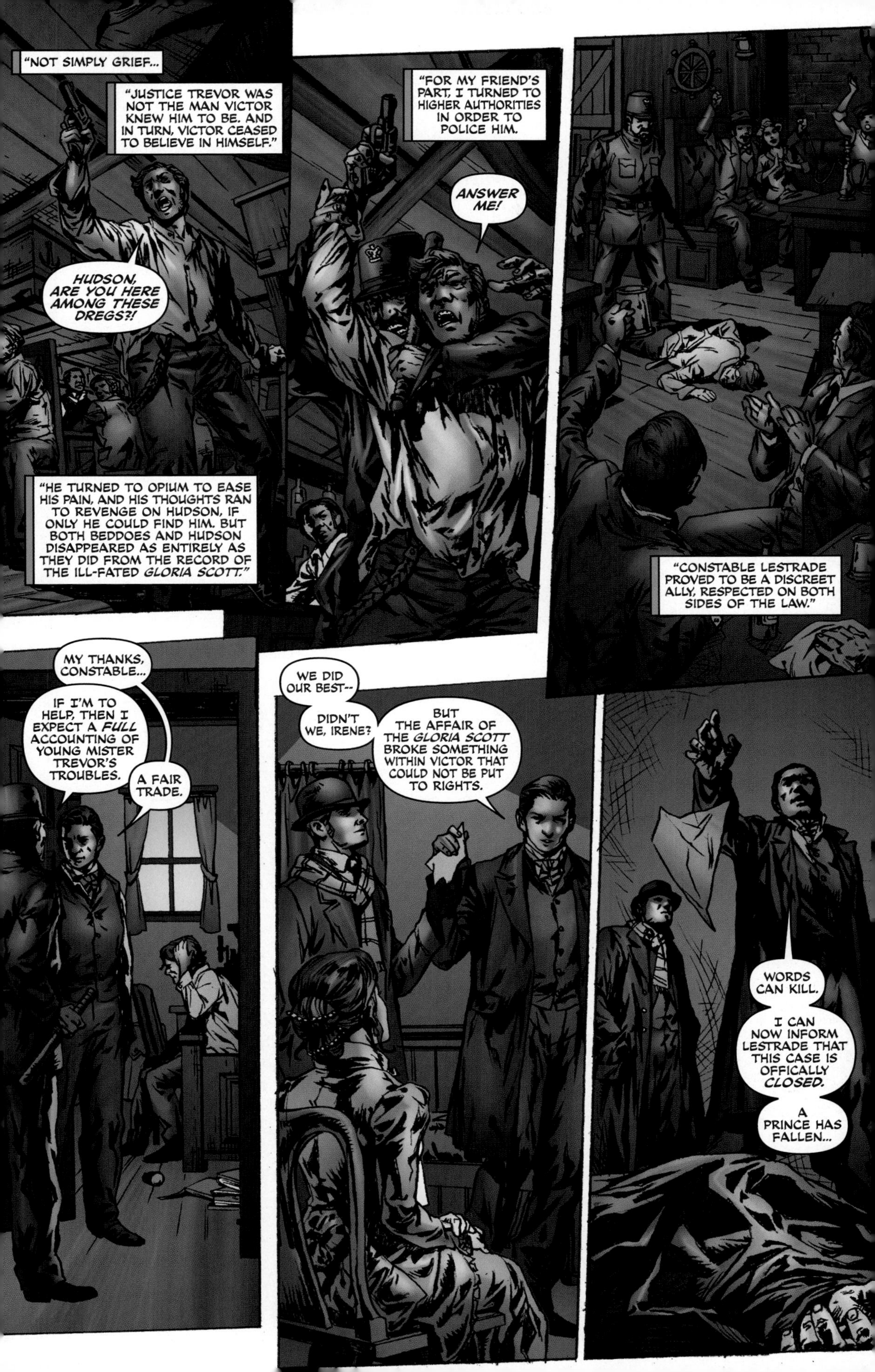
"NOT SIMPLY GRIEF...
"JUSTICE TREVOR WAS NOT THE MAN VICTOR KNEW HIM TO BE. AND IN TURN, VICTOR CEASED TO BELIEVE IN HIMSELF."
HUDSON, ARE YOU HERE AMONG THESE DREGS?!
"HE TURNED TO OPIUM TO EASE HIS PAIN, AND HIS THOUGHTS RAN TO REVENGE ON HUDSON, IF ONLY HE COULD FIND HIM. BUT BOTH BEDDOES AND HUDSON DISAPPEARED AS ENTIRELY AS THEY DID FROM THE RECORD OF THE ILL-FATED *GLORIA SCOTT*."
"FOR MY FRIEND'S PART, I TURNED TO HIGHER AUTHORITIES IN ORDER TO POLICE HIM.
ANSWER ME!
"CONSTABLE LESTRADE PROVED TO BE A DISCREET ALLY, RESPECTED ON BOTH SIDES OF THE LAW."
MY THANKS, CONSTABLE...
IF I'M TO HELP, THEN I EXPECT A *FULL* ACCOUNTING OF YOUNG MISTER TREVOR'S TROUBLES.
A FAIR TRADE.
WE DID OUR BEST--
DIDN'T WE, IRENE?
BUT THE AFFAIR OF THE *GLORIA SCOTT* BROKE SOMETHING WITHIN VICTOR THAT COULD NOT BE PUT TO RIGHTS.
WORDS CAN KILL.
I CAN NOW INFORM LESTRADE THAT THIS CASE IS OFFICALLY *CLOSED.*
A PRINCE HAS FALLEN...

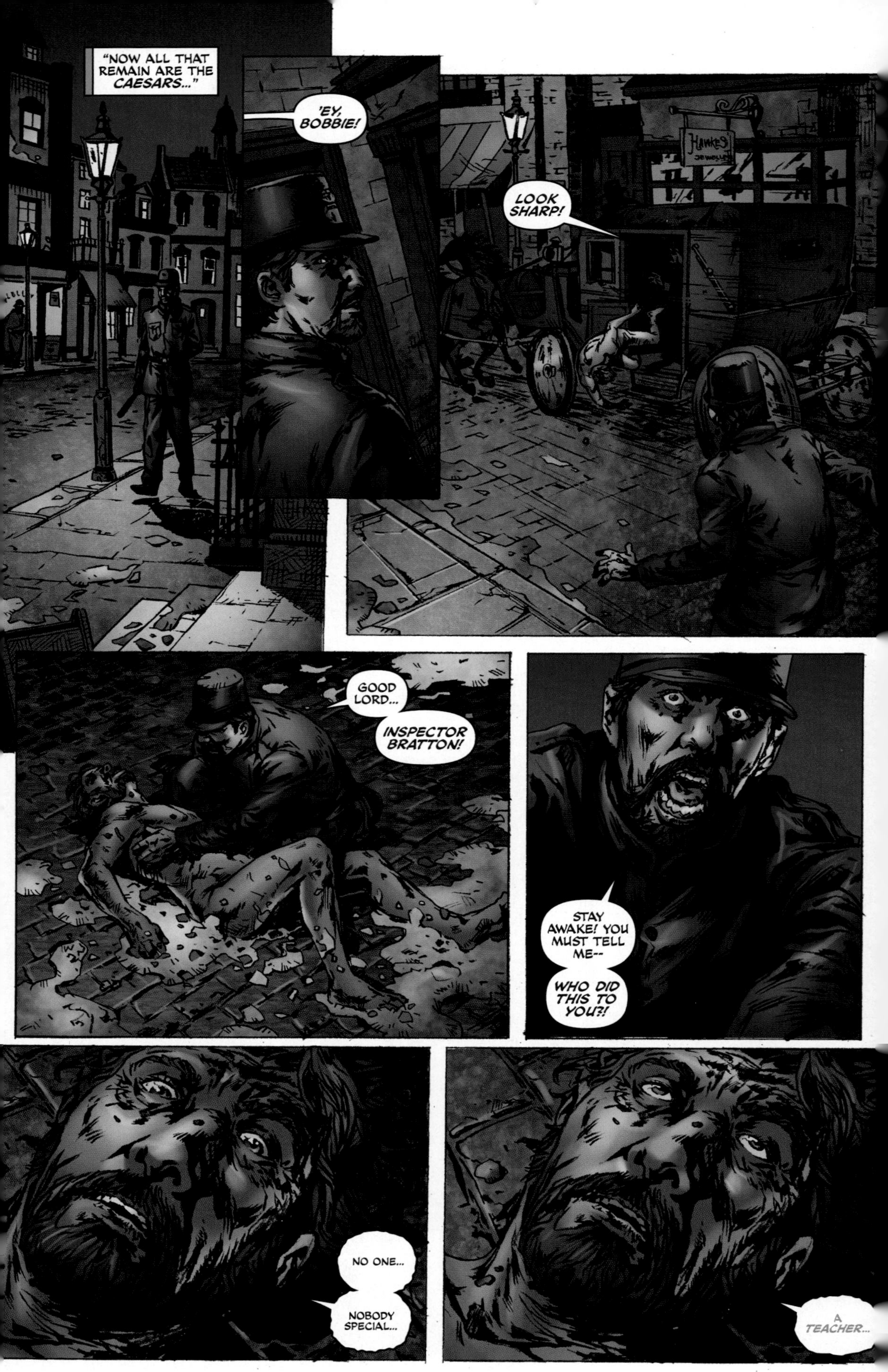
"NOW ALL THAT REMAIN ARE THE *CAESARS*..."
'EY, BOBBIE!
LOOK SHARP!
GOOD LORD...
INSPECTOR BRATTON!
STAY AWAKE! YOU MUST TELL ME--
WHO DID THIS TO YOU?!
NO ONE...
NOBODY SPECIAL...
A *TEACHER*...

AT UNIVERSITY...

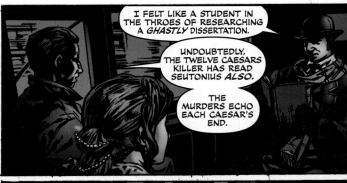

I FELT LIKE A STUDENT IN THE THROES OF RESEARCHING A *GHASTLY* DISSERTATION.

UNDOUBTEDLY, THE TWELVE CAESARS KILLER HAS READ SEUTONIUS *ALSO.*

THE MURDERS ECHO EACH CAESAR'S END.

THE *PATTERN* SOLVED, JUST NOT THE *PLANNER.*

I'LL ASSUME THAT THE DOOR IS LEFT *UNLATCHED* AS ALWAYS, SHERLOCK.

HOLMES? A WORD?

YOU HAVE MY SINCEREST *CONDOLENCES* FOR THE LOSS OF YOUR FRIEND.

BUT I REALLY DO THINK WE MUST PRESS ON WITH OUR DISCUSSIONS OF THE MOTIVES BEHIND THE MADMAN TERRORIZING LONDON.

YOUR PROFESSOR, THE MAN WHO LOANED ME THIS TOME, SEEMED KEEN ON YOUR ABILITIES TO ROOT OUT THE KILLER'S--

MY *PROFESSOR?*

THE NINTH CAESAR
VITELLIUS

IRENE!

TOOK YOU LONG ENOUGH, SHERLOCK...

SO MUCH FOR YOUR VAUNTED DEDUCTIVE PROWESS.

IN THE END, AND IN ALL PRACTICALITY, I HAD TO LEAVE THE MOST *TELLING* CLUE RIGHT AT YOUR DOORSTEP.

I WAS...

I'VE BEEN...

DISTRACTED.

CLUD

THAT'S QUITE ENOUGH!

CEASE THIS VIOLENCE OR I'LL PARSE MY OWN!

AND I ASSURE YOU THAT I'M QUITE THE CRACK SHOT.

ALLOW ME TO CALL YOUR *BLUFF*, DOCTOR WATSON.

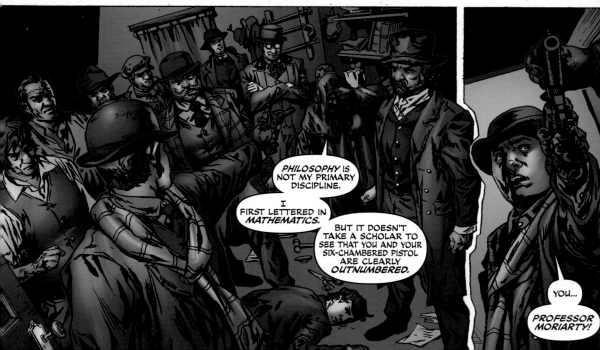

PHILOSOPHY IS NOT MY PRIMARY DISCIPLINE.

I FIRST LETTERED IN *MATHEMATICS*.

BUT IT DOESN'T TAKE A SCHOLAR TO SEE THAT YOU AND YOUR SIX-CHAMBERED PISTOL ARE CLEARLY *OUTNUMBERED*.

YOU...

PROFESSOR MORIARTY!

NOW THAT WE'VE DISPENSED WITH INTRODUCTIONS, SHALL WE BEGIN THE DISCOURSE?

ROME'S FAILURE WAS *INEVITABLE.*

THE CAESARS WERE FOOLS AND THE ROMAN MASSES MORESO FOR BLINDLY FOLLOWING THEIR INBRED LOT.

BRITTANIA FACES THE SAME END IF ITS CITIZENRY PERSIST IN SWEARING FEALTY TO ROYAL DUNCES AND THEIR PARLIAMENTARY PAWNS OVER THOSE *MOST* FIT TO RULE...

WHY DO WE FOLLOW THE MOST *POWERFUL* RATHER THAN THE MOST *EDUCATED?*

AND ARE THE TWO MUTUALLY EXCLUSIVE?

HOLMES, WAKE UP--

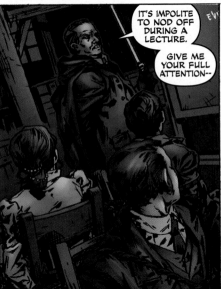

IT'S IMPOLITE TO NOD OFF DURING A LECTURE.

GIVE ME YOUR FULL ATTENTION--

GOOD V. EVIL

YOU MIGHT LEARN *SOMETHING...*

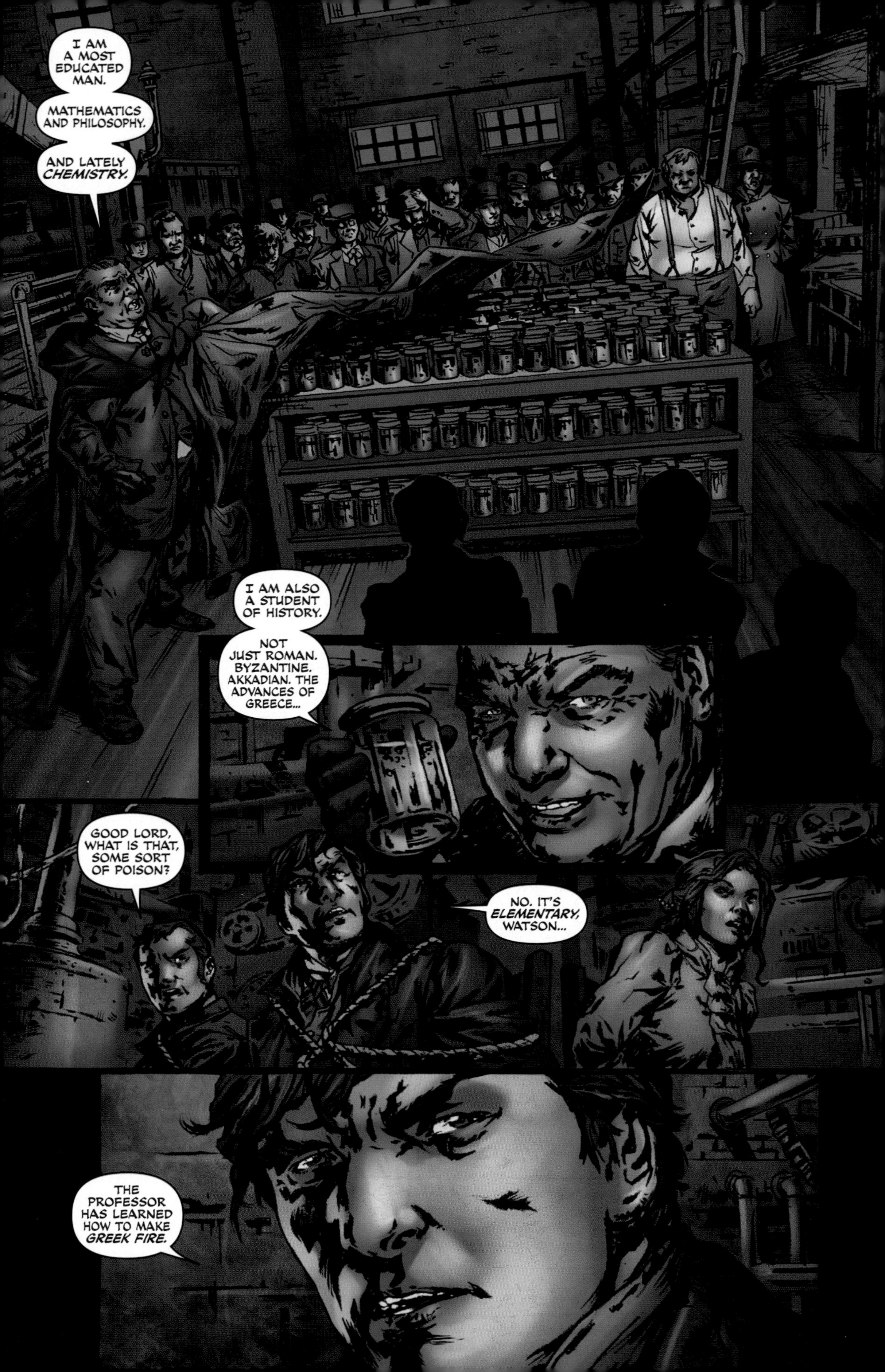
I AM A MOST EDUCATED MAN.
MATHEMATICS AND PHILOSOPHY.
AND LATELY *CHEMISTRY.*
I AM ALSO A STUDENT OF HISTORY.
NOT JUST ROMAN. BYZANTINE. AKKADIAN. THE ADVANCES OF GREECE...
GOOD LORD, WHAT IS THAT, SOME SORT OF POISON?
NO. IT'S *ELEMENTARY,* WATSON...
THE PROFESSOR HAS LEARNED HOW TO MAKE *GREEK FIRE.*

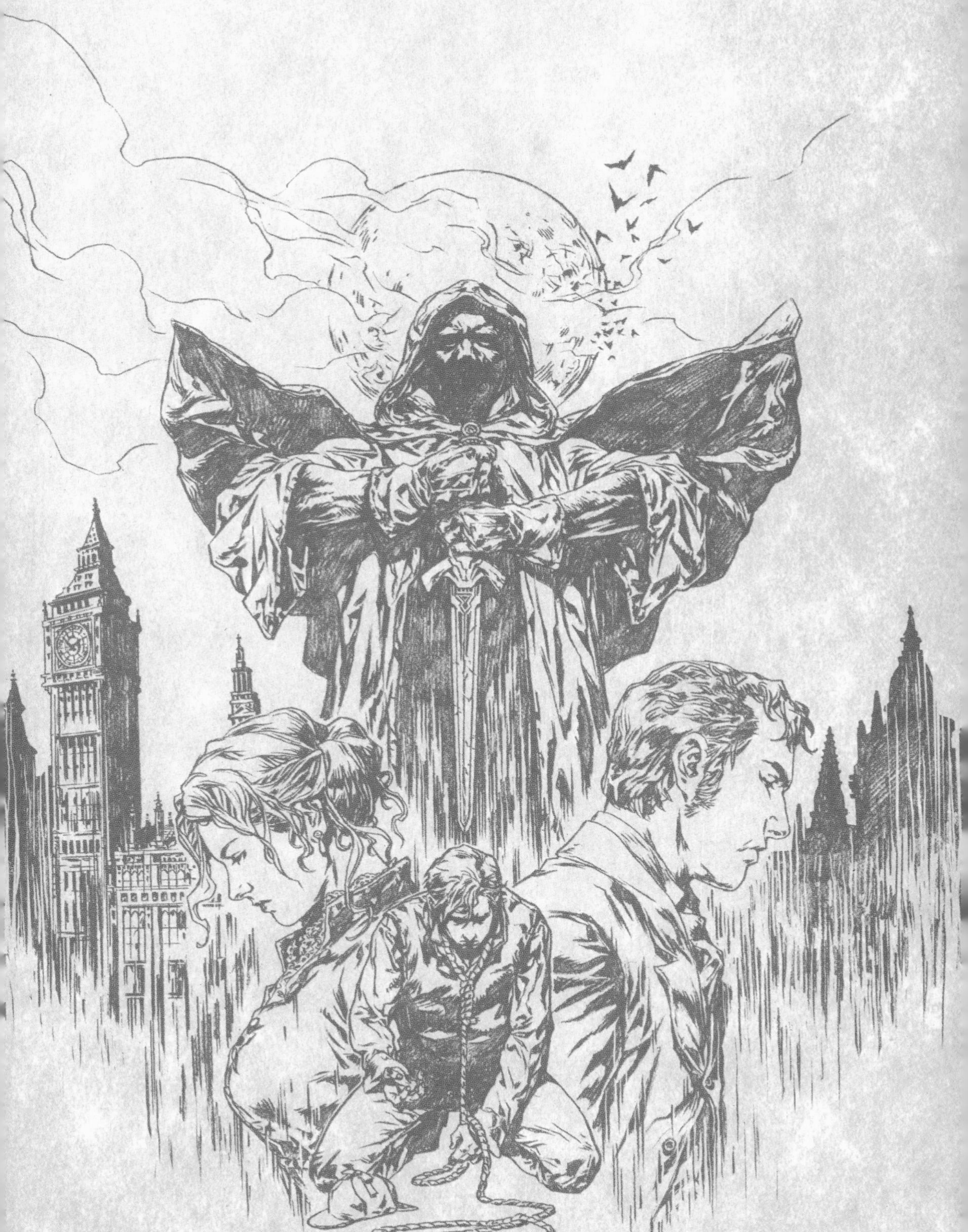

Cover by:
FRANCESCO
FRANCAVILLA

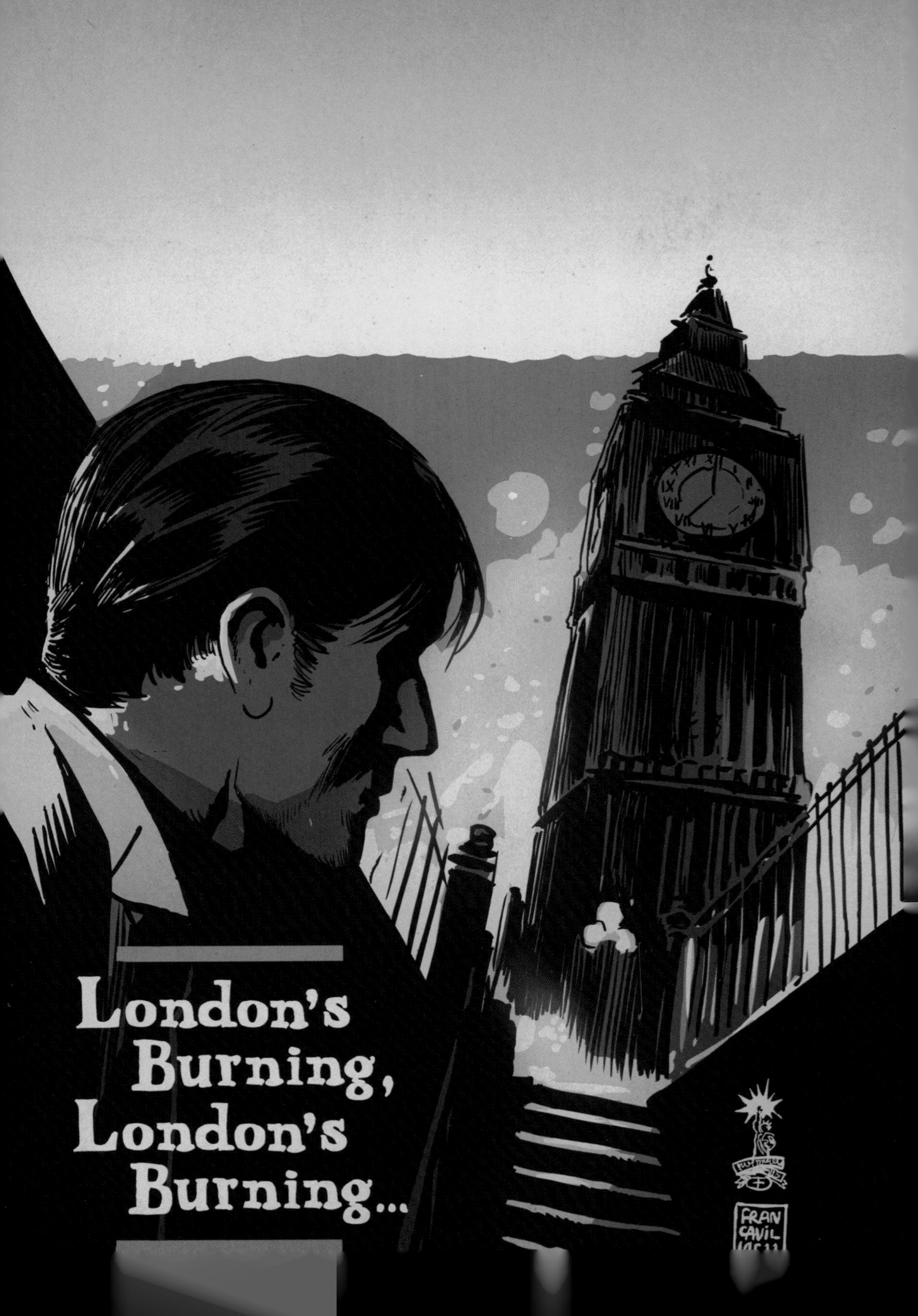
London's
Burning,
London's
Burning...

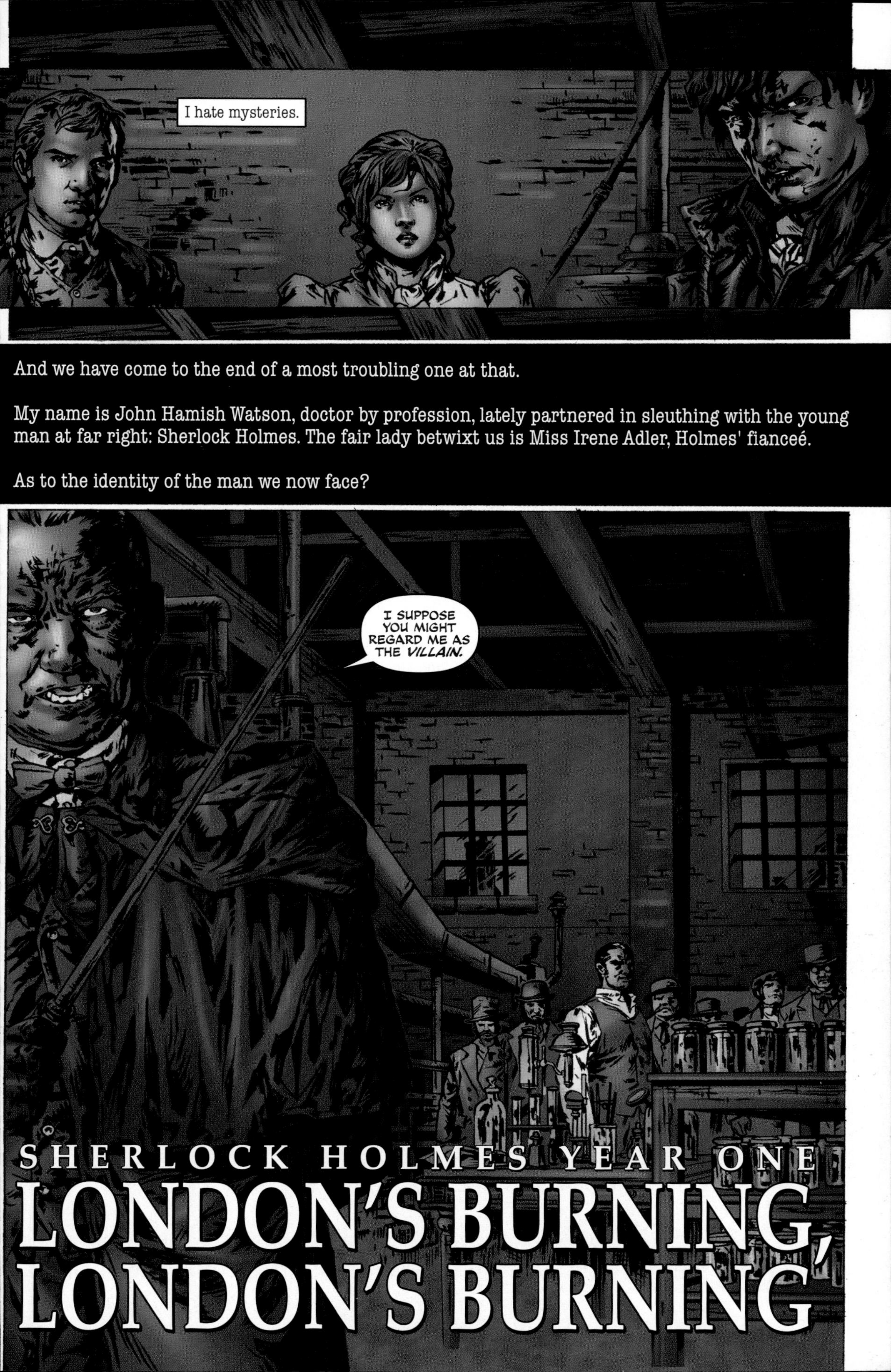
I hate mysteries.
And we have come to the end of a most troubling one at that.
My name is John Hamish Watson, doctor by profession, lately partnered in sleuthing with the young man at far right: Sherlock Holmes. The fair lady betwixt us is Miss Irene Adler, Holmes' fianceé.
As to the identity of the man we now face?
I SUPPOSE YOU MIGHT REGARD ME AS THE *VILLAIN.*
SHERLOCK HOLMES YEAR ONE
LONDON'S BURNING, LONDON'S BURNING'

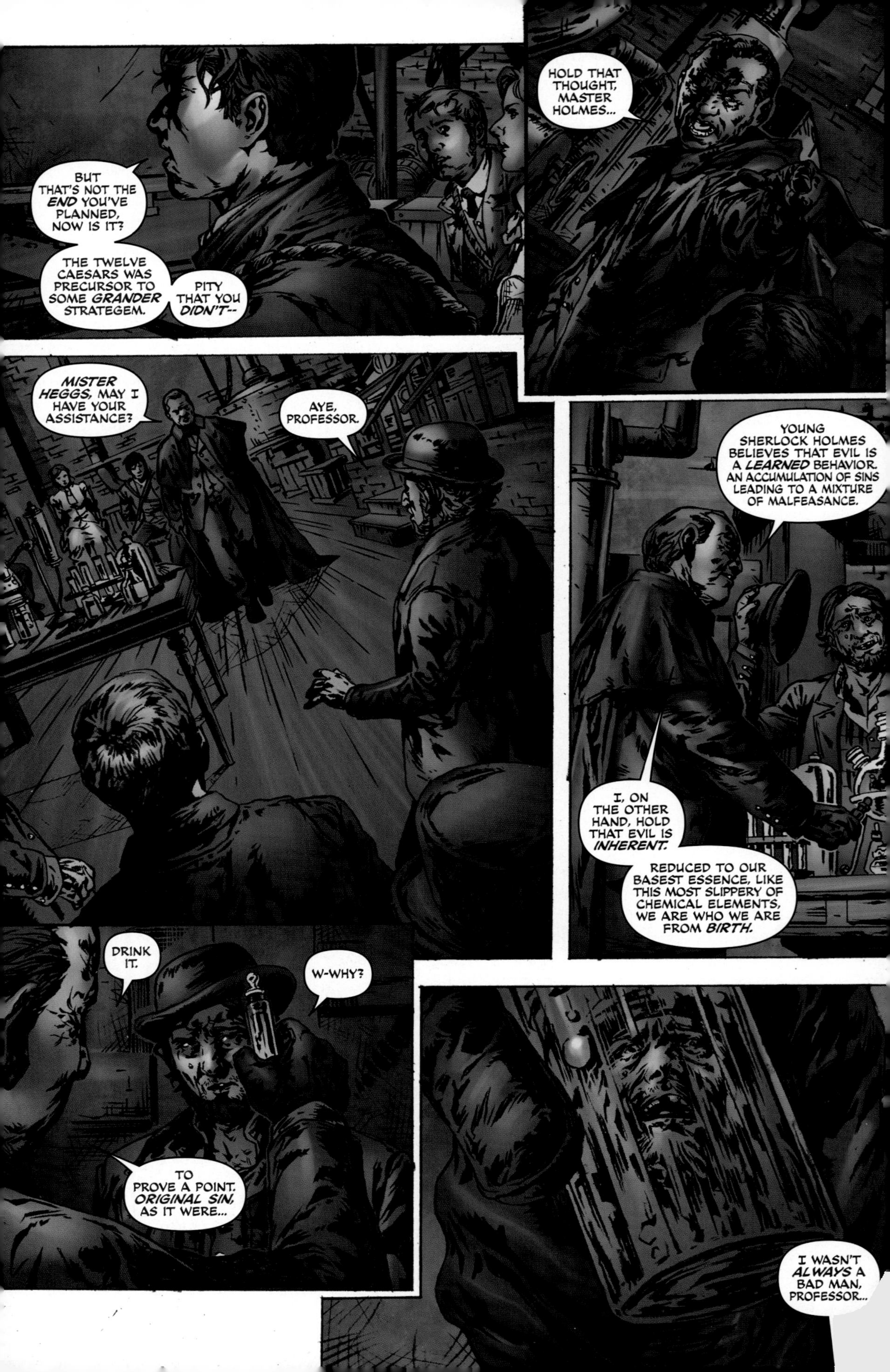
BUT THAT'S NOT THE *END* YOU'VE PLANNED, NOW IS IT?
THE TWELVE CAESARS WAS PRECURSOR TO SOME *GRANDER* STRATEGEM.
PITY THAT YOU *DIDN'T*--
HOLD THAT THOUGHT, MASTER HOLMES...
MISTER HEGGS, MAY I HAVE YOUR ASSISTANCE?
AYE, PROFESSOR.
YOUNG SHERLOCK HOLMES BELIEVES THAT EVIL IS A *LEARNED* BEHAVIOR. AN ACCUMULATION OF SINS LEADING TO A MIXTURE OF MALFEASANCE.
I, ON THE OTHER HAND, HOLD THAT EVIL IS *INHERENT.*
REDUCED TO OUR BASEST ESSENCE, LIKE THIS MOST SLIPPERY OF CHEMICAL ELEMENTS, WE ARE WHO WE ARE FROM *BIRTH.*
DRINK IT.
W-WHY?
TO PROVE A POINT. *ORIGINAL SIN,* AS IT WERE...
I WASN'T *ALWAYS* A BAD MAN, PROFESSOR...

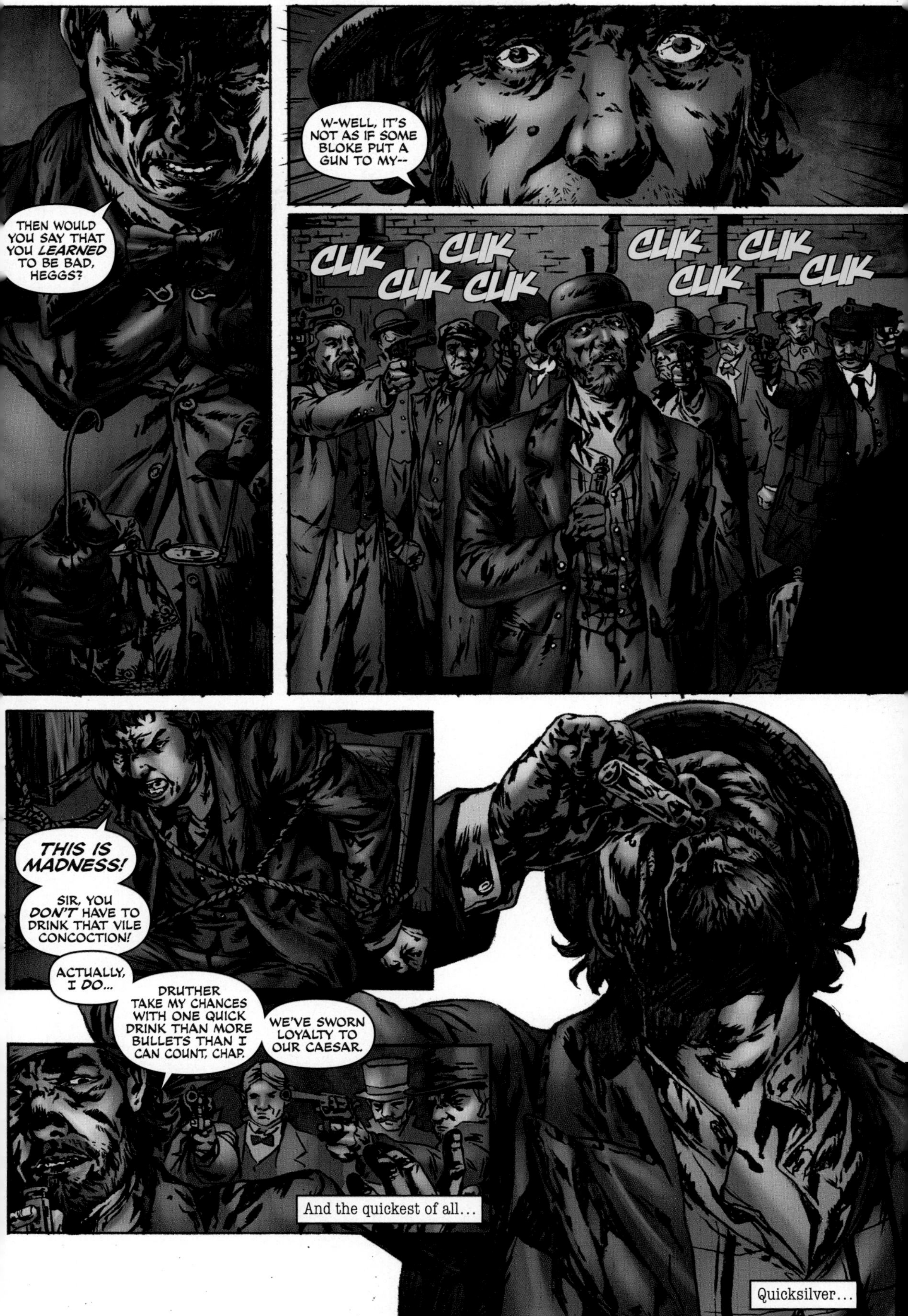
W-WELL, IT'S NOT AS IF SOME BLOKE PUT A GUN TO MY--
THEN WOULD YOU SAY THAT YOU *LEARNED* TO BE BAD, HEGGS?
CLIK CLIK CLIK CLIK
CLIK CLIK CLIK CLIK
THIS IS MADNESS!
SIR, YOU *DON'T* HAVE TO DRINK THAT VILE CONCOCTION!
ACTUALLY, I *DO*...
DRUTHER TAKE MY CHANCES WITH ONE QUICK DRINK THAN MORE BULLETS THAN I CAN COUNT, CHAP.
WE'VE SWORN LOYALTY TO OUR CAESAR.
And the quickest of all...
Quicksilver...

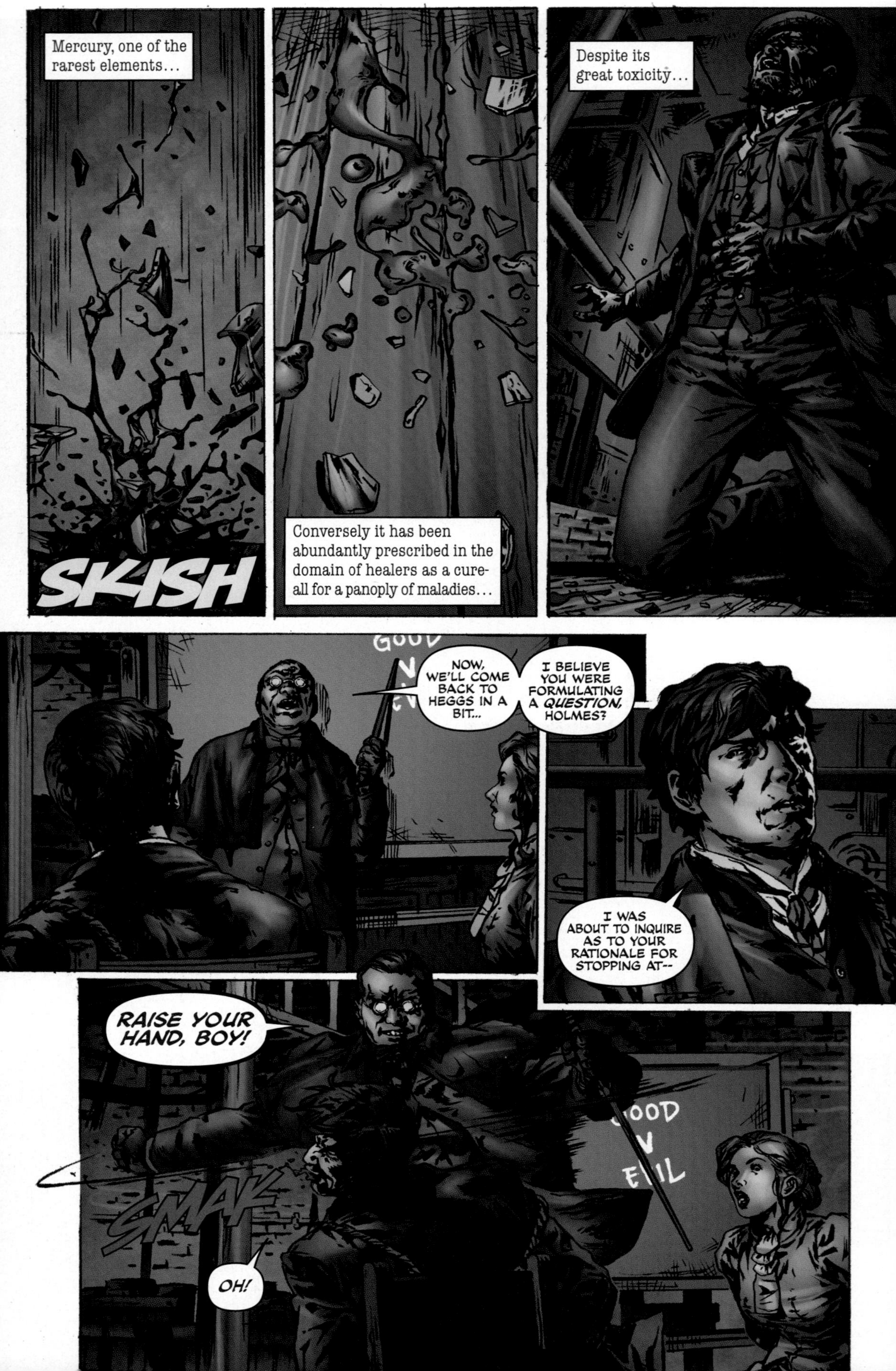
Mercury, one of the rarest elements...
SKISH
Conversely it has been abundantly prescribed in the domain of healers as a cure-all for a panoply of maladies...
Despite its great toxicity...
GOOD V EVIL
NOW, WE'LL COME BACK TO HEGGS IN A BIT...
I BELIEVE YOU WERE FORMULATING A QUESTION, HOLMES?
I WAS ABOUT TO INQUIRE AS TO YOUR RATIONALE FOR STOPPING AT--
RAISE YOUR HAND, BOY!
GOOD V EVIL
SMAK
OH!

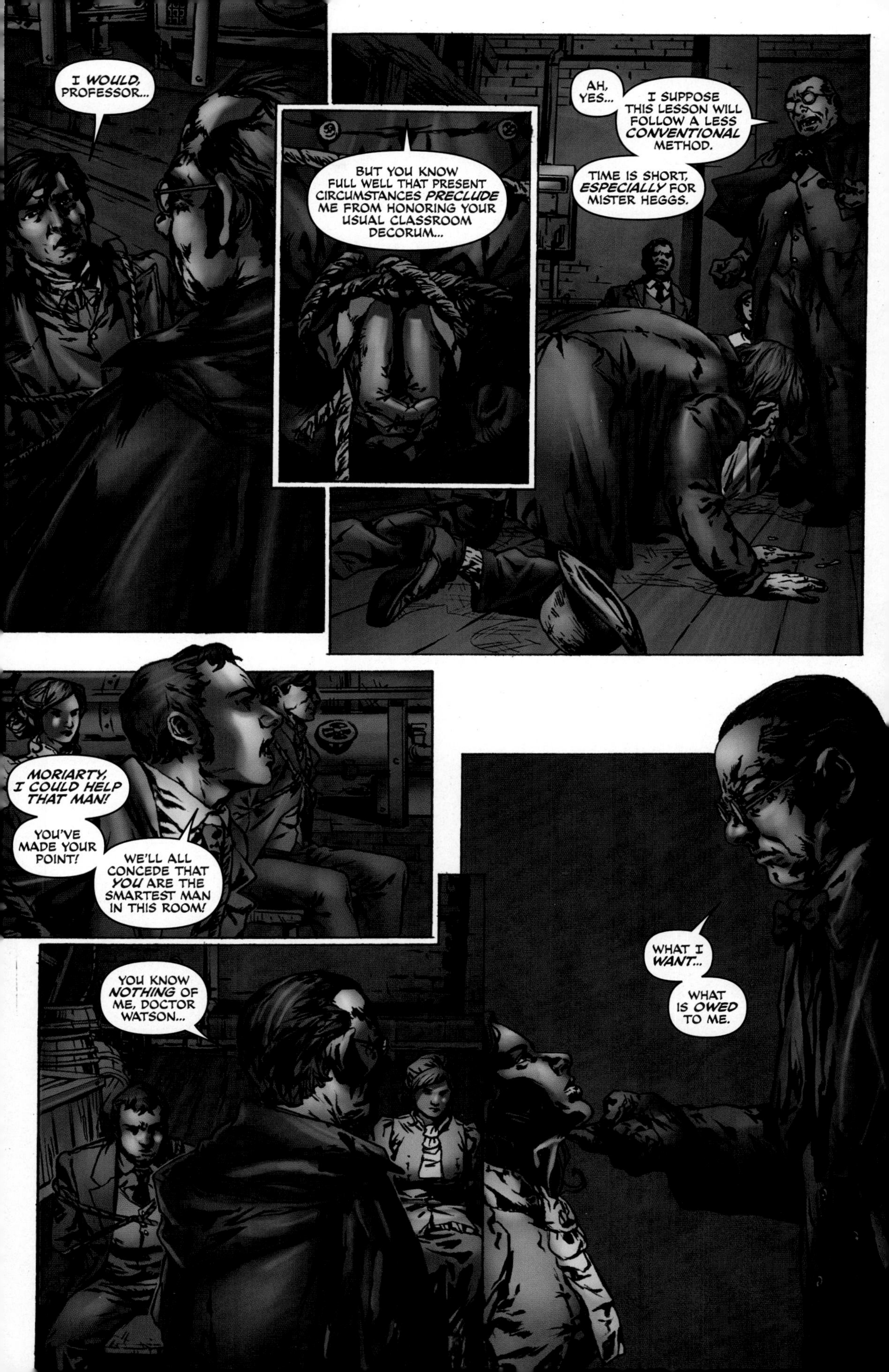
I WOULD, PROFESSOR...
BUT YOU KNOW FULL WELL THAT PRESENT CIRCUMSTANCES PRECLUDE ME FROM HONORING YOUR USUAL CLASSROOM DECORUM...
AH, YES...
I SUPPOSE THIS LESSON WILL FOLLOW A LESS CONVENTIONAL METHOD.
TIME IS SHORT, ESPECIALLY FOR MISTER HEGGS.
MORIARTY, I COULD HELP THAT MAN!
YOU'VE MADE YOUR POINT!
WE'LL ALL CONCEDE THAT YOU ARE THE SMARTEST MAN IN THIS ROOM!
YOU KNOW NOTHING OF ME, DOCTOR WATSON...
WHAT I WANT...
WHAT IS OWED TO ME.

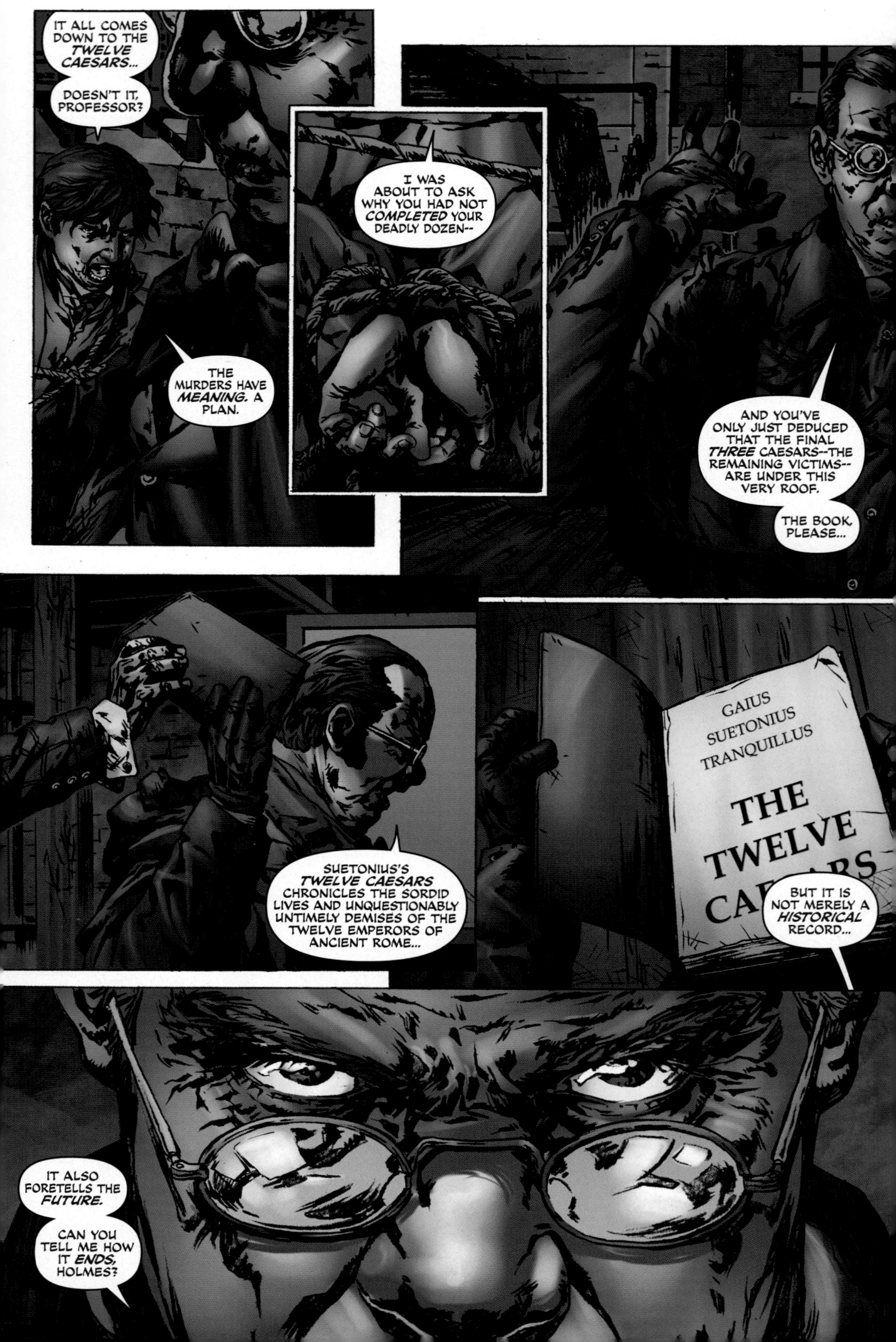
IT ALL COMES DOWN TO THE *TWELVE CAESARS*...
DOESN'T IT, PROFESSOR?
I WAS ABOUT TO ASK WHY YOU HAD NOT *COMPLETED* YOUR DEADLY DOZEN--
THE MURDERS HAVE *MEANING.* A PLAN.
AND YOU'VE ONLY JUST DEDUCED THAT THE FINAL *THREE* CAESARS--THE REMAINING VICTIMS--ARE UNDER THIS VERY ROOF.
THE BOOK, PLEASE...
SUETONIUS'S *TWELVE CAESARS* CHRONICLES THE SORDID LIVES AND UNQUESTIONABLY UNTIMELY DEMISES OF THE TWELVE EMPERORS OF ANCIENT ROME...
GAIUS
SUETONIUS
TRANQUILLUS
THE TWELVE
BUT IT IS NOT MERELY A *HISTORICAL* RECORD...
IT ALSO FORETELLS THE *FUTURE.*
CAN YOU TELL ME HOW IT *ENDS,* HOLMES?

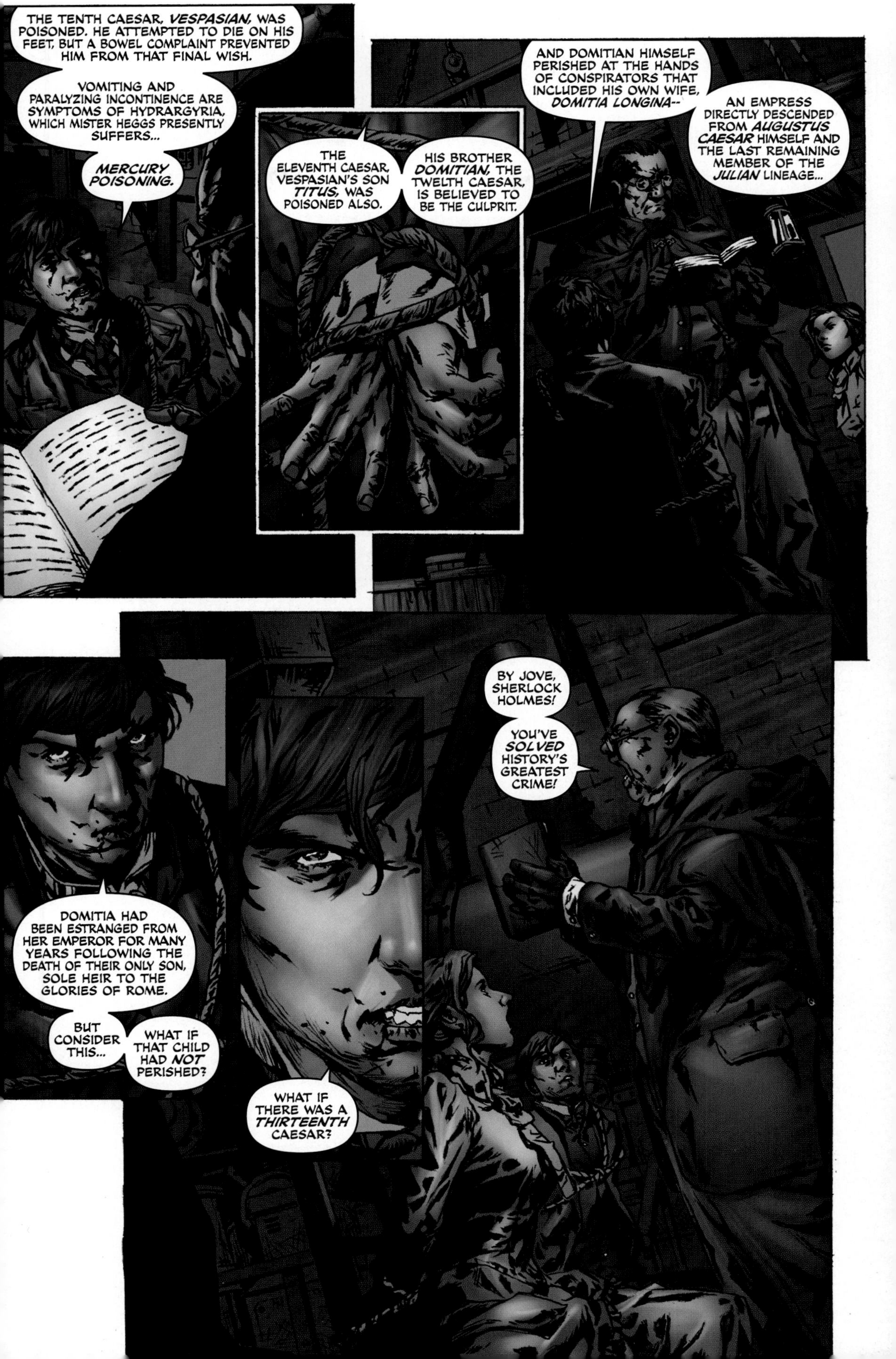
THE TENTH CAESAR, VESPASIAN, WAS POISONED. HE ATTEMPTED TO DIE ON HIS FEET, BUT A BOWEL COMPLAINT PREVENTED HIM FROM THAT FINAL WISH.
VOMITING AND PARALYZING INCONTINENCE ARE SYMPTOMS OF HYDRARGYRIA, WHICH MISTER HEGGS PRESENTLY SUFFERS...
MERCURY POISONING.
THE ELEVENTH CAESAR, VESPASIAN'S SON TITUS, WAS POISONED ALSO.
HIS BROTHER DOMITIAN, THE TWELTH CAESAR, IS BELIEVED TO BE THE CULPRIT.
AND DOMITIAN HIMSELF PERISHED AT THE HANDS OF CONSPIRATORS THAT INCLUDED HIS OWN WIFE, DOMITIA LONGINA--
AN EMPRESS DIRECTLY DESCENDED FROM AUGUSTUS CAESAR HIMSELF AND THE LAST REMAINING MEMBER OF THE JULIAN LINEAGE...
DOMITIA HAD BEEN ESTRANGED FROM HER EMPEROR FOR MANY YEARS FOLLOWING THE DEATH OF THEIR ONLY SON, SOLE HEIR TO THE GLORIES OF ROME.
BUT CONSIDER THIS...
WHAT IF THAT CHILD HAD NOT PERISHED?
WHAT IF THERE WAS A THIRTEENTH CAESAR?
BY JOVE, SHERLOCK HOLMES!
YOU'VE SOLVED HISTORY'S GREATEST CRIME!

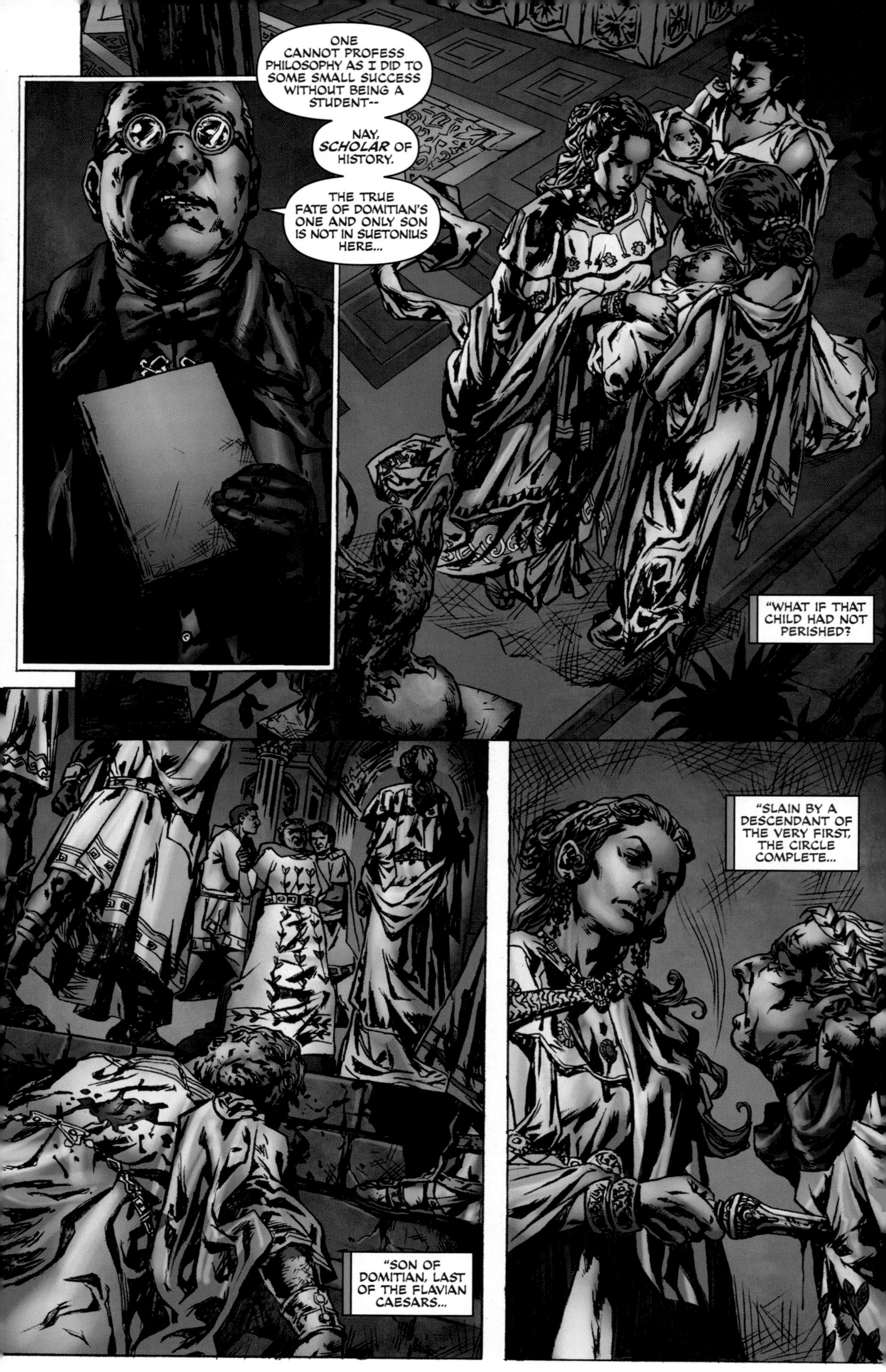

ONE CANNOT PROFESS PHILOSOPHY AS I DID TO SOME SMALL SUCCESS WITHOUT BEING A STUDENT--
NAY, *SCHOLAR* OF HISTORY.
THE TRUE FATE OF DOMITIAN'S ONE AND ONLY SON IS NOT IN SUETONIUS HERE...
"WHAT IF THAT CHILD HAD NOT PERISHED?
"SON OF DOMITIAN, LAST OF THE FLAVIAN CAESARS...
"SLAIN BY A DESCENDANT OF THE VERY FIRST, THE CIRCLE COMPLETE...

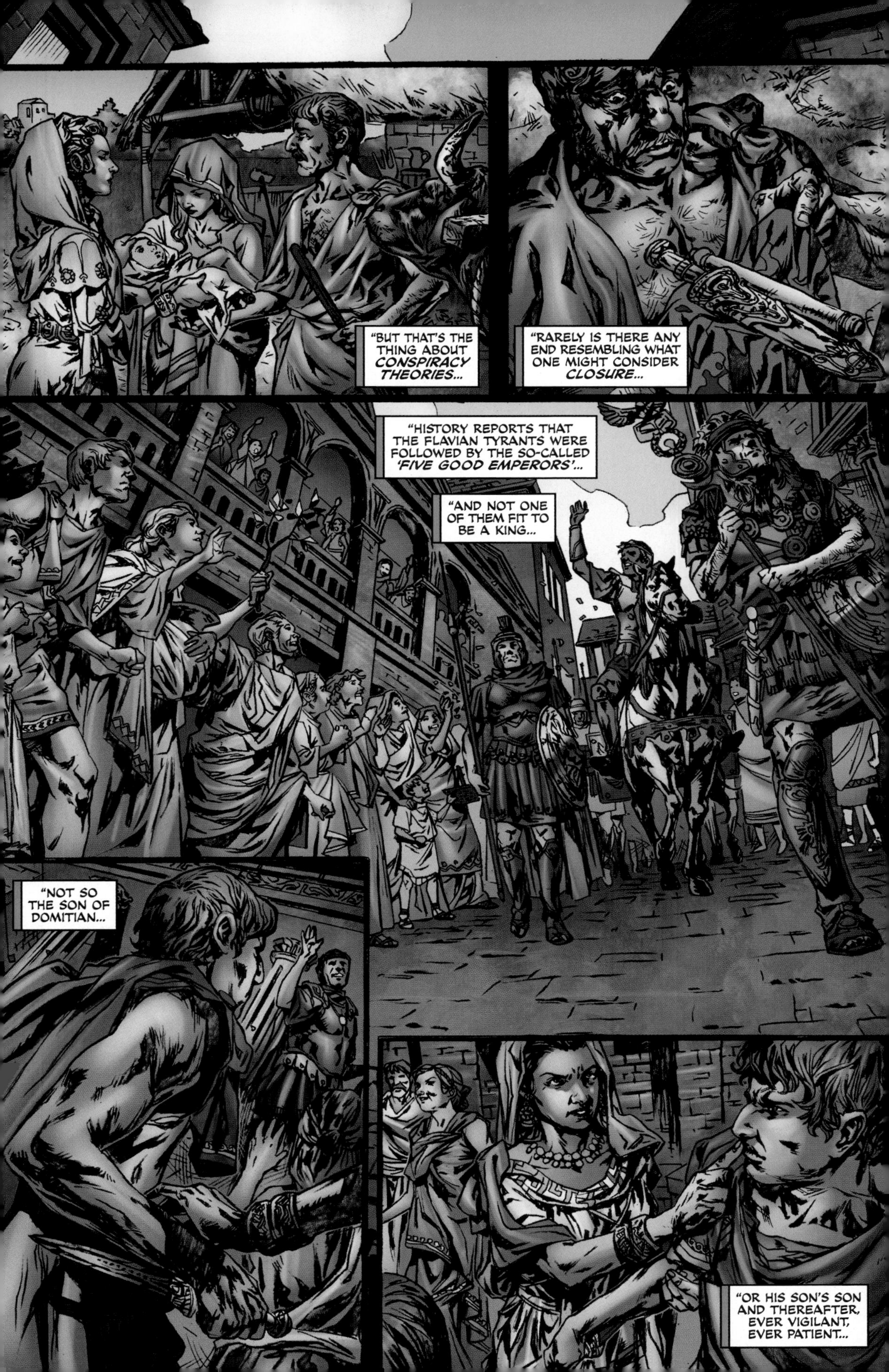
"BUT THAT'S THE THING ABOUT *CONSPIRACY THEORIES*...
"RARELY IS THERE ANY END RESEMBLING WHAT ONE MIGHT CONSIDER *CLOSURE*...
"HISTORY REPORTS THAT THE FLAVIAN TYRANTS WERE FOLLOWED BY THE SO-CALLED *'FIVE GOOD EMPERORS'*...
"AND NOT ONE OF THEM FIT TO BE A KING...
"NOT SO THE SON OF DOMITIAN...
"OR HIS SON'S SON AND THEREAFTER, EVER VIGILANT, EVER PATIENT...

MORITURI.

FROM THE LATIN...

FOR THOSE ABOUT TO DIE

"KNOWING FULL WELL WHAT AWAITS THE HEIRS TO THE TWELVE CAESARS..."

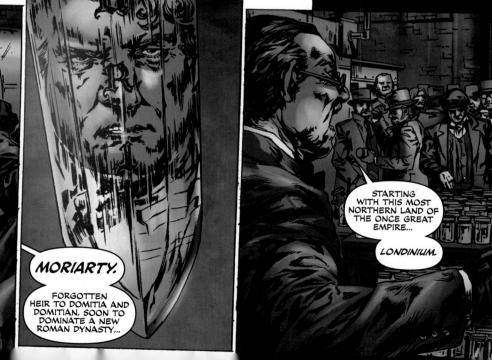

MORIARTY.

FORGOTTEN HEIR TO DOMITIA AND DOMITIAN, SOON TO DOMINATE A NEW ROMAN DYNASTY...

STARTING WITH THIS MOST NORTHERN LAND OF THE ONCE GREAT EMPIRE...

LONDINIUM.

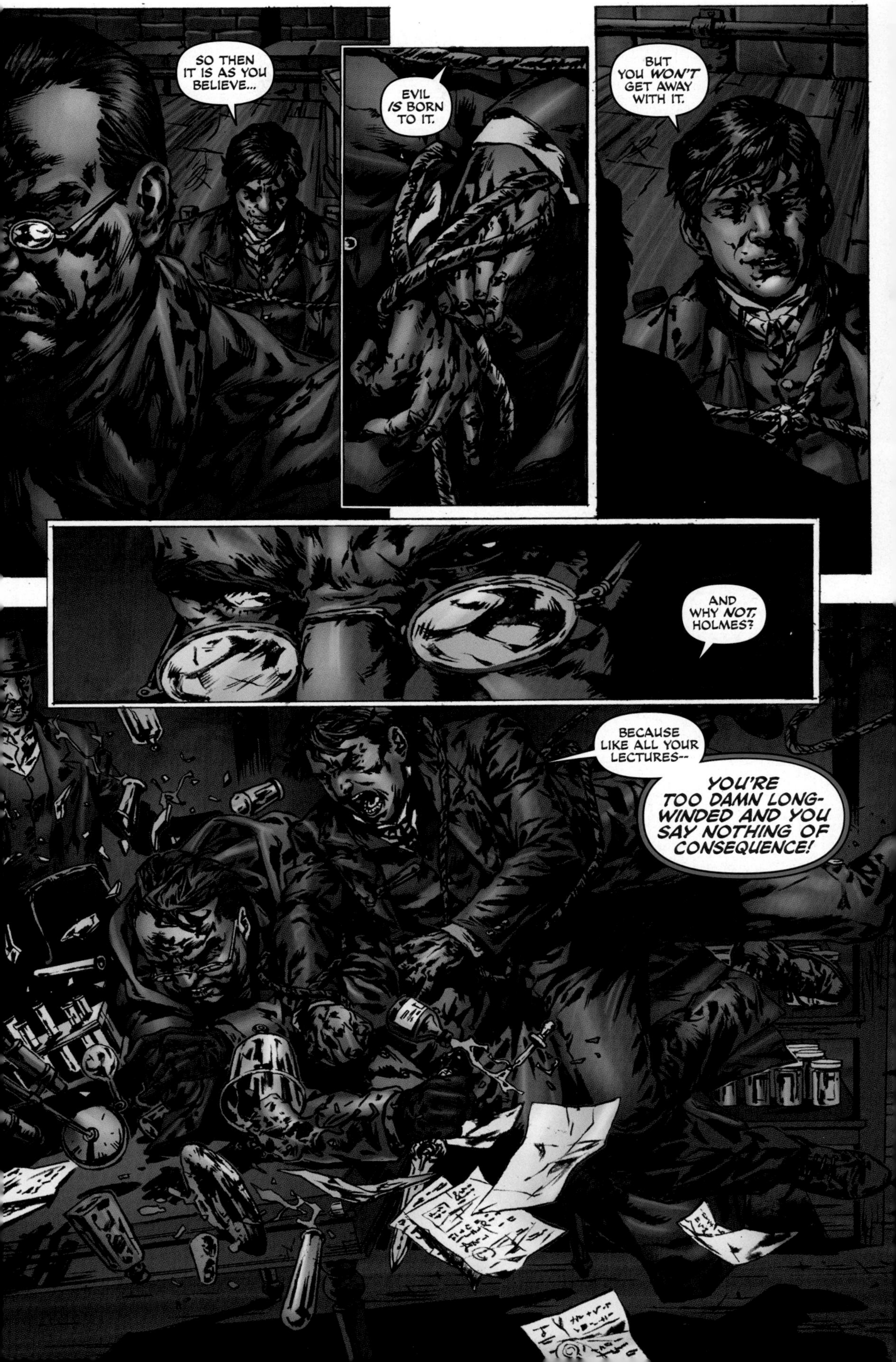
SO THEN IT IS AS YOU BELIEVE...
EVIL IS BORN TO IT.
BUT YOU WON'T GET AWAY WITH IT.
AND WHY NOT, HOLMES?
BECAUSE LIKE ALL YOUR LECTURES--
YOU'RE TOO DAMN LONG-WINDED AND YOU SAY NOTHING OF CONSEQUENCE!

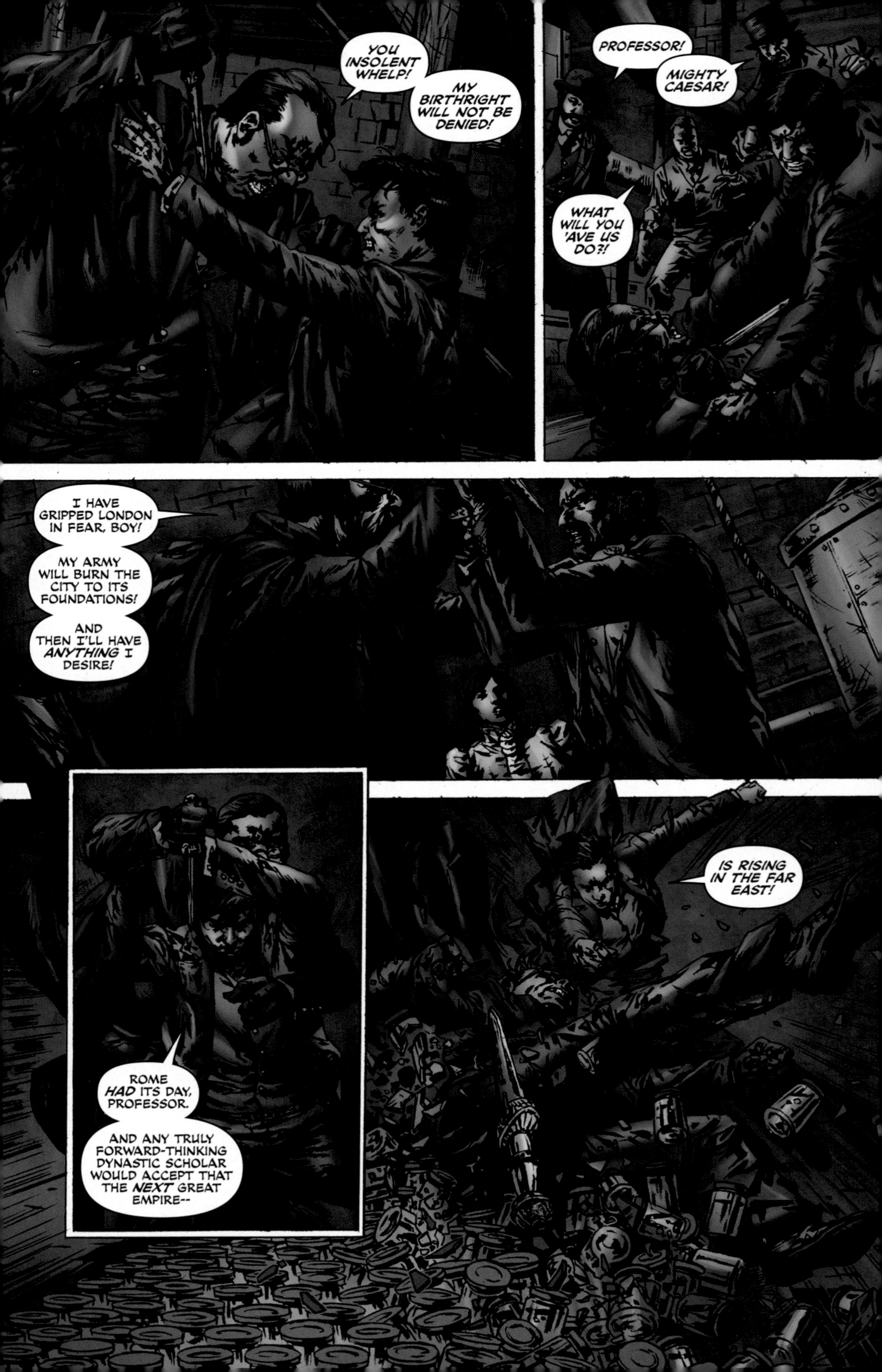
YOU INSOLENT WHELP!
MY BIRTHRIGHT WILL NOT BE DENIED!
PROFESSOR!
MIGHTY CAESAR!
WHAT WILL YOU 'AVE US DO?!
I HAVE GRIPPED LONDON IN FEAR, BOY!
MY ARMY WILL BURN THE CITY TO ITS FOUNDATIONS!
AND THEN I'LL HAVE ANYTHING I DESIRE!
ROME HAD ITS DAY, PROFESSOR.
AND ANY TRULY FORWARD-THINKING DYNASTIC SCHOLAR WOULD ACCEPT THAT THE NEXT GREAT EMPIRE--
IS RISING IN THE FAR EAST!

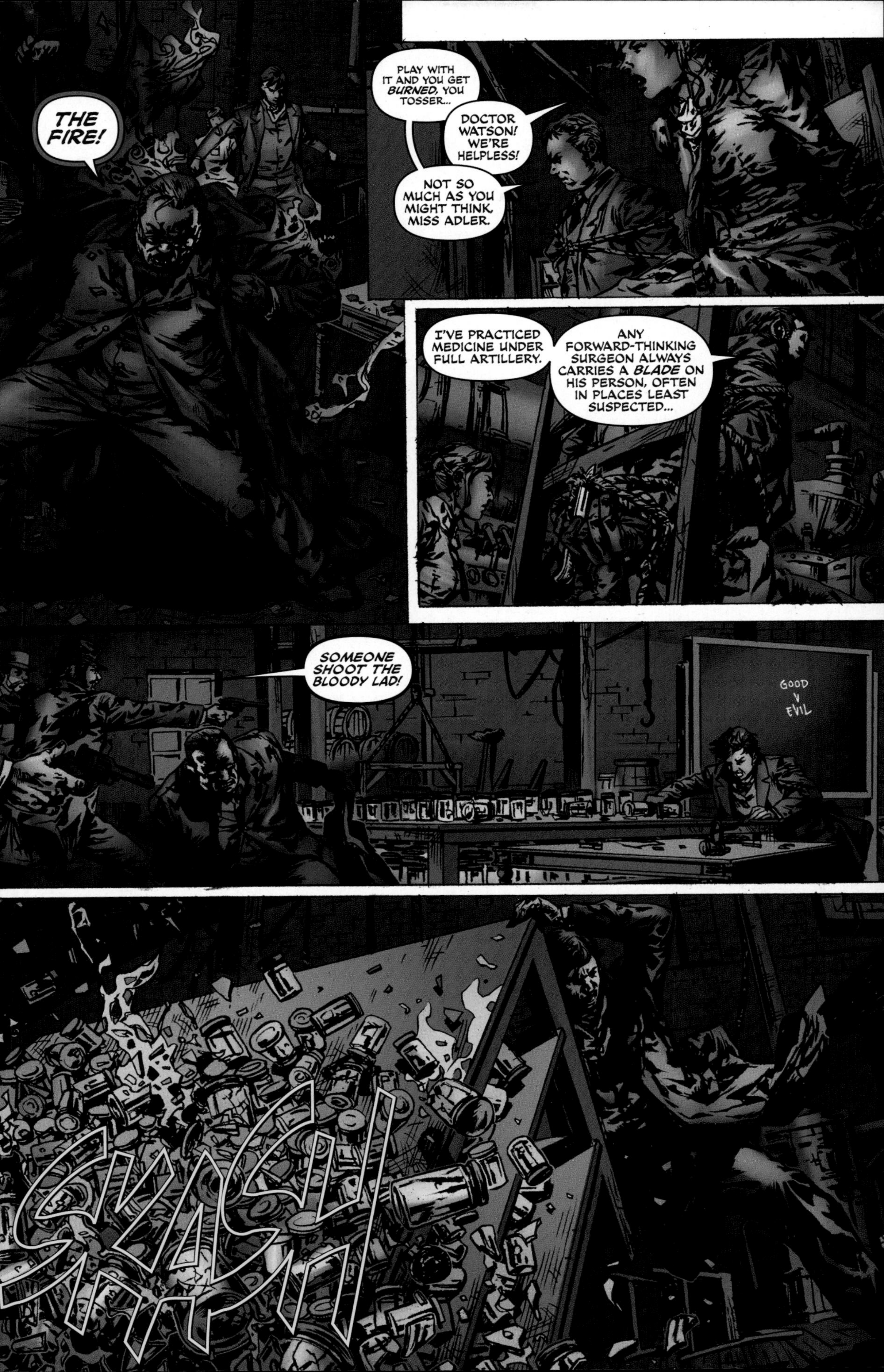
THE FIRE!
PLAY WITH IT AND YOU GET *BURNED*, YOU TOSSER...
DOCTOR WATSON! WE'RE HELPLESS!
NOT SO MUCH AS YOU MIGHT THINK, MISS ADLER.
I'VE PRACTICED MEDICINE UNDER FULL ARTILLERY.
ANY FORWARD-THINKING SURGEON ALWAYS CARRIES A *BLADE* ON HIS PERSON, OFTEN IN PLACES LEAST SUSPECTED...
SOMEONE SHOOT THE BLOODY LAD!
GOOD V EVIL
SMASH

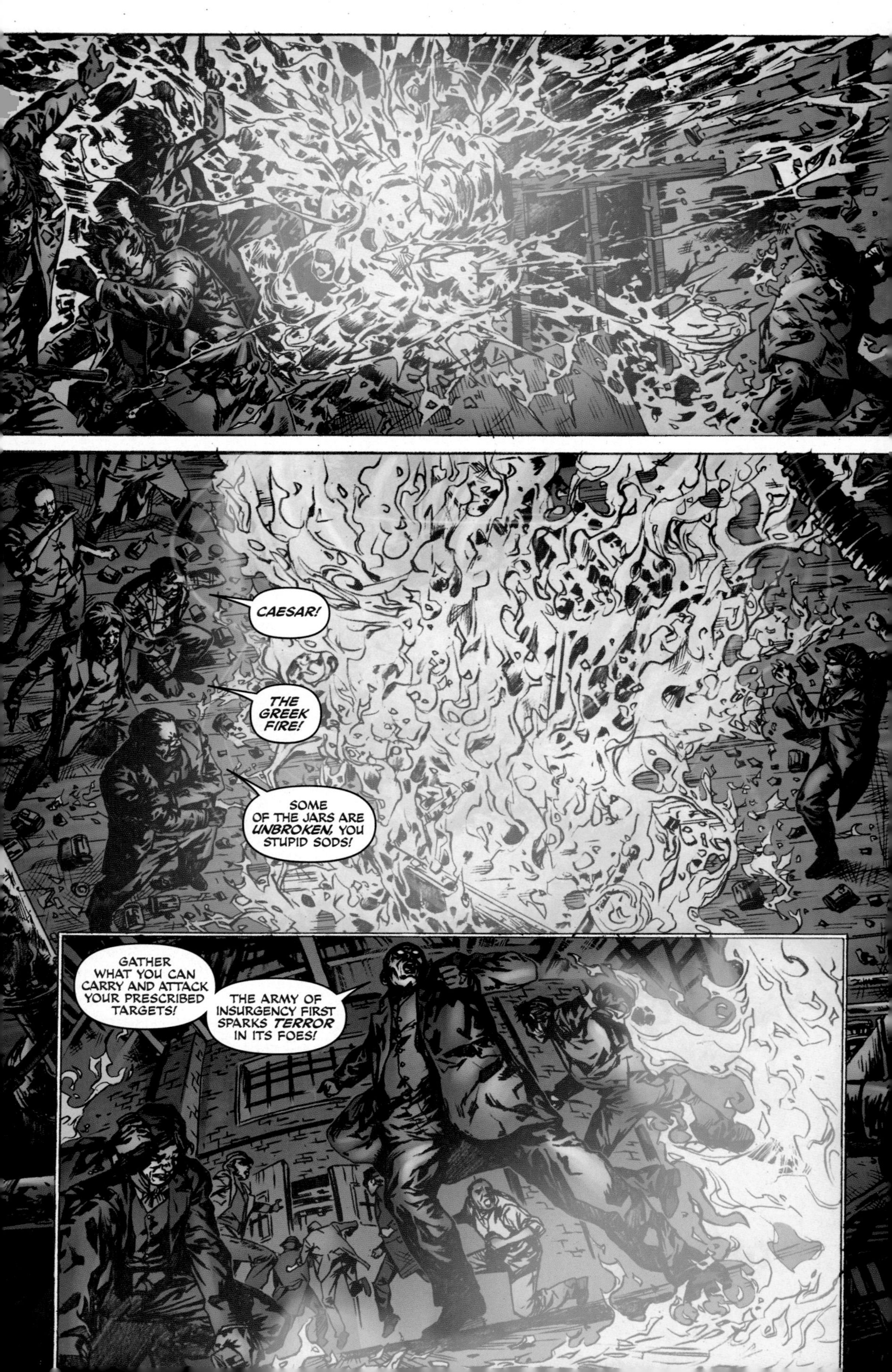
CAESAR!
THE GREEK FIRE!
SOME OF THE JARS ARE UNBROKEN, YOU STUPID SODS!
GATHER WHAT YOU CAN CARRY AND ATTACK YOUR PRESCRIBED TARGETS!
THE ARMY OF INSURGENCY FIRST SPARKS TERROR IN ITS FOES!

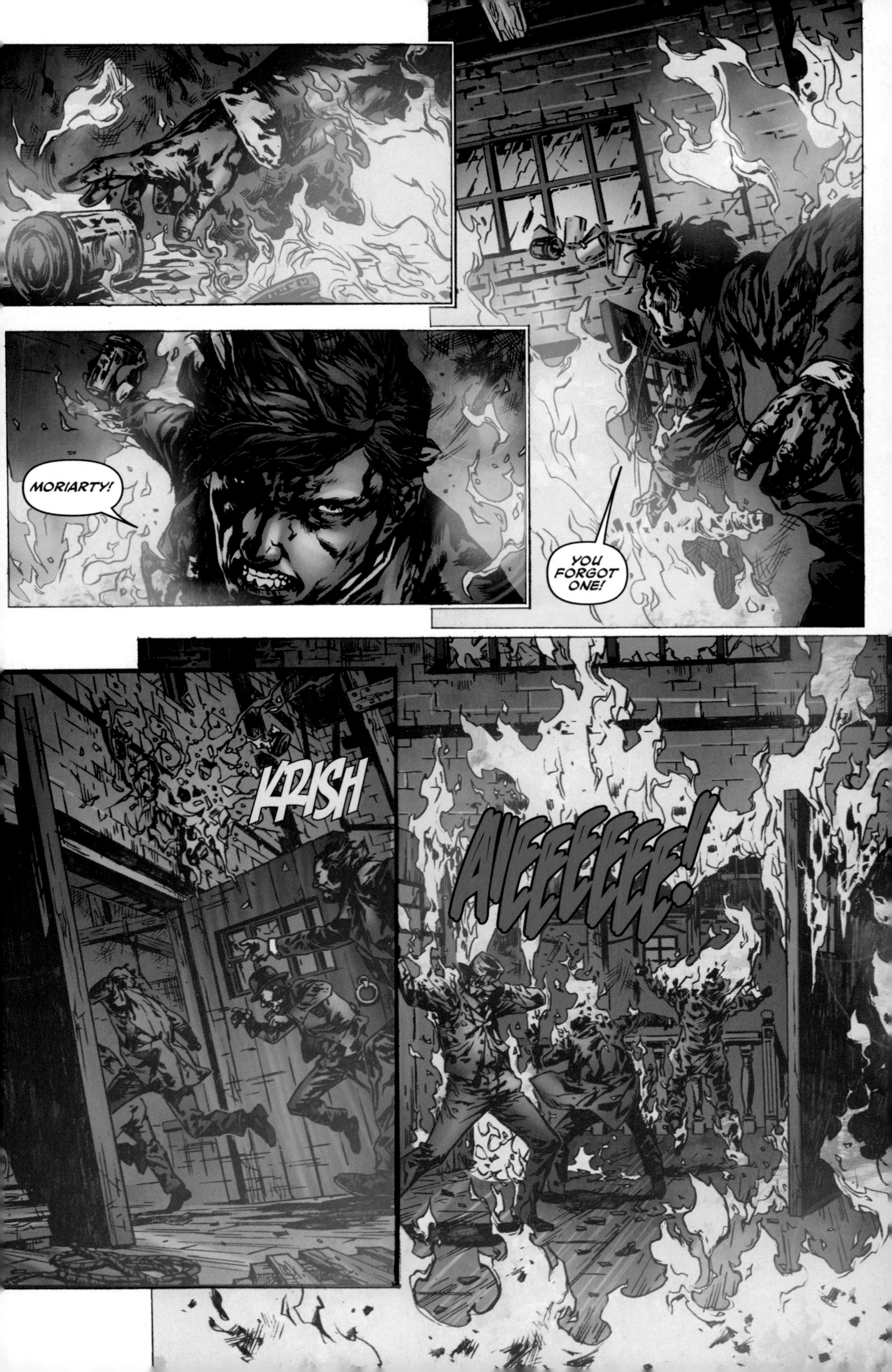
MORIARTY!
YOU FORGOT ONE!
KRISH
AIEEEEEE!

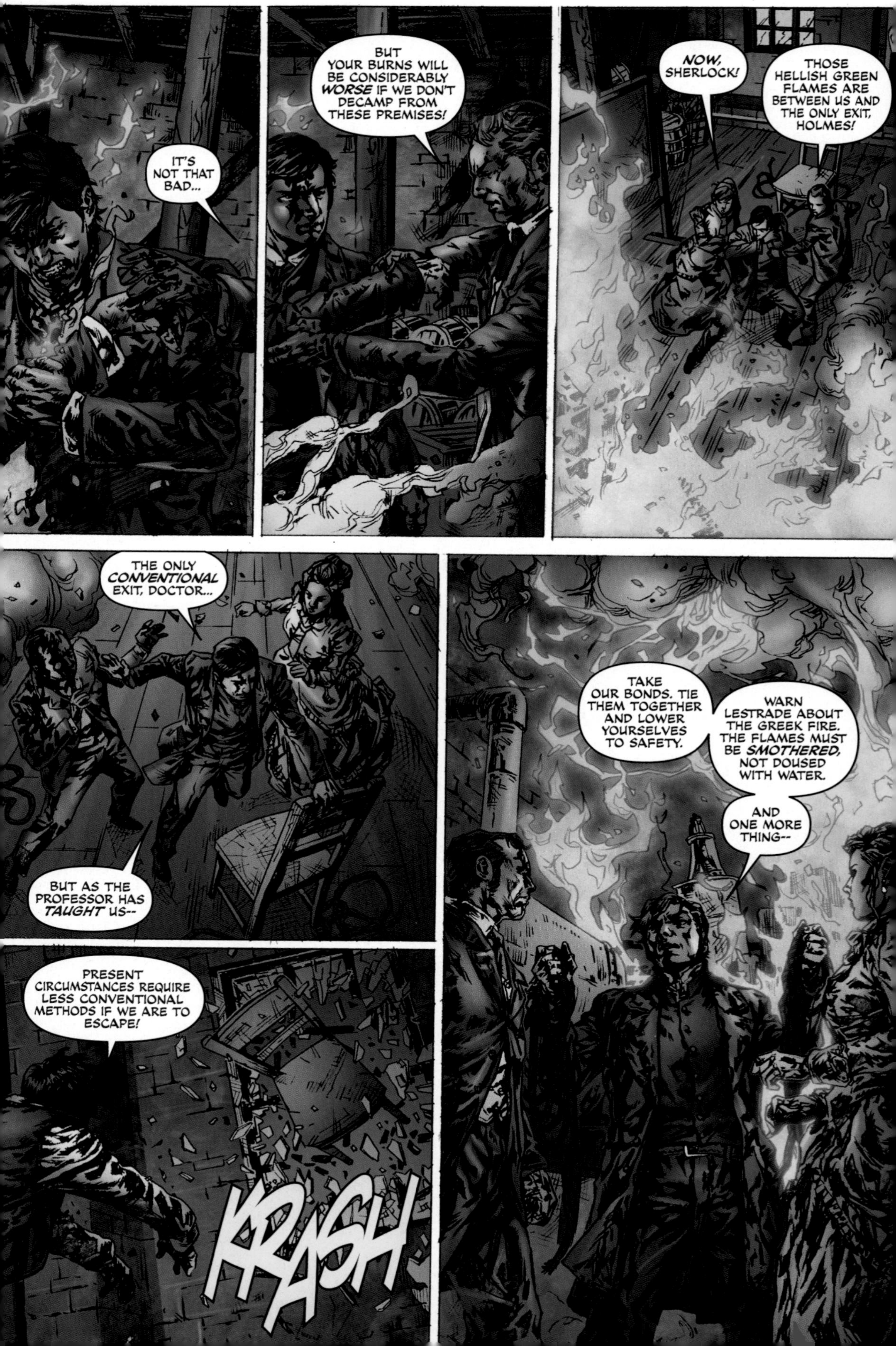
IT'S NOT THAT BAD...
BUT YOUR BURNS WILL BE CONSIDERABLY WORSE IF WE DON'T DECAMP FROM THESE PREMISES!
NOW, SHERLOCK!
THOSE HELLISH GREEN FLAMES ARE BETWEEN US AND THE ONLY EXIT, HOLMES!
THE ONLY CONVENTIONAL EXIT, DOCTOR...
BUT AS THE PROFESSOR HAS TAUGHT US--
PRESENT CIRCUMSTANCES REQUIRE LESS CONVENTIONAL METHODS IF WE ARE TO ESCAPE!
KRASH
TAKE OUR BONDS. TIE THEM TOGETHER AND LOWER YOURSELVES TO SAFETY.
WARN LESTRADE ABOUT THE GREEK FIRE. THE FLAMES MUST BE SMOTHERED, NOT DOUSED WITH WATER.
AND ONE MORE THING--

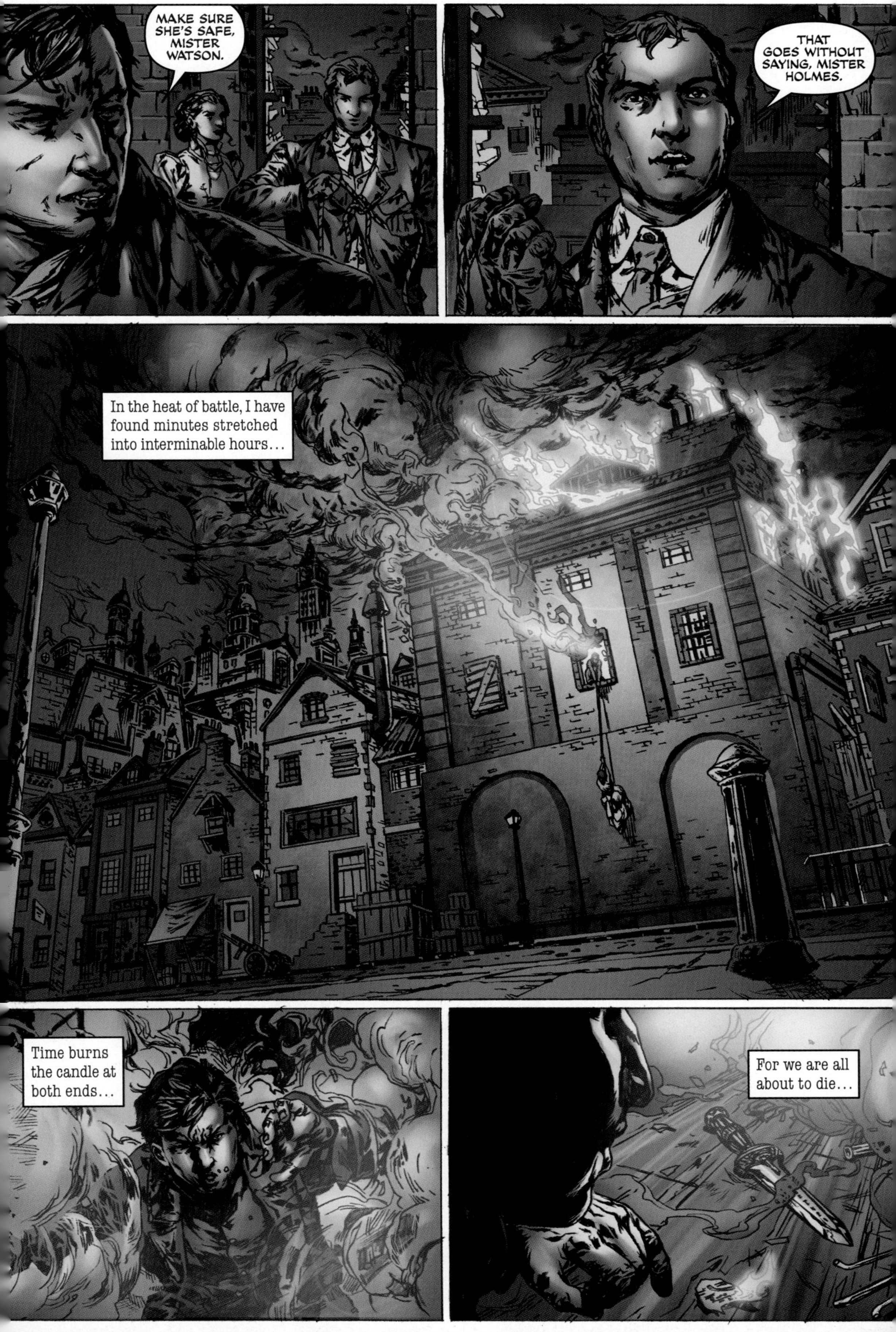
MAKE SURE SHE'S SAFE, MISTER WATSON.
THAT GOES WITHOUT SAYING, MISTER HOLMES.
In the heat of battle, I have found minutes stretched into interminable hours...
Time burns the candle at both ends...
For we are all about to die...

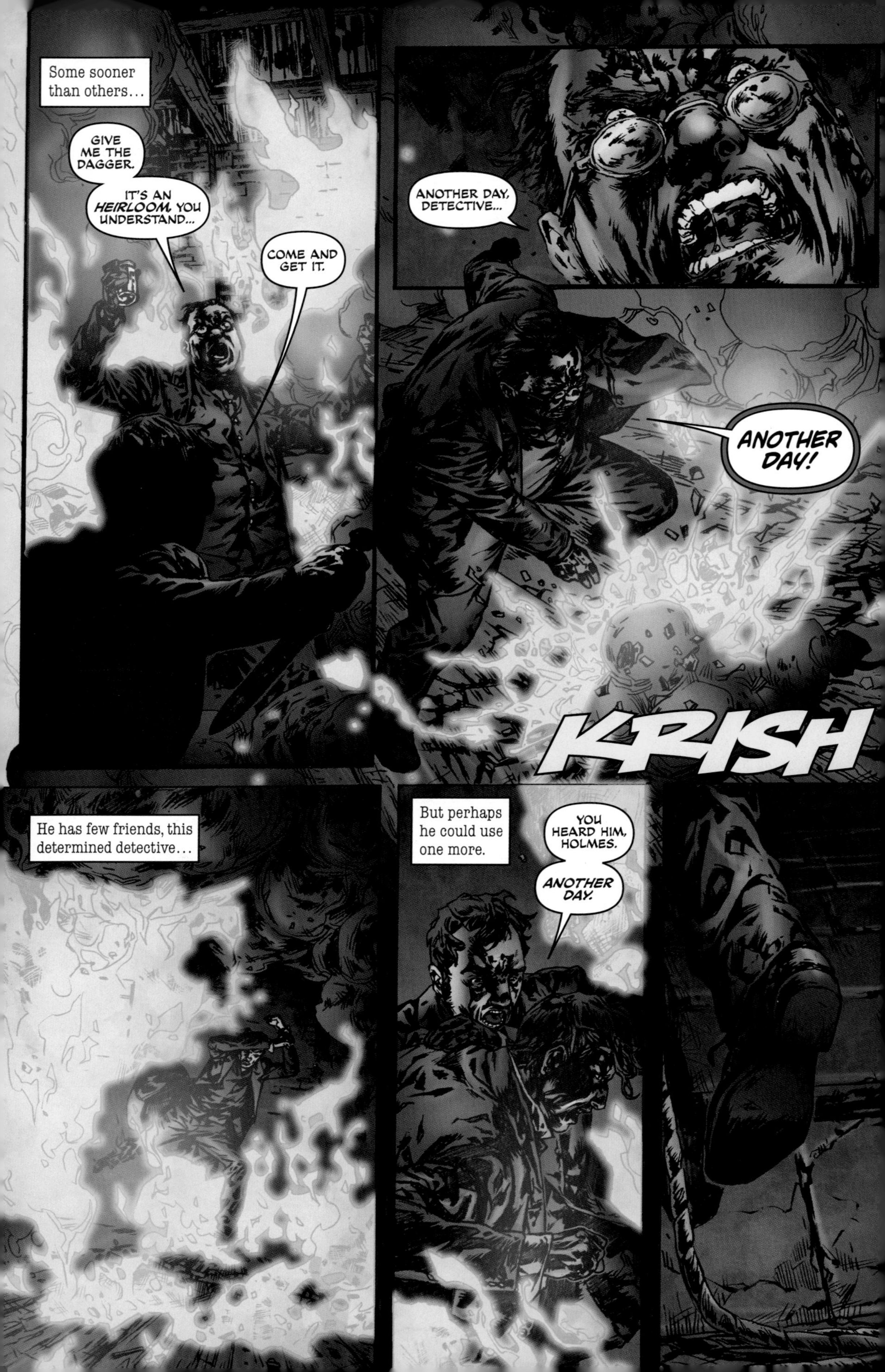
Some sooner than others...
GIVE ME THE DAGGER.
IT'S AN *HEIRLOOM*, YOU UNDERSTAND...
COME AND GET IT.
ANOTHER DAY, DETECTIVE...
ANOTHER DAY!
KRISH
He has few friends, this determined detective...
But perhaps he could use one more.
YOU HEARD HIM, HOLMES.
ANOTHER DAY.

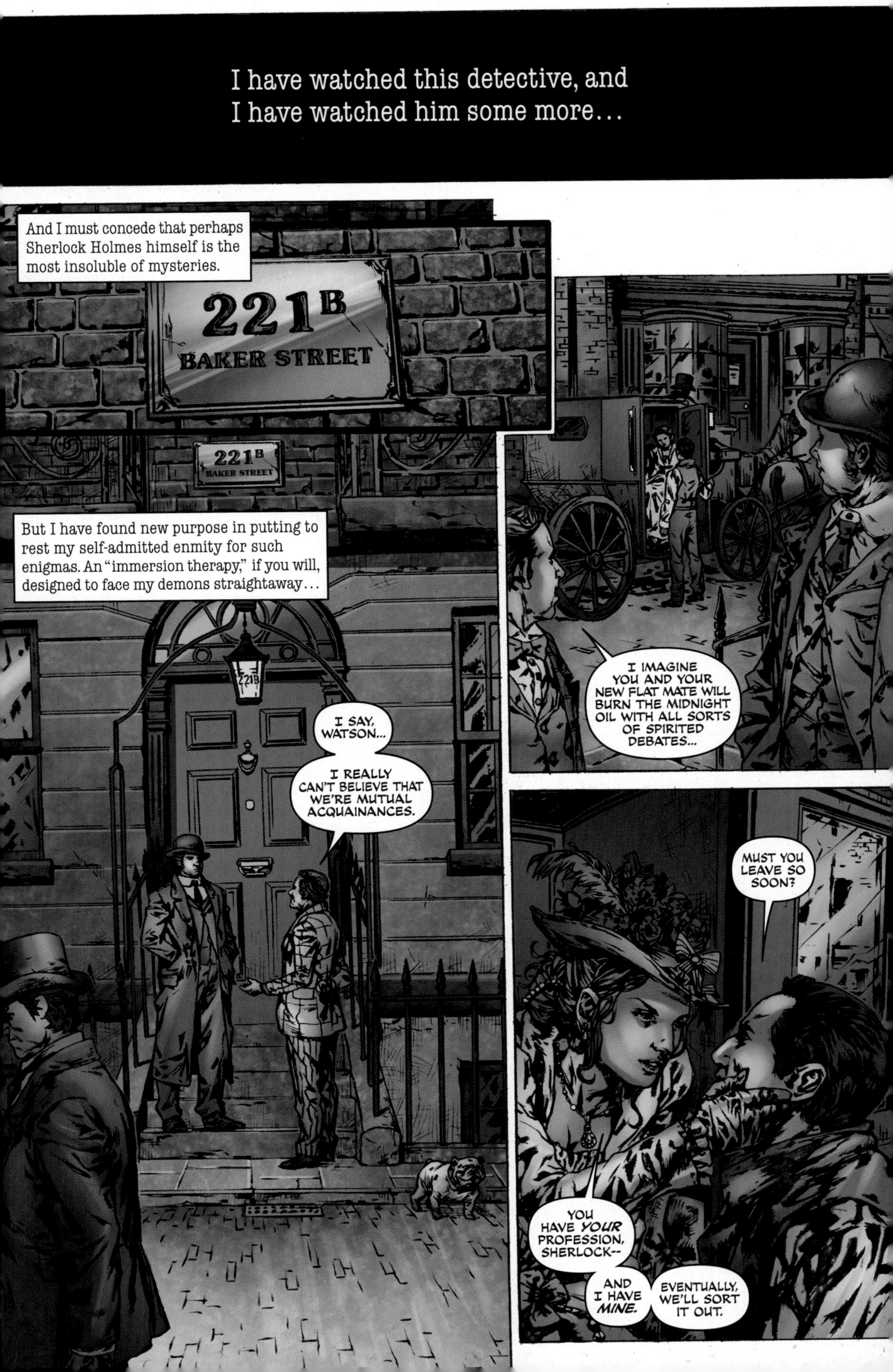

I have watched this detective, and I have watched him some more...
And I must concede that perhaps Sherlock Holmes himself is the most insoluble of mysteries.
221B BAKER STREET
221B BAKER STREET
But I have found new purpose in putting to rest my self-admitted enmity for such enigmas. An "immersion therapy," if you will, designed to face my demons straightaway...
221B
I SAY, WATSON...
I REALLY CAN'T BELIEVE THAT WE'RE MUTUAL ACQUAINANCES.
I IMAGINE YOU AND YOUR NEW FLAT MATE WILL BURN THE MIDNIGHT OIL WITH ALL SORTS OF SPIRITED DEBATES...
MUST YOU LEAVE SO SOON?
YOU HAVE *YOUR* PROFESSION, SHERLOCK--
AND I HAVE *MINE.*
EVENTUALLY, WE'LL SORT IT OUT.

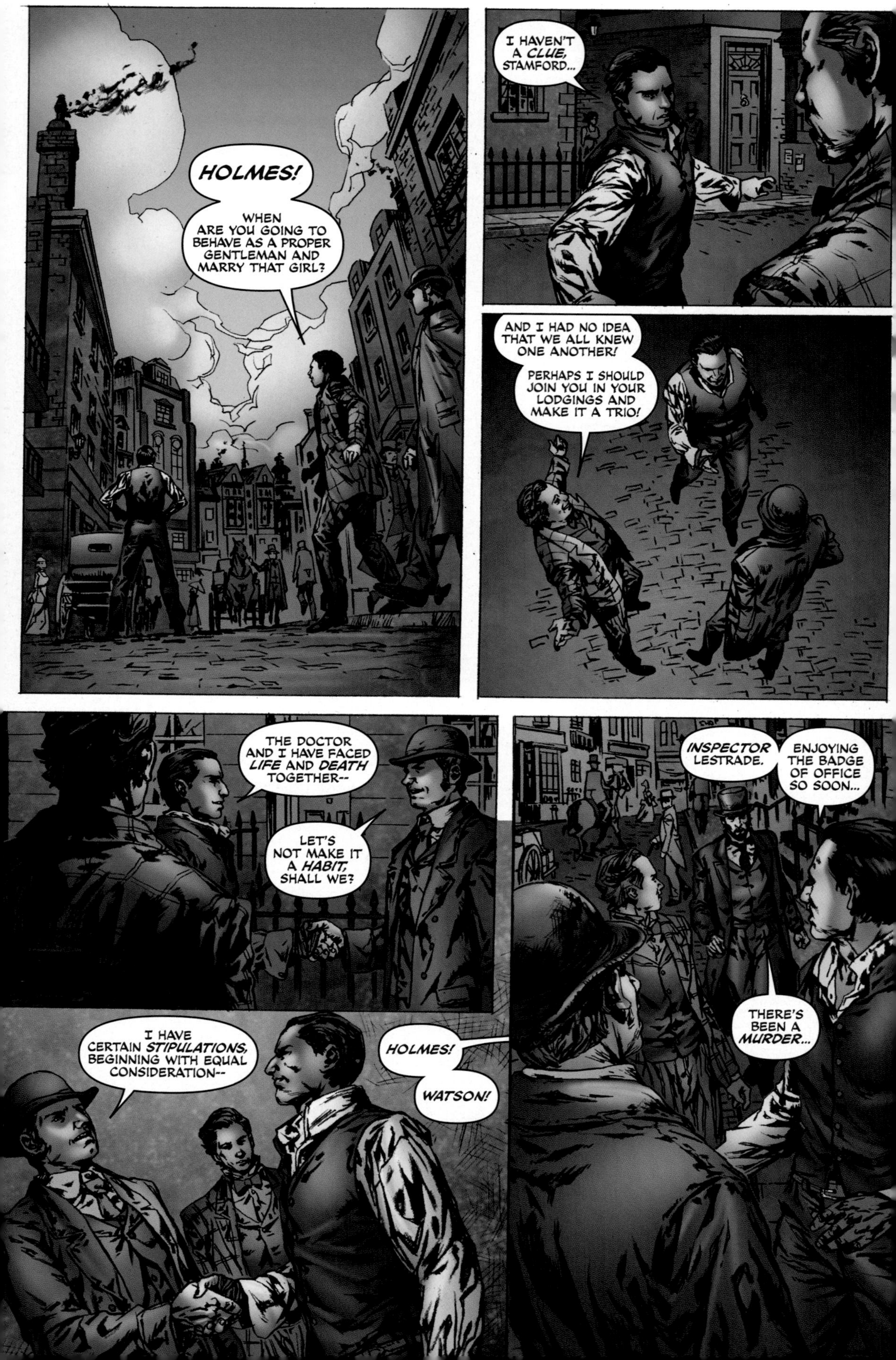
HOLMES!
WHEN ARE YOU GOING TO BEHAVE AS A PROPER GENTLEMAN AND MARRY THAT GIRL?
I HAVEN'T A *CLUE*, STAMFORD...
AND I HAD NO IDEA THAT WE ALL KNEW ONE ANOTHER!
PERHAPS I SHOULD JOIN YOU IN YOUR LODGINGS AND MAKE IT A TRIO!
THE DOCTOR AND I HAVE FACED *LIFE* AND *DEATH* TOGETHER--
LET'S NOT MAKE IT A *HABIT*, SHALL WE?
I HAVE CERTAIN *STIPULATIONS*, BEGINNING WITH EQUAL CONSIDERATION--
HOLMES!
WATSON!
INSPECTOR LESTRADE.
ENJOYING THE BADGE OF OFFICE SO SOON...
THERE'S BEEN A *MURDER*...

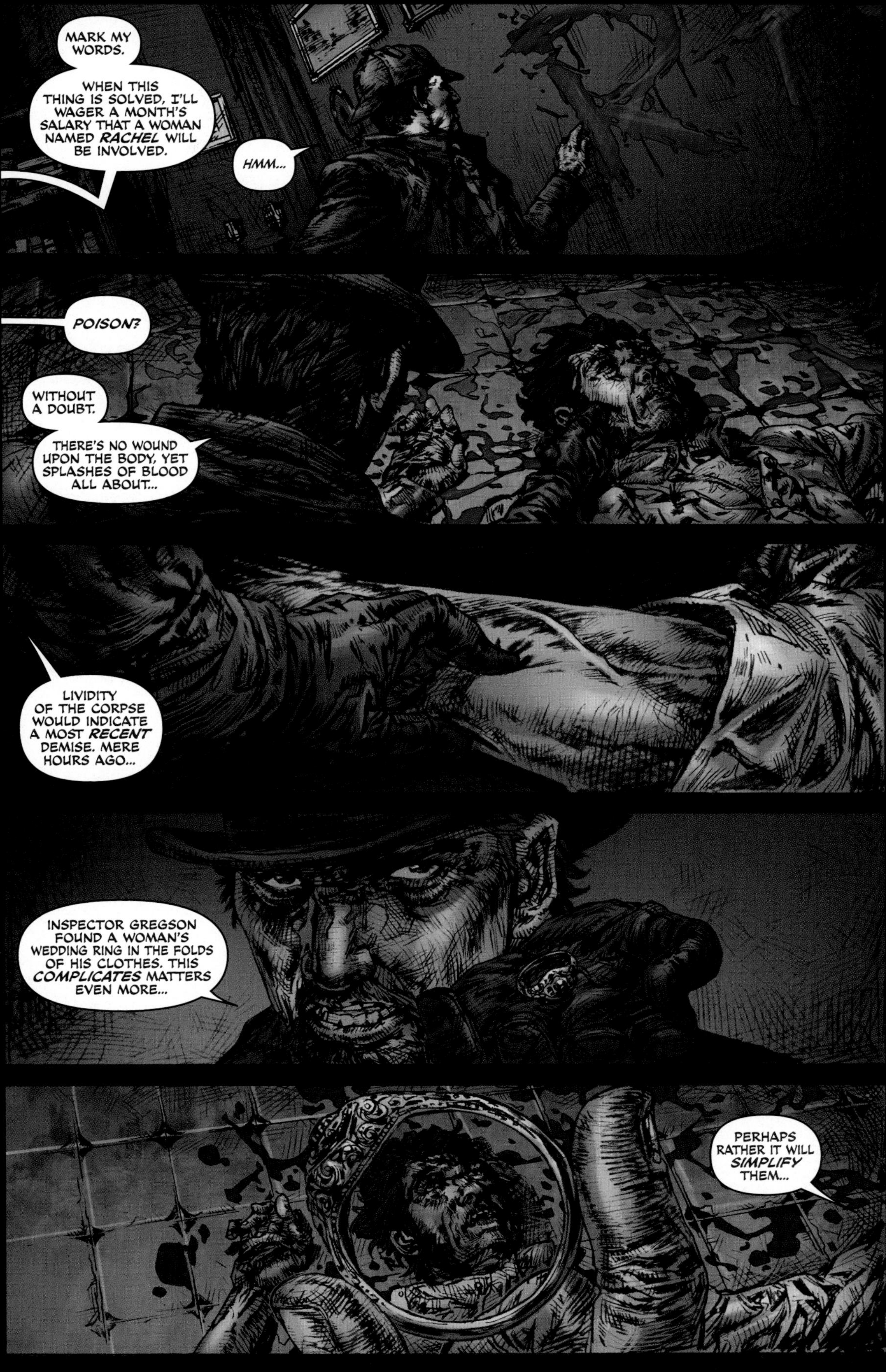
MARK MY WORDS.
WHEN THIS THING IS SOLVED, I'LL WAGER A MONTH'S SALARY THAT A WOMAN NAMED RACHEL WILL BE INVOLVED.
HMM...
POISON?
WITHOUT A DOUBT.
THERE'S NO WOUND UPON THE BODY, YET SPLASHES OF BLOOD ALL ABOUT...
LIVIDITY OF THE CORPSE WOULD INDICATE A MOST RECENT DEMISE. MERE HOURS AGO...
INSPECTOR GREGSON FOUND A WOMAN'S WEDDING RING IN THE FOLDS OF HIS CLOTHES. THIS COMPLICATES MATTERS EVEN MORE...
PERHAPS RATHER IT WILL SIMPLIFY THEM...

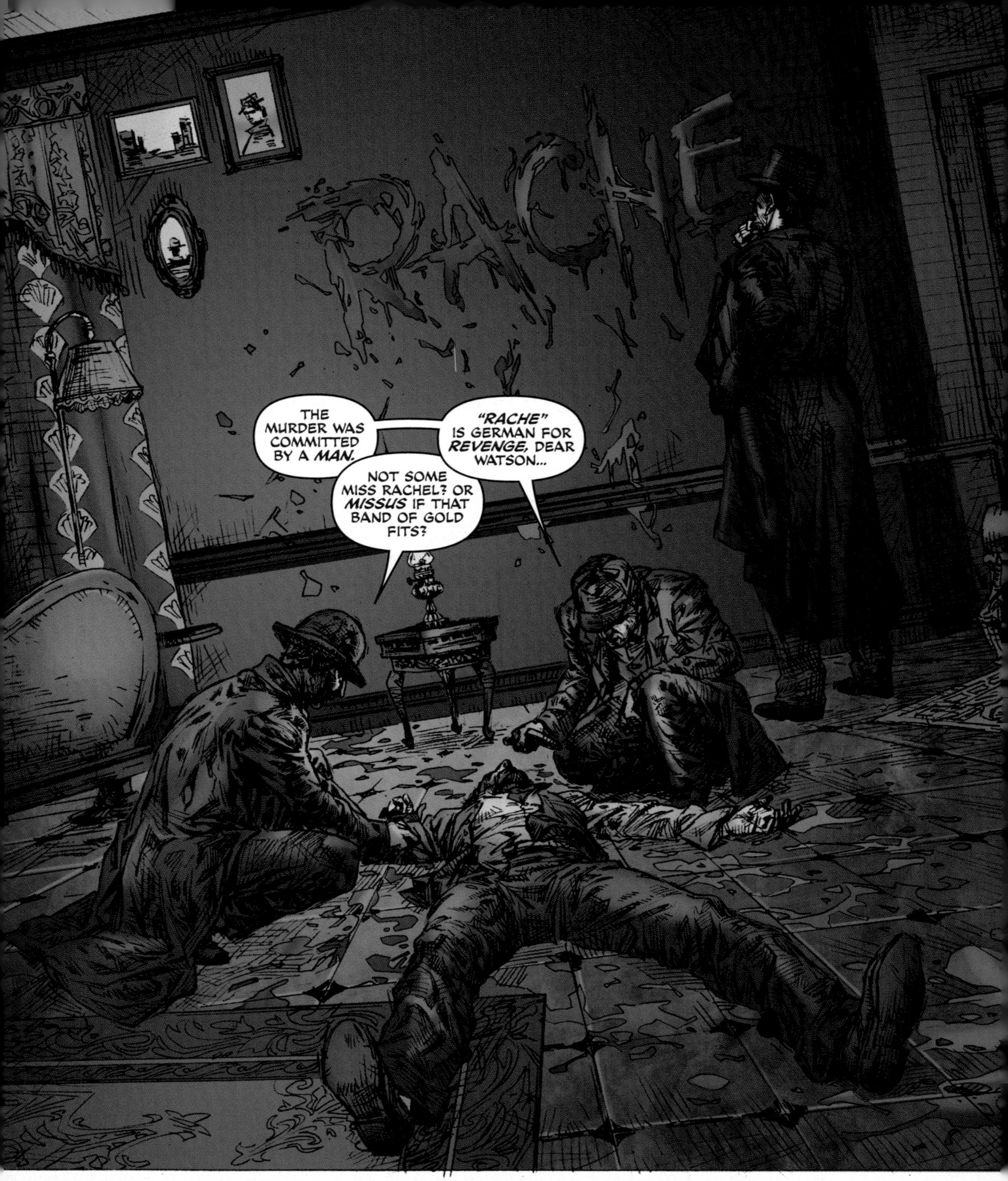
RACHE
THE MURDER WAS COMMITTED BY A *MAN.*
"*RACHE*" IS GERMAN FOR *REVENGE,* DEAR WATSON...
NOT SOME MISS RACHEL? OR *MISSUS* IF THAT BAND OF GOLD FITS?

In this strange case, (not) the first he solved in my presence (nor the last), Sherlock Holmes performed one of the greatest feats of deduction that henceforth would be known as…

A STUDY IN SCARLET

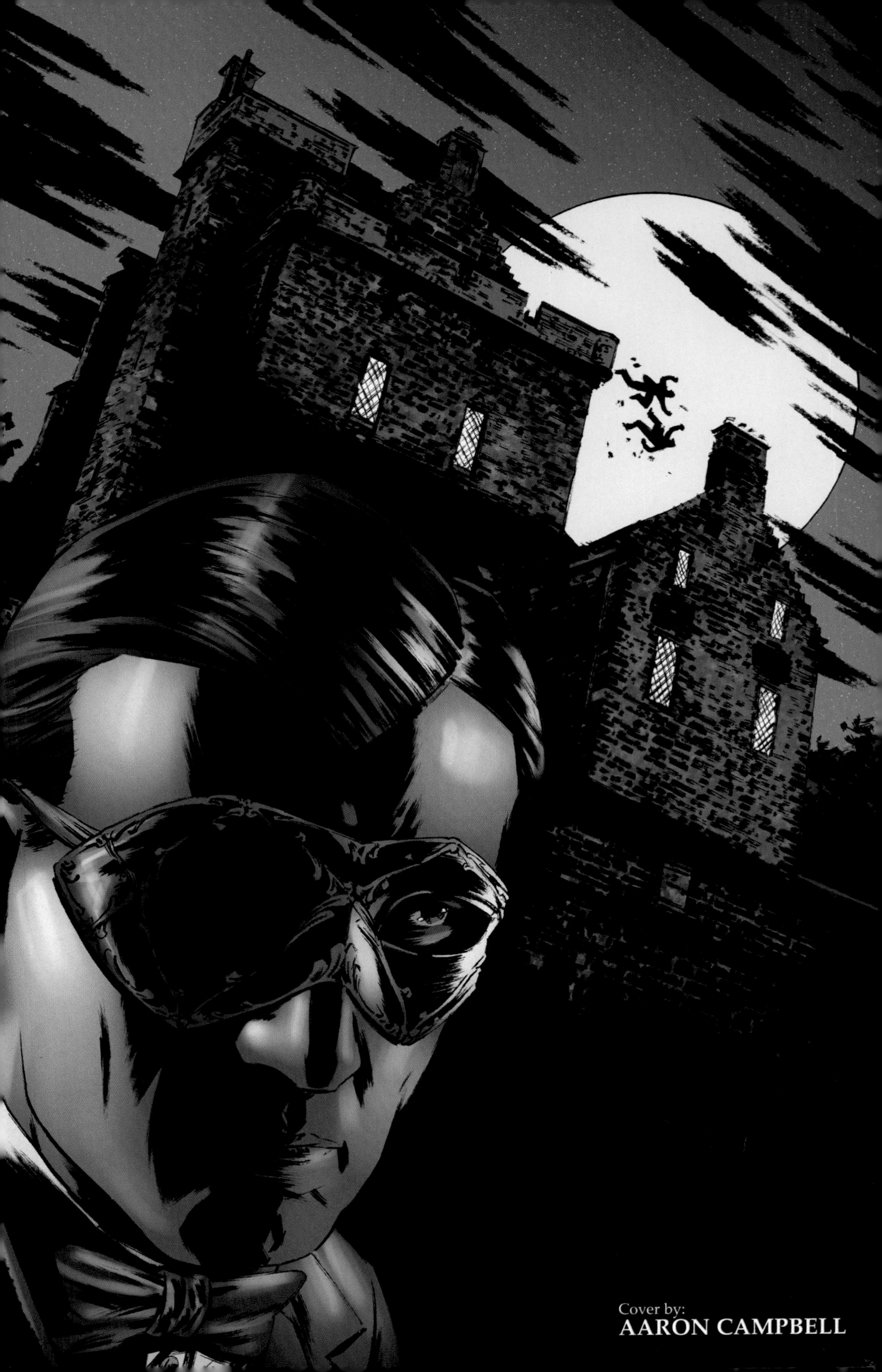

Cover by:
AARON CAMPBELL

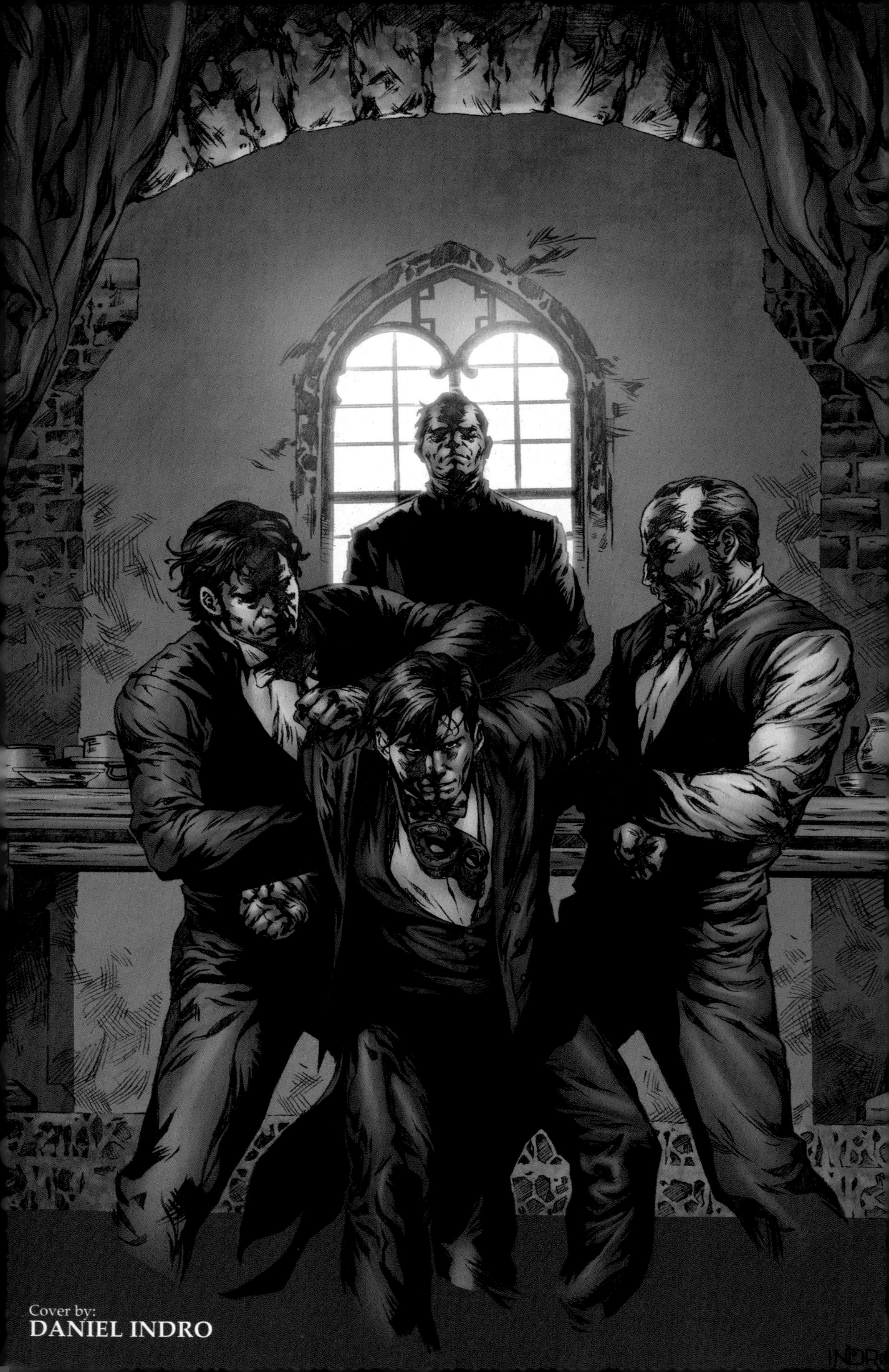

Cover by:
DANIEL INDRO

Cover by:
AARON CAMPBELL

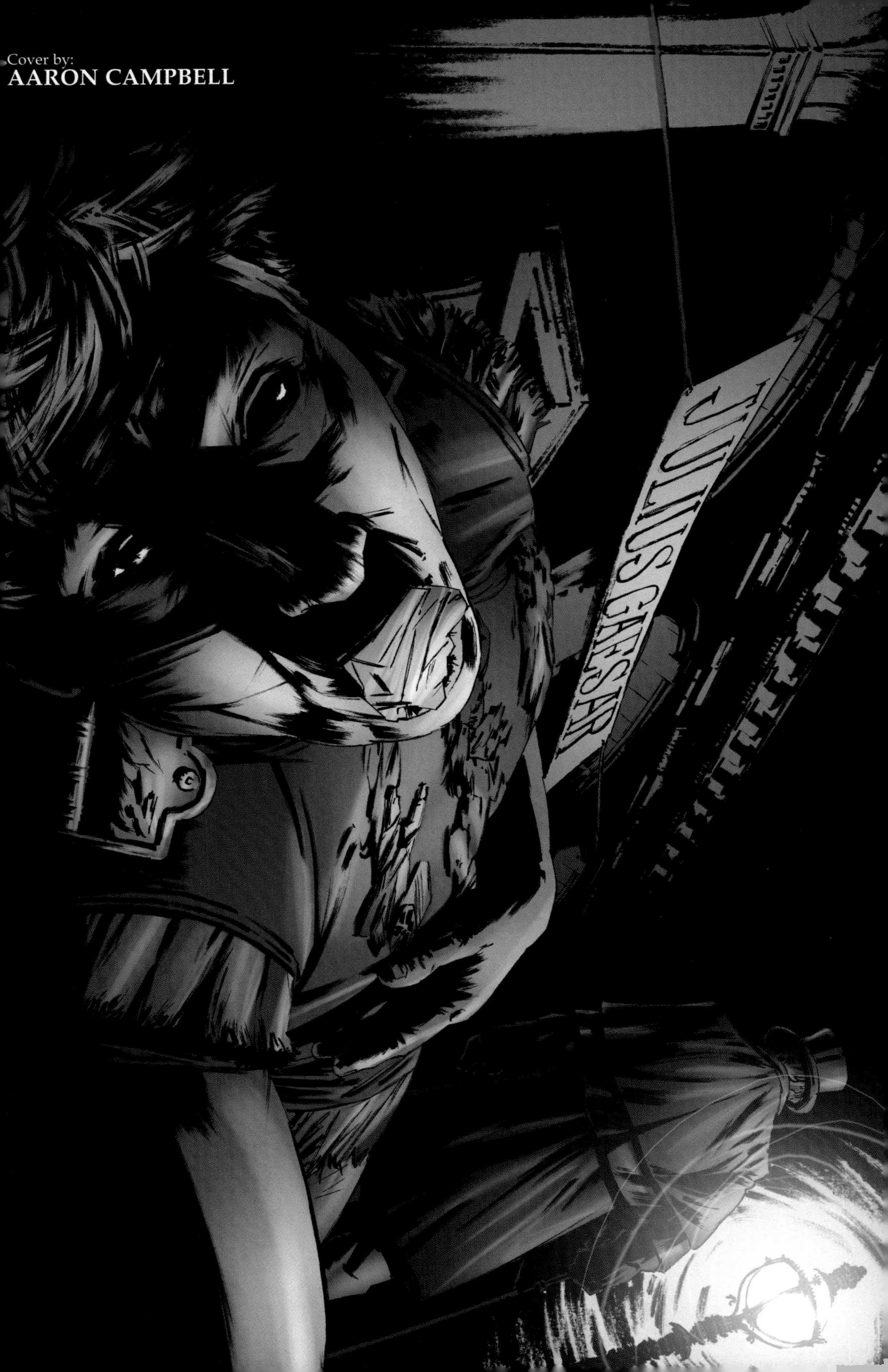
JULIUS CAESAR

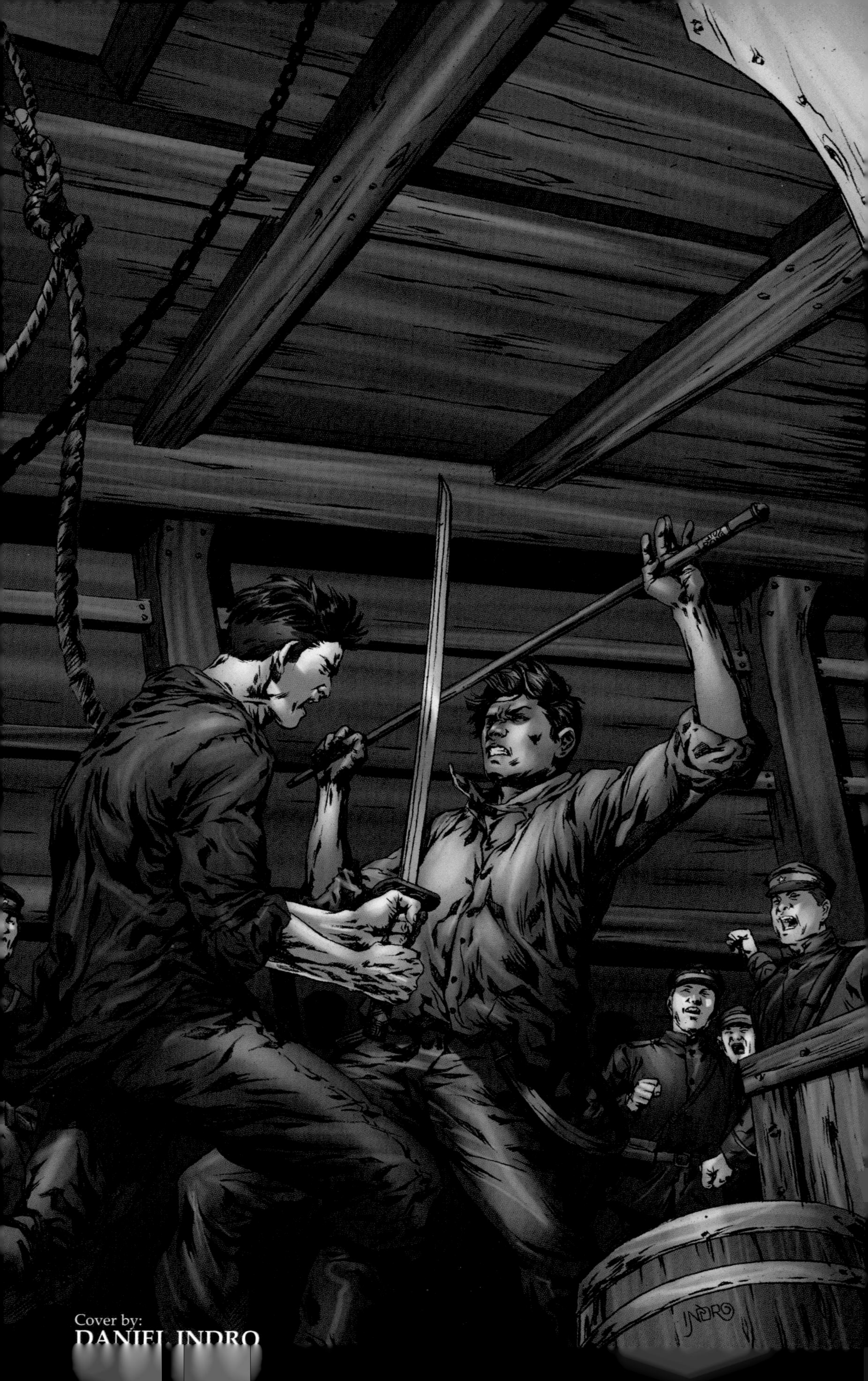
INDRO

Cover by:
DANIEL INDRO

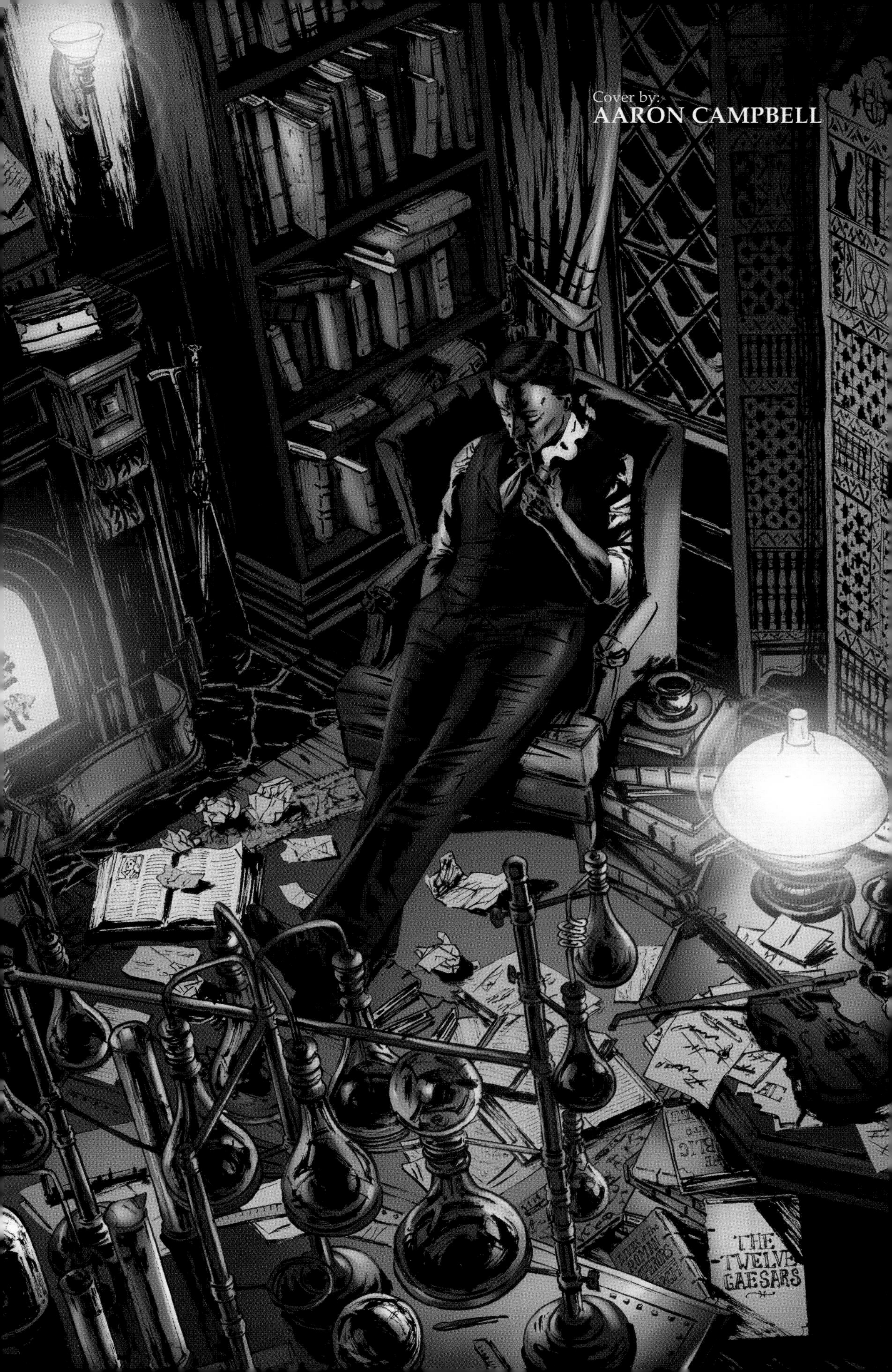
THE TWELVE CAESARS
Cover by:
AARON CAMPBELL

Cover by:
DANIEL INDRO

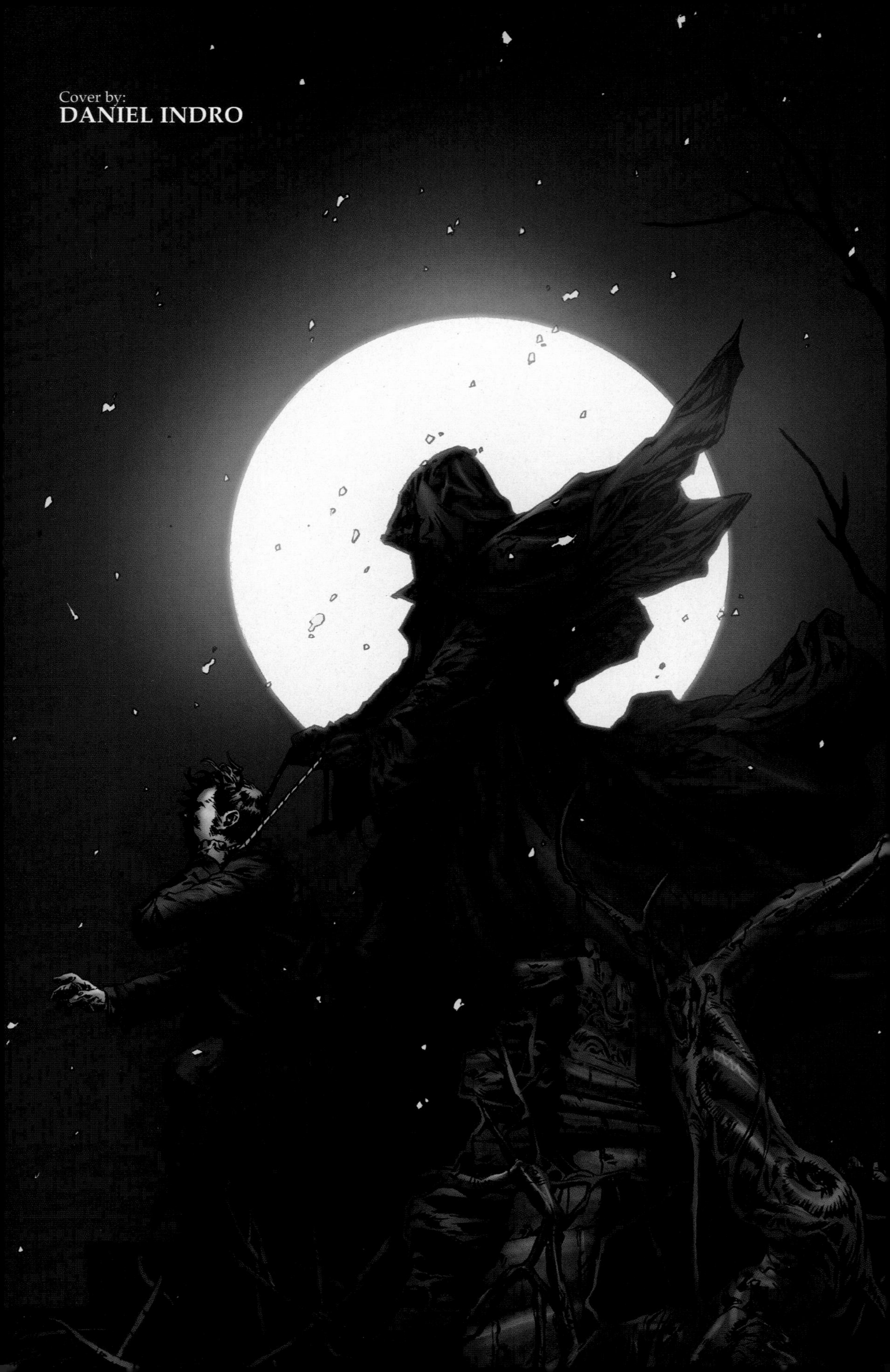

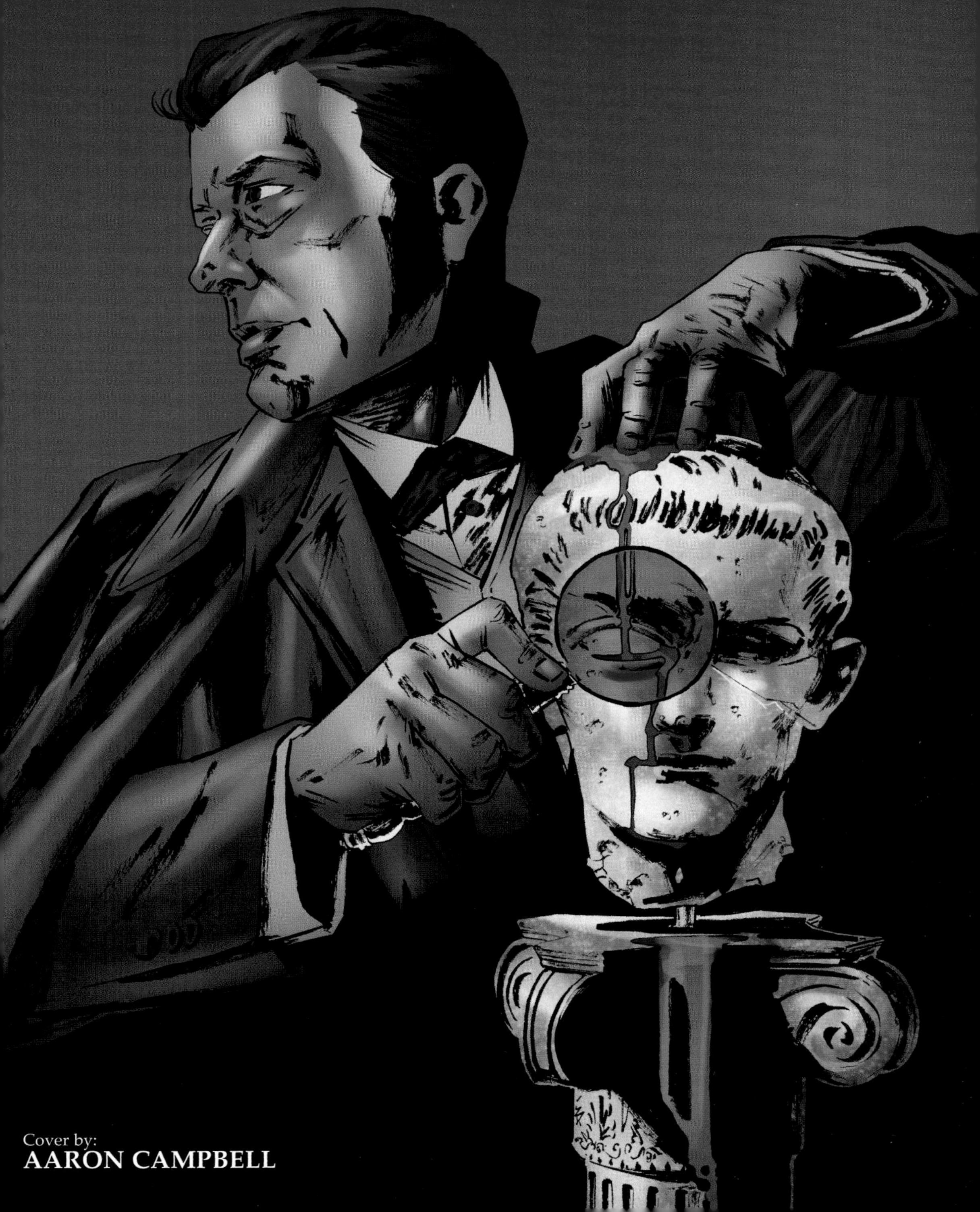

Cover by:
AARON CAMPBELL

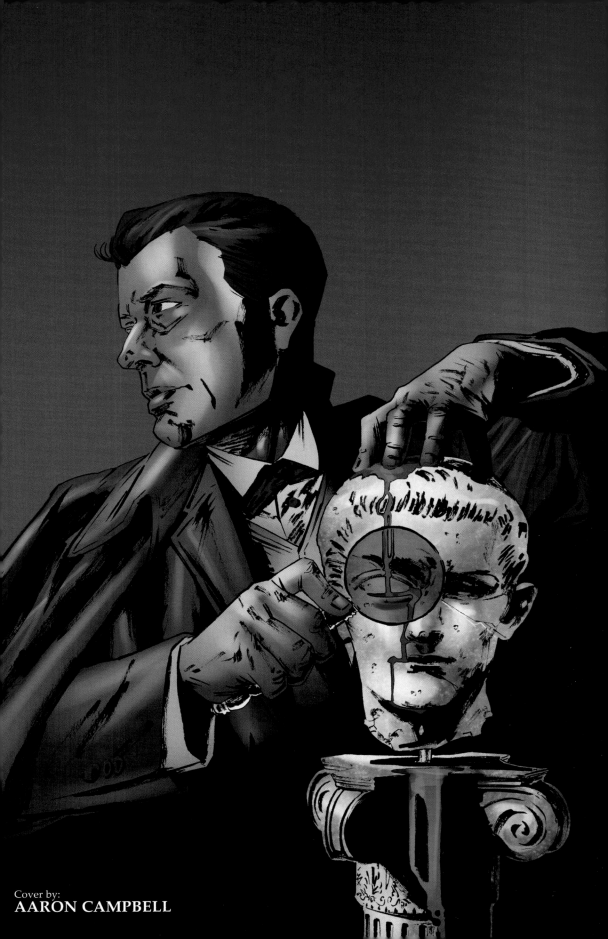

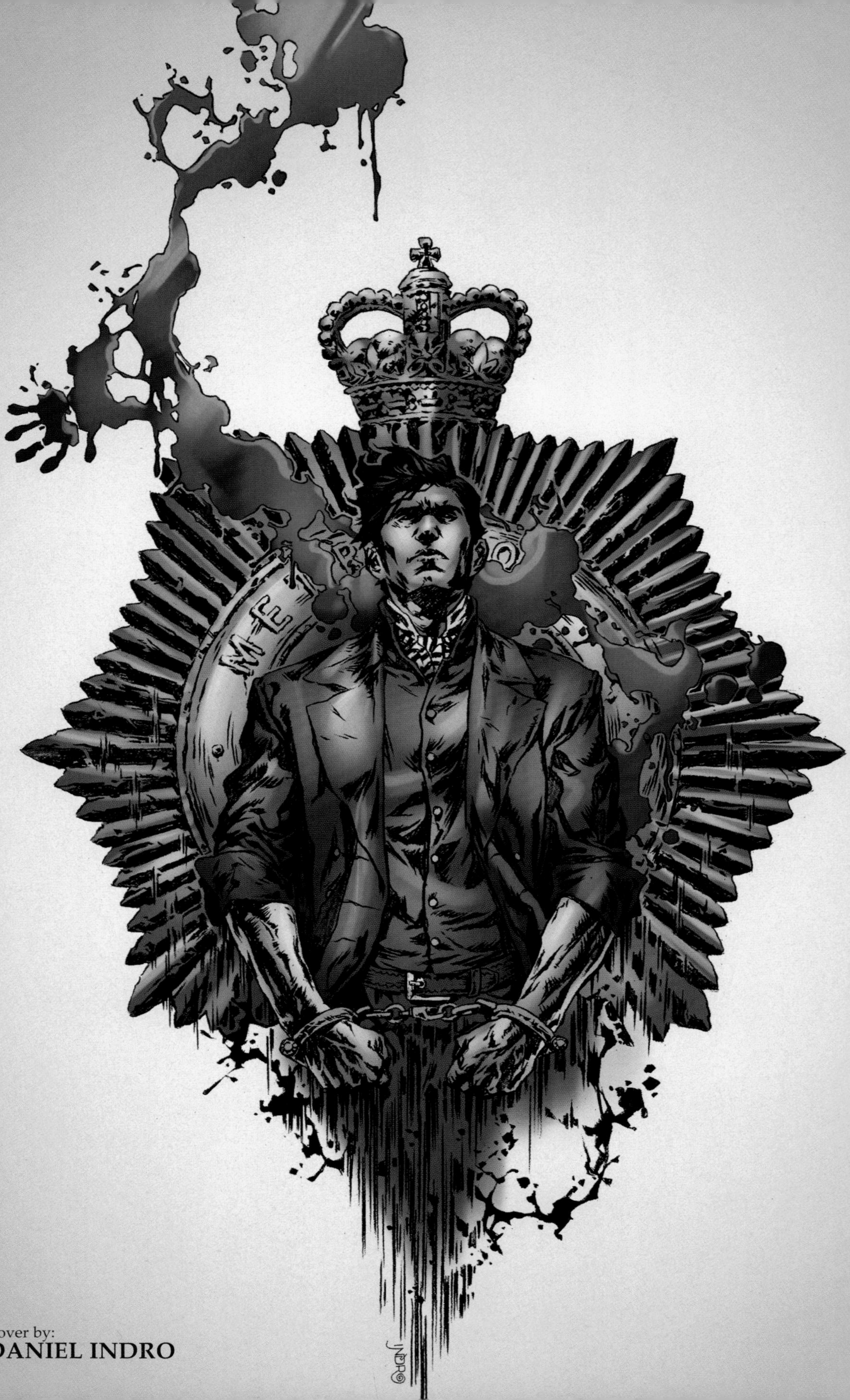

Cover by:
DANIEL INDRO

Cover by:
AARON CAMPBELL

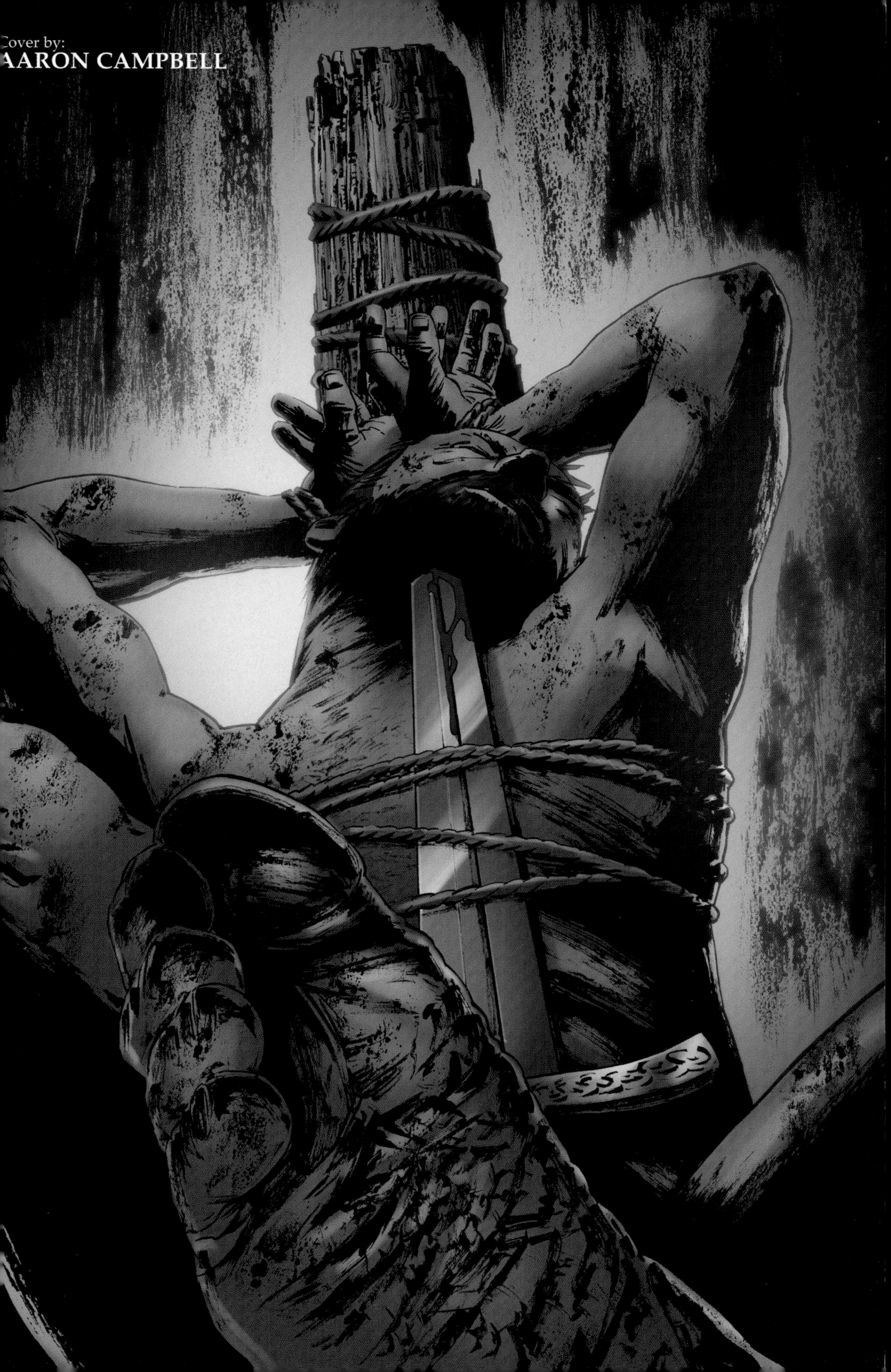

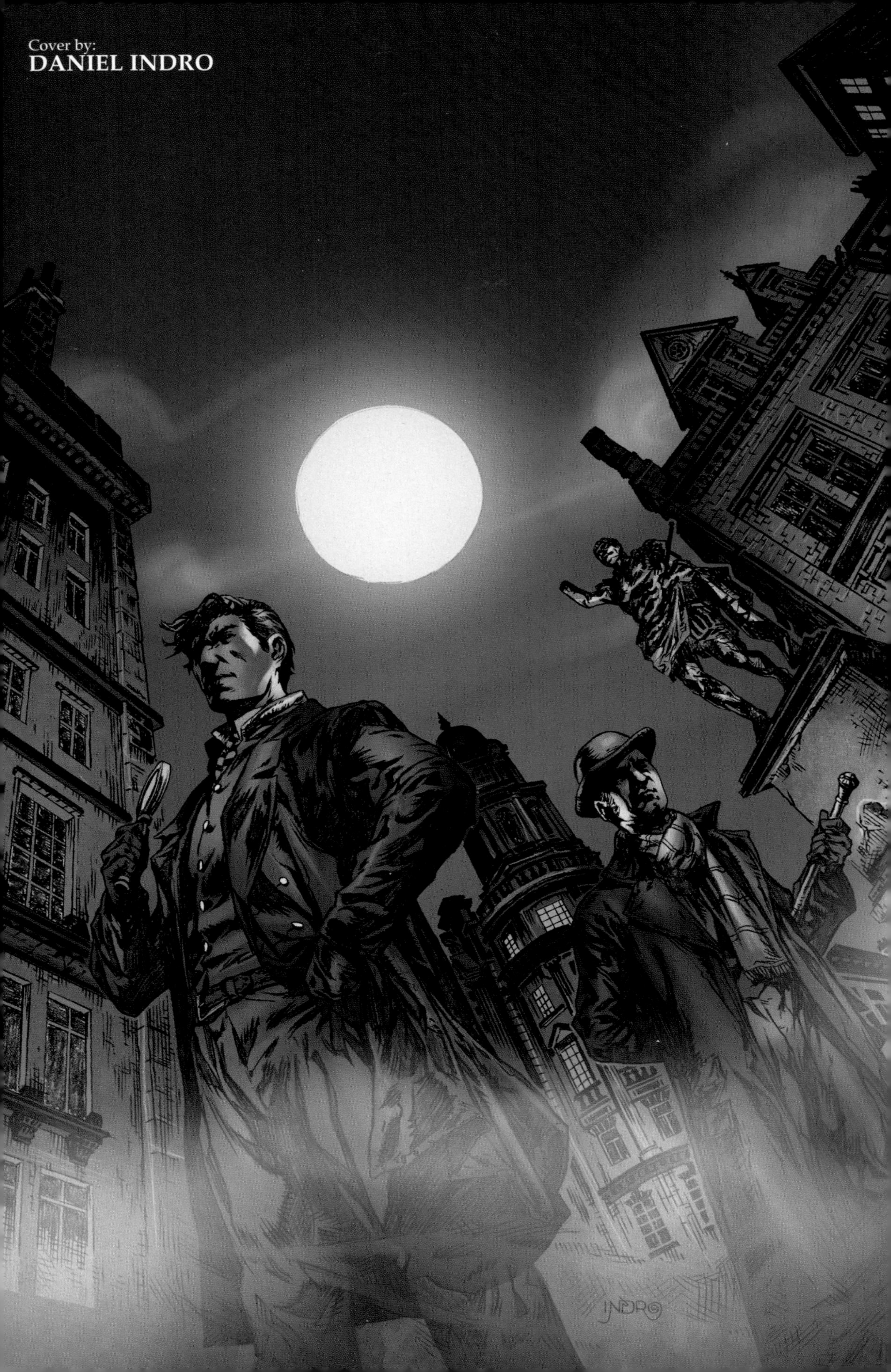
INDRO

Cover by:
DANIEL INDRO

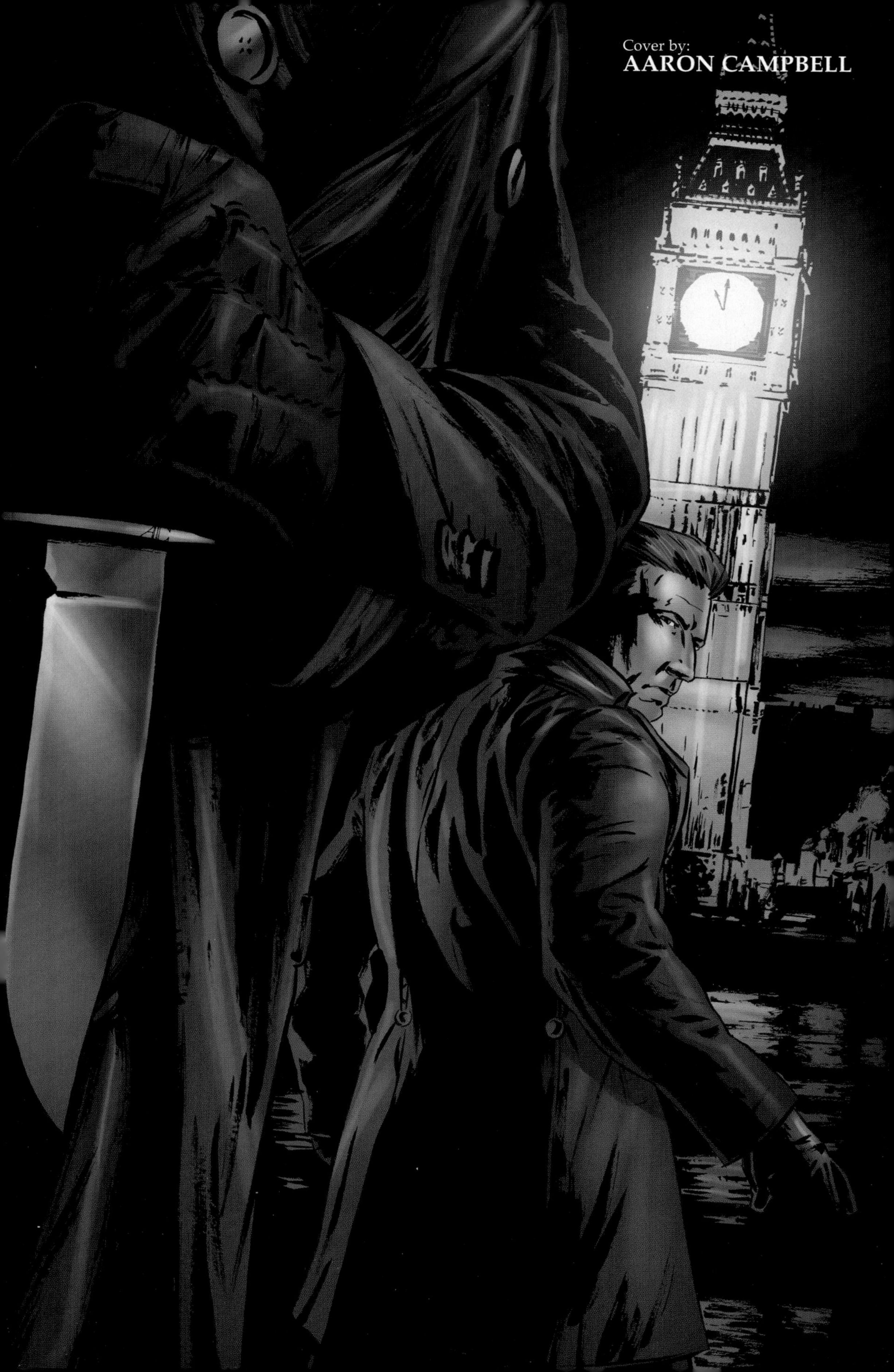

Cover by:
AARON CAMPBELL

Cover by:
DANIEL INDRO

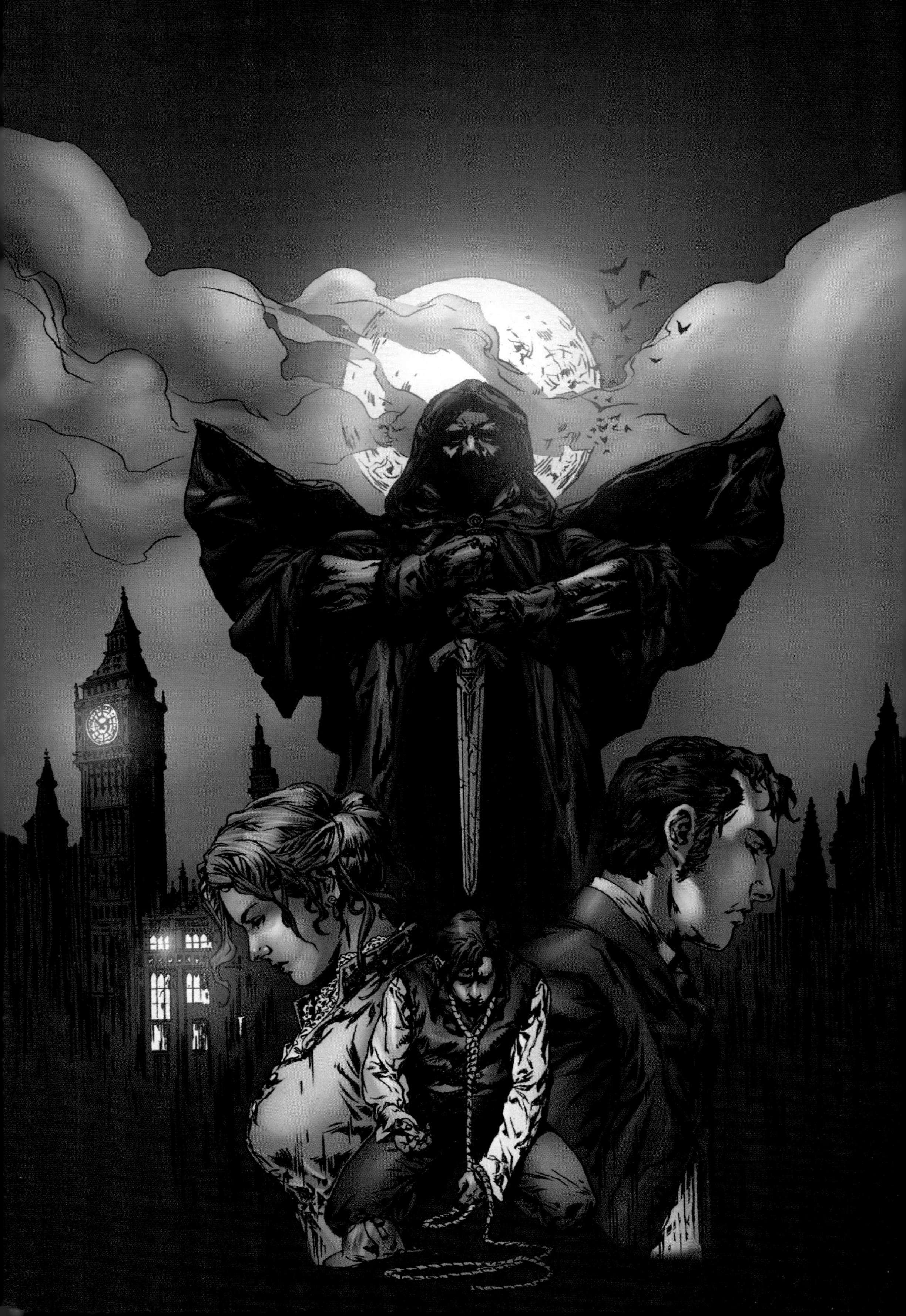